Training to Teach

A Guide for Students

SAGE
50
YEARS

THIRD EDITION

Training to Teach

A Guide for Students

EDITED BY **Neil Denby**

Los Angeles | London | New Delhi
Singapore | Washington DC

Los Angeles | London | New Delhi
Singapore | Washington DC

SAGE Publications Ltd
1 Oliver's Yard
55 City Road
London EC1Y 1SP

SAGE Publications Inc.
2455 Teller Road
Thousand Oaks, California 91320

SAGE Publications India Pvt Ltd
B 1/I 1 Mohan Cooperative Industrial Area
Mathura Road
New Delhi 110 044

SAGE Publications Asia-Pacific Pte Ltd
3 Church Street
#10-04 Samsung Hub
Singapore 049483

Commissioning editor: James Clark
Assistant editor: Rachael Plant
Production editor: Tom Bedford
Copyeditor: Audrey Scriven
Proofreader: Martin Noble
Marketing manager: Lorna Patkai
Cover design: Naomi Robinson
Typeset by: C&M Digitals (P) Ltd, Chennai, India
Printed and bound in Great Britain by Ashford Colour Press Ltd

First edition published 2008.
Second edition published 2012, reprinted 2014.

Library of Congress Control Number: 2015932149

British Library Cataloguing in Publication data

A catalogue record for this book is available from the British Library

ISBN 978-1-4739-0792-8
ISBN 978-1-4739-0793-5 (pbk)

This third edition of *Training to Teach* is dedicated to the memory of Dr Roger Crawford, a major contributor to the first two editions, who died peacefully at home in November 2014. Roger had recently retired as a Senior Lecturer in Education at the University of Huddersfield and will be missed by both former colleagues and students. He had worked abroad extensively, teaching in multicultural, urban secondary schools in New Zealand and Australia before returning to the UK where, alongside his career in Higher Education, he became a Chief Examiner for GCSE ICT and Functional Skills in ICT, and an Ofsted inspector for 11–18 schools and teacher training.

His writing is extensive, with publications including textbooks to support the teaching and learning of ICT and academic articles in practitioner publications and journals.

I remember Roger as one of life's gentlemen, who possessed a wry sense of humour. He turned many of his teacher trainees into excellent mentors, and stayed in touch with them over the years, showing interest in their progress and promotion. He was always supportive, always dedicated, and above all, someone who could call on a wealth of expertise, which he was always willing to share.

Dr Neil Denby
September 2015

CONTENTS

LIST OF TABLES AND FIGURES

Tables

Figures

ABOUT THE EDITOR

Neil Denby has been involved in teacher education for over eighteen years. He is a Fellow of the Chartered Institute of Educational Assessors and a Fellow of the Higher Education Academy. An experienced and successful author, he has written over two dozen texts at various levels from GCSE to postgraduate. He also has extensive experience teaching abroad, both in the Middle East and China. Recently retired from the School of Education and Professional Development at the University of Huddersfield, he now acts as an independent educational consultant. His research interests include using the abilities of gifted and talented pupils to enhance the learning experience; the importance of pupil voice in teacher-training partnerships; the promotion and impact of Master's-level PGCE requirements; and the encouragement of pupils from disadvantaged backgrounds into higher education.

ABOUT THE CONTRIBUTORS

Jan Barnes is a Senior Lecturer and Programme Lead for the Secondary PGCE in computing with ICT in the South West Wales Centre for Teacher Education at the University of Wales Trinity Saint David. She has previously taught ICT and Business Studies in both secondary schools and Further Education. In addition to her role in Secondary ITET she also teaches on Master's level courses and has a role in research. Her interests lie in the use of technology to support teaching and digital literacy, and the development of metacognition.

Nina Barnes is a Senior Lecturer in Education at the University of Huddersfield and teaches on the Secondary PGCE course specialising in Business Education. A graduate of the PGCE at Huddersfield herself, she has returned to the University after fifteen successful years' teaching at Sowerby Bridge High School in Halifax, West Yorkshire. Over the course of her employment Nina held the positions of Head of Year, Director of Sixth Form Studies, Assistant Headteacher and most recently Associate Deputy Headteacher with responsibility for Teaching and Learning. Nina has also worked as a subject and professional mentor to ITE students for the length of her employment.

Robert Butroyd is a Teacher Educator with nineteen years' experience. Prior to this he taught economics and business education in secondary schools for fourteen years, including schools in the West Midlands, Yorkshire and Galloway. His current research interests include action research, teachers' occupational experiences and pupil disengagement.

Sue Cronin is Deputy Head of the School of Teacher Education at Liverpool Hope University. She started her teaching career in Liverpool as a secondary mathematics teacher and taught in a variety of schools before joining the local authority supporting Gifted and Talented pupils across the city. Since joining Liverpool Hope Sue has worked on a variety of programmes linked to teacher education including Secondary PGCE Leader, and Coordinator of Mathematics Education. Her main research interests are around the areas of teacher education, mathematics education and creativity.

Matthew Crowther is Assistant Headteacher at Rastrick High School, a large academy-status school in Brighouse, West Yorkshire, in the north of England. He has a background in industry and is responsible for the school's technology specialism, timetable and whole school ITC, in addition to teaching economics, business studies and ICT.

Simon Evans has been involved in teacher training for over twenty years and is currently Director of Secondary Initial Teacher Education and Training at the South West Wales Centre of Teacher Education and Training. He is a Fellow of the Chartered Institute of Educational Assessors and a Fellow of the Higher Education Academy. Prior to this, he was a teacher and Head of Business and Economics in secondary schools in England and Wales. Simon is a Principal Lecturer in Education at the University of Wales Trinity St David and PGCE Tutor. He is also an examiner for other secondary PGCEs and an A Level Business examiner. His research interests include mentoring and coaching in developing teachers, assessment and thinking skills in Business and Economics, and the development of the Welsh Baccalaureate Qualification.

Angela Gault is Head of Education Partnerships and Lead Tutor for secondary Professional Studies in the Institute of Education at the University of Wolverhampton. She teaches on ITE and NQT Master's programmes and is an EdD supervisor. She taught English for over twenty years, mainly in Black Country secondary schools, and was a subject leader. Angela also worked for five years as a local authority school improvement consultant, providing CDP support to schools in challenging circumstances, before moving into Initial Teacher Education. She is interested in education policy and teachers' professional development.

Jonathan Glazzard is a University Teaching Fellow at the University of Huddersfield. He leads the primary initial teacher education provision and is also responsible for promoting effective teaching and learning across the university. Jonathan's research focuses on special education, inclusive education and disability. He believes in the power of education to transform the lives of pupils and he produces pedagogic research which promotes effective teaching and learning practices in schools and higher education.

Sandra Hiett is an independent researcher in arts education. She currently delivers initial teacher training at Liverpool Hope University on the Schools Direct programme, and was formerly PGCE art and design route leader and Artist Teacher MA programme leader at Liverpool John Moores University. Sandra is a founding partner of the Artist Teacher Associates, a continuing professional development organisation for arts-based educators. She is also deputy editor of the international *Journal of Art and Design Education* (iJADE) and a Fellow of the Research in Education for Creativity, Art and Performance (RECAP) at the University of Chester. Her main research interests include creativity, social justice and anti-racist education.

Michael Lamb is a former Head of History at a large academy school in Doncaster, in the north of England. He has had fourteen years' experience as a teacher, with eight years as Head of Department. He has recently moved to continue his career in Poole, Dorset. His love of teaching history and Newcastle United should not be held against him, as he needs history to remember when Newcastle United last won anything.

Joanne Pearson is Head of the Teamworks Teaching School Alliance in Calderdale, working across nursery, primary, secondary and special school settings to support teacher development and build research capacity. She also works as a tutor on the National Award for Special Needs Co-ordination and as a tutor for Teach First. Prior to her current post she was a university lecturer and secondary history teacher.

Jayne Price is Head of Division for Initial Teacher Education (Schools), Troops to Teachers Course Manager and Subject Coordinator for the secondary PGCE Music course in the School of Education and Professional Development at the University of Huddersfield. She taught for fifteen years as a music teacher and Head of Music in secondary schools in Derbyshire and Leeds, and spent the last two years of her time in school on the senior leadership team as CPD Coordinator with responsibility for staff training and development.

Ian Quigley is Assistant Headteacher at Sowerby Bridge High School, a multicultural comprehensive school in West Yorkshire. He is responsible for Curriculum and Assessment and has mentored ITT students and newly qualified teachers for many years. He is a Fellow of the Chartered Institute of Educational Assessors and a supporter of Burnley Football Club.

Rod Robertson is a Senior Lecturer in the School of Education at the University of Huddersfield. He worked for sixteen years in secondary schools as a Head of Department and Head of Faculty. He currently works on the ITE PGCE programme and also has experience of Teach First and Troops to Teachers. He has considerable experience of working with MA and PhD students, and of overseas teaching. His main research interests are leadership in secondary schools and Design & Technology as a secondary school subject.

Ed Southall is a lecturer in Education at the University of Huddersfield and teaches on the secondary PGCE course specialising in mathematics education. He also teaches maths at a large secondary school in Holmfirth. Ed is a former Assistant Headteacher and has held positions as both a Head of Mathematics and Head of ICT in previous roles. He has also worked as an education consultant in the Middle East.

John Trafford was until 2011 Head of the Department of Initial Teacher Education and Continuing Professional Development at the University of Huddersfield. Prior to this he was a secondary school French and German teacher, then languages tutor and PGCE course director at the University of Sheffield. Currently he is professional tutor and modern languages subject tutor to Teach First participants for Sheffield Hallam University. He is a former president of the Association for Language Learning.

Fiona Woodhouse is presently the coordinator of the Science with Biology, Chemistry and Physics PGCE courses at the University of Huddersfield. Previously she taught predominantly science and biology in schools for fifteen years, whilst additionally having a variety of responsibilities, before moving into initial and continuing teacher education. Fiona's main interests are in science subject pedagogy and in supporting teachers with classroom-based research.

FOREWORD

In 2007 the influential report on some of the highest achieving education systems in the world produced by McKinsey and Company noted that the quality of teaching within these countries was the single biggest determinant of their success. The extensive field of research on school effectiveness and improvement, the findings produced by our inspection bodies and the practical wisdom of teachers all point to the same conclusion.

Initial teacher education plays a pivotal and often underestimated role in this process of engendering outstanding teaching. Recent reports from the British Education Research Association/Royal Society of Arts on practice in the various national systems of the United Kingdom have sharpened our understanding of the critical role played by teacher education in career-long professional learning.

In particular they point to the importance of university-led programmes developed in partnership with schools that provide excellent settings for students to engage in 'clinical practice' models of work-based learning. At the heart of this process, they argue, should lie research-informed knowledge which provides trainee teachers with a sound basis for critical reflection on their own emerging practice.

This excellent textbook provides exactly the type of primer that is needed for these foundations to be securely in place. It is suffused with practical wisdom and research-based knowledge in equal measure and presented in a lively and engaging format.

It is a pleasure to commend it both to students taking their first steps into the great profession of teaching and to their tutors and mentors who have the privilege and the great responsibility of working with them.

David Egan
Professor of Welsh Education Policy,
University of Wales Trinity Saint David

ACKNOWLEDGEMENTS

SAGE would like to thank the following reviewers whose feedback helped to shape this new edition:

Branwen Bingle, University of Worcester

Caroline Crolla, University of Reading

Liam Cullinan, Perry Beeches The Academy

Marion Hobbs, Edge Hill University

Sarah Martin-Denham, University of Sunderland

Lizana Oberholzer, The Buckingham Partnership SCITT

CHAPTER 1

LEARNING TO TEACH: AN INTRODUCTION

Neil Denby

Introduction

Education is characterised by change. It is a constant kaleidoscope of competing policies and initiatives which means that any education text that wishes to retain and expand its market share needs to be subject to regular updates. The second edition of *Training to Teach* was published in 2012, just as the new teaching standards were applied, and as key policies like Every Child Matters and the Diplomas faded from prominence. Since then, government policy has brought about a number of changes – to schools, to qualifications and examinations, and to teacher training. Currently the sector faces changes to A levels and GCSEs, to other forms of testing such as coursework and controlled assessment, to the ways that progress in schools is measured and managed, to new policies on inclusion, even to the way that schools are funded. The very structure of the sector has changed as the number of different school types and training routes has also multiplied.

This edition includes revisions to all the chapters in the second edition, to bring them in line with current education policies and outlooks. In some cases these revisions (for example in those chapters on inclusion, assessment and securing a teaching post) have been major. New research and reading have been introduced where further discussions and analysis have been published. In addition, there are six new chapters, designed to target areas of growing concern or emphasis. These are as follows:

- **School-based training.** This chapter discusses the pros and cons of learning to teach 'on the job' in a school setting, through new routes into teaching such as School Direct and Troops to Teachers. In particular it focuses on learning from observation (of self and others) and from the mentoring process (this chapter therefore subsumes the previous edition's chapter on mentoring). It also includes the importance of SMART targets, measures of progress towards targets, and of making progress through reflection.
- **Classroom management.** This chapter, although based in part on the previous chapter on Classroom Management and Behaviour Strategies, focuses more directly on developing a classroom presence and on creating a positive learning environment through utilising key tools, such as the use of voice and awareness of the power of body language.
- **Behaviour strategies in challenging classrooms.** The focus here is on how, as a teacher, you can recognise and support children in crisis and develop the skills to de-escalate inappropriate behaviour in the classroom. This chapter will also help you to recognise and develop your own role as a practitioner in providing the 'classroom experience'.
- **Inclusion.** This chapter expands on the second edition's chapter on English as an Additional Language by widening its focus to include children with Special Educational Needs, new and current policies on inclusion, and strategies for successfully teaching children with disabilities.
- **Using digital technologies in teaching strategies.** This chapter recognises the significance of new media, including social media, on children and young people, and therefore their impact on education. It therefore includes advice on the use and abuse of social media and specifics on online safeguarding. It also looks at the use of interactive whiteboards and the use of image and voice capture technology.
- **Harnessing creativity in the classroom.** The joy of effective teaching can often be found in the activities and learning tools that children and young people can be encouraged to use in the classroom. This chapter explores the idea of creative approaches to teaching and suggests some ideas and activities that might harness pupils' creative abilities to enhance learning.

Which country?

The UK does not have a single system of education, nor of teacher-training. Scotland, Northern Ireland and Wales each have their own systems. In Scotland, there are undergraduate and postgraduate university routes for primary and secondary. Whilst the

General Teaching Council (GTC) for England has been abolished, the Scottish professional body (GTC Scotland) still flourishes and you must be a member of it before you can teach in Scotland. The Scottish equivalent of the Disclosure and Barring Service (DBS) is the Protection of Vulnerable Groups (PVG) Scheme, which carries out similar checks into previous convictions and cautions. A key part of the training process in Scotland is the first or induction year. The Teacher Induction Scheme guarantees a one-year teaching post in a Scottish local authority, with teachers on a reduced timetable and supported by a mentor. Non-university routes do not exist in Scotland. In Wales there are Graduate Teacher Training (GTP) routes and trainees in Wales can access certain routes in England. There is a General Teaching Council for Wales and a different set of teacher standards to attain. In Northern Ireland the equivalent to the DBS is AccessNI and teachers must be registered with the GTC Northern Ireland. Courses in Initial Teacher Education (ITE) in Northern Ireland are university based.

When it comes to teaching your subject, remember that the National Curriculum only applies in England, so if you intend to teach in any of the other Home Countries, you will need to investigate the position and status of your subject. Also, Ofsted is peculiar to England. In Wales ESTYN is the inspectorate, in Scotland it is Education Scotland, and in Northern Ireland the Education and Training Inspectorate (ETI) is the relevant body.

Despite these differences most of the content of this book will be relevant to most teacher training routes, in particular those chapters on professionalism, classroom behaviour and learning, digital technologies, inclusion, assessment, child protection, differentiation and creativity.

Which route?

If you decide that you really want to teach, you probably already have a good idea of the age range in which you want to specialise. Training is specific to an age range, although broadly speaking you will train to teach in primary education (4–11 years old), secondary education (11–18 or 19 years old) or the post-compulsory or Further Education sector (19+). The country in which you wish to train will also have a significant bearing on the training you receive, and perhaps more importantly, on the costs of such training. If you normally live and decide to train in Wales, for example, you may gain financial support from a Welsh Government Fee Grant, a Learning Grant, or from Tuition Fee Support. In England, various designated shortage subjects may receive tax free bursaries as an incentive to students to teach a particular subject. In Scotland, the situation for Scottish residents is different again. A quick web search will let you know what is currently available.

The two usual points of entry to a teaching qualification are at undergraduate or postgraduate level. You will need at least two 'A' levels in appropriate subjects (depending on the training institution) as well as a Grade C or better (there is talk of raising this to Grade B) in English and mathematics at GCSE. For primary teaching you will also require a GCSE pass in a science subject. This is because primary teachers (and also some Key Stage 3 teachers, for which a similar requirement may be in place) are required to teach across the breadth of the curriculum. Undergraduate training courses are usually three or four years of full-time study and will lead to a degree in Education.

Postgraduate entrants will already have a degree in an appropriate subject. (Some subjects are difficult to align with the school curriculum so think carefully about specialising in law or psychology, for example, before applying to teach business education or mathematics.) One of the most popular routes into teaching is the one year Postgraduate Certificate in Education (PGCE), which will also include some work at Master's level.

You may also, of course, already be teaching as an 'unqualified teacher' in the independent sector, in which case you can opt for an 'Assessment Only' route, where a portfolio evidencing your knowledge, skills and progress may be presented. If you are an overseas trained teacher (OTT) there may also be shorter routes available to qualified teacher status (QTS).

Entry onto all teacher training courses is now also dependent on your passing the professional skills tests in English and mathematics. Without doing so, a training provider will not be allowed to accept you onto a course of study.

Your decision to teach shows that you have already recognised that the rewards of teaching far outweigh the hard work and effort that go into training and into becoming an effective classroom practitioner. More than that, though, you have also accepted that you are about to set out on a lifelong journey of learning and discovery.

You will have recognised that, as individuals, we never stop learning, but that as children and young people we need to be equipped with the skills and competencies to enable learning to take place. You will be entering one of the most hard-working, dedicated and rewarding professions.

Up to 35,000 people train to be teachers each year, spread over higher education institutions (HEIs) such as universities and teacher training colleges, employment-based routes, 'SCiTTs' (School-based Initial Teacher Training), Teach First (currently based in challenging schools), GTPs (Graduate Teacher Programmes) and RTPs (Registered Teacher Programmes). Other routes are available through training schools, or by recruiting candidates with previous experience in industry or the armed forces. Intending teachers can choose the route that is most appropriate to their own needs, circumstances and experience.

Each route involves different levels of funding and support, from academic or practice-based personnel. Each receives more or less emphasis (and funding support) depending on the political colour of the government in office, or the specific leanings of the current Education Minister. All will equip the student or trainee teacher with generic skills and capabilities that are transferable into all classrooms. Some will need skills that are more attuned to primary, or those with special needs, or examination biased teaching; others will operate in the private sector, as subject specialists in secondary education, as peripatetic support, and even as consultants. The issues of assessment, subject knowledge, classroom management and behaviour, preparation, pedagogy, differentiation, innovation and creativity in the classroom are all – along with numerous others – central to the operation of the successful teacher. For a qualified teacher, depending on the circumstances, each of these will be more or less central or peripheral, but all will be present.

This book is designed to be of use to anyone either contemplating teaching or who has already joined a teacher training course. It will also be of value to those on post-compulsory (16+) courses who are aiming for QTLS (Qualified Teacher, Learning and Skills), which, from 2011, as outlined in the Wolf Report (DfE, 2011), will also allow them to teach in schools. It is designed and written to give you an overview of requirements for good practice, and to point you towards specific further reading, reflection, study and practice. Appropriate reference is made to underpinning theory, and features are used to link this to practical applications in the classroom and to the important areas of professional studies – the core classroom knowledge and skills that are at the heart of all teacher training courses.

Features

The specific standards required by government change from time to time, but the underlying knowledge and skills that a set of standards represents do not. The new Part One Standards, as revised in 2011 and applied from September 2012, are the current required standards that must be reached for those aiming for QTS. The 2012 Standards for Qualified Teachers refer to teaching and responsibilities under eight headings:

- Set high expectations which inspire, motivate and challenge pupils
- Promote good progress and outcomes by pupils
- Demonstrate good subject and curriculum knowledge
- Plan and teach well structured lessons
- Adapt teaching to respond to the strengths and needs of all pupils
- Make accurate and productive use of assessment
- Manage behaviour effectively to ensure a good and safe learning environment
- Fulfil wider professional responsibilities.

Part Two Standards refer to 'personal and professional conduct' under three headings:

- Teachers uphold public trust in the profession and maintain high standards of ethics and behaviour, within and outside school
- Teachers must have proper and professional regard for the ethos, policies and practices of the school in which they teach, and maintain high standards in their own attendance and punctuality
- Teachers must have an understanding of, and always act within, the statutory frameworks that set out their professional duties and responsibilities.

The current Standards are detailed in Appendix II, and specific links are made to them at the start of each chapter. Each chapter is written with one or more of the specific areas of knowledge or expertise linked to the Standards in mind. As well as these specific references, the chapter content will also often cover elements of other Standards. Teaching is a holistic activity, and it is difficult to completely separate the skills and knowledge required to, for example, maintain a positive and productive classroom, into separate micro-managed features. Trainee teachers will find it a useful and instructive learning exercise to link this chapter content to whichever standards, requirements and expectations are in place.

You will find that some concepts, ideas and policies are so important that they are mentioned in many different contexts. This means that, although a concept or policy might have a chapter to itself, it will also be mentioned in other places as relevant. Child protection issues, for example, although they have a chapter of their own, are also mentioned in several other places. This just serves to underline their importance.

Each of the boxed features you will find in every chapter has a specific function or purpose. At the end of a chapter, there is a bullet-pointed summary to help you remember and apply what you have learned. The group exercise is an idea for an activity or discussion that can take place during university- or college-based learning sessions, or can be adapted for use if you are on a non-HEI-based training route. The individual reflection is a prompt for you to think about your own practice and progress, and how you can improve. There is a short list of focused, key reading – in general reduced to particular articles, webpages or chapters of books to make it manageable, but a full list of references is also provided. The 'application to teaching' is a suggestion for a lesson plan or technique that will help you underpin the particular standard or standards that are the focus of the chapter in either a primary or a secondary context. In each chapter there are also several 'thoughts'. These are tips, ideas or thought-provokers to encourage thought and reflection on your part.

In addition to the text here, there is a companion website, available at no charge, to accompany the book. The website (https://study.sagepub.com/denby3e) contains additional material to help you understand and apply the concepts, knowledge and skills explained in the text. On the site are direct links to some of the reading – in particular to journal articles and other Sage publications – along with presentations on some of the key points explained in the chapters. You may add to these presentations and adapt them for your own use, both as aids to learning and to teaching. The reading will help to provide depth to your professional studies and, in addition, support assignment writing where this is a part of your course.

How do I qualify to be a teacher?

At present, you need to achieve the standards required to gain Qualified Teacher Status, with the current standards being those published in September 2012. This is the accreditation that will enable you to teach in state-maintained and special schools in England and Wales. The requirements in Northern Ireland and Scotland are slightly different, so if that is where you intend to train you will need to check those requirements. You will not need the QTS qualification if you wish to teach in the independent sector – you will, however, still need the knowledge and skills explored in this book. Your initial teacher training (ITT) provider will recommend you for QTS to the Department for Education (DfE). The award is automatic: no further study is required. To gain accreditation you must follow a course of initial teacher training and meet all of the standards as set out by the government body responsible. These standards are a set of statements that specify, in a formal way, the knowledge, understanding, skills and experiences that you must demonstrate. They provide the first stage in a continuum of teacher development from trainee to qualified teacher status (on successful completion of the induction year) through to excellent and advanced skills teachers. Teacher training standards can be grouped under three headings:

- **Professional values and practice.** Regarding the attitudes and commitment expected of anyone qualifying to be a teacher. Fairness, honesty, integrity and mutual respect will feature highly.
- **Knowledge and understanding.** Regarding the required and expected levels of subject knowledge from the teacher, along with expectations of what pupils should achieve.
- **Teaching.** These relate to the skill set needed to deliver effective lessons, such as managing a class, assessment and monitoring progress. Teaching standards in Wales are similar but cover some issues specific to Wales. In addition, in order to teach in England, you must pass the QTS skills tests in numeracy, literacy and information and communications technology (ICT).

Primary or secondary?

Compulsory schooling in England and Wales is divided into four key stages, sandwiched between pre-school learning and post-16 education. You will train to teach at least two key stages. At present, the stages are:

- Age 0–3: Pre-school
- Age 3–5: Early Years Foundation Stage (EYFS)
- Age 5–7: Years 1 and 2; Key Stage 1
- Age 7–11: Years 3, 4, 5, 6; Key Stage 2
- Age 11–14: Years 7, 8, 9; Key Stage 3
- Age 14–16: Years 10 and 11; Key Stage 4
- Age 16–19: Post-16: Years 12 and 13; VIth form or post-compulsory education; Key Stage 5

The role and importance of your subject specialism are greater at secondary level than at primary. At primary your 'specialism' is the core curriculum.

To teach primary at Key Stage 1 or 2 you will train to teach all the national curriculum subjects – the core made up of English, mathematics and science, plus the designated foundation subjects. You will be expected to have a good knowledge of all subjects. (The only exception to this 'general' rule is modern foreign languages. Because every Key Stage 2 pupil in England is entitled to study a foreign language it is possible to train as a primary teacher specialising in languages.) The teaching and learning emphasis is therefore on a range of subjects, but to a level appropriate for children of this age group.

At secondary (Key Stage 3, 4 and post-16) you will be expected to be a subject specialist, in a national curriculum subject or an accepted non-national curriculum subject (such as economics, psychology or business education) in which you have an appropriate and relevant degree. In some subjects, such as mathematics and physics, where there are shortages of teachers, you can undertake an enhancement course to improve your subject knowledge to the required level. Details of all courses, requirements and training routes can be found on the appropriate Department for Education website, where the links to current routes are housed.

A thought

If you are teaching secondary, go and watch a primary teacher at work. You will be amazed at their energy, ingenuity and enthusiasm. Of course, the opposite case holds if you are training at primary level!

Application to secondary teaching

When introducing yourself to a new class it is essential that you learn names. Children and young people respond much more readily when spoken to by name. You could make this part of a game or exercise, supply labels, or make learners state their name before answering a question. A seating plan will also help you to remember.

The reflective practitioner

You are entering a profession where lifelong learning is an expectation. Innovation and experimentation will always be a part of your working life. This is just one reason why the skills you will gain in the classroom and through your study should be augmented by further professional development. You will find that you go through a number of stages on your way to becoming a confident classroom practitioner.

Fuller (1969) suggests a three-stage model of teacher training. Initially, the trainee has a concern about 'self' – how am I doing? How will I cope? What will the kids think of me? Secondly, a concern about tasks is developed – how are my lesson plans? Have I prepared enough material? What about my marking? Finally, the focus turns to the learners, first as a class, then as individual learners – how well is so-and-so doing? What extra materials might help? How can I explain this more clearly? Each stage of this development requires you to reflect on your progress, i.e. to think about the journey, where you are, where you want to be, and what is going to take you to the next stage. As one who delivers education, you are a practitioner; as one who considers how they can improve and move forward, how they can learn from their own and others' experience, you are reflective. Your goal is therefore to become a reflective practitioner.

The student teachers in Buitink's (2008) study of 'what and how trainee teachers learnt' realised there was a range of issues on which to reflect. They approached thinking about their teaching based on a combination of different factors, such as dealing with pupil behaviour, variation within the lesson, pupil motivation, responding to the context, paying attention to pupil development and backgrounds, their own role as teachers and their necessary instructional skills. The pupils' learning process also became increasingly important (2008: 123). Stephen Lerman (2013: 52) provides a comprehensive description of reflective practice as:

> Developing the skills of sharpening attention to what is going on in the classroom, noticing and recording significant events and 'working' on them in order to learn as much as possible about children's learning and the role of the teacher.

GROUP EXERCISE

Consider Fuller's three stages of trainee teacher development. Talk about these with a qualified teacher in post and see if they agree with the stages. Discuss the intermediate stages that might also take place and how you could manage them.

Application to primary teaching

Look at the factors that Buitink's trainees thought might have a significant effect on their teaching. What other factors do you think you could add, that would be of particular importance in the primary and early years setting? Plan a lesson to take at least some of these factors into account.

Reading and writing

In order to progress and reflect, you must read extensively. While each chapter will introduce you to some key texts, you will need to find others for yourself. Should you find an area particularly useful or interesting, use your library service to find out more about it. A good starting point is often the list of references that the writer of a chapter, article or book has cited. As with any 'social science', education has its different theorists who may not agree with one another. You will need to consider what each one is saying and how it applies to your own set of circumstances before making your own judgement as to which theorist you feel is correct. In time you will develop your own theories and methods that are particular to your needs and those of your learners'.

You will be expected to write at a reasonably high level. On many teacher training routes you will not only have the opportunity but also be positively encouraged to write at Master's level. You will find this (and subsequent professional development) easier if you are used to reading widely.

Some things of which you should be aware!

There are several features which single out education and training from other professions and you will encounter many of these within the pages of this book. Three key areas are particularly apposite to education: external factors; change as the norm; and the use of specialised terminology and acronyms.

External factors

Unlike other professions where the professional can often take the lofty position that s/he is the expert, in education everyone is an expert. All have been to school and therefore all will have an opinion on some aspect or other of education. You must learn to take this in your stride and not be put off by the many times a parent, governor or friend will tell you that 'this is how it should be done', or 'this is what really works', or the even more traditional 'in my day ...'. Ignore them. You are doing the best possible job for these young people, in this situation, here and now.

Your effectiveness will also increase or decrease in relation to the circumstances in which you are teaching. Social and economic circumstances, for example, may have a huge effect on a child's ability to learn and their ultimate attainment. Research (Blanden and Machin, 2007) suggests that social class is still the most powerful influence on educational attainment, even to degree level: 44 per cent of the richest fifth of the population have degrees, compared with just 10 per cent of the poorest fifth. The authors of this Sutton Trust report state that both attainment and behaviour are affected by social class, and movement from one class to another has slowed to a standstill since 1970. Two other hypotheses are suggested by Hout (2006, 2007). These are Maximally Maintained Inequality (MMI) and Effectively Maintained Inequality (EMI) (see also Lucas, 2001, 2009) which argue that inequality in education will remain. Boliver (2011: 230) explains why:

> ... those from more advantaged socioeconomic backgrounds are better placed to take up the new educational opportunities that expansion affords (MMI) and to secure for themselves qualitatively better kinds of education at any given level (EMI).

These arguments say that, effectively, the better-off will secure places at better institutions so that even if, quantitatively, it looks like more people are attending, say, university (this study was based on the tertiary sector), qualitatively, the most sought after places at the most prestigious institutions will still be populated by those from better-off socio-economic groups. Boliver used empirical data from the past forty years of UK education to prove this has been the case in the past and remains so today.

A thought

How important do you think social and economic circumstances are to educational attainment? What other external factors do you think might be important? How might you mitigate their effects?

Change as the norm

There is never a moment when there is not some change being proposed, implemented, monitored, measured or assessed. As this book was being written, a whole basket of changes was being proposed. These included:

- a new National Curriculum, in place from September 2014, with further changes in 2015, 2016 and 2017
- new English, mathematics and science tests for Years 2 and 6 from 2016
- suggestions that larger class sizes do not affect progress and may be used to make education budgets more 'efficient'
- a push for more academies to be formed, outside local authority control, and for more 'Free Schools' to be established

- the establishment of a different way to measure the progress of pupils in secondary school (Progress 8)
- financial capability introduced as a National Curriculum subject area
- the raising of the school-leaving age incrementally from 16 to 18 years old
- a possible move to a two-year PGCE as standard, along with the removal of the controversial policy that allows some schools to employ unqualified teachers
- an emphasis on the teaching of reading through a system of synthetic phonics
- resit opportunities for candidates at GCSE and GCE limited
- modular examination courses reconstituted to rely on a final examination
- a reduction in the role of coursework or controlled assessment in examinations, in many subjects, its complete removal
- the application of a new SEND (Special Educational Needs and Disabilities) Code of Practice.

INDIVIDUAL REFLECTION

Which of the changes described here is likely to have the most effect on your teaching? Think about how you can alter your teaching to take this into account.

Recent changes in education include new teaching routes and sets of standards, along with new GCSE and AS and A level courses written to new subject criteria. Some subjects (like modern foreign languages and mathematics) may find that they have a more secure place in the curriculum; others (such as media studies and psychology) that they are no longer in favour. Coursework and its manifestation as Controlled Assessment will play a much reduced role in examinations. All the changes and innovations are aimed at the long-term vision of improving schools and producing a step-change in the way parents and families are supported to deal with the new challenges faced by young people in the twenty-first century.

Specifically with regard to educational attainment targets, 90 per cent of children are expected to develop well across all areas of the Early Years Foundation Stage profile by age 5, 90 per cent of children should reach or exceed expected levels in English and mathematics by age 11, 90 per cent should achieve the equivalent of five higher level GCSEs by age 19 (with 70 per cent achieving at least two A' levels or equivalent) while every young person will have the skills for adult life and further study.

In 1972 the school leaving age was raised to 16. In 2013 it rose to 17, and by 2015 it will be 18. Young people aged 16–18 will not have to stay in school necessarily, but will have to be in some form of training. The policy was one of the last Labour government's and was adopted by the incoming Liberal/Conservative coalition government. At the time it was announced 11 per cent of 16–18 year olds were NEETs (Not in Employment, Education or Training), and the policy is, at least in part, to counter this trend. (There are novel ways to police such leaving ages: in Canada, for example, under-18 year olds are denied a driving licence unless they can prove they are in education or training.)

Terminology

'Children and young people' is now the preferred nomenclature for pupils or any young person in an educational setting. In this book, to save using the entire 'children and young people' phrase at every turn, we tend to use it sometimes, but at other times refer to 'pupils', 'children', 'young people', 'students', or even 'learners'. You can presume that these terms are interchangeable. Trainee teachers are generally referred to as 'trainees', although the book addresses the reader directly whenever possible. Teachers are also referred to as 'practitioners'.

You will find that education is rife with 'TLAs' – no, not teaching and learning assistants (although they are, of course, TLAs), but Three Letter Acronyms. Examples include AQA, HMI, CPD, QTS, QCA, ICT and ZPD, along with other codes such as 'Key Stage 3', 'Key Stage 4' and 'Early Years'. If someone uses one of these, whether it is at a meeting, on your placement or during taught sessions, they will be doing so in the expectation that everyone in the audience recognises and understands that acronym. However this is seldom the case. If you don't know what an acronym stands for, don't be afraid to ask. Often you will find that you are one of many who did not know, as new terms are coined almost on a daily basis. There is a list of some of the terms in most widespread use in Appendix I at the back of the book, along with space for you to add others as they are invented.

And the reason you are taking up teaching?

You will remember what it was all about when Shawn (sic), Kylii (sic) or Leeza (sic) (for it will be they) come up to you on the last day of term and say 'Thanks, Sir', 'Thanks, Miss'; when you have sweated over a trip, through the minefield of health and safety, travel sickness and the emotional trauma of being more than five miles from home, and the last kid off the bus, in the dark, says 'That was great, Miss, I've never seen anything like that before, can we go again?'; when the examination results are published and your quiet pleasure is greater in the D grade that your 'failing' student achieved rather than the A grade that your top student gained. As teachers, we each have the potential to have a huge influence on the lives and outlooks of all those we teach. If we have been effective, we will loom large in their memories; if we've been fair, we'll be remembered with respect; if we've been kind, or humorous, we'll be remembered with affection. Pupils will come up to you years later and say 'Hi Sir, remember me?'

Summary

- Qualified Teacher Status (QTS) is the accreditation that enables you to teach in state-maintained and special schools in England and Wales.
- To achieve QTS, you must show that you are competent and professional in line with current teaching standards.
- You will train in primary or secondary, and across at least two key stages.
- You will aim to become a reflective practitioner and a lifelong learner.
- You are entering a profession where, in spite of numerous external factors, you will have the power to change young people's lives.

Key reading

Buitink, J. (2008) 'What and how do student teachers learn during school-based teacher education?', *Teaching and Teacher Education,* 25 (1): 118–27.

Review of Vocational Education – The Wolf Report (2011) DFE-00031-2011.

The Education Act (2011). London: HMSO.

Lerman, S. (2013) 'Reflective practice', in B. Jaworski and A. Watson (eds), *Mentoring in mathematics teaching*. London: Routledge.

The current Standards for Qualified Teacher Status.

References and bibliography

Blanden, J. and Machin, S. (2007) *Recent changes in intergenerational mobility in Britain*. London: Sutton Trust.

Boliver, V. (2011) 'Expansion, differentiation, and the persistence of social class inequalities in British higher education', *Higher Education,* 61 (3): 229–42.

Buitink, J. (2008) 'What and how do student teachers learn during school-based teacher education?', *Teaching and Teacher Education,* 25 (1): 118–27.

DfE (2011) *Review of Vocational Education – The Wolf Report*. DfE-00031-2011.

Fuller, F. (1969) 'Concerns of teachers: a developmental conceptualization', *American Educational Research Journal,* 6: 207–26.

Hout, M. (2006) 'Maximally maintained inequality and essentially maintained inequality: cross-national comparisons', *Sociological Theory and Methods,* 21 (2): 237–52.

Hout, M. (2007) 'Maximally maintained inequality revisited: Irish educational mobility in comparative perspective', in B. Hilliard and M.N.G. Phadraig (eds), *Changing Ireland in inter national comparison*. Dublin: The Liffey Press.

Lerman, S. (2013) 'Reflective practice', in B. Jaworski and A. Watson (eds), *Mentoring in mathematics teaching*. London: Routledge.
Lucas, S.R. (2001) 'Effectively maintained inequality: education transitions, track mobility, and social background effects', *American Journal of Sociology,* 106: 1642–90.
Lucas, S.R. (2009) 'Stratification theory, socioeconomic background, and educational attainment: a formal analysis', *Rationality and Society*, 21 (4): 459–511.

Visit https://study.sagepub.com/denby3e for extra resources related to this chapter.

Part I

PROFESSIONAL ATTRIBUTES

This opening section is designed to give information and advice on the way you are expected to behave and develop as a professional. The chapters naturally fall together to give a picture of the professional life of the teacher – one who has a number of constituencies to satisfy. At the centre are the children and young people you will teach. With them comes an intricate web of others (individuals, frameworks and institutions) with which you must work. These are accompanied by a set of expectations such as professional behaviour, the ability to communicate, team working, reflecting and learning.

You will not just be a teacher but also a role model, a surrogate parent (*in loco parentis*), an adviser and a learner, expected to keep up to date with the latest in theory and practice. Some of these expectations will be laid down in duties and regulations, covered by professional bodies and even legislation. Keeping children safe, for example, is a legal duty. Some are more to do with how you work and interact with colleagues such as specialist support staff and your own mentors. All are central to how you are perceived – by other professionals, by society, but most importantly, by the children in your charge.

CHAPTER 2

RELATIONSHIPS WITH CHILDREN AND YOUNG PEOPLE

Robert Butroyd

Standards linked to this chapter include...

1. Set high expectations which inspire, motivate and challenge pupils

   - establish a safe and stimulating environment for pupils, rooted in mutual respect
   - set goals that stretch and challenge pupils of all backgrounds, abilities and dispositions
   - demonstrate consistently the positive attitudes, values and behaviour which are expected of pupils.

(Continued)

(Continued)

Teachers' Standards Part 2: Personal and Professional Conduct

Teachers must demonstrate consistently high standards of personal and professional conduct. Teachers uphold public trust in the profession and maintain high standards of ethics and behaviour, within and outside school, by:

- treating pupils with dignity, building relationships rooted in mutual respect, and at all times observing proper boundaries appropriate to a teacher's professional position
- having regard for the need to safeguard pupils' wellbeing, in accordance with statutory provisions
- showing tolerance of and respect for the rights of others
- not undermining fundamental British values, including democracy, the rule of law, individual liberty and mutual respect, and tolerance of those with different faiths and beliefs
- ensuring that personal beliefs are not expressed in ways which exploit pupils' vulnerability or might lead them to break the law.

Introduction

The Standards make it clear that as a teacher it is expected that you will become a role model for the children you teach. You will need to 'demonstrate consistently high standards of personal and professional conduct' and 'maintain high standards of ethics and behaviour'. This includes sensible advice to keep your own personal beliefs to yourself rather than 'promote' them, and to tolerate and respect others' rights. As a teacher you are in a position of power over pupils who, at any age, may be considered to be vulnerable and easily manipulated. Primary school children in particular may have views and opinions that could be swayed by those of their teacher (with whom, in many cases, they will spend more time than with their parents). Secondary school children may appear to have more 'street-cred' but are often just as vulnerable. It is easy for you to subconsciously and inadvertently imprint a view on a child so it is imperative that you behave professionally and neutrally in all situations.

This is one of the reasons why it is so important to the teaching profession to have teachers from all walks and sectors of society and the community – so that they can provide positive role models for those sections of the community with which they most identify themselves. As a teacher, you will be a role model, so it is incumbent on you to become a positive role model – this means not allowing pupils to witness those traits or behaviours that might detract from such a model. Pupils observe teachers, even when they are off guard. Whether they like it or not pupils learn from the ways in which teachers carry out their role, how they behave towards them and towards other adults. This does not necessarily mean that you have to conform to a stereotype as you can (and should) still be yourself. New teachers may struggle with the idea of being a role model but can still be successful. Others, with the confidence of experience, may be more relaxed about their role and nonetheless successful. As a teacher you need not lead the life of a saint – indeed if you imply that you do then many pupils will be lost to you. Pupils and teachers need to develop an awareness of their 'audience' and 'appropriate' behaviour.

This chapter will set you on your way to developing the values, attitudes and behaviour that will help you encourage children to achieve their full educational potential.

Protection, safeguarding and the hidden curriculum

Protection and safeguarding are major concerns for those who care for children and young people. The Education and Inspections Act 2006 required schools to promote children's wellbeing. The notion of wellbeing is underpinned by an exploration of values: being healthy; staying safe; enjoying and achieving; making a positive contribution; achieving economic wellbeing. These values, and others related to protection and safeguarding, are evident in the curriculum, the organisation of the school day, the selection of teaching materials, methods and lesson content. This might be termed the hidden curriculum. Subsequent planning continues to focus on the needs and safety of the child, thus the 2007 Children's Plan claims that government has:

> ...been listening to parents, teachers, professionals, and children and young people themselves. [It] heard that while there are more opportunities for young people today than ever before, parents want more support in managing the new pressures they face such as balancing work and family life, dealing with the internet and the modern commercial world, and letting their children play and learn whilst staying safe. (HMSO, 2007: 3)

This chapter focuses on another aspect of the hidden curriculum: teachers and their relationships. These relationships can on occasions be difficult, particularly with pupils. Pupils are perhaps wise to be wary of teachers who are felt to 'pry' too much into what they really think, if those teachers are responsible for assessment and discipline and can compel pupils to work in groups, speak in public or conform to other forms of social behaviour. While pupils view teachers' motives with a certain degree of scepticism, they want relationships with integrity, relationships where teachers listen and respond to pupils' interests and motivations.

Communities

Teachers do not operate in a vacuum. Many schools can draw upon communities that promote educational values, while others draw upon communities that, because of parental experiences of education, or a number of other factors, do not. When investigating the school or schools where you will be training it would be worthwhile to look at the key indicators for the community in which each is based. On the one hand, a school may be placed in an affluent area, with many parents of professional status, where education is valued, encouraged and not stymied by economic necessity. On the other hand, a school could have many pupils with above average levels of deprivation as measured by indicators of relative poverty and deprivation: such indicators include workless households, single parent households, and levels of qualifications for preceding generations. In such a community, leaving school and beginning to earn a living may have a much higher priority than qualifications and further education. In some cases, for example, education may be valued, but young people in relative poverty must make the difficult choice between remaining in education in hopes of enhancing their future income, as opposed to becoming economically active (i.e. entering the jobs market) as early as possible. In these circumstances those little things which attempt to create a unity of identity in a school – specific rules of personal appearance, restricted access to parts of the building, pronouncements in assembly – can become negative influences on pupils' experiences, who can then become resentful of the school and its teachers. A school's ethos, or set of values, is thus important and can be instrumental in promoting positive values.

> A school's ethos can help pupils to develop expectations of responsibility and self reliance, to consult, to be honest about other people's feelings, and to respect each others' needs and desires. (Bigger and Brown, 2013: 9)

As a teacher you should strive to maintain your own approach, to maintain your integrity, but this can be a struggle. It is not intolerance to difference, it is more self-censorship. Ofsted, parental views, management teams, colleagues, syllabus constraints and poor resources are often cited as reasons for an inability to explore different pedagogies and different approaches to relationships. The numerous influences on such relationships have been the subject of research. For example, Buzzelli et al. (2008), looking at the difficulties of teaching science in an early years setting, measured teachers' cultural and ethical views of the nature of science alongside those they expected outside of this realm, and found that teachers' personal values and those they expected of scientists were not the same. So does this point to dual standards, or just a development of classroom practice? Research (Bigger and Brown, 2013) shows that children benefit from 'their total set of experiences in school'... 'stemming as much from how they are taught as what they are taught'. Whilst they will collect both information and values from numerous sources, including family, their peers and the media, school plays a more important and central role – it is, after all, the place where most young people spend the majority of their formative years:

> ...school can be a place where experiences and values are integrated, discussed and shaped into a meaningful philosophy of life. All curriculum subjects can contribute to this, within a whole-school ethos which promotes personal and social development. (Bigger and Brown, 2013: vii)

Resources are accumulating on a number of websites that you can draw on to develop your practice. These change from time to time but include government-sponsored, teacher group-sponsored, newspaper-supported, and commercial sites.

Intellectual challenge

Pupils, like teachers, wish for relationships that are comfortable in an environment that is positive. An exploration of values in education raises fundamental questions about the curriculum, pedagogy and relationships. This can be a cause of insecurity for teachers and pupils alike. Exploration of these issues needs to focus upon improvements to teaching and learning, and to take place in circumstances that are supportive and non-threatening.

Sometimes you will have to challenge deep-seated beliefs. One example is 'boys are better at computers than girls'. An exploratory study of 135 male and 166 female secondary students (Vekiri, 2010) showed that boys' and girls' beliefs in their ability on computers (ICT) were affected by teacher and parent expectations, and by whether teaching and learning were perceived (by the pupils) as being creative and useful, much more than by their gender. So you modify your views, change your tactics, and move on.

Teaching is often about compromise, full of dilemmas created by the tension between the intentions of the teacher and the demands of the school. This is one of the things that makes teaching intellectually challenging, and rewarding. The concept of the teacher as role model, the nature of friendship, and the impact of school rules on teaching, are indicative of some of these dilemmas.

A thought

You will be advised many times about the necessary separation that you will need to achieve between your private life and your 'public' life as a schoolteacher. This is particularly important in an information age where many of our social interactions may take place online. Sharing risqué or 'amusing' incidents and circumstances via social media will quickly become an issue if pupils can gain access to your postings,

(Continued)

(Continued)

tweets etc. You must also beware of sending out mixed messages. For example, how can you promote safety if you drive too fast; how can you promote healthy living if you can be seen smoking a cigarette outside the school gates? Is your life as a person (social or otherwise) more important than your professional role? In this context, think about the advantages and disadvantages of living within the school catchment area.

Teacher as role model?

Research into teachers' attitudes shows some marked differences. Barry was a teacher with thirty years' experience and saw himself as unconventional. He enjoyed being his 'natural self'', even to the extent of using language that some might consider inappropriate in a classroom. When asked about this he said that he had not considered it before, but that on reflection he felt that it created a type of 'intimacy' with the pupils and prevented him sounding 'too pukka'. His pupils (whose names have been changed) had no difficulty with this, and indeed were glad that Barry could be seen as a 'person':

James: ... you feel he is more like you.

John: I like him, he's a good teacher. Other teachers are more stuck up.

Mary: He relates to you.

John: He gets on the same level so that you can understand.

This approach contravenes all that young teachers are told about the techniques a teacher should employ, and Barry recognised this:

> I really cannot consider myself a proper teacher. I suppose that gets through. I mean that I am not credible myself as a proper teacher ... somebody who has got the rhetoric and the solemnity that you expect. I can remember when I started teaching at school there were solemn rebukes that did the job. Nobody is frightened of me. I feel that you have got to have a few missiles to carry around to be a proper teacher and I haven't got any. I'm sort of naked in the conference chamber. [Laughter]

June had three years' experience and a more conventional approach to the notion of the teacher as a role model than Barry:

> It is part of what you do. I also look at other teachers as role models. That is how people learn. I'm not sure that you always agree with them. You discard some bits and concentrate on the bits you like, and hopefully that is what the kids do as well. They get out what they like and discard what they don't.

June's class dealt with some very important ethical issues, mainly concerned with the nature of domestic violence. This required June to monitor effectively and provide an appropriate framework and stimulus for learning. 'Her influence can be seen from the following pupil comments:

Q: What sort of person do you think the teacher would like you to grow up to be?

Joanne: A friendly and kind person because she is like that now.

Kate: Helpful, she likes to help you out when you are stuck with things.

Andy: She gets along with us all and she is nice, and she is supportive of people who do not understand the work as much. So, she would like us to be like, helpful.

According to June, pupils 'get out what they like and discard what they don't'. Pupils are active evaluators, not the passive receivers of models. What are the implications for this in the way that, as a teacher, you behave towards pupils and adults?

A thought

How do you think you come across as a role model to pupils? What sort of ethos do you think you are projecting? You could check this out with friends and colleagues to see if they agree with you! Do you talk to pupils in the same way that you talk to adults who enter a learning situation? Consider why there might be differences and how your pupils might perceive these.

Friendship?

Teachers will often keep a deliberate distance between themselves and their pupils. However, an effective teacher needs to pursue quite deep and emotional issues. Colin, with twenty-four years' experience, looks back wistfully at the nature of the teacher–pupil relationship:

Q: What values underpin your lessons?

A: I'm not quite sure, maybe friendship. Maybe friendship between children and adults is frowned on ... It should be friendly.

Relationships are complex, as in many walks of life. Here, Colin's pupils talk about teacher relationships in general:

Q: When a teacher shouts at you what sort of effect does it have on you?

John: I think it's funny.

Q: Why?

John: I don't know, it's just funny when you see them lose their rag, and see them get right mad and uptight when it's over little things and you should have a laugh about it. But they get really mad and upset, and we don't understand why.

Q: Why is it funny?

John: Because we are only kids. When they were little they would have messed about as well, but they take it right serious if someone throws a rubber across [the] classroom or something like that. [I] just laugh.

Q: Why do you think that teachers shout?

John: So we get on with our work and that we get good grades.

Kate: Because they think that it will teach us, but it doesn't. If they just said it politely and stuff like that.

John: Talked to us like friends.

Kate: Yeah.

Friendship implies a relationship of equals. Despite the best efforts of many teachers and pupils, their relationships are underpinned by the power of a teacher over a pupil. There are many disadvantages in this uneasy relationship. Children usually find themselves in a disadvantageous power situation; they are used to having rules imposed and being passive recipients rather than proactive instigators. Often they are not used to being asked for an opinion, so may be unsure as to what is expected of them if this occurs. There are also issues when the child response runs counter to 'accepted wisdom'. As Wood (2003: 368) suggests:

> What pupils say may also clash with dominant discourses about effective practice, both at the macro-level of government policy, and the micro worlds of schooling.

For example, Flutter and Rudduck (2004: 94) refer to the opinion of a Year 10 boy, who when asked what he could change in his experience of the school from Year 7, stated:

> I'd change everything because it's just been a waste of time really – me being at this school.

Is Colin unreasonable in wishing to have warmer relationships with his pupils? How does schooling intervene to make closer relationships more difficult?

A thought

As a person you will relate on various different levels depending on with whom you are relating. You will relate differently to friends, colleagues, family, peers etc. Think about these different roles and their application to your teaching. Which of them can you safely take into the classroom? Which class? What sort of situation?

School rules

The intention of teachers to make pupils do things that they don't want to do can be a point of conflict. Barry, when asked if there was anything about school rules he did not like, had this to say:

Barry: Anything that gets in the way of getting the kids the best results, and most of them do. I know that they are not intended to, but the effects are, if you are going to give kids detention for chewing gum, for having their shirts out.

Q: For wearing the wrong coloured footwear?

Barry: Yes. It's an irrelevance to my concerns.

Barry expresses a controversial point of view. But it is a view reflected by his pupils, those in 'middle ability' groups, where a sense of frustration and grievance can be more apparent:

Q: Some people think that they should be teaching you about right and wrong. Do you think that it is the place of the school to do that?

Marisa: Yeah, but we don't have rules like that, we just have 'don't carry coats in school, don't chew gum, don't wear earrings, don't wear make-up'. It's totally irrelevant to the teaching.

Kerry: They're not positive things, they are negative things.

Q: What do you mean by positive things?

Kerry: Well, they don't treat you level-headedly. They look down on you.

Marisa: In assembly, like with one teacher it's all about what we are doing wrong, not about what we are doing right.

Jez: One teacher says, just like 'don't chew gum'. They only have them so you like don't break bigger ones. They could say like 'don't take drugs', but then you'll go out and do that and go onto bigger things. But if they have like stupid little ones like 'don't chew gum'. I know what I mean. [Laughter]

Q: What sort of school rules would you like to see?

Kerry: A lot of encouragement.

For these pupils many of these smaller issues, such as dress, coats, gum, which some teachers may argue can help in the smooth running of the school and create habits among pupils they think will help in later life, are viewed as negative intrusions that make little sense from the pupils' point of view, other than to suggest the all-powerful 'school'.

Application to secondary teaching

If education is to be truly inclusive, then this should be reflected in the relationship teachers have with young people. There is a range of roles to be filled within a school, and you need to be clear about your role. This may change depending upon the context. After-school clubs, breakfast clubs, extra-curricular activities, such as school plays, sports teams, and even the teaching of different subjects at different times of the week, require different roles, different personae, fulfilled by the same person. Do you understand the boundaries and purposes of your different personae? Do pupils understand boundaries and purposes? Do you need to be clear beforehand? Desirable though this might be, is it always possible? How do you develop young people's understanding of multiple selves (see below), and their development of appropriate behaviour?

Applications to primary and early years teaching

A useful exercise when first establishing yourself in a classroom is to have the pupils create a set of rules. In this way, you can generate a discussion of what is positive and what is negative, have a good idea of what works and what doesn't, and allow the pupils to have ownership of the rules (a powerful tool). Small groups of pupils can devise five rules each that are shared with the rest of the class to form a master list. This list can then be put into order of priority and created as display material. You will be surprised at the amount of conformity and understanding of social norms even in quite young children. Beware (particularly with younger children) of their ideas of appropriate rewards and punishments. They can be particularly venal with rewards and vicious with punishments!

Rules for behaviour in the classroom can be formal or informal. We can sometimes take these for granted, and when pupils transgress our response can sometimes be curt and incomprehensible, particularly to younger children. Researching with pre-school children, Sylva et al. (2003) found that it was important for children and teachers to engage in 'sustained shared thinking', preferably on a one-to-one basis. One benefit of this was to encourage children to be more assertive, and more rational by allowing them to talk through conflicts.

GROUP EXERCISE

In your group, or with colleagues, consider why those in the 'middle ability' groups may be more concerned with school uniform than other students. Do you think that Barry is right to talk of school uniform as an irrelevance? What do you think pupils mean when they say they consider some school rules to be negative? What other examples can you list of 'negative' school rules (from your own experience or from your placement)? What examples can you give of positive school rules? Younger pupils may be developing their language and interpersonal skills. When you see behaviour you do not approve of how do you handle it? Do you explain your actions? Do you allow young children to explain theirs?

Theory

Intrinsic and instrumental values

Dewey (1966) offers some clarity in the area of values. He argues that educational values are often coincidental with educational aims. He also makes a useful distinction between two types of educational value: intrinsic and instrumental. This distinction between intrinsic values, which are ends in themselves, and instrumental values, which are means to ends, is an important one. Educational aims may have value, and perhaps revered for that reason. However, if they are instrumental values then the purpose of their inclusion in any curriculum, hidden or formal, may appear obscure and irrelevant if the end, the intrinsic value, is hidden behind an instrumental value. It is also important to recognise that a value is not inherently intrinsic or instrumental. As 'occasions present themselves' a value may move from one classification to another. For example, examination success may be an instrumental value, in that it enables a successful student to gain access through further study or employment to the work or lifestyle that offers (intrinsic) satisfaction. However, on achieving examination success that achievement may offer intrinsic value in itself. Whether a value is intrinsic or instrumental depends upon individual perception and the 'occasion'.

INDIVIDUAL REFLECTION

The bullet points below indicate a range of values teachers said they touched upon in a particular subject context. It is not possible to say that these values are explored in all classrooms, because this depends upon the relationship to pedagogy. For example, curiosity may remain an aim of the curriculum, but could remain untouched in the classroom. Equally, science can be taught in a way that constantly helps pupils explore their own life circumstances, but this may not be in the syllabus. What is clear is that the potential for engagement with values in subject matter is enormous:

- *Illustrative values in science* – curiosity; exploration; cooperation; respect; learn about life; learn about the way things work; tolerance; reasoning; independence; questioning things that are taken for granted.
- *Illustrative values in English* – power of language; love of literature; pleasure in reading; tolerance; sympathy; understanding; anti-racism; discovery of the inner person; independence; developing potential; appreciation of different cultures; discussion of important issues; respect for individuals.

What do you think these values mean? Do you agree that they are likely to be evident in your teaching? What role do you think you should have in exploring these values with pupils?

Multiple selves

Cairns (2000) points to the changing nature of values throughout a person's life. Context is therefore crucial to understanding values. A key question to consider is the relative importance of contexts, and whether the identity, or self, remains constant in each context. Life history research suggests that the context of other aspects of a teacher's life does impact upon their' self-identity. So it is worth considering 'what else do I do?' and how this impacts on your role as a teacher. Layder (2006), referring to the work of Goffman, talks about the way individuals distance themselves from their roles in order to reduce tension, and the way that individuals act out different roles in different aspects of their lives. Both teachers and pupils have multiple roles to play. Investigating co-operative learning with younger children, Boekaerts et al. (2008) found evidence that, although the role of the teacher is important, it is tempered by pupil ethnicity (particularly in multi-ethnic classrooms), pupil prior knowledge, and the teacher's own experience with co-operative learning techniques.

Substantial self – situational self

An understanding of the teacher's self-image is also a notable factor in the knowledge and skills upon which teachers depend. Nias's (1989, 1996) work with primary teachers offers some insight into how teachers maintain and adapt their values. The substantial self 'comprises the most highly prized aspects of our self concept and the attitudes and values which are salient to them'. In new situations the values of the substantial self are protected through the development of the situational self, such as the individual's teacher identity or being in the teacher role.

The teacher's problematic

The theme of pupil resistance to what they see as unreasonable intrusions is evident in the writings of Woods (1979, 1980, 1990). He examines pupil behaviour and the strategies for coping that underpin it. He also draws parallels between the behaviour of pupils and that of teachers. For example, he examines the use of laughter from the point of view of the teacher. Laughter can be used to control a situation, sometimes to subvert it, and often to do both. He recognises that teachers can be drawn between two models of the teacher: the bureaucrat and the person. Sachs and Smith (1988) refer to this as the 'teacher's problematic' and recognise that they are tempted to oscillate between both.

Summary

- Values permeate the curriculum, pedagogy, schooling and relationships.
- Values can be implicit or explicit, instrumental or intrinsic.
- As teachers we are not always aware of the values that we transmit.
- Pupils interpret values and are not simply passive receptors.
- We need to be aware of values and consider their impact.
- Values create dilemmas and these cannot always be resolved.
- Teachers have to make decisions taking into account tension between the demands of the school and their own intentions.

Key reading

Butroyd, R. (2007) 'Denial and distortion of instrumental and intrinsic value in the teaching of science and English: its impact upon fifteen Year 10 teachers', *Forum*, 49 (3): 313–29.

Day, C., Kington, A., Stobart, G. and Sammons, P. (2006) 'The personal and professional lives of teachers: stable and unstable identities', *British Educational Research Journal*, 32 (4): 601–16.

Vekiri, I. (2010) 'Boys' and girls' ICT beliefs: do teachers matter?', *Computers & Education*, 55 (1): 16–23.

References and bibliography

Bigger, S. and Brown, E. (2013) *Spiritual, moral, social, and cultural education*. London: David Fulton

Boekaerts, M., Oortwijn, M. and Vedder, P. (2008) 'The impact of the teacher's role and pupils' ethnicity and prior knowledge on pupils' performance and motivation to cooperate', *Instructional Science,* 36 (3): 251–68.

Buzzelli, C.A., Donnelly, L.A. and Akerson, V.L. (2008) 'Early childhood teachers' views of nature of science: the influence of intellectual levels, cultural values, and explicit reflective teaching', *Journal of Research in Science Teaching,* 45 (6): 748–70.

Cairns, J. (2000) 'Schools, community and the developing values of young adults: towards an ecology of education in values', in J. Cairns, R. Gardiner and D. Lawton (eds), *Values and the curriculum*. London: Woburn, pp. 52–73.

Cullingford, C. (1991) *The inner world of the school*. London: Cassell.

Dewey, J. (1966) *Democracy in education*. New York: Free Press.

Flutter, J. and Rudduck, J. (2004) *Consulting pupils: what's in it for schools?* London: RoutledgeFalmer.

HMSO (2007) *The Children's Plan: building brighter futures,* Cm 7280. London; HMSO.

Layder, D. (2006) *Understanding social theory* (2nd edn). London: Sage.

Nias, J. (1989) *Primary teachers talking*. London: Routledge & Kegan Paul.

Nias, J. (1996) 'Thinking about feeling: the emotions in teaching', *Cambridge Journal of Education*, 26 (3): 293–306.

Sachs, J. and Smith, R. (1988) 'Constructing teacher culture', *British Journal of Education,* 9 (4): 423–36.

Sylva, K., Melhuish, E., Sammons, P., Siraj-Blatchford, I., Taggart, B. and Elliot, K. (2003) *Research brief: The Effective Provision of Pre-School Education (EPPE) Project: findings from the pre-school period*. Available online at www.ioe.ac.uk/projects/eppe

Vekiri, I. (2010) 'Boys' and girls' ICT beliefs: do teachers matter?', *Computers & Education*, 55 (1): 16–23.

Wood, E. (2003) *The power of pupil perspectives in evidence-based practice: the case of gender and underachievement,* Research Papers in Education, 18 (4): 365–83.

Woods, P. (1979) *The divided school*. London: Routledge & Kegan Paul.

Woods, P. (ed.) (1980) 'Pupil strategies', in *Explorations in the sociology of the school*. London: Croom Helm.

Woods, P. (1990) *The happiest days? How pupils cope with school*. London: Falmer.

Useful website

Department for Education: www.education.gov.uk

Visit https://study.sagepub.com/denby3e for extra resources related to this chapter.

CHAPTER 3

PROFESSIONALISM, THE PROFESSIONAL DUTIES OF TEACHERS AND LEGAL REQUIREMENTS

Fiona Woodhouse

Standards linked to this chapter include...

Teachers' Standards Part 2: Personal and Professional Conduct

A teacher is expected to demonstrate consistently high standards of personal and professional conduct. The following statements define the behaviour and attitudes which set the required standard for conduct throughout a teacher's career.

Teachers uphold public trust in the profession and maintain high standards of ethics and behaviour, within and outside school, by:

- treating pupils with dignity, building relationships rooted in mutual respect, and at all times observing proper boundaries appropriate to a teacher's professional position

(Continued)

(Continued)

- having regard for the need to safeguard pupils' wellbeing, in accordance with statutory provisions
- showing tolerance of and respect for the rights of others
- not undermining fundamental British values, including democracy, the rule of law, individual liberty and mutual respect, and tolerance of those with different faiths and beliefs
- ensuring that personal beliefs are not expressed in ways which exploit pupils' vulnerability or might lead them to break the law.

Teachers must have proper and professional regard for the ethos, policies and practices of the school in which they teach, and maintain high standards in their own attendance and punctuality.

Teachers must have an understanding of, and always act within, the statutory frameworks which set out their professional duties and responsibilities.

Introduction

The complex art of teaching consists of more than many practitioners at first realise. It is a professional activity and this concept of professionalism is embedded in the Teachers' Standards. Several research studies over time (Helsby, 1996; Groundwater-Smith and Sachs, 2002; Leaton Gray and Whitty, 2010) have clearly indicated the importance of professionalism to teachers.

Teachers have to work within the statutory and non-statutory frameworks that inform practice in most schools. It is essential that, as a teacher, you have an understanding of your own professional role within the context of these frameworks. This chapter will give you an overview of the professional nature of the teaching role and of the various frameworks currently of importance and within which you will have to work.

The teacher as a professional

The concept of the teacher as a professional is a much debated one. It is an international issue and research stems from many countries around this construct of teaching. Bransford et al. (2005: 11) believe it is critical that teachers see themselves as professionals: 'It is important for teachers to understand their roles and responsibilities as professionals in schools...'. They give examples of why teaching should be considered a profession. However, commentators such as Hargreaves (1994) and Caldwell and

Spinks (1998) consider teachers as the providers of a quality service, while Hoyle (2001) comments that the perception of teachers as professionals is one which fluctuates in society. Hilferty (2008: 162) focuses on the 'set of knowledge, skills and values that guide professional practice'. Sachs (2003) considers different types of teacher professionalism. A definition of professionalism in teaching is therefore a fluid concept – is it a product of the current Standards or some intrinsic understanding that you as a beginning teacher hold? Can you define what you understand as professionalism or do you need this defining for you? What roles do the government, society, the media and the teaching profession itself play in creating this fluid and changing concept of teacher professionalism? Goepel (2012) discusses the changing concept of professionalism with the introduction of the 2012 Teaching Standards.

A thought

Is teaching a profession? And does it require thinking about at a deeper level or is it a function anyone can do? A recent NQT commented that their course had been much better than others they could have selected as it was more practically based. They could now manage the class better than the other NQTs and didn't see the need for having to understand the theories on behaviour and learning. So what is teaching for you – simply managing a class or a vocation?

A job of many parts

As a teacher, you need to be able to apply your knowledge of content and of transmission effectively to develop your pupils fully (Hoyle, 2001). Good teachers have professional insight, which is based on their knowledge of theory linked with experience in the classroom. They can deliver effective teaching strategies and interventions using their knowledge, skills and experience. A 'professional' teacher uses the skills of a theorist, an artist, a technician and a performer to deliver a complex service. The teacher's role also combines the work of a communicator, manager and critical researcher. Additionally a teacher needs to be a good planner, motivator and, moral leader and within the complex school systems a reliable team member. The skilled practitioner also displays professional accountability, or what Hoyle and John (1995) call 'professional responsibility'. This means, as a teacher, not only being part of the formal quality assurance structure, but also taking responsibility for your own quality as a professional.

Hegarty (2000) points to the teaching 'moment' being core to the work of the skilled practitioner. This moment occurs when a teacher interacts with learners to stimulate and direct learning: when the culmination of all the teacher's knowledge, skills and experience enables pupils to learn and make good progress.

The Hegarty model uses teacher' 'insight' to deliver knowledge, skills, experience and research into the teaching moment. He argues that '... what is essential is that the teacher relates the knowledge that is used in that particular situation and does so by generating a new insight specific to the situation' (Hegarty, 2000: 462). The model is an idealised concept and all of its components and facets may not be present for every teaching situation, but it does provide a range of cognitive and skill-based components which as a practitioner you may draw upon in constructing your teaching behaviour.

Theory

The skilled practitioner takes theory, reflects upon it, and then turns it into applied theory or knowledge which can be used in learning. Theory sets the rules which are applied to specific activities, as opposed to the equally important practical knowledge generated by working alongside an experienced practitioner (Carr, 2003).

Professional knowledge

A teacher therefore requires knowledge, which Winch (2004) calls 'professional knowledge'. He identifies three areas of knowledge that make up this professional requirement and suggests these are acquired during a foundation period:

1. *Appropriate subject knowledge, which is underpinned by systematic unified theory.* It is difficult to teach something which one has not fully mastered (as you have no doubt discovered already!). Winch warns against believing that elementary subject knowledge is required to teach pupils who have generally modest academic attainments and argues that actually the reverse may be the case.
2. *Pedagogic knowledge.* Skilled practitioners require a wide range of pedagogic knowledge to enable them to apply or transmit subject knowledge. Hegarty (2000) calls this 'craft knowledge' as it encompasses knowledge of teaching. Park and Oliver (2008) refer to this as pedagogical content knowledge (PCK), which is a body of knowledge unique to the teaching profession. For instance, a teacher needs to have understanding of the use of formal and informal assessment or the art of differentiation. They require knowledge of the structures of how pupils learn and how to motivate and manage individuals and classes.

3. *A mixed bag labelled 'other knowledge'*. This includes knowledge about individual pupils, including their home background, knowledge of the curriculum, and the skill necessary to navigate the often complex array of teaching materials, study programmes, and guidance and information from the media.

Knowledge of self and a positive view of self-concept are important to teachers' survival and professional growth. The belief you have in your subject is also important as it will impact, often subconsciously, on how you teach that subject.

Experience

As a skilled practitioner you will use a wide range of learning experiences to improve the quality of your performance and generate new insights (see below). You will also experience an accumulation of insights that will not only draw from your knowledge and skills but also help you develop them. This will give personal meaning to the learning situation, which is strongly influenced by a teacher's own experiences and working environment (Helsby, 1996). Critical reflection of learning outcomes is fed back into the model to enhance performance and development (see Chapter 8). A skilled practitioner will start to seek out new experiences from which to learn from day one and will continue to do so throughout their career.

Skills

Whilst a comprehensive knowledge base is important, skills are also vital. The skills required of a good teacher are both comprehensive and demanding. Even the 'best' practitioners are still acquiring skills late in their careers. Teaching skills range from the use of complex verbal and non-verbal communication strategies (see Chapter 11) to various methods of using knowledge. They require teacher ability in ICT, media and improvisation in planning complex pupil activities, and include diagnostic, problem-solving and decision-making skills, along with motivation and classroom control (see Chapters 9 and 10). All these and more make for an excellent practitioner.

Research

Good teachers will continually seek out ways of improving practice. Stenhouse (1975) advocated that teachers should become research practitioners as a way of providing empirical knowledge and self-improvement. This action-research approach tends to make the full-time educational researcher more of a collaborator than a leader. Stenhouse even argues that it is a teacher's professional responsibility to deliver research from the classroom. Others champion teachers as reviewers and practical samplers of others' research. According to some commentators, as a teacher you should review current theory proactively and where appropriate apply it in practice. All Post Graduate Certificate in Education courses must include Master's level work to encourage the proactive use of research in the development of professional practice. Linked to this is the key skill of being reflective (see Chapter 8), which is bound up with insight.

Insight

Insight closes the circle and is the reflective process: it is the application of judgement which makes sense out of the situation and leads to personal development. Insight in this context enables trainees, and teachers, to learn from their experience. Hegarty (2000: 461) argues that teachers need to build a bank of insights from their experiences, which can be adapted to bring insight into new teaching moments:

> Different situations need to be approached with different sets of insights, which in turn need to be completed in different ways. Intelligent practical behaviour therefore, calls for a large repertoire of incomplete sets of insights, skill in selecting appropriately from them, and the ability to generate fresh insights which complete the set in an illuminating way.

What does 'being a professional' look like?

Being a professional practitioner is multi-dimensional and requires a complex array of attributes. Teaching is a lifelong journey along which – as you travel – you will continue to acquire and develop the skills and knowledge that will help you maintain and develop good practice in the classroom. Central to all of this is your own construct of being a professional and how this impacts on your daily life as a teacher. This will be a challenging but rewarding journey.

The Part 2 Standards that were listed at the beginning of this chapter refer to the professional nature of a teacher in three sections. Firstly, they are required to demonstrate consistently high standards of personal and professional conduct. As a teacher you must uphold public trust in the profession and maintain high standards of ethics and behaviour, within and outside school, in detailed ways: these will include key words like 'dignity', 'respect', 'boundaries', 'safeguarding' and 'tolerance', and instructions to ensure your personal beliefs do not exploit pupils or undermine 'fundamental British values'. This is challenging, and begs the question how do you behave and how can you evidence this? And in addition, what implications does this have for you outside of your school life, both with friends and in public?

GROUP EXERCISE

In small groups of three to four, choose one of the frameworks, pieces of guidance or legislation outlined in Table 3.1 on page 44 and provide a clear overview of the key aspects of this in relation to teaching for everyone else. You will need to cover:

- what the key elements of the Act or guidance are
- how these will impact on teaching in general
- what implications these will have in the classroom for you and the rest of the group as teachers
- how your placement schools have responded to the Act or guidance.

Secondly, you are required to 'Have proper and professional regard for the ethos, policies and practices of the school..., and maintain high standards in [your] own attendance and punctuality'. So you need to be clear about the ethos of the school you are in and ensure you work as part of a team alongside your peers in that school.

Thirdly, you must know and act within all the statutory frameworks that apply to teaching. These are explored below.

Statutory frameworks

This is a changing and complex area. The government produces legal frameworks and non-statutory guidance that advises you further on how you should work within schools. These are regularly updated, with amendments to Acts as further initiatives are introduced. Education is a continuingly evolving profession – change is normal, so amendments and additions are varied and numerous. Over recent years the range of types of schools has increased and consequently your employer may not follow and work within all of the frameworks below. If you are in an academy, or 'free' school, you will still find versions of each, although they may be part of the school's own documentation, or system of governance or finance.

Teachers' Standards

The Teachers' Standards (DfE, 2012) govern trainee teachers working towards Qualified Teacher Status (QTS), Newly Qualified Teachers (NQTs) and Teachers with QTS. It states these at the beginning of the standards document. So what about unqualified teachers and those working in independent schools, 'free' schools and academies?

Are these standards for all teachers or just some? You will find that most 'schools' do work within these frameworks or very similar. In the standards it does state:

> 'School' means whatever educational setting the standards are applied in. The standards are required to be used by teachers in maintained schools and non-maintained special schools. Use of the standards in academies and free schools depends on the specific establishment arrangements of those schools. Independent schools are not required to use the standards, but may do so if they wish. (2012: 9)

Local Authorities

Local Authorities (LAs) are the employers of community and controlled schools and most authorities will embed the relevant frameworks, but may also have policies which are individual to them with which you will need to comply once you take up employment with them.

Governing bodies

The governing body of a school is the main employer for those teachers who will eventually work in Foundation and Voluntary Aided schools, academies and Trust schools. For teachers in the independent sector this may be the governing body or the owner.

School policies

All schools must have clear policies on issues such as bullying, behaviour and child protection. These will have been developed in response to the Acts and guidance issued but designed specifically for the school and its setting. As a teacher you will have a responsibility to know and follow these, as well as at times review and develop them.

Application to primary and early years teaching

A key part of your role – both as a teacher and as a professional – will be to ensure the health and wellbeing of the young people in your care (see Chapter 4). There are many reasons why, in this age group, children might be withdrawn, tearful or uncooperative. They could have fallen out with a friend, have toothache (or another pain), lost a pet, or been unfairly blamed for a misdemeanour. They could be hungry, tired, too hot, too cold, suffering from eyestrain, or even a learning difficulty. You will need to develop a 'caring' strategy in order to find out the real reason behind unusual or recalcitrant behaviour, and a set of steps that will allow you to decide when to take an issue further because you believe there is a problem, or abuse, that outside agencies will need to deal with. This is a dangerous tightrope to walk, but walk it you must, with the welfare of the child at the heart of your actions.

Main frameworks

For the other statutory documents of which you need to be aware, go to the government website (www.gov.uk/government/collections/statutory-guidance-schools) where the Department for Education's statutory guidance publications for schools and local authorities are laid out in detail. This statutory guidance is issued under legislation so it must be followed. At present there are policies in the following areas:

1. Administration and finance
2. Admissions
3. Assessment
4. Behaviour and attendance
5. Curriculum
6. Early Years Foundation Stage
7. Governance
8. Involving parents and pupils
9. Looked after children
10. Safeguarding children and young people
11. Special educational/health needs
12. Staff employment and teachers' pay
13. 16–19 education and work experience

Some of these frameworks may be modified by government nationally, or by individual schools, as long as staff agree.

The School Teachers' Pay and Conditions Document (STPCD) 2014

This document is one of the most important frameworks as it sets out your responsibilities as a teacher. Classroom teachers should carry out their professional duties under the reasonable direction of the head teacher. Fifteen professional duties are specifically included in the document and are grouped under the following headings: whole school organisation, strategy and development; health and safety and discipline; management of staff and resources; professional development; communication and working with colleagues and other relevant professionals.

A thought

The School Teachers' Pay and Conditions Document section 7 outlines the 15 professional duties of a teacher. What do you think this should cover? Should they be the same regardless of the age group being taught? Who do you think should decide on what these duties are – our professional bodies, the government or employers?

The first of these duties is that of teaching. This involves the preparation and development of courses of study, teaching materials, teaching programmes and individual lessons – within the context of the school's plans, curriculum and schemes of work – and then teaching the pupils to whom you are assigned. You will need to assess, monitor, record and report on the learning needs, progress and achievements of those pupils. This assessment could be in the form of oral or written reports, or references about individual pupils or groups of pupils, and includes participating in the arrangements for preparing pupils for public examinations, and in assessing, recording and reporting any assessments required as part of these examinations as well as supervision of them during examination work.

The second three duties come under the heading of whole school organisation and development. You will be required to contribute to the implementation of the school's policies, practices and procedures, and support the vision of the school. Also set out clearly is the requirement to work with others (see Chapter 5) on the curriculum and pupil development, and to teach classes (subject to conditions) to cover colleagues.

Application to secondary teaching

The recent SEND Act has embedded at its core the idea of quality first teaching: this has implications for you as a classroom teacher in having responsibility for ensuring that the needs of all the pupils in your care are met. Look carefully at the 'SEND code of practice: 0 to 25 years', speak with the school designated SENCo, and ensure that you have strategies in place to support all pupils and are aware of the conditions that some of those pupils might have. What are inclusive strategies for pupils with hearing or visual impairments for your subject? How can you support pupils with dyspraxia and dyslexia in your subject? Remember also that behaviour is now excluded from SEN issues.

The next two requirements are for you to be responsible for promoting the general safety and wellbeing of individual pupils and to maintain good order and discipline in the classroom. Under the heading management of staff and resources you are asked to direct and supervise support staff and where appropriate other teachers. You must contribute to the recruitment, selection, appointment and professional development of support staff and other teachers, and are also responsible for the deployment of resources to them. Further duties involve your own professional development. You are required to participate in the arrangements for appraisal (see Chapter 8) both of yourself and colleagues as outlined in the regulations. You must also be able to communicate and consult with pupils, parents and carers. Finally you are required to work with colleagues and other relevant professionals within and beyond the school.

These duties outlined in the school teachers' pay and conditions document will then be developed and amended within your individual school context, depending on the nature of the school in which you are employed.

Additionally this document gives details on your working time for those in maintained schools. You should be available for work for 195 days in any school year, of which 190 are days on which you are required to teach pupils. You will have to be available to work for 1,265 hours as directed by the head teacher (often referred to as directed time). This time does not include any time for the preparation of teaching materials and similar work required to enable you to discharge the duties as outlined in the 15 requirements.

INDIVIDUAL REFLECTION

Consider the statements below which came from the (now defunct) General Teaching Council for England's code of professional practice (2006) and reflect on how you carry these out in the classroom:

- First and foremost, teachers are skilled practitioners.
- Teachers place the learning and wellbeing of young people at the centre of their professional practice.
- Teachers respond sensitively to the differences in the home backgrounds and circumstances of young people, recognising the key role that parents and carers play in children's education.
- Teachers see themselves as part of a team, in which fellow teachers, other professional colleagues and governors are partners in securing the learning and wellbeing of young people.
- Teachers entering the teaching profession in England have met a common professional standard.

National legislation and guidance

Table 3.1 outlines some of the key areas of legislation and guidance of which you need to be aware.

Table 3.1 Legislation and guidance for teachers

Teacher's Standards	www.gov.uk/government/publications/teachers-standards
The School Teachers' Pay and Conditions Document (STPCD) 2014	www.gov.uk/government/publications/school-teachers-pay-and-conditions-2014
The Education (School Teachers' Appraisal) (England) Regulations 2012	This outlines the procedures for the appraisal of teacher's' performance. www.legislation.gov.uk/uksi/2012/115/pdfs/uksi_20120115_en.pdf
Education Act 1996, 2002, 2011	Each successive Education Act has many implications for teachers. Further details of current legislation can be found via the DfE website. The 2011 Act was introduced to put teachers at the heart of school improvement and reform aspects of the education system. It included a comprehensive review of the curriculum. There is also guidance from the Education Secretary available online to help support schools and teachers. It includes information on a wide range of subjects, including the 2010 White Paper (on which the 2011 Act is based), School Teacher Review Body (STRB), SEN provision, maintained schools and the curriculum.
Children Act 2004 (amending the *Children Act 1989*)	In all schools there will be policies that have been developed to address aspects of this Act, which deals with the wellbeing of children. It includes the requirement for teachers to be familiar with the procedures in school for dealing with issues such as suspected child abuse. The Act contains a wealth of requirements and guidance. Further details on it and its successors can be found online.
Every Child Matters 2003	Although the spotlight has moved away from *Every Child Matters* and its terminology it has been fundamental in shaping educational policy since its publication and has underpinned much of the recent change in education and will continue to do so over the next few years. This guidance was published with the *Children Act 2004* and there are many commonalities between them. The key aims are for every child, whatever their background or circumstances, to have the support they need to: stay safe be healthy enjoy and achieve make a positive contribution achieve economic wellbeing. For information on policies, guidance, case studies and resources consult the website http://webarchive.nationalarchives.gov.uk/20130401151715/https://www.education.gov.uk/publications/standard/publicationdetail/page1/cm5860

Education and Inspections Act 2006	This Act considers many aspects that will have been incorporated into various policies found in schools. For instance this Act advises about the role of Ofsted in the inspection of schools. For some additional clarification of this see: www.gov.uk/government/uploads/system/uploads/attachment_data/file/314095/Post-legislative_assessments_of_the_2006_acts.pdf
SEND code of practice: 0 to 25 years (15 August 2014) Previously: *SEN and Disability Act (SENDA) 2001* and the *Special Educational Needs Code of Practice* (DfES, 2001) Education for children with health needs who cannot attend school (17 May 2013) Inclusive schooling: children with special educational needs (1 November 2001) SEND: managing changes to legislation from September 2014 (28 August 2014) Supporting pupils at school with a medical condition (1 September 2014)	There has recently been updated statutory guidance in this area. Together these give the requirements and guidance on the identification and assessment of pupils with special educational needs. Once a pupil has been identified as an SEND pupil then there needs to be intervention in the form of personalised provision. Details of the various statutory guidance are indicated below and can be found at www.gov.uk/government/collections/statutory-guidance-schools#special-educational-health-needs
Safeguarding children and young people (2014)	This guidance is about child protection and safeguarding children. There are four main statutory guidance issues which need to be consulted in this important area in ensuring the wellbeing of children: Keeping children safe in education (15 October 2014) Promoting the education of looked-after children (23 July 2014) Supervision of activity with children (10 September 2012) Working together to safeguard children (21 March 2013). See www.gov.uk/government/collections/statutory-guidance-schools#safeguarding-children-and-young-people
Race Relations Act 1976 and *Amendment Act 2000* *Sex Discrimination Act 1975* *Equality Act 2010*	These Acts both have elements in them relating to pupils. It is unlawful to discriminate against a pupil on sex or racial grounds. More information on the Equality Act (Race Relations Act and Sex Discrimination Act) can be found on the websites www.equalityhumanrights.com/ and www.gov.uk/browse/education
Disability Discrimination Acts 1995 and 2005 *Disability Equality Duty 2006*	It is unlawful to discriminate against disabled pupils. Schools and colleges must not treat disabled pupils less favourably than non-disabled pupils. For more information on the Disability Equality Duty you can look at the website of The Equality and Human Rights Commission website at www.equalityhumanrights.com

(Continued)

Table 3.1 (Continued)

Health & Safety at Work Act 1974	The main responsibility lies with your employers who need to take reasonable care for the health and safety of their employees, however employees also have a duty to take reasonable care of their own health and safety and of those affected by this, namely pupils. Teachers need to make themselves aware of LA and school policies, and some departments, e.g. science and D&T, may have additional ones. You need to report any hazards of which you become aware and record details of any incident. Along with the *Health & Safety at Work (HASAW) Act* are: *Management of Health & Safety at Work Regulations* *First Aid Regulations* *Electricity at Work Regulations* *Control of Substances Hazardous to Health (COSHH) Regulations.* Further details can be found on the Health and Safety Executive website at www.hse.gov.uk/
The Department for Education's statutory guidance publications for schools and local authorities	See the website www.gov.uk/government/collections/statutory-guidance-schools for statutory guidance on: 1. Administration and finance 2. Admissions 3. Assessment 4. Behaviour and attendance 5. Curriculum 6. Early Years Foundation Stage 7. Governance 8. Involving parents and pupils 9. Looked after children 10. Safeguarding children and young people 11. Special educational/health needs 12. Staff employment and teachers pay 13. 16–19 education and work experience

Summary

- Teaching is a complex professional activity, with skills which you will discover, develop and hone over the years.
- The Teachers' Standards outline what is required to be 'professional'. This is then partly underpinned by legislation and guidance and set in the context of your own school.
- Professionalism is also constructed from our own experiences and expectations – our own professional nature.
- As you develop your professionalism you will need to:
  - understand what it means to be a professional as a teacher
  - be aware of and work within the frameworks and guidance that underpin your profession
  - consider new guidance which impacts on the profession.

Key reading

Goepel, J. (2012) 'Upholding public trust: an examination of teacher professionalism and the use of Teachers' Standards in England', *Teacher Development: An International Journal of Teachers' Professional Development,* 16 (4): 489–505.

Hegarty, S. (2000) 'Teaching as a knowledge-based activity', *Oxford Review of Education,* 26 (3 & 4): 451–65.

Pollard, A. (2014) *Reflective teaching in schools*. London: Bloomsbury.

Sellars, M. (2014) *Reflective practice for teachers*. London: Sage.

References and bibliography

Bransford, J., Darling-Hammond, L. and LePage, P. (2005) *Preparing teachers for a changing world: what teachers should learn and be able to do*. San Francisco, CA: Jossey-Bass.

Caldwell, B. and Spinks, J. (1998) *Beyond the self-managing school*. London: Falmer.

Carr, D. (2003) *Making sense of education*. London: Routledge.

Department for Education (DfE) (2012) *Standards for qualified teachers*. Available online at www.gov.uk/government/publications/teachers-standards

Groundwater-Smith, S. and Sachs, J. (2002) 'The activist professional and the reinstatement of trust', *Cambridge Journal of Education*, 32 (3): 341–58.

Hargreaves, D. (1994) 'The new professionalism: the synthesis of professional and institutional development', *Teaching and Teacher Educator,* 10 (4): 423–38.

Helsby, G. (1996) 'Defining and developing professionalism in English secondary schools', *Journal of Education for Teaching,* 22 (2): 135–48.

Hilferty, F. (2008) 'Theorising teacher professionalism as an enacted discourse of power', *British Journal of Sociology of Education,* 29 (2): 161–73.

Hoyle, E. (2001) 'Teaching: prestige, status and esteem', *Educational Management & Administration,* 29 (2): 139–52.

Hoyle, E. and John, P. (1995) *Professional knowledge and professional practice*. London: Cassell.

Humphreys, M. and Hyland, T. (2002) 'Theory, practice and performance in teaching: professionalism, intuition, and jazz', *Educational Studies,* 28 (1): 5–15.

Leaton Gray, S. and Whitty, G. (2010) 'Social trajectories or disrupted identities? Changing and competing models of teacher professionalism under New Labour', *Cambridge Journal of Education*, 40 (1): 5–23 (DOI: 10.1080/03057640903567005).

Park, S. and Oliver, J.S. (2008) 'Revisiting the conceptualisation of pedagogical content knowledge (PCK): PCK as a conceptual tool to understand teachers as professionals', *Research in Science Education,* 38: 261–84.

Sachs, J. (2003) *The activist teaching profession*. Oxford: Oxford University Press.

Stenhouse, L. (1975) *An introduction to curriculum research and development*. London: Heinemann.

Winch, C. (2004) 'What do teachers need to know about teaching? A critical examination of the occupational knowledge of teachers', *British Journal of Educational Studies,* 52 (2): 180–96.

Visit https://study.sagepub.com/denby3e for extra resources related to this chapter.

CHAPTER 4

CHILD PROTECTION ISSUES

Jonathan Glazzard

Standards linked to this chapter include...

Teachers' Standards Part 2: Personal and Professional Conduct

Teachers uphold public trust in the profession and maintain high standards of ethics and behaviour, within and outside school, by having regard for the need to safeguard pupils' wellbeing, in accordance with statutory provisions.

Introduction

Recent inspections of schools and initial teacher training have focused heavily on the institutional systems and processes designed to safeguard children. The safeguarding agenda has also permeated every aspect of the children's workforce. Current discourses around childhood perceive children as both innocent and vulnerable and therefore in need of protection. Within current policy, exposure to risk is viewed negatively and children are protected from all forms of danger. These discourses contrast sharply with the way children were treated in the past and this represents a substantial shift in thinking about children. Such a shift in values is both necessary and a feature of a civilised society. All teachers need to know about how to safeguard children from danger and how to identify possible signs of abuse, and this chapter – whilst unable to answer questions about all aspects of safeguarding – will provide you with a basic overview of child protection issues.

Legislative context

Section 175 of the Education Act 2002 places a duty on maintained schools to promote and safeguard children's welfare, and schools have both a moral and legal duty to promote children's wellbeing, to protect them from harm, and to respond to child abuse. In addition to this legislation the Teachers' Standards (DfE, 2012) explicitly state that *all* teachers are responsible for safeguarding children's wellbeing. Schools' legal duties are detailed in *Keeping Children Safe in Education* (DfE, 2014). Within this statutory guidance *safeguarding* is defined as:

> ... protecting children from maltreatment; preventing impairment of children's health or development; ensuring that children grow up in circumstances consistent with the provision of safe and effective care; and taking action to enable all children to have the best outcomes. (DfE, 2014: 4)

Within the context of this statutory guidance the term *children* includes everyone under the age of 18. The guidance states that action should be taken to protect a child who is suffering or is likely to suffer significant harm. Additionally action must be taken to promote the *welfare* of children who are in need of additional support, even if they are not at immediate risk (DfE, 2014: para 3).

The statutory guidance makes everyone who comes into contact with children responsible for safeguarding them and puts the onus of identifying children who need help onto staff. Staff must be aware of signs of abuse and know what to do in each case, always acting in the interests of the child. Systems within schools, including governance, must all have safeguarding at their heart (DfE, 2014). The DfE also details instances of poor practice (DfE, 2014: 19).

Definitions and symptoms of abuse

There are four main categories of abuse: physical, neglect, sexual and emotional.

Physical abuse

Physical abuse can be defined as 'actual or likely physical injury to a child or young person' (Lindon, 2008: 44). Physical abuse could be the result of a direct attack or the direct failure of an adult to safeguard a child from injury or suffering (Lindon, 2008). Examples of physical abuse include the following: hitting; shaking; biting; burning; squeezing; suffocating (full or partial); poisoning; rough handling; and the inappropriate use of drugs, alcohol or prescription medication (Lindon, 2008). This is not an exhaustive list. Adults have a responsibility to protect children from violence and adults who know about risks of violence to children but fail to protect them can be prosecuted. This extends to adults who whilst not directly responsible for causing injury do not act to prevent it.

The causes of physical abuse are varied. Physical abuse of children can arise from family stress or an inability to manage a child's behaviour appropriately, resulting in frustration. The causes can also be more deep-rooted and may stem from an adult's own background (Lindon, 2008). Symptoms may be physical (such as bruises, bite marks, scratches). Additionally, children who have been exposed to physical abuse may be aggressive and violent towards other children and display challenging behaviour.

Neglect

Neglect is a term used to describe a persistent failure to care for children's physical and emotional needs. Children suffering from neglect may experience the following:

- a lack of food
- a lack of appropriate clothing (e.g. unclean clothing, or the lack of warm clothes)
- a lack of love and care
- a lack of attention on the part of the parent or carer to a child's cleanliness
- a lack of warmth
- being left to look after themselves at home.

This is not an exhaustive list. Children can also experience neglect from practitioners if there is a lack of attention as regards their physical and emotional needs.

Sexual abuse

According to Lindon (2008: 55) 'Sexual abuse is defined as the actual or likely sexual exploitation of a child or adolescent, who is dependent or developmentally immature.' The victims of such crimes are not able to give their consent and can be manipulated in a variety of ways. The perpetrators, who may be male or female, abuse their power and prey on vulnerable children and adolescents. However, the majority of abusers are male. It is often the case that most perpetrators of sexual abuse know their victims – they may be a family member or friend, or someone known to the family. They may try to convince their victims that the sexual behaviour is normal or they may bribe their victims with gifts. The perpetrator always holds power over the victim and this power increases as the exploitative relationship develops (DfE, 2014). Lindon (2008: 56) argues that:

> Anyone who abuses a child usually builds a web of coercion to try to prevent discovery and reduce the likelihood that a child or young adolescent will be believed. But sexual abusers are especially keen to force apparent cooperation and to impose secrecy; they know they are breaking an important social taboo.

The symptoms of sexual abuse are varied and could include:

- change in a child's behaviour
- rejection of physical contact
- evidence of bruising and marks in the genital area and/or other areas of the body
- drawings which demonstrate advanced sexual knowledge
- overtly 'forward' relationships with other children
- rocking
- being withdrawn
- stained underwear
- pain when going to the toilet
- use of inappropriate language.

Girls are more prone to sexual abuse than boys. Abuse can include full sexual intercourse, oral or anal sex. Additionally adults may fondle or masturbate children or ask children to perform these acts on them. Sexual exhibitionism, where adults perform sexual acts in front of children, is also a form of sexual abuse. Any act that involves the sexual exploitation of young or vulnerable people is classified as sexual abuse. This extends to the possession of inappropriate images of children and young people and any form of child pornography.

Some young people who are being sexually exploited do not demonstrate any external signs of this abuse (DfE, 2014). Sexual exploitation can include cyberbullying and grooming, unwanted pressure from peers to engage in sexual activities, and seemingly 'consensual' relationships. However, the imbalance of power in the relationship is critical in marking out sexual exploitation.

Emotional abuse

Emotional abuse has been defined as 'any form of direct ill-treatment or neglect [which] affects children's sense of security and trust' (Lindon, 2008: 39). This can include:

- verbal attacks which damage a child's sense of self
- unrealistic adult expectations of children
- continuous 'put downs'
- continuous verbal threats
- observing domestic violence within the home, even if not directly affected.

The damage to the child's self-concept can be evident in their behaviour. They may appear withdrawn or cry frequently. They may lack confidence or seek attention. Additionally, they may demonstrate aggressive behaviour towards others.

No one trait is evidence of any form of abuse and the symptoms of each form of abuse will vary from child to child. Unless a child makes a direct disclosure, practitioners – including teachers – will have to use their professional judgement in cases where they suspect that a child may be the victim of abuse. This is a major professional responsibility and one that is daunting for both teachers and trainees. If you are having any doubts about suspected abuse you should consult the Designated Person or the head teacher at your school rather than staying silent. Not speaking out could have major implications for your career if it later became apparent that a child was being abused and that you had suspected this but had taken no action. In all cases, you must never speak to the parents or carers directly.

Application to secondary teaching

Case study 1

Heather is a 15-year-old pupil and attends a local comprehensive school. Her English teacher, James, notices over several weeks that Heather has developed an interest in him. She frequently attempts to stay behind at the end of lessons to talk to him. James has also noticed that Heather is becoming increasingly flirtatious with him in class and has begun to ask him questions about his interests outside of school. Several of the other pupils have noticed her behaviour and have started to make jokes about it.

- How do you think James should deal with this situation?
- How can schools and teachers take steps to prevent such situations occurring?

Case study 2

You are a teacher in a large secondary school and you have noticed that one of your colleagues (who is also a friend) has developed an unhealthy relationship with one of the pupils. Your colleague and the pupil have exchanged telephone numbers and they have started to send text messages to each other. You also discover that your colleague is also sending messages to this pupil on a social networking site.

- How would you begin to address this situation?

Case study 3

Sam is a gay 14-year-old pupil at your school and he has approached you for help. It appears that he has been the victim of verbal abuse in the schoolyard at break-times and this is beginning to escalate. At first Sam ignored the abuse, but the perpetrators have threatened physical assault and as a result he now feels unsafe. He approaches you to ask for help.

- How would you address Sam's situation?
- How can issues of homophobia be addressed on a whole-school level?

The role of the Designated Person

The Designated Person is responsible for ensuring that the school safeguarding policy is followed and all employees should be aware of who has this role. This person will act as a source of advice and training and will refer concerns relating to specific children to other agencies. The Designated Person will coordinate action regarding referrals, liaise with the head teacher over policies and investigations, keep themselves up to date with training, and be able to contribute to case reviews. In addition he or she will ensure that other stakeholders (such as parents) are aware of safeguarding policies and be responsible for keeping detailed and secure records, including their transfer to receiving schools or institutions.

Schools must nominate a Designated Governor for child protection whose role is to ensure that the school is compliant in its legal duties to safeguard the welfare of children. The Designated Governor should review the safeguarding practices at least annually to check compliance with policy and legislation.

GROUP EXERCISE

Teachers have to be able to work in collaboration with other professionals, particularly when working with vulnerable children and in cases where children are being abused. These could include:

- the police
- social services
- local authority personnel e.g. Local Safeguarding Boards
- medical professionals
- Education Welfare Officers.

This is not an exhaustive list. As a group, research into the roles and responsibilities of other professionals who you may be required to work with in the future. Disseminate the information to your colleagues in the form of a short presentation.

Safe recruitment

Schools (and teacher training providers) must ensure that all appropriate background checks have been carried out on all staff and volunteers who have unsupervised access to children. No person should be allowed to work in a school until the outcome of such checks is satisfactory. Schools must carry out their own criminal record checks (DBS checks – the Disclosure and Barring Service) and ensure that the references which have been provided to support employment are authentic.

The Bichard Report in 2004, which inquired into the circumstances surrounding the Ian Huntley case, led to important changes in the law in relation to vetting and barring systems. Anyone who is disqualified from working with children or vulnerable people should not be granted employment, and anyone with a criminal background will be detected through vetting systems.

Employers will need to make decisions about whether the nature of an applicant's criminal background makes them unsuitable to work with children: in teaching there is no such thing as 'spent' cautions or convictions. Trainee teachers and other students are vetted by their training provider and schools should not request additional checks. Additionally, those from other organisations who are visiting the school in a professional capacity do not need to be vetted by the school since they will have been vetted by their own organisation.

A thought

Effective and safe recruitment processes are essential for protecting children from exposure to people who may present risks. It is also important for checks to be carried out on visitors such as volunteers. Visitors to schools and early years settings can enhance the educational experience for children. Think carefully about how education providers can strike the right balance between being vigilant and being friendly.

Dealing with a disclosure of abuse

Disclosures of abuse from children can occur at any point during your training and teaching career. Be familiar with the school safeguarding policy which will give specific advice on how to deal with such situations. Stay calm and do not transmit feelings of embarrassment, shock or anger to children. Ensure that you follow the school policy precisely and:

- offer reassurance to the child
- tell the child you are pleased he or she is speaking to you
- do not offer assurances of confidentiality but explain to the child that in order to help them you will need to tell other people
- tell the child who you will pass the information on to
- listen to the child and let them talk
- remember that children tend rarely to tell lies about abuse but they may have tried to tell others about it and not been believed
- tell the child that it is not his or her fault
- check that you have understood correctly what the child is trying to tell you by repeating the information back
- praise the child for speaking to you
- reassure the child that he or she has a right to be safe and protected
- do not tell the child that what they have experienced is dirty, naughty or bad
- do not offer any comments about the alleged offender – your role is to listen to what the child has to say and to remain neutral
- at the end of the conversation thank the child for speaking to you and remind them who you are going to pass the information on to and why this is necessary

- remember that children may retract what they have said so it is important to keep a written record of the disclosure
- following the disclosure, make a detailed record of the conversation using the child's own words only – ensure that you do not add your own interpretation or personal opinion
- never speak to a child's parents or carers about the disclosure.

Following the disclosure it is important to pass the information on to the head teacher and/or the Designated Person who must report this to social services immediately. The disclosure could have an emotional impact on practitioners so support systems should be available in the school to help staff cope with this distressing process.

Dealing with concerns

Concerns could arise from observing injuries which appear to be non-accidental or through suspicions that a child may be at risk of harm. Concerns could also stem from children making direct disclosures or implying that they may have been abused. Additionally, concerns or allegations against members of staff also need to be taken seriously. In these instances teachers must not investigate suspicions. They should record what they have heard or seen, including the date and time, and share their concerns with the Designated Person and/or head teacher. All information must be treated confidentially and must be stored in a locked filing cabinet or on a password protected computer. If members of staff fail to report concerns then this could be regarded as a disciplinary issue. If there is a concern or allegation about the head teacher this should be reported to the Chair of Governors. Specific child protection cases should not be discussed at governors' meetings due to the confidential nature of such cases and the need to protect individual children and alleged abusers.

A thought

Education providers have a duty to protect the safety and wellbeing of children. However, it is important that children are exposed to a certain element of risk. They need to be exposed to risk and and to be taught how to manage risk as a valuable preparation for adult life. There is little to be gained by 'wrapping children up in cotton wool'. How can providers strike a balance between protecting children and giving them some exposure to risk? How can we empower children to keep themselves safe? The notion of giving children some responsibility for their own safety is a way of viewing children as active social agents.

Confidentiality

All staff working in school need to understand the importance of maintaining confidentiality, particularly in the context of child protection issues. The purpose of confidentiality is to protect the child. It is not appropriate to offer children assurances of confidentiality as the information will be shared with other professionals in order to help them. As a general principle, information should only be shared on a 'need to know' basis and any breaches of confidentiality can be dealt with through disciplinary procedures.

Whistle blowing

All employees have a responsibility to raise matters of concern about the behaviour of other members of staff. This is not an easy thing to do but children's welfare and safety must be regarded as the first priority. You may feel that you are being disloyal to a colleague and you may be worried that you will face discrimination and harassment as a consequence of raising a concern. You may also be worried that you have misinterpreted a situation. Fear of repercussions or fear of not being believed often prevents people from whistle blowing. It is important to remember that your first duty is to protect children's safety and education, and you should follow the school's policy on whistle blowing in these instances. Raising your concerns may help to prevent a problem from getting worse and may protect and reduce the risks to others.

Whistle blowing can be used to expose members of staff who demonstrate inappropriate conduct towards colleagues. This could include cases of bullying, harassment, and direct and indirect discrimination. It can be used to expose any member of staff (paid or voluntary) whose behaviour or conduct towards children, colleagues and parents presents a cause for concern.

As a trainee teacher whistle blowing is particularly problematic. You may be worried about how your colleagues in school will perceive you if you raise a concern, and you may also have concerns about whether making the decision to whistle blow will impact negatively on school assessments of your performance. In such instances you should discuss your concerns with your provider link tutor or consultant who can advise you on how to proceed.

If you wish to raise an issue about a colleague in school you should voice your uneasiness, suspicions or concerns sooner rather than later. As a trainee teacher you should be able to raise concerns with your mentor or professional tutor. However, if your concerns are not taken seriously or taken forward it will be necessary to approach the head teacher. If you wish to raise concerns about the head teacher you should first raise the issues with your mentor and/or tutor and if these are dismissed or not acted upon it will be necessary to contact the Chair of Governors.

In all instances it is important that you get a satisfactory response. If you are not happy with the response you receive then express your concerns in writing, outlining the context, event(s), times, dates and names. If the head teacher fails to act on the information then you should send the written record to the Chair of Governors, keeping a confidential copy for your records. It is not your role to prove what is true in such situations; however you need to be able to demonstrate that you have sufficient grounds for raising a concern. In all instances you should follow the guidance issued by your training provider.

The school policy on whistle blowing should explicitly state that no action will be taken against you if the concern proves to be unfounded. You have raised the issue in good faith. However, malicious allegations may be treated as a disciplinary offence.

The importance of training

The Designated Teacher or head teacher is responsible for ensuring that all members of staff, including new colleagues, receive comprehensive training in child protection. All staff will be expected to participate in Local Authority safeguarding training and attend refresher courses. The Designated Person will be expected to attend a refresher course once every two years.

Allegations about members of staff

Concerns about the conduct of a member of staff should be reported to the Designated Person, who will then make decisions about each situation on a case-by-case basis in consultation with the head teacher. In some situations – for example if a child has been injured in school – the school should inform the parents and carers immediately. In cases where the allegation is made against a member of staff, the Local Authority Designated Officer (LADO) should be informed of all allegations made. Additionally parents and carers should be kept informed about the progress of any investigation and the outcomes. Some parents or carers may be happy for the child to continue to stay in the school but teachers and other practitioners must not discuss the case with the parents during on-going investigations.

Record keeping

Accurate and timely record keeping is vital and there should be a clear record of:

- any allegation made
- how it was followed up
- how it was resolved
- who was involved in making any decisions.

Information sharing

Schools are not investigating agencies but have a duty to pass on any concerns to other agencies which investigate allegations of abuse. All information about the alleged perpetrator and victim should be shared.

Timescales

Cases should be resolved quickly as they can cause considerable anxiety for both the alleged perpetrator and the alleged victim.

Suspension

The head teacher will evaluate the possible risk of harm posed by an accused person and may consider an immediate suspension.

Monitoring progress

The local authority designated safeguarding officer should regularly monitor the progress of cases in liaison with the head teacher and any external agencies involved with the case.

Concluding a case

In the case of teachers and other practitioners who have been the subject of a false allegation, head teachers will need to decide upon a strategy which will facilitate a return to work. If a child has made a false allegation against a parent or a member of staff, schools will need to consider how they are best able to support the child, and in such circumstances the child should not be discriminated against. The child's well-being is the most important priority in such situations.

Application to primary and early years teaching

Young children often seek reassurance from practitioners if they are hurt or distressed. They may approach known adults for comfort and perhaps seek reassurance in the form of hugging. Additionally they may try to 'cuddle up' to practitioners during story times or they may try to sit on their laps. In the early years also some children will need to be changed, particularly when they have soiled themselves. In such circumstances it is important to have a clear policy in relation to what is appropriate and what is not in order to protect both staff and children. No adult should ever place him or herself in a vulnerable position and it is certainly not appropriate to be left alone with a child. The safeguarding policy should stipulate clear guidelines on 'touch' and all practitioners and parents should be made aware of this policy.

Creating a safe school

All adults should regard safeguarding children's welfare as a key professional duty. Within a safe school relationships between adults and between adults and children are based on mutual respect. All staff, including trainees, are expected to follow the school behaviour policy. If you have difficulties in managing the behaviour of a specific pupil or group of pupils you must discuss strategies to support you in this process with your mentor and other colleagues.

You will need to find out about the school policy on physical contact with children. Trainees are often advised to refrain from any physical contact with children in order to protect themselves from allegations of abuse. However, you will have to use your own discretion and make a professional judgement, particularly in situations where young children may be distressed and seek reassurance from you. Generally, it will be appropriate to comfort children in these situations but this should be appropriate to the age and maturity of the child. If you are working with very young children you will need to find out about the school policy on whether it is appropriate to hold hands with children. Adults must not *initiate* physical contact unnecessarily. As a general rule:

- adults should avoid being left alone with a child, especially where a door is closed
- if you need to speak to a child privately conduct the meeting in a shared area where you can be seen or ask another adult to be present
- only use physical restraint as a last resort to avoid injury
- never sit young children on your lap
- children should be discouraged from hugging adults.

A thought

Head teachers have a duty to inform colleagues in school about the safe use of information and communication technology. The growth of social networking sites has made it possible for teachers and other practitioners in school to communicate more easily. What are the dangers associated with this? How can senior leaders educate staff to comply with safeguarding policies, whilst preserving the rights of colleagues to use such forms of communication?

Teachers and other practitioners working in school must behave professionally at all times. Children should be taught explicitly about the importance of positive relationships and feelings, and should be encouraged to develop inclusive attitudes so that relationships are harmonious. All discrimination and harassment must be challenged regardless of whether the perpetrators are children or adults. Children should be explicitly taught about issues related to e-safety through the taught ICT curriculum. Trainee teachers are expected to be familiar with the school policy on safeguarding/ child protection and the policy on whistle blowing.

Photographing children

The use of cameras is common in schools for recording evidence of children's learning and also for recording special events such as stage productions or sports' days. Children must not be photographed if parents have not given their permission to allow this. Additionally, schools must not use photographs of children on the school website or allow images of children to be included in press releases without permission from parents or carers. Note that schools cannot be held accountable for photographs of children or video footage taken by other parents during school functions. The use of flash photography should be avoided as this could dazzle children or be dangerous for children with specified conditions.

Trainee teachers should discuss the school policy on recording digital images of children with their mentors. Sometimes it is appropriate to blur faces or to take shots from behind a child so that the face is not recorded. Information relating to a child's full name should not be recorded next to a photograph and photographs of children should not be transported between home and school, even if stored on a personal laptop computer.

Safeguarding pupil data

Teachers and trainee teachers should take all steps to ensure that pupil data are kept secure. This includes data relating to pupil attainment, individual education plans, behaviour plans or reports. This information should be stored in school in a locked cupboard. If the data are transferred between home and school the child's name and date of birth should not be linked to the data and electronic data related to pupils' attainment, achievement and progress should only be stored on a password protected computer.

Cybersafety

Children and young people need to be trained in safe practices on the internet. Although there will be experts in your school whose job this is, you will still need your own knowledge and awareness. You will need to know the problems in order that you can recognise them and then act on them. Children need to know how to be secure and safe online, and how to deal with modern problems such as cyber-bullying, identity theft and online grooming. These can have serious consequences for children.

Teachers also need to be aware of their own profiles and internet usage. As a student, it may be that pictures of you in a compromising position on a night out are both fun and funny. As a professional, you may well find that pupils who have taken a dislike to you (or even who have just taken an interest in you) will access your social networking account and spread both pictures and rumours. You will therefore need to protect your online identity and access to social networking and video and photo-sharing sites.

Cyberbullying, the *Guardian* reported in November 2009, is as common as name-calling amongst children. In a survey conducted by the Teacher Support Network with the Association of Teachers and Lecturers (ATL), it was reported in March 2010 (at the ATL Conference) that more than one in seven teachers had been a victim of cyberbullying by pupils or parents, and almost half were aware of a colleague who had been targeted.

Other problems and offences arise as pupils find new uses for technology. Examples include filming lessons and uploading them to sites with commentaries, persuading teachers and pupils into situations and positions that are open to misinterpretation and then distributing photographs, and taking indecent images which are then emailed or texted round (called 'sexting'). Advice to help children (and teachers) safeguard against such problems includes:

- don't publish your address or phone number on networking sites
- use complex passwords that have both letters and numbers in them, and don't use the same password for everything – your highest level passwords should be particularly complex and changed regularly
- try not to log in on public machines – if you do, log off properly and erase the history
- only make virtual friends with people you actually know, not strangers.
- never take a stranger's description of themselves as 'genuine' – if ever you are in any doubt about how genuine someone is, or about the information they want, report them.

There is a lot of free advice and even training available via various organisations such as the police, charities, internet companies and broadcasters. For example, you can enrol the help of the BBC's Tracy Beaker, or the cartoon rabbit 'Dongle' for younger children, use videos and resources provided by the police through the Child Exploitation and Online Protection Centre (CEOP), or visit the sites of child-centred charities such as Childnet and Kidscape. CEOP, for example, provides a range of resources for teachers and other professionals working with young people. There are films, presentations, games, lesson plans and posters covering a range of issues, from grooming by child sex offenders to cyberbullying. A good starting point is Chatdanger (www.chatdanger.com) which provides child-friendly advice on safeguarding linked to mobile phones, chatrooms, email, instant messaging (IM) and online games. The child-focused CEOP site is at www.thinkuknow.co.uk. Current links are included at the end of the chapter.

The Byron Review (Byron, 2008) highlights concerns raised by children about the internet, including the ease with which pornographic material can be accessed and the risks of online bullying. Byron also identifies the dangers associated with children's use of violent video games and online gaming. The review recommends that all new teachers should be trained in e-safety and that Ofsted inspections should focus on this area as a key priority. Byron recommends that all children, parents, teachers and trainee teachers are educated about e-safety and emphasises that e-safety should be seen as a national priority.

Avoiding risks and applying common sense

It is good practice for all staff to sign a code of conduct as part of the induction process. All staff should be aware of the dangers associated with the following:

- working alone with children
- the use of physical interventions
- giving and receiving gifts from children and parents
- contacting children through private telephones (including texting), e-mail, MSN, or social networking sites
- disclosing personal details inappropriately
- meeting pupils outside school hours or school duties
- entering into social friendships with pupils
- dealing with sensitive information about children.

Trainees, teachers and all other colleagues in school should be aware of the dangers of crossing professional boundaries.

INDIVIDUAL REFLECTION

Some schools now use CCTV cameras so that children and staff are under continuous surveillance, and some nurseries have developed systems to enable parents to log in to a password protected computer system to access live coverage of the day-to-day events as they unfold within a setting. This can be beneficial as parents are able to observe their child and the interactions which take place between practitioners and children. Additionally, the use of technology can help to safeguard practitioners as it offers a reliable record of what has happened on a day-to-day basis. However, such practices also raise specific concerns about children's right to privacy and the perpetual use of surveillance. There is also no guarantee that the use of CCTV will protect children from the perpetrators of child abuse. What do you think the advantages and disadvantages are of such practices? What are the ethical implications and the dangers of using technology in this way?

Male and gay practitioners

Male practitioners working in the early years sector are particularly vulnerable as a result of prejudices in society which exist around the motivations of males who choose to work with young children. Additionally, prejudices can be magnified if the employee is gay, lesbian, transsexual, transgender, or has had gender reassignment. Bullying, discrimination or harassment could be directed from children, parents or colleagues. Within these circumstances the leaders of schools and early years settings should take steps to safeguard the employee from bullying, harassment or discrimination. All employers have a duty to ensure equality of opportunity for employees under the Equality Act 2010.

Female Genital Mutilation (FGM)

Education professionals need to be alert to the possibility of a girl either being at risk of Female Genital Mutilation (FGM) or having already suffered it (DfE, 2014). Victims are likely to come from those communities which are known to practise FGM: potential victims may not even be aware of the practice within their community.

FGM comprises the removal of or injury to the external female genitalia for non-medical reasons. The practice is illegal in the UK. Possible warning signs could include:

- prolonged absence from school and a change in behaviour on return
- the child may find it difficult to sit still and may be uncomfortable
- the child may complain of pain between her legs
- the child may have frequent infections and experience bleeding
- the child may be known to belong to a community that practises FGM.

UK communities that are most at risk of FGM include the Kenyan, Somali, Sudanese, Sierra Leonean, Egyptian, Nigerian and Eritrean. Non-African communities that practise FGM include the Yemeni, Afghani, Kurdish, Indonesian and Pakistani.

Summary

- Symptoms of abuse can vary from child to child and no one symptom can be taken as an indicator of abuse.
- All practitioners must receive training in how to recognise possible abuse and the specific procedures on how to report abuse and be familiar with the school safeguarding policy.
- Abuse can be subjective and value-laden: what constitutes abuse for one person may not be viewed as abuse by another person. This can be dangerous as the symptoms may get overlooked. If in any doubt discuss your concerns with the Designated Person.

- Abuse can take place via electronic means – such as cyberbullying via mobile phones or social networking. Be aware of, and prepared to educate about, the problems.
- Never place yourself in a vulnerable situation. If in doubt, enlist the support of a colleague as an observer.

Key reading

Byron, T. (2008) *Safer children in a digital world: a summary for children and young people.* Nottingham: DCSF.

Department for Education (DfE) (2014) *Keeping children safe in education: statutory guidance for schools and colleges*. London: DfE.

Department for Children, Schools and Families (DCSF) (2010) *Working together to safeguard children: a guide to inter-agency working to safeguard and promote the welfare of children.* Nottingham: DCSF.

Dillenburger, K. and McKee, B. (2009) 'Child abuse and neglect: training needs of student teachers', *International Journal of Educational Research,* 48 (5): 320–30.

References and bibliography

Byron, T. (2008) *Safer children in a digital world: a summary for children and young people.* Nottingham: DCSF.

Department for Education (DfE) (2012) *Standards for qualified teachers*. Available online at www.gov.uk/government/publications/teachers-standards

Department for Education and Skills (DfES) (2007) *Safeguarding children and safer recruitment in education*. London: DfES.

Lindon, J. (2008) *Safeguarding children and young people*. London: Hodder.

Macpherson, P. (2011) 'Safeguarding children', in A. Hansen (ed.), *Primary professional studies.* Exeter: Learning Matters, pp. 134–49.

Maslow, A.H. (1943) 'A theory of human motivation', *Psychological Review,* 50: 370–96.

Useful websites

CBBC Stay Safe: www.bbc.co.uk/cbbc/help/web/staysafe
Child Exploitation and Online Protection Centre: www.ceop.police.uk/
Google Family Safety Centre: www.google.co.uk/familysafety/
Kidscape: www.kidscape.org.uk/cyberbullying/cyberbullyingchildrenyoungpeople.shtml
NSPCC:
www.nspcc.org.uk (this site provides useful advice on the signs of abuse and neglect)

Visit https://study.sagepub.com/denby3e for extra resources related to this chapter.

CHAPTER 5

COMMUNICATION AND COLLABORATION

Rod Robertson

Standards linked to this chapter include...

5. Adapt teaching to respond to the strengths and needs of all pupils

- know when and how to differentiate appropriately, using approaches which enable pupils to be taught effectively
- have a secure understanding of how a range of factors can inhibit pupils' ability to learn, and how best to overcome these
- demonstrate an awareness of the physical, social and intellectual development of children, and know how to adapt teaching to support pupils' education at different stages of development

- have a clear understanding of the needs of all pupils, including those with special educational needs; those of high ability; those with English as an additional language; those with disabilities; and be able to use and evaluate distinctive teaching approaches to engage and support them.

8. Fulfil wider professional responsibilities

- make a positive contribution to the wider life and ethos of the school
- develop effective professional relationships with colleagues, knowing how and when to draw on advice and specialist support
- deploy support staff effectively
- communicate effectively with parents with regard to pupils' achievements and wellbeing.

Introduction

Your school placement experience will quickly show you that schools are busy and complex places. When first encountering the school and the classroom you may become bewildered by the many interactions you are expected to become involved in. It will soon become apparent that classrooms and schools are not only populated by teachers and those that they teach. The school community includes Learning Support staff, Pastoral Officers, Education Welfare Officers, and a plethora of other professionals (not to mention the colleagues supporting in premises management, catering, administration support and so on) (see Chapter 7). If all of these adults are to bring about the most effective practice, from which pupils are to benefit, then collaboration, co-operation and sharing of effective practice must take place before, during and after formal lesson times. As a teacher, you will also be expected to communicate effectively with parents and carers. It is important that you see the need to be proactive in all of these opportunities for communication and collaboration.

Understanding expectations

If you are to understand your role as a teacher within a particular primary or secondary setting then you will need to ensure that what is expected of you in the context of current government legislation and schools has been made clear. The necessary procedures and protocols should be made explicit at the outset. However, if this hasn't happened during your initial induction period it is vital that you seek clarification.

Understanding what is expected of you as a teacher is just as important as communicating, collaborating and co-operating effectively with children, young people, colleagues, parents, and carers.

Communicate

Communicating effectively with children and young people – building relationships

Most of your communication with young people and children will be in group contexts within the confines of the classroom – however you will also constantly find yourself communicating with children and young people as you move to and from your classrooms and around the school. In this context you must see every situation where you encounter pupils, in your role as a teacher, as an opportunity. Seizing these opportunities to build relationships with children and young people will pay dividends for all. Communicating the notion that you are approachable is vital if you are to encourage children and young people to see you, and indeed all teachers like you, as people who are interested in their wellbeing. The 'student voice' (and children of all ages have a right and a desire to be listened to) should be acknowledged in both formal and informal contexts – and of course teachers are presented with many opportunities to hear what children are saying about their school experiences (Mitra and Gross, 2009).

A thought

Take the opportunity with a small group of pupils to ask them what was the 'best' experience they have had at school so far. Remind them this could be any activity, including after school clubs and school trips. Listen carefully to what they say, as they will very soon start describing events and the people involved as well as what these people said and did. Consider what the pupils say about teacher involvement in these events – usually teacher participation or organisation is intrinsically linked to enjoyment of the activity. List the ways in which pupils see their contact with teachers as positive and then try to build these into your lesson planning whilst avoiding the negative.

You must never forget your role as responsible adult and teacher; however this should not stop you being creative in your interactions with children and young people. Pupils will *perceive the boundaries* you set if you make these explicit. They will also *continue* to *perceive* these boundaries if you consistently adhere to these in your interactions with pupils. Lack of clarity and inconsistency will confuse young people and this confusion can lead to 'blurred boundaries'. Children and young people are capable of accepting that teachers (or any adults they encounter) have different personalities, interests, opinions and beliefs – but when teachers give out 'mixed messages' they are likely to become confused and unsure about what is appropriate.

Communicating effectively with colleagues – building relationships

As a teacher you should constantly be developing effective communication skills and making sure that these are not just manifesting themselves in the classroom but also in any forum where you are talking with, and sharing with, colleagues, parents and carers.

It would be useful to acquire the organisation chart for your school to understand individuals' roles and responsibilities. Accessing the Staff Handbook will also help you understand any protocols and procedures that are in place. In addition, the school's calendar of meetings will allow you to prepare for any necessary input that you will need to make. For example, if there is an expectation that you should attend a regular meeting with teaching and learning support colleagues to discuss forthcoming projects and planned work, then you will need to know this in order to plan and prepare.

However, in a more pragmatic context, perhaps you may be expected to brief a Learning Support Assistant (LSA) about a particular project that they will be working on with a pupil who will be in your class. It is absolutely vital that before the first lesson of this project you meet with the LSA to discuss with them the work to be covered – this may only take a few minutes but still has to be planned into the busy working day (i.e. it is not effective planning/teaching to 'grab' a minute at the start of the lesson to explain a complicated set of worksheets/resources). It is especially important that you are aware of, and follow, policy. For example, if there is a policy within the school that states all new resources that are to be used with classes/individuals should be forwarded to the Special Needs Coordinator (SENCO) before the lesson you will need to know about this and act accordingly!

A thought

Colleagues will often be willing to ask you to clarify something you have communicated to them if they are unsure what you meant. However children and young people are not always willing to do this. It is therefore important that you are sensitive to the non-verbal clues that children exhibit that may tell you they are unclear about what you have communicated (i.e. if you detect an individual or group looking doubtful about what you have said, get them to repeat back in their own words what has been said or asked of them).

Communicate effectively with parents and carers

It is vital that you know the formal ways (e.g. letter, detention slip, report card, Home/School Consultation Evening) by which the school communicates with parents and carers. It is also useful to know if other less formal ways are allowed. For example, it may be entirely appropriate (i.e. the school allows this) to telephone a parent. However, many schools will have a formal procedure for how to record the time, date, reason, and outcome of the telephone call, and it is your responsibility to be aware of this (as well as the school's responsibility to make you aware). Some schools will have a policy where the need to contact the parent is discussed with the relevant pastoral member of staff (e.g. form tutor) before that contact is made. Of course it is entirely possible that the school will not permit any telephone communication with a parent or carer unless it is instigated by a member of staff with a pastoral role, so do be aware of this.

When communicating with parents and carers it is important that at the outset of the communication they are made aware of the reason for the communication. Also, it should always be possible to give them an opportunity to ask any questions or seek further clarification (perhaps from someone else) at the conclusion of the meeting or telephone call.

Any face-to-face meeting must at all times be cordial but professional. The parent or carer must see you – the teacher – as approachable and concerned about the progress and wellbeing of the young person. In face-to-face meetings you can't underestimate the importance of communicating to the parent or carer that you know the pupil well and that you have an understanding of the abilities, achievements, and areas to be developed.

Application to secondary teaching

This demonstrates to children the need to follow instructions carefully. Construct a simple model using building blocks (they can be held together with double-sided sticky tape if the blocks don't have their own locating pins). Hide this model behind some card and then give clear instructions that will allow the children to make the model (e.g. '... place red block on top of blue block with one corner of blue block pointing to the right...'). After the instructions have been completed show the children the model you have originally made and allow them to compare their models.

An alternative method of doing this is to pair the children, ask them to sit back to back and allow one child to build a simple model, and then give instructions that will allow their partner to make a copy (the children building the copy will obviously need identical blocks to the ones used in the model initially built by their partner). Children will enjoy doing this activity, however if you don't have a big enough supply of building blocks then it is possible to choose only a few pairs of children and then allow groups to watch the pairs giving and receiving instructions, although many will ask can they have opportunity to be both instruction giver and receiver – they are not always content just to be spectators!

Collaboration and co-operative working

Collaboration is when you work alongside others to achieve a common goal. Co-operation is where you plan together (and interlink with others) but don't then necessarily work alongside another professional to achieve that which is planned for.

Inherent in this is the acknowledgement that when meeting with colleagues, parents and carers, you are doing so in a spirit of both collaboration and co-operation. For example:

- An LSA that you are meeting with (and who you will be working with) may know of an effective strategy another class teacher uses with a particular behaviour or child. Remember, they may be supporting this child throughout the school day and are therefore able to observe how the child responds to different teaching styles. Obviously, it would be foolish of you not to listen to the suggestions that are made.
- A parent may suggest that their child really likes your lessons but does need to have longer to write the homework into the homework planner. You should be able to reassure the parent that you will make a little more time available to allow this to happen – and then make sure you do!
- You manage to cure Liam's pencil tapping habit (low level disruption) by giving him some Blu-Tack to play with. This occupies his hands but does not adversely affect his concentration (or the learning of others). Make sure that colleagues are aware of your strategy, perhaps at staff briefing time.

A thought

Is there a difference between collaboration and co-operation? When do you work best with others – is it when *they* are working with *you* to achieve something you see (they see or you both see) as important? To demonstrate a commitment to collaborative and co-operative working you will need to be involved in projects where colleagues work together to achieve a common (agreed) aim and not just your interests.

Team working

To be an effective teacher you must accept that working independently in an educational setting is never an option. Teachers must constantly seek advice and information from a range of colleagues. You should also expect to be consulted (you are an expert, after all) and to be a willing source of information and advice for colleagues and others involved in the education or wellbeing of the young person.

Children and young people will be quick to discern whether or not the teachers they encounter are communicating effectively with each other. They will know because an effective dialogue will consistently communicate school expectations. This ongoing communication is also a key element in building and sustaining the team.

The reality of 'sharing effective practice' suggests that you should expect to make public, for others, strategies that you, as a teacher, find work well in your teaching situations. Practice can be shared formally or informally, or even via a shared space such as a web forum – a practice used with design students to mixed effect by Chiu (2010). Such sharing provides your colleagues with the possibility of putting these strategies in place in their own teaching. However, if you are to be truly collaborative then you should be looking for this to be reciprocated. You should expect your colleagues to inform you of what works for them (being forthcoming yourself encourages this) and to reflect on these practices to determine how you might utilise them in your own context. We all need to be proactive if we are to identify opportunities to work together and maximise the benefits of these opportunities.

As a teacher, you should never lose sight of one of your primary roles and one of the primary outcomes you should desire – the support of learning. Remember that it is usually inefficient if more than one person is undertaking the same function. In this context you must be aware of how separate but complementary roles interlink. For example, as a teacher it would be ineffective for you to spend all of your time supporting a particular child to the exclusion of the other children in a class. It is your role instead to collaborate with the allocated LSA to allow him or her to support the child appropriately.

Communication

Barnard (1948) suggested the following:

- Everyone should know the channels of communication.
- Everyone should have access to a formal channel of communication.
- Lines of communication should be as short and direct as possible.

Barnard, although writing some sixty years ago, saw the need for everyone to be clear about the channels of communication (see Chapter 11 for Mehrabian's view). He also implied that whilst there should always be access to a formal channel of communication there were often more expedient ways of arriving at a decision. For example, waiting for the next departmental meeting on the calendar may present problems if it is important to have a decision about a relatively minor matter before you meet with a class.

Thody et al. (2000) presented a model to help understand communication – it placed the individual at the centre of the model and had, radiating concentrically from this, 'values', 'attitudes', 'skills' and 'rationality'.

Thody et al. suggested that as your 'values' are closer than your attitudes and skills then these 'values' will have more effect on your communication. Consequently, because your commitment to rationality (your desire to be objective, logical, etc.) is further removed from your values and attitudes this has less impact on your communication. This perhaps should make you aware of how your values and attitudes may have a disproportionate impact on how effectively (and objectively) you might communicate with colleagues, parents and carers. Effective practice comes about by a commitment to objectivity!

New technologies are also key to communication and collaboration between teacher and student. One study (Kearns and Frey, 2010) found that the younger the participant, the more receptive they were to new technology, and the more use they made of it. This particularly applied to mobile technologies. Students are 'digital natives' (Schmuck et al., 2014) who have used digital technologies since an early age to handle information through multiple sources and in different formats – often out of sequence. Teachers tend to be 'digital immigrants' who have adopted IT skills later than in their formative years. As a new trainee or beginning teacher, you may be a 'digital native', so should take every opportunity to use formats like VLEs, videos, vines and blogs to enhance your levels of collaboration with your pupils. Always be aware of issues of privacy and safety (see Chapter 4 and Chapter 19).

Collaboration

Brown et al. (1999), in the context of school effectiveness, highlighted 'types' of schools. They identified the following types:

- **Type A schools** – those schools which give opportunities for collaboration and where department priorities correlate with the school development plan. These are considered to be effective schools.
- **Type B schools** – those schools where there are fewer opportunities for collaboration. These are less effective schools.
- **Type C schools** – those schools where there is little collaboration. These are schools where effective practice is very much less evident.

Of course we would all like to be in effective schools and Brown et al. (1999) provide us with one test (are there opportunities for collaboration?) we can apply to determine if we are likely to be in an effective school! This test could quite appropriately be applied to a department or faculty context.

Leonard and Leonard (2003) tell us that from their research '… teachers themselves value attributes of collegial enterprise that are based upon strong customs of routine professional interaction …'. Leonard and Leonard make explicit that teachers value regular interaction with colleagues in a climate of collegiality. In its truest sense collegiality is when colleagues are allowed to meet, discuss and arrive at a decision based on a consensus of those who have taken part in the discussion. This is very much focused on the setting where the discussion has taken place (i.e. teachers arriving at the best decisions for the children and young people in their school).

Applications to primary and early years teaching

At the outset of a series of lessons remind pupils about the need for clear communication (i.e. use words like 'transmit' and 'receive'). Reiterate to the pupils your rules for the classroom (e.g. pupils listen when you talk, the pupils listen when another pupil is talking, no shouting out, etc.).

Demonstrate clear communication by showing pupils semaphore (communicating using arm signals) – there is only a need to do this for simple letters of the alphabet. Provide the class with a worksheet with various letters and their semaphore equivalent. Allow two small groups of pupils, located at opposite ends of the class, to send simple messages back and forward (obviously without talking). Allow other pupils to observe. At some point in the proceedings allow two pupils to unfurl a large piece of cloth or card that obscures the person sending the message from the person receiving, and explain this is what happens when you get a breakdown in communication. Pupils of all ages enjoy this activity and it often generates lots of discussion about the basics of effective communication. You can root the subject of the communication in your own subject or use it as a vehicle for setting classroom norms.

Managing conflict

When collaboration fails, this can lead to deep problems unless the resulting conflict is resolved. This section addresses the issue of managing conflict when communicating and collaborating with colleagues. An effective teacher never ignores any conflict that arises when working with colleagues. It is better to think of 'managing' conflict rather than 'resolving' conflict – this is because some believe conflict is 'normal' and even productive if managed effectively.

Whilst organisations will have established grievance procedures that can be engaged with, a number of approaches can be adopted to manage conflict before it becomes part of a formalised process. Two strategies that can be used are Purkey et al's 'Six Cs' (2010) and 'CUDSA'.

Purkey et al. (2010) identified some principles to be followed to manage conflict. These are easy to remember as they are based on 'six Cs' – Concern, Confer, Consult, Confront, Combat and Conciliate. In the first instance Purkey et al. suggested it is a matter of Concern if the issue or source of conflict won't take care of itself and/or there is a legal, moral or safety issue related to the conflict. They argued that it is important to initially Confer with the person with whom the conflict exists. It is suggested this is done in private and informally. If this initial meeting does not prove positive then those involved should Consult: this involves a more formal approach to discuss what had been previously agreed, and to seek clarification if there has been some misunderstanding from the earlier informal meeting. If the situation still exists after this third stage then it is necessary to Confront in an assertive manner (i.e. calmly, self-assuredly, confidently, and in the spirit of give and take) and not aggressively (angrily, explosively, and in a domineering manner). The penultimate stage is to Combat by, for example, seeking another solution, actively 'giving space' to the person involved, or asking another colleague for advice or help. Finally Purkey et al. suggested Conciliate, and this involves mending wounds and restoring relationships.

A slightly easier to remember approach to conflict management is 'CUDSA' (its origins are uncertain, but experienced teachers – and others – have used the approach for more than twenty years). Confront the conflict, Understand the other's position, Define the problem(s), Search for and evaluate alternative solutions, and Agree upon, implement and evaluate the best solution. Whichever approach you adopt it will be useful to have in your repertoire a conflict management tool that you can turn to when required.

Teams

When first discussing the concepts of teams and 'team learning' it is instructive to look at the work of Tuckman (1965) and Belbin (1981). Tuckman was seeking to throw light on the 'stages' a team goes through when working together. Have you been aware of or experienced these team 'stages'?

- **Forming** – team members coming together, or a new member joins the team.
- **Storming** – team members experiencing initial tension between themselves.
- **Norming** – team members have a sense of the compromises that are necessary to act as a team.
- **Performing** – the team works collaboratively to achieve a goal or to work towards a target.

Tuckman suggested that a team must move through these stages in order to perform effectively. In this regard it is important to accept that whilst the 'storming' stage may be difficult it is necessary if you and the team are to ascertain your team 'norms' and thus perform better. There is also a fifth stage that is often forgotten – adjournment – when the team breaks up or a number of members leave the team. Of course this necessitates the team re-forming (even if some of the initial members are still present) and then moving through these stages again. You should not underestimate the number of times you will have to do this throughout your career.

Belbin was more interested in looking more carefully at the individuals that contribute to team effectiveness. He identified the following 'types' of team member through their positive and negative aspects:

- **Company worker** – is dutiful and hard-working *but* may lack flexibility.
- **Chairman** – appears self-confident, has a strong sense of objectives *but* of ordinary 'intellect'.
- **Shaper** – is dynamic and will challenge complacency *but* can be impatient.
- **Plant** – displays individualistic tendencies *but* may disregard protocols.
- **Resource investigator** – constantly curious and will willingly contact people *but* may lose interest after a period of time.
- **Monitor-evaluator** – sees being prudent and discreet as important *but* lacks inspiration.
- **Team worker** – sees being social as important and has the ability to respond well to changes *but* can be indecisive.
- **Completer-finisher** – is orderly and conscientious *but* will not readily 'let go' of the task.

Belbin was suggesting that for the team to function most effectively each of these roles needs to be taken. In the context of schools this may be a little complicated because as a teacher you will be a member of more than one team. You are likely, for example, to be a member of a subject department and faculty whilst at the same time being a form tutor and consequently a member of a pastoral team. Further on in your career you may lead one team (as a Head of Year), be a junior member of another (management), and a player in another (subject department). You will need to play a different role in each and play each of those roles effectively – this versatility is just one of the juggling acts that goes with being a good teacher! More recently Salo (2008) has contributed to the discussion of team work and school organisation. Salo has revisited the issue of the micropolitics of schools, namely the many (and sometimes) competing goals that individuals and groups have within schools. It is therefore vital that teachers 'learn' to work together collaboratively. Cooke et al. (2008) also provide an interesting and comprehensive review of research and advances in team theory and team behaviour over the last fifty years.

INDIVIDUAL REFLECTION

Select a period of two to three weeks in which there are a number of staff/department meetings where you will be in attendance. Reflect on the actual collaboration and co-operation that appears to take place – is this genuine or contrived? Is expediency the motivator for most discussions that take place? Then ask yourself how well planned the meetings were and how well prepared you were for them, i.e. was there a published agenda for the meeting (along with meeting papers) and did you (and others present) read the papers before the event?

Team learning

Hall (2001) highlighted the concept of 'team learning' and suggested that this (and personal effectiveness) was brought about by:

- **Appropriate team culture** – each individual recognises and identifies with the culture of the team.
- **'Team self-talk'** – open discussion within the team of concerns and ideas.
- **Group vision** – this has been arrived at, and is shared by all team members.
- **Stimuli for group learning** – there are ongoing opportunities to develop team identity and learning is seen as important.

Hall went on to explain how these elements are interdependent. For the team to be effective individuals must therefore acknowledge that they have an active part to play in bringing about and subsequently sustaining the team.

GROUP EXERCISE

In a small group (2–3) plan a lesson (that all involved will subsequently teach if possible) using a previously agreed lesson planning format:

- In the first instance agree the objectives for the lesson.
- After these have been agreed the group is to split up for about 30 minutes – each individual is to plan the lesson using the agreed lesson objectives.
- The group then re-forms to agree the final lesson plan (bringing together the individual plans) with all members to take responsibility for the outcome. If possible this small group should team teach this lesson.
- Together reflect on the lesson *outcomes* and the *process* of arriving at the lesson plan.

Summary

- It is important to communicate to children and young people that you are interested in their wellbeing.
- Know your school's policies and procedures for communicating with colleagues and parents or carers.
- Be proactive when meeting with colleagues and parents or carers – prevention is better than cure.
- Always prepare in advance for any meeting that you are to attend.
- At the outset of any interaction (meeting) you should agree the reason for the meeting.

- At the conclusion of the meeting you should clarify what you understand to be the outcome and future implications.
- Team working is at the heart of any effective school.
- Effective and proactive team members are at the heart of an effective team!

Key reading

Brown, M., Boyle, B. and Boyle, T. (1999) 'Commonalities between perception and practice in models of school decision-making in secondary schools', *School Leadership & Management,* 19 (3): 319–30.

Muijs, D. and Reynolds, D. (2010) *Effective teaching evidence and practice* (3rd edn). London: Sage. Chapter 4, 'Collaborative small group work'.

Kearns, L. R. and Frey, B. A. (2010) 'Web 2.0 technologies and back channel communication in an online learning community', *TechTrends*, 54 (4): 41–51.

References and bibliography

Barnard, C. (1948) *Organisation and management.* Cambridge, MA: Harvard University Press.

Belbin, R.M. (1981) *Management teams: why they succeed or fail.* London: Heinemann.

Brown, M., Boyle, B. and Boyle, T. (1999) 'Commonalities between perception and practice in models of school decision-making in secondary schools', *School Leadership and Management,* 19 (3): 319–30.

Cooke, N. J., Rosen, M. A. and Salas, E. (2008) 'On teams, teamwork, and team performance: discoveries and developments'. *Human Factors: The Journal of the Human Factors and Ergonomics Society*, 50 (3): 540–7.

Department for Education and Skills (2004) *Every Child Matters: Change for Children*. London: DfES.

Hall, V. (2001) 'Management teams in education: an unequal music', *School Leadership and Management,* 21 (3): 327–41.

Kearns, L. R. and Frey, B. A. (2010) 'Web 2.0 technologies and back channel communication in an online learning community', *TechTrends*, 54 (4): 41–51.

Leonard, L. and Leonard, P. (2003) 'The continuing trouble with collaboration: teachers talk', *Current Issues in Education* [online], 6 (15). Available at http://cie.ed.asu.edu/volume6/ number15/

Mitra, D.L. and Gross, S.J. (2009) 'Increasing student voice in high school reform: building partnerships, improving outcomes', *Educational Management Administration and Leadership,* 37 (4): 522–43.

Muijs, D. and Reynolds, D. (2010) 'Collaborative small group work', in *Effective teaching evidence and practice* (3rd edn). London: Sage.

Purkey, W.W., Schmidt, J.J. and Novak, J.M (2010)' *From conflict to conciliation: how to defuse difficult situations*. Thousand Oaks, CA: Corwin.

Salo, P. (2008) 'Decision making as a struggle and a play', *Educational Management Administration and Leadership,* 36 (4): 495–510.

Schmuck, T.H., Haber, P., Mayr, M. and Lampoltshammer, T. (2014) 'Management of collaboration in education', *INTED2014 Proceedings*, 1588–1595.

Thody, A., Gray, B. and Bowden, D. (2000) *The teacher's survival guide.* London: Continuum.

Tuckman, B.W. (1965) 'Development sequence in small groups', *Psychological Bulletin,* 63 (6): 384–99.

Visit https://study.sagepub.com/denby3e for extra resources related to this chapter.

CHAPTER 6

SCHOOL-BASED TRAINING

Simon Evans

Standards linked to this chapter include...

4. Plan and teach well structured lessons
   - reflect systematically on the effectiveness of lessons and approaches to teaching
   - contribute to the design and provision of an engaging curriculum within the relevant subject area(s).
5. Adapt teaching to respond to the strengths and needs of all pupils
   - demonstrate an awareness of the physical, social and intellectual development of children, and know how to adapt teaching to support pupils' education at different stages of development.

(Continued)

(Continued)

8. Fulfil wider professional responsibilities
   - develop effective professional relationships with colleagues, knowing how and when to draw on advice and specialist support
   - take responsibility for improving teaching through appropriate professional development, responding to advice and feedback from colleagues.

Introduction

Training to be a teacher is very much a 'hands-on' experience, with much of the training based in the classroom. This has always been the case, with even the traditional PGCE trainee based roughly twice as long in partner schools as at the HEI.

Trainees on traditional routes also have the benefit of learning from each other, sharing practice and providing mutual support networks, and also a personal tutor who is concerned for their welfare. To get the best out of training your school needs to be able to recreate these circumstances, through support, such as excellent mentoring, and by taking on groups of trainees.

On some routes you might also find yourself with a teaching load or timetable expectation that is much larger than that of 'traditional' trainees. This makes the management of time and the ability to set priorities not just key but essential skills. This chapter briefly describes the alternative routes into teaching, and then details the principles of successful mentoring that will help you become an organised and effective teacher.

Effective teachers constantly adapt their practice in a creative and innovative manner which aims to enthuse and inspire learners. Argyris and Schön (1975) advocate a 'reflective practitioner' model of learning to teach, and state:

> '... reflection is essential to educators' capacity to think not only about their practice but also about how they think, their implicit theories, and the sense they make of their experiences'. (Kortman and Honaker, 2002: 25)

It may be difficult, perhaps impossible, to achieve this reflective practice without the support and focus provided by a skilled mentor in school.

A diversified training market

At the time of writing (this is important, as change is rapid and often unpredictable), in both England and Wales major curriculum change continues apace alongside imminent national reviews and reports into initial teacher training, led by Sir Andrew Carter in England and Professor John Furlong in Wales. The landscape described might therefore look rather different in years to come, but informed opinion suggests that greater, not less, diversification of pathways is expected.

University-led training is offered by universities and colleges based in Departments or Schools of Education and delivered in long-standing partnerships with schools and colleges. This provision leads to a PGCE or BA Ed, usually with associated Master's modules which confer MA credits. Two or three extended periods of teaching experience are integrated with university-based study of subject and phase-specific pedagogy.

School-led training is based almost entirely within a school or consortia of schools for the duration of the training. Candidates are selected by the schools and are based there during their training, but may spend periods of teaching experience at other schools to broaden their practice. Often university partners undertake the quality assurance, assessment and theoretical aspects of this provision. School-centred initial teacher training (SCITT) is offered by schools which have been granted government approval to train their own teachers and award Qualified Teacher Status (QTS). SCITTs may also offer a PGCE usually with university accreditation. The School Direct programme is an employment-based route offered by a group of schools (with a university or SCITT) which may be salaried to support the training of career-changers. Applicants may be recruited to School Direct with a particular post in mind for them.

Teach First is an educational charity aimed at tackling the impact of poverty and disadvantage through education. It aims to train applicants with outstanding degrees to teach in socially disadvantaged schools in England and Wales. Around 2,000 graduates in selected subjects are trained through the Teach First scheme each year.

Troops to Teachers is aimed at training qualified and experienced military service-leavers who have the requisite qualities to become teachers. Through the quality assurance and accreditation procedures of universities, the scheme may lead to a PGCE.

Controversially, there are also routes into teaching which require no specific training or teaching qualification. For a thorough consideration of the available routes visit www.education.gov.uk/get-into-teaching/teacher-training-options

With such a variety of approach to training teachers growing so quickly, academics and commentators have worried about the capacity of the system to ensure the quality and parity of all routes. This concern has been exacerbated by the variety of recruitment, entry, accreditation, inspection and financial support packages (or not) applicable to the different routes. There is also some debate about the efficacy of this diversified market in improving the pool of applicants, which was its prime intent. Well-respected teaching recruitment analyst and advisor, Professor John Howson, has revealed recently that for 2014-15 in England 1,300 teacher training places were unfilled, with School Direct filling only 57% of its fee-based places and 71% of salaried places, and SCITTs filling 79% of their places (Howson, 2014).

A thought

To become successful and self-motivated teachers, 'Trainee Teachers need support in school from mentors who are qualified to do the job and are able to devote time to it' (Blandford, in Child and Merrill, 2005) to encourage and enhance this self-motivation. In fact, Wright argues that – given the recent proliferation of initial teacher training models – the role of mentor has assumed a greater significance than ever: 'Theirs [mentors] is arguably the single biggest contribution in establishing the quality of the teaching profession' (Wright, 2010: 1). How important is mentoring to your development?

What is mentoring?

A school-based mentor should be an experienced practitioner who has taken on the role of supporting your development. The term 'mentor' is originally derived from Greek mythology. Homer's *Odyssey* describes how, before leaving to fight in the Trojan Wars, Odysseus entrusted Mentor with the care of his household. For ten years Odysseus's son Telemachus profited from Mentor's advice, encouragement and spiritual guidance. Eventually the word came to have its current meaning: an experienced, trusted adviser and counsellor.

A thought

A good mentor allows the learner to make mistakes, encourages the self-management of the learning process, and should be adept at assisting in the evaluation process by being an effective questioner and listener without being judgemental. Clearly, any colleague of the trainee teacher might become a mentor in the broad, informal sense. Indeed, Zey (1988) distinguishes these informal mentoring relationships which emerge by chance from the formal mentoring arrangements which might be determined by the school or ITT provider. These informal mentoring links may be beneficial, and even preferable in some cases, as their self-selecting nature grows from a degree of mutual trust. Could such informal mentoring conflict with the formal role that is usually directly related to the award of QTS?

Murray (2001: xiii) defines mentoring as 'a deliberate pairing of a more skilled or more experienced person with a less skilled or less experienced one, with a mutually agreed goal of having the less skilled person grow and develop specific competencies'. Hughes (2010: 96) regards the mentor as 'someone usually involved in a professional relationship with an initial teacher training student or new teacher…', adding 'that the mentor has a greater knowledge than the trainee of the work involved and uses this to guide, support and advise the trainee'. Parsloe (1999) suggests that a good mentor is someone who is a good motivator who can advise and instruct without interfering or imposing solutions. Wright (2010) concludes that to do this effectively mentors not only model and explain their own teaching practices to trainees, but also analyse and question them.

The DfES (2006) outlined 10 principles for effective mentoring and coaching which have also been endorsed by the Welsh Government (developed by the Centre for the Use of Research and Evidence in Education, CUREE). These describe coaching and mentoring as being 'a learning conversation' with an experienced practitioner to help you identify and clarify your learning needs and support you in your gradual development as a teacher. Mentors should help you to reflect on, review and refine your practice, and provide you with opportunities to develop and extend your teaching repertoire through the sharing of planning and by observing them or other practitioners. They should broker support and contributions from fellow professionals where necessary to access specialist skills and expertise that will enable you to extend your knowledge. They should also create a learning environment which encourages you to 'take risks' and innovate while helping you to develop your skills in an atmosphere of mutual trust. However large your timetable commitment is, your school is failing you if your mentor does not initiate a professional dialogue that supports you to reflect on your practice.

Application to primary and early years teaching

In the primary classroom, you may be working very closely with your mentor in both planning and delivering lessons. Indeed, you may be with your mentor for the majority of your time and it may be difficult for you to develop a sense of independence or be seen as a 'real teacher' by the children. You must plan to develop some lessons on your own, and then deliver these without the support of your mentor. Young children may find it hard to ignore the presence of their normal class teacher, thus making observation difficult. For teaching and observations to be uninterrupted, it may be wise to establish some 'Do not disturb' agreements with the pupils to allow this part of mentoring to proceed effectively.

The mentoring principles see the learning environment as a low-risk one in which mistakes are viewed as a natural part of the process of learning and becoming an effective teacher, not as opportunities for blame or angst. Mistakes and weaknesses must be recognised, revealed and targets agreed, but at the same time, strengths and successes should be acknowledged and celebrated. School-based mentors, however skilled, can only help you so much – the world's most effective trainer is you (MacLennan, 1999: 33). Your mentor should encourage you to make your own choices, decisions and mistakes (Kortman and Honaker, 2002: 20). Your progress then depends crucially on your own ability to reflect and self-evaluate. You will need honesty and insight to recognise your strengths and weaknesses and the conviction and proactivity to undertake change.

Effective mentoring

Partner schools should know that there is far more to mentoring than merely observing a trainee teacher and then following up with a feedback session. Several frameworks for trainee teacher and mentor development have been described over the years, and one of the most enduring and influential is that designed by Maynard and Furlong (1995). This describes the stages that trainee teachers might pass through on their journey to becoming capable teachers along with appropriate mentoring strategies at each stage:

Stage 1: Early idealism. Here a trainee might hold some quite romantic, idealised views about pupils and their own role as a teacher. They will often believe that that they have some higher moral purpose and are there to 'make a difference' and 'put something back into society'. While these are certainly worthy beliefs, they may not always contribute to a realistic appraisal of what is possible in the early stages of learning to teach and to operate effectively in the classroom.

At this stage, a sensitive mentor will provide a strong model for you through his or her own teaching and temper any idealism with purposeful observation and collaborative teaching opportunities, with a focus perhaps on rules, routines and structured lessons.

Stage 2: Personal survival. At this stage, early idealism is balanced with a realistic evaluation of the sheer scale of the task facing the trainee in developing all the skills and understandings needed to teach well and simply 'survive' in the classroom. A trainee's primary focus will often and necessarily be centred on their own 'performance': how do I appear as a teacher; how am I presenting myself to pupils; how am I coming over to colleagues; what is my voice like; will the pupils like me; will they behave? There may also be a natural obsession with 'personal survival' in contemplating the complex demands of a teacher training course: how can I prepare lessons and write assignments; how do I shift roles seamlessly between trainee teacher and learner; can I get through until the end of the day/week/term/year? Again, these are legitimate concerns, but an obsession with personal survival, if continued, is likely to lead to rather closed, defensive teaching, focused only on your needs as a trainee and not those of the pupils or the learning.

At this stage, effective mentors will provide plenty of reassurance and perspective. They will supply advice and guidance about how to become more economic in planning and preparation, and begin shifting the focus of reflection from what you are teaching towards what the pupils are learning.

Stage 3: Dealing with difficulties. At some point in the venture of teacher training, most trainees will come to a sobering realisation of the scale and complexity of the difficulties they face in making progress. This is often an emotional and somewhat dispiriting moment. Skilled mentors and teacher trainers are attuned to the possible pressure points in the year when this is likely and to the signs. For many trainees, this may feel like an overwhelming obstacle and they may come to question fundamentally their aspiration to be a teacher. However, Maynard and Furlong's model suggests that this is a quite normal stage that needs to be passed through in the process.

Here, an effective mentor might take on the roles of 'counsellor' – helping you to realise and reconnect with your original ambition to be a teacher – and 'appraiser' – identifying what you are already doing well and giving priority to those aspects in which it is possible to make tangible progress relatively quickly.

Stage 4: Hitting a plateau. One way that trainees often progress from the 'difficulties' stage is by finding a narrow range of lesson formats and types of teaching and learning which appear to 'work' for them. These are then repeated ad infinitum because they work, feel comfortable, and take the pressure off the trainee. Perhaps lessons become dominated by a series of structured worksheets, or a 'presentation – activity – plenary' format. Once again, there is nothing wrong with doing more of what is seen to work, but the great danger is in repeating a limited repertoire of approaches which will bore the pupils and trap the trainee on 'the plateau', preventing innovation and growth.

At this point, a mentor will perhaps take the role of 'critical friend' in pointing out the current narrowness of range in your teaching and in encouraging greater risk, creativity and imagination. He or she will try to shift your thinking from being overly focused on aspects of the teaching to concentrate on the potential learning gains to the pupils by widening your repertoire of strategies. Maynard and Furlong suggest that there are two particularly useful and underused mentoring strategies at this stage of a trainee's development. Firstly, trainees are encouraged to return to classroom observation, but now with a specific focus on how pupils are learning within lessons, rather than how teachers are teaching. Secondly, trainees are involved with small groups of pupils within lessons as they engage with activities and tasks in order to make notes on how they gain understanding of particular tasks or concepts.

Stage 5: Moving on. In this final stage of the model trainees are prompted, challenged and supported to 'move on' from the relative comfort of 'the plateau' and to experiment and innovate with a broad range of approaches and strategies. They begin to question and investigate the fundamental grounds for their practice and ask 'What kind of teacher am I going to be?' There is greater focus on the development of learning and progression in their subjects and a deepening understanding of the complexities of teaching and learning, including their social, moral and political dimensions.

The mentor's role is now arguably that of collaborator and co-enquirer with the trainee. A mentor might ask you challenging, research-based questions designed to initiate a deeper exploration of children's learning, progression and understanding in their phase or subject. Many initial teacher training programmes reflect this co-enquiry stage by scheduling small-scale research, lesson study or problem-based assignments for trainees during the latter parts of the programme. Often the mentor is involved in the assignment as a kind of sponsor come guide, with a genuine spin-off benefit to the school or department from the research learning gained.

A thought

The idea of the reflective practitioner has been influential for many years (Argyris and Schön, 1975). However, Wright (2010) has helpfully clarified that this is not a passive process such as silently regarding your reflection in a mirror or mulling things over deeply in your mind. Rather, it is best thought of as an active, targeted and iterative development facilitated through focused conversation with your mentor or colleagues. Wright calls this 'dynamic reflection'.

Dialogic review

A study by Stopp (2008) into trainee teachers' reflections on their progress suggests that a useful development of the conventional mentor 'feedback' to trainees post-lesson is the process of 'dialogic review'. This replaces the usual discursive evaluation of the lesson observed with a 'simple sequence of open questions focusing upon trainees identifying and evaluating their own professional development' (Stopp, 2008: 5). These questions and their sequence were found to be well-received by trainees and to promote a broader and more engaged approach to self-evaluation than straight mentor feedback, so are useful to trainees in extending the process of reflection:

What do you feel pleased about in terms of your development so far? This helps you identify where you feel you have made progress and begins self-evaluation in a positive context.

What are you currently trying to focus on improving? This prompts you to identify your current targets and reinforces the fact that you are a learner who is 'on the move' yourself.

What do you think will be your next priority for development? This pushes you to synthesise all of the messages distilled from evaluation and reflection to put the next steps in order of priority.

How might you go about this? This asks you to select a strategy and the support/resources needed to undertake this successfully.

Dialogue with peers can also produce positive results – it is an extension of 'learning by teaching' that allows you to learn from your fellow trainees. You should make specific time (other than social time) available to share successes and how they can be spread, and any difficulties and their possible solutions. This can also provide an emotional release if such discussions are held without mentors present so that you are not limited by the strictures of formal meeting structures. In a school setting, such meetings can also put you back in touch with the fact that you are still a trainee, and there are others like you!

Setting goals and challenges

The key to good reflection and evaluation, and thus to making progress, is setting SMART targets (i.e. Specific, Measurable, Achievable, Realistic and Time-related). Part of your organisational skill should be in setting your own SMART targets. This may be after discussions with your mentor but they need to be 'owned' by you and not specified or imposed, otherwise you will feel little commitment towards achieving them.

Writing clear targets is a skill in itself and an effective mentor will assist you with this. 'Improve my questioning skills' is so open and vague a wish as to be virtually useless as a target. It gives you no guidance as to how to go about the task and you have no way of assessing whether it is achieved. However, 'Next lesson, prepare a list of key questions at all levels of Bloom's taxonomy and pose questions to pupils with the aid of a seating plan' is a much smarter target, and contains within it a clear strategy as to how you will go about trying to improve your questioning skills. You will be able to assess whether and how well this has been achieved, and whether or not it assists you in improving your questioning.

This SMART target has within it the opportunity for you to write a variety of questions at differing levels of learning complexity, to think about possible pupil answers and anticipate pupil difficulties or misconceptions, to develop probes and follow-ups for these misconceptions, and to discuss all of these collaboratively with your mentor prior to the next lesson. Your mentor then conducts a focused observation of your questioning in the next lesson, providing fertile ground for an evaluative mentoring discussion and the targeting of subsequent steps in refining your questioning skills.

A key mentor skill is to ensure that targets are both manageable and bespoke: manageable, as the feeling of tangible progress on a well-selected number of practical goals clearly attained is much more motivating than the sense of helplessness that might be inspired by myriad well-intentioned, but ultimately unachievable targets; bespoke, so that instead of statements directly lifted from the professional standards, you write in a personal, rather than bureaucratic, language.

GROUP EXERCISE

Peer review some recent evaluations with your mentor, peers or colleagues. Have you set SMART targets or are they too vague? Have you set yourself too many targets or at too taxing a level of demand? Discuss this with your peers and rewrite some of the weaker targets in a SMART format. If you have set yourself too many targets, which could be dispensed with at this stage or subsumed within other targets? Traffic-lighting the targets with highlighters can work very well here, i.e. green for good, amber ones to be improved, and red for those to be rejected at this stage.

Observations

Two main types of classroom observation will be crucial in identifying ways of improving your practice. Firstly, you will observe experienced practitioners, and secondly, your mentor will make observations of you with the aim of supporting you with future training and developmental opportunities.

Observing other practitioners

A key aspect in becoming an able teacher is the process of learning from observing the practice of others. It is therefore essential that school-based routes provide the opportunity for such observations. Guided observation will help you move your perspective from that of the pupils to that of a teacher, and it will also help you 'see' what is happening in classrooms. Guided observation should be related to the Teachers' Standards and your targets. These will include observations of both pupils and teachers. Observation of pupils is included as:

> '... by studying what pupils do, observers can learn a great deal not only about the impact of teaching on the learner, but about the child's perspective and the influence that individual and groups of children have on the lesson'. (Wragg, 1994: 87)

Observing other teachers does not necessarily mean that you just observe them teaching – you could, for example, observe them supervising an activity outside the classroom, consulting at a parents' evening or school event. Alternatively you might observe them by focusing on a specific area, such as working with learning support assistants, classroom management or their use of questioning. It is important for you to develop a structure for note taking or to use an observation pro-forma to focus this process. Typical focus points might be how:

- teaching assistants are used to support teaching and learning
- SEN, EAL, G+T or Pupil Premium children are supported
- teachers differentiate to encourage learning and to motivate pupils
- classroom or behaviour management is used
- assertive discipline can be used as a tool for classroom management
- behaviour modification encourages effective discipline and control in the classroom
- teachers manage time, the room layout, whole-class and group work, and different activities to ensure that pupils' interest and attention are maintained
- the teacher at different points manages transition effectively during the lesson, day or week
- pupil and teacher talk takes place and is managed.

When observing it is important to try to suspend your natural inclination to rush to make a judgement of what you are seeing, because this may close down your thinking and perhaps confirm prior assumptions that you have carried with you into the lesson. The observation is incomplete until you discuss it sensitively and professionally with the person being observed, being conscious that being observed may be stressful for any teacher, even experienced ones. The person being observed should be able to provide explicit commentary on aspects of practice and engage you in asking questions about the strategies and resources adopted in the lesson. However, the skills of experienced teachers may have become so deeply embedded in what they do that they are barely conscious of them. The discussion may therefore need to tease out some of these tacit skills to make them more explicit.

Another effective observational activity is to observe your peers. This can be a useful and non-threatening method for focusing on specific areas. It provides you and your peers with an opportunity to discuss any issues that arise and thoughts on the strategies used and adopted.

A thought

Peer or self-review of targets is a great way to reveal trends and patterns in your development. Are the same targets appearing all the time? If so, this suggests that this is a key issue for you and one that you have yet to get to grips with. For example, you may find the conclusions of lessons difficult to manage successfully. You either always run out of time or are reluctant to disturb the pupils when they are engaged productively in the main learning activity. Discuss this with your mentor and consider how you might address this target successfully. For example, you might observe other teachers in the school who are successful with conclusions and discuss with them how they deal with them. Your mentor can then observe your next attempt at a concerted conclusion to the lesson to assess progress.

Observations by mentors of your practice

Observations of your teaching are an important process for all stakeholders in your progress. They assure the training provider of a systematic training, they assist in quality assurance of the school mentoring, they provide targets which can be actioned and reviewed, and of course they contribute to your assessment.

Although mentors have a right to expect every lesson you teach to be thoroughly well-planned, 'surprise' observations are not recommended in the literature. Both you and your mentor 'should have a shared overview of your progress to date and what you need to work on now and what your future developmental needs are' (Brooks and Sikes, 1997: 103). Your mentor turning up unannounced is unlikely to contribute to this. A clear focus for the observation, agreed with the mentor, ties in with the experiential learning cycle of 'planning – implementing – reviewing', and links closely with the notion of reflective practice. Wright (2010: 24) suggests the following simple cycle of observation:

1. **Observation** – an initial lesson observation identifies that the trainee needs to expand and extend question types.
2. **Feedback** – this is discussed in feedback and progressive sequences of questions are suggested.
3. **Dynamic reflection** – the trainee undertakes some reading on question types and observes other teachers who are known to deploy questions skilfully.
4. **Lesson planning** – the trainee and mentor identify a lesson next week which offers the opportunity to use a wider range of questions. The lesson plan, including explicit questioning sequences, is jointly reviewed by trainee and mentor. This is indicated as a personal target on the lesson plan.
5. **Subsequent observation** – the mentor carries out a focused observation concentrating particularly on the trainee's questioning skills and judging and commenting on any progress. The cycle then continues with similar or related targets.

To support the observation, you should provide your mentor with all the documentation required for completion (e.g. a copy of the lesson plan, lesson activities and materials, observation record or other assessment criteria). The mentor will usually stay for the complete lesson or for a negotiated part of the lesson (for example, it could be that the focus was just the starter or plenary, or the management of a task).

Following the observation, meet with your mentor for feedback. Immediately after the lesson is probably too soon, with your emotional response to how it went perhaps overwhelming your capacity to analyse dispassionately. Too delayed a meeting will inevitably lead to memories of precise instances being lost. Collaborative discussion following an observation will help you and your mentor identify where progress has been made and what the next training and development activities might be. This process will also support you in developing a self-evaluative, reflective approach to your teaching. It is a useful exercise for you to make your own written evaluation prior to the collaborative discussion, if there is time, for example by annotating the lesson plan, and to expect the first question asked by your mentor to be 'How do you think it went?'

A good mentor will aim to discuss only the previously agreed focuses for the observation, and should allow you the opportunity to respond to and rationalise your actions. As a good trainee you will accept positive criticism and be open to discussion rather than overly defensive. Use the mentor's observation notes to help you reflect further.

Application to secondary teaching

Concluding lessons successfully and ensuring that learning and progress have been achieved by pupils are notoriously complex, difficult teaching skills. Try this 'topping and tailing' activity:

- Share a lesson plan yet to be taught with your mentor, giving him or her the aims and objectives and the introductory phases but withholding the concluding parts of the lesson. Ask your mentor to plan the plenary activities, assessment tasks and conclusion of the lesson. Later you can compare and discuss your approaches to see whether this has improved your ways of conceptualising the concluding phases.
- Undertake a parallel activity with one of your mentor's lesson plans. Given their early part of the plan, how would you chose to conclude it so that the learning is genuinely consolidated and concluded successfully?
- A further development is to actually teach and evaluate the lessons produced.

Using technology as a mentoring tool

As well as being observed by your mentor, modern technologies, video and webcams and CCTV systems in classrooms can enhance the mentoring experience. For example, IRIS Connect is one of several electronic systems used for classroom observation. Teachers can be recorded teaching and then use the recordings to inform development of their professional practice. The idea behind the system is that it is in the control of the individual teacher, participation is voluntary, and the recordings and data are the property of the teacher and can be saved or deleted by that teacher on a password-protected website. These, and other systems, can be particularly powerful in mentoring also, however great care does need to be exercised in relation to the confidentiality, safeguarding and data-protection of the footage stored and viewed.

Summary

- Teacher training relies on being largely 'hands-on' and classroom-based.
- There are many alternative routes into teaching, each with unique demands.
- The effectiveness of teacher training is linked to the effectiveness of mentoring.
- Dialogue – with mentors, colleagues and peers – can help shape experience and progress.
- Goals and challenges should be SMART, and owned by the trainee.
- Observations by you and of you are key parts of your training.

Key reading

CUREE (2005) 'National framework for mentoring and coaching'. Available at www.curee.co.uk/mentoring-and-coaching

Pearson, L., Wilson, V. and Cameron, D. (2010) 'An introduction to mentoring'. Teacher Training Resource Bank [online]. This is now archived at http://webarchive.nationalarchives.gov.uk/20101021152907/http://www.ttrb.ac.uk/ViewArticle2.aspx?Keyword=mentors&SearchOption=And&SearchType=Keyword&RefineExpand=1&ContentId=16378

Stopp, P. (2008) 'From feedback to dialogic review: an approach to appropriate matching of mentoring and coaching feedback'. Paper presented at BERA, Heriot Watt University, Edinburgh, 3-6 September.

Yeomans, R. and Sampson, J. (eds) (1994) *Mentorship in the primary school.* London: Falmer.

References and bibliography

Argyris, C. and Schön, D.A. (1975) *Theory in practice: increasing professional effectiveness.* San Francisco, CA: Jossey-Bass.

Brooks, V. and Sikes, P. (1997) *The good mentor guide: initial teacher education in secondary schools.* Buckingham: Open University Press.

Child, A. and Merrill, S. (2005) *Developing as a secondary school mentor: a case study approach for trainee mentors and their tutors.* Exeter: Learning Matters.

Department for Education and Skills (DfES) (2006), 'Coaching in secondary schools' (DVD-ROM), *Secondary National Strategy for School Improvement.* Norwich: DfES.

General Teaching Council for England (2004) *The learning conversation.* London: GTCE.

Howson, J. (2014) http://johnohowson.wordpress.com/page/2/?blogsub=confirming (last accessed 01/01/15).

Hughes, S. (2010) 'Mentoring and coaching: the helping relationship', in T. Wright (ed.), *How to be a brilliant mentor: developing outstanding teachers.* London: Routledge. Chapter 7.

Kortman, S.A. and Honaker, C.J. (2002) *The best mentoring experience.* Dubuque, IA: Kendall Hunt.

MacLennan, N. (1999) *Coaching and mentoring.* Aldershot: Gower.

Maynard, T. and Furlong, J. (1994) 'Learning to teach and models of mentoring', in D. McIntyre, H. Hagger and M. Wilkin (eds), *Mentoring: perspectives on school-based teacher education*. London: Kogan Page.

Maynard, T. and Furlong, J. (1995) *Mentoring student teachers: the growth of professional knowledge*. London: Routledge.

Murray, M. (2001) *Beyond the myths and magic of mentoring: how to facilitate an effective mentoring process*. San Francisco, CA: Jossey-Bass.

Parsloe, E. (1999) *The manager as coach and mentor*. London: Institute of Personnel & Development.

Stopp, P. (2008) 'From feedback to dialogic review: an approach to appropriate matching of mentoring and coaching feedback'. Paper presented at BERA, Heriot Watt University, Edinburgh, 3–6 September.

Wragg, E. (1994) *An introduction to classroom observation*. London: Routledge.

Wright, T. (ed.) (2010) *How to be a brilliant mentor: developing outstanding teachers*. London: Routledge.

Zey, M. G. (1988) 'A mentor for all reasons', *Personnel Journal*, 67 (1): 46–51.

Useful websites

CUREE: www.curee.co.uk/mentoring-and-coaching

DfE Get Into Teaching: www.education.gov.uk/get-into-teaching

Visit https://study.sagepub.com/denby3e for extra resources related to this chapter.

CHAPTER 7

UNDERSTANDING THE ROLES OF SPECIALIST COLLEAGUES

Matthew Crowther and Michael Lamb

Standards linked to this chapter include...

8. Fulfil wider professional responsibilities

- make a positive contribution to the wider life and ethos of the school
- develop effective professional relationships with colleagues, knowing how and when to draw on advice and specialist support
- deploy support staff effectively
- take responsibility for improving teaching through appropriate professional development, responding to advice and feedback from colleagues
- communicate effectively with parents with regard to pupils' achievements and wellbeing.

Introduction

Schools are micro versions of society and as society is diverse and complex so are schools. No two pupils are the same; members of the same family are often different and will make you very aware of this fact. If pupils from the same family are different then other pupils are even more so. They have both different educational needs and different social needs. Schools need to be recognised as communities where care and guidance and progress are paramount. Within schools every single person who comes into contact with a child has a responsibility for promoting the learning and welfare of that child. As you are about to embark on a career in teaching you need to understand that this is more than the subject you love to teach, that it is about teamwork with other colleagues you will come across in your school. As someone embarking on a career in teaching you need to understand the roles and responsibilities of your fellow colleagues in meeting the needs of young people and how that may impact on you as you enter the profession.

Despite the many – and inevitable – changes in government policy, it remains clear that colleagues, governors, parents and carers must not operate in isolation but instead work together to improve pupil progress and promote learning both in school and beyond. This chapter aims to provide insights into the many, varied and ever-changing roles that exist in schools. In addition, it will highlight the wealth of knowledge and expertise that will enhance your role as a classroom practitioner and help you with your own professional development. For most teacher training courses, initial acceptance is dependent on your having undertaken a period of observation or shadowing. If you have not had this opportunity, make it a priority. Keep a journal of your experiences as this will be good evidence for your professional teaching files. Show colleagues within this shadowing experience your journal thoughts and ask them to comment on and sign what they have seen as extra evidence.

The ethos of the school

The ethos of the school is the way that it would wish to be perceived by the outside world. All schools will have mottos and mission statements that are essentially similar in nature, and so you will find that schools are striving, thrusting, reaching, aspiring, succeeding … You need to look a little deeper to find out what kind of school it really is – what is happening beneath the surface? This is a question you can answer with a little research. Is it a results-driven school with high performing pupils and the expectations that come with this? Is the pastoral side more important, with the school perhaps being in a more socially deprived area where producing well-rounded and responsible members of society is as important if not more important than the results? What is the ethnic make-up of the school? What is the gender split of the school? Look at the most recent Ofsted reports on the school, the Department of Education information on the school, and the school's own website and prospectus. Try to see beyond the superficial claims of the motto or mission statement to find out the true ethos of the school, because in order to be a successful member of that school this is information you will need to access.

A thought

As you enter the teaching profession you should familiarise yourself with the true ethos of your training school and its surroundings. It may be some years since you last spent any time in a school environment. In the school where you are training, you should identify the key staff and arrange to have a short meeting to reacquaint yourself with their roles. Also, look at the school day and the curriculum. What are the changes – and which of these are significant? The quicker you can familiarise yourself with the surroundings, the easier your early transition into school will become.

Colleagues within schools

Some specialist colleagues are based in schools. A range of colleagues will have key responsibilities in assisting you in your role as a teacher. These colleagues will cover a wide range of areas, such as curriculum development, special educational needs, inclusion and pastoral duties. This builds on the roles and responsibilities within each teaching department that will be based around the classroom and the curriculum.

The curriculum

School curricula have been developed to provide broad, personalised teaching that is accessible to all children and young people. Ideally, a balanced curriculum should enable young people to learn successfully (including enjoying the experience) and achieve their potential. They should also be able to take their place in society as confident individuals and responsible citizens. They should therefore learn to stay safe and healthy and the curriculum should give them the skills to lead fulfilling lives. These range from the basics of developing numeracy skills within mathematics and literacy skills within English (and all other subjects) to more specialist learning such as playing an instrument (often taught by a peripatetic teacher) or speaking a foreign language. Different colleagues have different roles in giving pupils a more fulfilling school experience.

It is the role of senior management, usually a curriculum deputy, and the heads of teaching departments to ensure that the curriculum provided meets the above aims. Although in the majority of cases the curriculum is very much predefined, it must still cater for the range of abilities and needs of the pupils at your school. This includes those with special educational needs, the gifted and talented, those on pupil premium, and pupils from different social, moral, cultural and linguistic backgrounds. Catering for these groups must be evident in both planning and teaching the curriculum. Colleagues who can assist you with building on your delivery of the curriculum include fellow teachers, curriculum managers and departmental heads.

Fellow teaching colleagues will have a vast range of experience and will be happy to offer advice and help on planning teaching and learning strategies. Some schools will have Leading Practitioners (LPs), i.e. teachers who have constantly demonstrated a high level of expertise and effectiveness in their teaching. As well as this LPs will probably have additional duties in the modelling and improving of teaching and learning. They will work with the head teacher to develop, implement and evaluate the school policies, practices and procedures. These are therefore important colleagues to work with as they are the best at their profession, and this is why the Secretary of State for Education is keen that the best teachers should be promoted rapidly.

It is important as a teacher new to the profession that you draw on the experiences of other teachers and other curriculum specialists. Classroom observations are vital to this process.

Observation

Part of your training will be your observation of other colleagues. Treat this seriously – it is a vital part of your learning and an opportunity which many teachers on full timetables do not have. Observation allows you to see a range of teaching and learning strategies, not just in your own subject area but also across the curriculum. Cross-curricular observation is rewarding, as other subject area colleagues may demonstrate particular strengths or techniques that can be incorporated into your own teaching. One aspect of teaching that needs a particular focus is planning. By planning ahead and discussing your planning with the head of department or experienced colleagues you will have the opportunity to think about how you can maximise the welfare and achievement of all your pupils. Again, self-evaluation of and reflection on your planning are critical. To begin with in teaching, after every lesson and observation, use a reflective journal to comment on how you think the lesson went: this should then be used within your mentor or line manager meetings. Using a Red, Amber, Green (RAG) system is a quick and effective way to highlight what is effective within your teaching and what needs improving. RAG is increasingly used in schools to show progress – of teachers, subjects and departments. Red = a target set but not reached, Amber = working towards that target, Green = that target met. This will make it easier for you to spot patterns within your teaching and areas for improvement.

One of the more recent additions to curriculum staff is that of Cover Supervisors. Following an agreement between the government and teaching unions to minimise the times when teachers are expected to cover lessons during periods of colleague absence, schools have appointed their own cover teachers. Traditionally cover or supply teachers were obtained through supply agencies, but many schools have now invested in their own specialised supply teachers who can keep the continuity of lessons going despite teacher absence. In larger schools there may be several such Cover Supervisors.

Special educational needs and inclusion

SEN and inclusion dovetail into curriculum development. Schools work hard to ensure that the curriculum on offer provides effective learning opportunities for all pupils, whatever their needs. This is based around the following three key elements:

- Setting suitable learning challenges, where all pupils can experience success in learning through teaching that is suitable to their individual abilities.
- Responding to pupils' diverse learning needs, whether it be boys and girls, physical disabilities, pupils from different ethnic groups and social and cultural backgrounds or linguistic capabilities.
- Overcoming potential barriers to learning and assessment for individuals and groups of pupils, by ensuring that teachers make provision for SEN pupils to be able to participate in assessment activities.

Birkett (2003) states that teachers have a responsibility to support pupils with highly complex needs. Children and young people in mainstream school include disabled students and students with learning difficulties. Trainees often do not have the detailed knowledge of issues that other teachers may have gained from experience. Dillenburger and McKee (2009) investigated trainee awareness of child abuse and neglect (CAN), and concluded that there was an urgent need for the inclusion of pre-service child protection training programmes for, in particular, those in Initial Teacher Education and Early Childhood Studies.

With the Children and Families Act of 2014, Special Educational Needs (SEN) has changed within schools. Behavioural difficulties have been removed as an SEN category and pupils will no longer have statements based on their behaviour. Poor behaviour, it is assumed, arises from pupils' learning difficulties not being properly met. Pupils now have an Educational, Health and Care (EHC) plan. The focus of the EHC plan is to make sure that pupils achieve their best, become confident individuals, and make a successful transition into adulthood.

Senior management and colleagues have a legal responsibility to make sure that both the curriculum and special educational needs policy within a school meet the needs of pupils. The main aim of special needs is that all children reach their full potential in school despite any disabilities or learning needs. All pupils should make a significant level of progress. As a teacher there are many ways in which this can be achieved. The appropriate specialists to advise on a school's policy towards SEN are lead colleagues such as the SEN coordinator (SENCO) or inclusion manager. SENCOs and their teams may create and distribute resources to help a teacher with special needs pupils, and such resources may also be other colleagues. These can include a specialist higher-level teaching assistant (TA) or teaching support; technical support such as laptops; or even simple classroom strategies to deal with the special needs within your classes. As a teacher you must plan on how best to utilise such colleagues and resources within your lessons. Lee (2002) identified several factors that influence working with TAs, and included some of the following from a teacher's point of view:

- clarity of role for the TA
- time for teachers and TAs to collaborate
- guiding the TA on strategies to use with pupils
- communicating effectively with the TA.

As part of the process, you should evaluate the effectiveness of the resources that have been used to help SEN pupils. From this, you can begin to develop strategies for individual pupils. All teachers are essentially SEN teachers. They have a responsibility to their pupils as within any one class there can be a range of special educational needs. By speaking with and observing, not just members of your department, but also colleagues across the school, and by using the expertise of the SEN coordinator, you can effectively arm yourself with a range of strategies to help focus your teaching and understanding around inclusion and special educational needs. A main strategy you need to use is an effective seating plan which will help you learn pupils' names and teach them more effectively. Your class seating plan should be marked in groups, with SEN, Gifted and Talented (G and T) and less able pupils highlighted within it. Use your own codes so that the information remains confidential to you. Your teaching should then be adapted to each of these groups.

Application to secondary teaching

For the classes you will teach you should investigate any special educational needs that the children have and how these may impact on your planning and teaching. Many students are included on the SEN register and it is important as an effective classroom practitioner that your teaching takes account of their individual needs. How could you differentiate your lesson to accommodate their needs? How might you tailor your resources? Do you need to change your teaching style? Being inclusive in your teaching is an important aspect if you are to engage all students and help them learn and achieve.

Pastoral system

All schools have a pastoral system which usually consists of a pastoral deputy head and learning managers (traditionally heads of year or heads of house – it is important you find out which system your school uses as soon as you join), along with form tutors who are in daily contact with the pupils. Forms may be constituted horizontally (in year/age groups) or vertically, with members of each age group in the same form. The latter is designed to provide better social interaction and has been described as a way 'to enhance and stabilise relationships' (Beckett and Wrigley, 2014: 218). Each pupil is different and each has different learning and emotional needs of which both you and the school must be aware. The role of the pastoral team is to promote an environment within school where positive teaching and learning can take place. The team has a particular duty to monitor the mental and physical welfare of all students and to transmit concerns to other colleagues. This is achieved by supporting pupils' welfare, monitoring behaviour and achievement, and ensuring that all pupils feel secure. Form tutors must learn to listen to pupils with as much respect or 'equality' as would be the case with adults (Denby, 2007).

As a teacher you have a responsibility to report any pupil concerns regarding behaviour, learning or other student welfare issues to the relevant pastoral colleague so that interventions and strategies can be used in order to support pupils. The National Association for Pastoral Care in Education (www.napce.org.uk) has lots of useful information. Tucker, on the NAPCE site, states that a wide range of professionals bring together a rich mix of skills for the benefit of children and young people. Professionals such as counsellors, behaviour therapists, educational psychologists, social workers, youth workers and police officers can all be involved with pupils at school (Tucker, 2014). As one who is new to the profession you are unlikely to come across or be directly involved with many of these professionals, but you need to be aware of them and their roles and how they may be involved with the pupils you are teaching.

A thought

Think about the type of information you may need on a class, including SEN data, prior attainment and achievement levels, predicted targets and rates of progression. Once you have compiled this information for your group what does it tell you about the class you are teaching? How can these data inform your planning and preparation? You may need to seek advice from your colleagues about the best methods to plan and carry out your teaching, particularly if the group concerned has many different needs.

In order to better understand your classes and build a relationship with key colleagues you should start with one of your classes to compile information about your pupils. Make sure that you speak with all the colleagues who have some impact on that class. Schools are data rich environments these days, and you will have access to massive amounts of data on every child from SEN needs to target grades for your subject.

Data managers (assessment)

Although covered in greater detail in Chapter 23 it is important in this context to recognise the increasing role of data within the management of a successful school. Teachers are expected to use a wide variety of data and there are specialist colleagues within your school who have overall responsibility for the production and dissemination of data. Schools are data rich environments and as a new teacher it is important to familiarise yourself with the data and how these are used. Talk to colleagues who are responsible for data so that you can improve your teaching through a better understanding of your pupils. Data do not only cover assessment but also behaviour, however be aware that behaviour is no longer a part of SEN. They facilitate the accurate use of interventions and teaching and learning strategies for pupils who are either underperforming or exceeding expectations.

Most schools will use a Management Information System (MIS) to collate the academic and behavioural data on students. This has led to the creation of MIS managers who can support you in compiling, analysing and disseminating data about students and their achievement. Understanding how to access data on individual students within school will help inform your planning and teaching strategies by enabling you to accurately assess a student's progression. Progress is now more important than final attainment so constant tracking of data with pupils is key.

Administration, technical support and caretaking colleagues

Schools have a whole range of support staff including administration and technical colleagues, buildings and caretaking staff. Often administration colleagues will come to your aid when you need to write letters to parents, organise events, or deal with external agencies. Be aware that standard letters may already exist within the school system. You should also understand that each school that you work in will have different protocols with letters and other communication with parents so it is very important that you learn what these are and follow them carefully. The administrative staff or more senior and experienced teaching colleagues will be able to help you with this. Never be afraid to ask, as communication with other school colleagues is vital to a successful school. These administrative staff will also be vital in your future teaching career if you want to organise trips and visits and risk assessments need to be written.

Someone within the administrative staff with have a responsibility for trips and visits and thus will have experience of what needs to be done for these. Other specialist roles include examination officers (who track and manage the examination entries and requirements), technical colleagues (such as IT specialists), and caretaking staff (who assist with the management of physical resources).

Your main focus will be teaching and learning – efficient administration and other support will make sure that it stays that way.

External colleagues

At one time, *colleagues* within education just meant fellow teachers, but not any more. Schools form a hub that is part of the wider community: they are not just dependent on teachers and support staff within them but also engage with a range of outside agencies and individuals who can all be considered 'colleagues' in contributing to the education and welfare of children. These external colleagues encompass parents and carers as well as health, social and justice professionals.

INDIVIDUAL REFLECTION

Take three individuals as examples from one of the groups you are teaching, and from your knowledge of their circumstances list any external colleagues who have been involved in their education. Sort these by order of priority and consider why particular colleagues are more important to particular young people. Repeat the exercise at your next placement. What does this tell you about the children in each school? What conclusions can you draw from this?

Parents and carers

The children in your care come from many differing backgrounds. The nuclear family, with both parents involved in the welfare of the child, may be the exception rather than the rule. Making assumptions about mothers and fathers is not wise, as many children will be cared for in different circumstances and by different people. Parents/carers[1] have a pivotal role in the development and wellbeing of children and young people. The communication channels between schools and carers should always be open. As a teacher, you will usually formally communicate through the school's reporting system and at consultation evenings. However, it is important to understand that the role carers have is

[1]To avoid repetition and as both are 'carers', this term is used to refer to both groups.

a key one, and that consequently their involvement in school and education is vital. If a school views parents and carers as partners, this results in positive interaction between the school's professionals and its pupils' parents (Addi-Raccah and Ainhoren, 2009).

The relationship between schools and carers therefore needs to be positive. Communication between schools and families is becoming more frequent and thus more important, while also possibly losing some of its 'formal' edge. With all communication with carers via email, letter or telephone you must make sure, firstly, that you are contacting the appropriate person, and secondly, that you are following school protocols. To effectively deal with carers the following areas need to be considered:

- Staff must be approachable, communication must be two-way, and possible ethnic, social and cultural issues must be dealt with positively and sensitively.
- Carers and school staff can learn from one another and develop a relationship where both parties understand their role in promoting pupils' achievement.
- Carers from all social backgrounds should be involved in their child's progress and have an opportunity to express their views on the care and education being provided.
- Challenges and barriers such as busy or inactive carers must be overcome through creating flexibility within the communication process.

Application to primary and early years teaching

At the primary and early years stages, the idea of the 'red book' – a record of an individual's progress – was developed so that parents can track their child's development in key areas like mathematics and English. Find out how far this has been taken in your placement school, and then develop your own 'red book' in which you record each pupil's progress in key areas such as mathematics, reading, writing, comprehension and language skills. This will give you a much more in-depth idea of the learning needs of your class.

GROUP EXERCISE

Review with your peers some of your experiences of dealing with colleagues. Some schools have different approaches to different issues and also a wider range of colleagues than others. Collect information on colleagues and processes in your placement, and via discussion compare this with what is available in other schools. Suggest an agreed list of priority colleagues, and then make sure that you know exactly what each of these does in your placement schools.

Extended Services

As schools branch out into more intensive community work an area called Extended Services or Extended Schools has developed. Extended Services Coordinators exist in some schools to build partnerships with other external agencies that you may come across through your involvement with pastoral duties. Extended Services aims to help meet the needs of children, young people, their families and community by bringing agencies together and putting them in touch with children and families. Schools can no longer work in isolation if they are to become a focal point of the local community.

Extended Service Coordinators will develop a wide range of activities that are specifically suited to the needs of their community. This could involve working closely with many of the school's stakeholders to foster closer relationships and improve opportunities, not just for students but their families as well. By opening a school's facilities outside of normal hours this allows a wider range of people to access the resources available.

Parent Teacher Associations are common in the majority of schools. In 2007, the National Foundation for Educational Research (NFER) (www.nfer.ac.uk/) found that 83% of primary schools and 60% of secondary schools had a PTA or its equivalent. The role of the PTA is to encourage co-operation between home and school and education authorities. When you start at your school find out whether it has a PTA and what their key agenda items are for them to improve the school.

Governing Bodies

A Governing Body (GB) exists in all state schools and in many (not all) cases may also be the employer. The GB has statutory responsibility for pay and appraisal and makes the final decisions on pay. Once you have qualified, it will be the governors who will decide if you are entitled to an increase in salary as they will also decide the head teacher's level of pay. These decisions are based on appraisals which, under the School Teachers Pay and Conditions Document (STPCD), consider progression based on performance (see Chapter 8). Governors must be confident that the appraisals and pay policy are being applied fairly. Governors have three main roles and responsibilities. Firstly, they have, as a 'critical friend', to hold the head teacher to account for the educational performance of the school. Whilst the head teacher manages the performance of staff, the GB manages that of the head teacher. Secondly, they set the school's vision, strategic direction and ethos and work to achieve this. Thirdly, they oversee the financial performance of the school and make sure the school budget is being used correctly and effectively. When you start at your new school find out who the teacher staff governor and the associate staff governor are and ask them about their roles. Although a lot of what is discussed at governor meetings is confidential, these staff governors will be able to tell you a lot about the inner workings of the school because all school development plans and visions for the future of the school start with the school governors.

A thought

Have you considered investigating the background to the local community which your school serves? A lot can be gained by considering what the needs of the local community may be and how you and the school can cater for their needs. It is worthwhile taking the time to find out information about the catchment area, local community interests, and some of the social, cultural and economic backgrounds to the communities around the school. You may be surprised that by gaining a greater understanding of the community this can help inform your teaching and improve relationships with students and their families.

Social Services

As an external agency, Children's Social Services may be called upon to intervene and support the school and specific pupils where there are children in need and looked-after children (children in care). Pastoral colleagues will involve Social Services if they believe a young person to be at high risk from harm, or if they need looking after by the local authority, or if a pupil is seeking adoption.

Children's Social Services form part of a wider menu of support that can be provided through school depending on the level of need of the pupil. Pupils and their families may have contact with Social Services and a social worker due to being at risk or needing local authority intervention, so familiarising yourself with the needs of each pupil is paramount. The school will be central to all services as teachers spend significantly more time with children than their families do and can have considerable input into the welfare of the child.

Other important colleagues may include the school nurse, trained counsellors, educational welfare officers (EWOs) who work to find out whether difficulties outside school are contributing to the child's classroom problems or attendance, student key workers and mentors. These may provide confidential health advice, promote healthy living through the Healthy Schools Initiative, or give additional support to pupils, carers and school in promoting student welfare.

Conclusion

Schools are not islands. They are part of a complex structure of experts, agencies and interested parties. All colleagues should be valued equally for their knowledge, experience and expertise. It is crucial for you to get to know who all these key individuals are by name as they may be very important for you within your teaching career. Teamwork makes for a more successful teacher and a more successful educational environment.

Summary

- There is a vast range of colleagues with whom, as a teacher, you will have a professional relationship.
- These individuals carry an enormous amount of knowledge and expertise and provide guidance and support so that you can promote teaching and learning and pupil welfare for the benefit of all.
- By utilising these colleagues' experience both your professional development and the pupils' learning experiences will be much improved.
- Schools are very much a focal point for the local community and must have a greater involvement in bringing children, parents and the community together.

Key reading

Information about roles and responsibilities in schools, including references to the SEN coordinator role and a link to the SEN Code of Practice, may be found on the relevant government websites.

The National Curriculum Online website contains the National Curriculum inclusion statement, inclusion statements by subject, and other inclusion materials published by the QCA. It is available via the National Archive (http://nationalarchives.co.uk).

Addi-Raccah, A. and Ainhoren, R. (2009) 'School governance and teachers' attitudes to parents' involvement in schools', *Teaching and Teacher Education,* 25 (6): 805–13.

References and bibliography

Addi-Raccah, A. and Ainhoren, R. (2009) 'School governance and teachers' attitudes to parents' involvement in schools', *Teaching and Teacher Education,* 25 (6): 805–13.

Ajegbo, K. (2007) *Diversity and citizenship: curriculum review.* Nottingham: DfES.

Beckett, L. and Wrigley, T. (2014) 'Overcoming stereotypes, discovering hidden capitals', *Improving Schools,* 17 (3): 217–230.

Birkett, V. (2003) *How to support and teach children with special educational needs.* Hyde: LDA.

Denby, N. (2007) 'Ensuring more accurate responses from child respondents in school-based research', Hawaii International Conference on Education, Pepperdine University, CA.

Dillenburger, K. and McKee, B. (2009) 'Child abuse and neglect: training needs of student teachers', *International Journal of Educational Research*, 48 (5): 320–30.
Lee, B. (2002) *Teaching assistants in schools: the current state of play*. Windsor: NFER.
Tucker, S. (2014) *Pastoral care in education: an international journal of personal, social and emotional development*. Birmingham: Routledge Taylor Francis Group.
www.nfer.ac.uk/nfer/publications/ASO01/ASO01part9.pdf

Visit https://study.sagepub.com/denby3e for extra resources related to this chapter.

CHAPTER 8

DEVELOPING SKILLS FOR CAREER PROGRESS

Nina Barnes and Jayne Price

Standards linked to this chapter include...

3. Demonstrate good subject and curriculum knowledge
   - demonstrate a critical understanding of developments in the subject and curriculum areas, and promote the value of scholarship.
4. Plan and teach well structured lessons
   - reflect systematically on the effectiveness of lessons and approaches to teaching.
8. Fulfil wider professional responsibilities
   - take responsibility for improving teaching through appropriate professional development, responding to advice and feedback from colleagues.

Introduction

During your teacher training you will be asked to critically reflect on your teaching and your experiences in school; for some trainees this will form part of the Master's level studies for their postgraduate teaching qualification. This key skill will be used to analyse the impact of your teaching on pupils' learning throughout your career, to enhance your practice and shape your professional development. This chapter introduces you to the critical and reflective thinking skills and processes which will support your career progression during your early professional development and beyond, and then looks at the form that such career progression might take.

Reflective practice

Reflective practice is set out in the theories of Schön (1983) and exemplified by such writers as Ghaye and Ghaye (1998), McEntee et al. (2003) and Farrell (2004). These theories emphasise the commonality of experience of professionals who are all called upon to exercise judgement and sensitivity in highly complex situations. You will join a group of professionals who need to develop 'situational understanding' by incorporating systematic reflection and self-evaluation into their practice. Schön (1983: 42) describes this as 'a reflective conversation with the situation'. Day (2002: 56) refers to three kinds of reflection:

- **reflection about action** (the goals and practices of one's profession)
- **reflection on action** (weighing competing viewpoints and then exploring alternative solutions)
- **reflection in action** (drawing upon experience and knowledge).

The processes of critical reflection include considering the context and values that shape professional practice. As part of your reflection, you might consider the extent to which the findings are unique to a particular context and you will explore the underlying values that shape the origins and development of the professional practice in question. Critical reflection requires critical engagement with the ideas of those in 'authority'. These are people with a wide range of experience and expertise. They have often undertaken practical research studies and the published findings are regarded as the starting point in building up a body of understanding. Critically reflecting on your own practice requires you to consider how your practice is underpinned by these theoretical frameworks, to interrogate the impact on the pupils' learning and to provide evidence to support this analysis. You will also reflect on your own learning and development and how this has enhanced your professional development.

GROUP EXERCISE

Understanding what the word 'critical' means in this context will help to make your reflections more powerful. In groups of three, think critically and discuss the following statement: **'Good teachers are born and not made'.**

What did you consider when you were discussing this question? Which of the following critical thinking processes did you use?

- **Identifying, assessing and exploring context** – i.e. considering the statement in the context of the current debate about the best way to train teachers through school-based vocational routes or university-based academic routes.
- **Questioning meaning, assumptions and definitions of terms** – you might have discussed and identified a definition of a 'good teacher'.
- **Being sceptical, looking for evidence, recognising limitations** – did you explore what might be the evidence for the statement, perhaps in light of your own experiences? You should also analyse what other authors and practitioners think, focusing on the published evidence.
- **Generating alternative viewpoints and considering other possibilities** – you may have considered which teaching skills can be taught or developed through initial and continuous professional development and which might be considered 'personality traits' that are perhaps innate.
- **Systematic unpicking of ideas** – critical reflection is characterised by a systematic approach and the careful development of a coherent argument, where assertions and conclusions are supported with evidence both from professional practice and the literature.

Engaging with the literature to support the development of professional practice

There are several kinds of literature including theory, research, practice and policy. Different types of literature will tend to emphasise claims to different kinds of knowledge and have different sets of strengths and limitations:

- **Theoretical knowledge** – deals with systems of interrelated concepts. It may well draw from other writers' work.
- **Research-based knowledge** – is based on focused and systematic enquiry using various methods of data collection and analysis resulting in a set of research findings. It is important to consider the nature of the research and whether it has

been commissioned by a particular body, such as the DfE. This can influence the findings of the research.

- **Practice-based knowledge** – concerns knowledge of everyday activity, such as professional practice. This may be implicit know-how, i.e. used without awareness. Reflection is the means whereby this knowledge is brought into full consciousness in order to inform and challenge practice.
- **Policy literature** – policy makers tend to emphasise practice knowledge. A policy is based on a set of values and assumptions in keeping with a particular political ideology. It is important to critically review this literature in relation to theory and not assume it is ideal.

Developing your confidence to read critically is a skill that you will develop during your teacher training. For non-critical readers, sources provide 'facts' and the purpose of reading is to absorb these facts in order to develop an understanding of the topic under investigation. Non-critical readers are most interested in identifying the main points raised in the text, and their literature reviews are likely to consist of restatement and summaries of what different authors have said. As a critical reader you will recognise that a source contains only *one* version of the facts, and that in order to gain a full understanding that text must be interrogated, the reasoning and evidence provided must be evaluated, and the author's values and perspectives taken into account. Critical readers use the literature to develop a coherent argument and their writing is characterised by the interpretation, evaluation, comparison and contrasting of alternative viewpoints and synthesis.

Learning to engage in critical analysis and reflection within academic enquiry necessitates a questioning approach to your studies. It requires an interrogative tactic to be used to examine the literature. This is particularly relevant in terms of government policy documents. Literature should be accessed from different sources, recognising that a wider viewpoint gives a more balanced perspective. To demonstrate 'mastery' of the subject area you will need to read widely enough to be able to identify the key debates in the area, the key research questions and the conclusions from previous research, as well as compare and contrast different perspectives from different authors and identify those authors who agree with each other. Critical analysis will help you identify where knowledge is 'thin' or where aspects of your own practice provide an alternative viewpoint to the one given.

The following techniques characterise good use of the literature in academic written work:

Restatement – outlining what the text says using a mixture of direct quotation, paraphrase and summary. It's good practice to summarise rather than to rely too much on the quotation of authors' work. Remember to carefully follow your provider's policy on referencing and citations.

Description – outlining what the text does as well as what it says: for example, 'Wiliam (2011) takes a historical perspective on the development of formative assessment in schools'.

Interpretation – outlining the significance of the text you are referring to: for example, 'Black and Wiliam (1998) *made a strong case* for a new emphasis on the use of formative assessment in the classroom, *presenting evidence of significant improvements* in outcomes for pupils'.

Synthesis – recognising that different sources are making the same or similar claims or arguments. Here you would summarise the main argument and then cite the authors who agree with each other in your reference.

Contrast – a balanced argument is presented by contrasting the different views inherent within the literature.

The development of an argument – using the literature to develop a coherent argument: for example, 'No area of education policy is as contentious – or as consistently newsworthy – as assessment (Mansell and James, 2009). Rightly or wrongly assessments have become the bedrock of educational accountability; they are the predominant means by which students themselves gauge their competency (Royce Sadler, 2007), with summative assessment data also providing parents with key information when it comes to school selection (GTCE, 2011).'

Criticality – when discussing the literature, a critical approach is adopted by raising questions, highlighting any weaknesses or limitations, by introducing other authors' criticisms and tentatively suggesting constructive solutions.

A thought

Consider the following paragraph from a written assignment and identify the main weakness in the writing:

'Music is a subject which has had its place in the curriculum questioned in the past. Thankfully, however, Music is now starting to be seen as a subject which contributes to the whole curriculum and rightly deserves its place there. One advantage of Music is that it is a highly accessible subject to all pupils because of the range of genres, styles and traditions and instruments, so there is effectively something for everyone.'

This paragraph is full of assertions – statements are made as fact without any support from references to the literature or professional practice. It therefore leaves the reader asking questions such as: How does the writer know that the place of music in the curriculum has been questioned? What evidence is there to support the claim that music is highly accessible? Who sees music as a subject that contributes to the whole curriculum? Making assertions is the absolute enemy of criticality so avoid doing so at all costs.

In order to develop this critical approach to the literature, you must consider how to read key sources and take notes in order to generate the information you need. Suggested strategies include the use of different coloured highlighter pens to identify recurring themes across different sources, using a table to record contrasting opinions, recording your own reactions to the claims made by the author as you are reading, and finally summarising in your own words the key points made. Academic reading is about developing your understanding of the key debates, and then reaching for your own informed viewpoint.

Applying learning to evaluate and inform practice

During your training, you will be expected to apply the critical understanding gained from a theoretical perspective to evaluate and inform your professional practice. This includes the application of conceptual ideas and research findings.

Becoming a reflective practitioner means taking responsibility for your own academic learning and having the motivation to inform both your own and others' practice. Key to this element of training is using the ideas and theories you have established from your reading and course lectures to engage in a critical dialogue with colleagues and evaluate and inform practice using a more knowledgeable approach. The underlying principle is to provide you with skills of critical analysis and deepening understanding of professional practice to give you the confidence to develop strategies for the improvement of your own professional practice.

Key to this is interrogating your practice in terms of pupils' learning and progress. You might need to gather some data in order to consider this effectively. For example, to evaluate the extent to which the pupils can connect their learning, you may ask pupils:

What was the lesson mainly about?

What did you think you were supposed to be learning and what did you learn?

Do you see connections with other work you've done?

Did you enjoy the lesson?

If the lesson was being taught again to a similar group how could it be improved?

When evaluating the stimulus and variety of tasks and activities, you might ask another adult to observe, focusing on a particular pupil or group:

How were the pupils introduced to the activity?

Was there a motivational highlight?

Was the level of challenge appropriate?

Was there a balance between active and passive tasks?

Were pupils enthusiastic and on task?

How well did they work collaboratively?

When evaluating learning you may engage in self-reflection or a shared reflection with your mentor:

Did pupils learn what was expected and what evidence shows this?

How did teacher knowledge support learning?

How did pupil and teacher activities facilitate learning?

Application to secondary teaching

Children and young people can benefit from their own 'reflective' learning. You should encourage them to think about their own development needs at various stages in their school career. Options at Year 9, examination choices post-GCSE and intended destinations post-sixth form are all good points at which to encourage reflection. They need to be encouraged to develop responsibility for enhancing their own profile. This can be drawn as a flowchart and may help them to make decisions if they know the consequences of these. For example, if, at 14, they decide not to take a science subject, they could discover that careers as either a primary school teacher or Royal Navy officer are suddenly out of reach. Careers software can help to provide the information.

Application to primary and early years teaching

Younger children can also think about their own development. They could try to imagine where they would like to be in five or ten years' time. They can have great fun imagining themselves as astronauts, pop singers or Formula 1 drivers. The exercise is then to track backwards over the five- or ten-year period to see which skills, knowledge and experiences they would need to develop if they were going to achieve their ambition.

Continuing Professional Development

Schools are encouraged to ensure that staff are appropriately developed so that they remain confident practitioners through their careers. In education areas such as new examinations and assessment methods and changes to responsibilities and expectations are being joined by new theories, new policies and inevitably new priorities. These require updated knowledge, skills and expertise, meaning that Continuing Professional Development (CPD) is an integral part of the school budget. CPD consists of reflective activity designed to improve an individual's attributes, knowledge, understanding and skills. It both supports individual needs and improves professional practice. Bell and Gilbert (1996) define the three key areas of professional learning and therefore teacher development as personal, social and occupational. Thus all of your development activities should fall into one or more of these categories and sometimes into all three.

Blandford (2001) outlines the key issues which schools need to work towards when deciding CPD requirements. These include reflecting on experiences, individual and collaborative research and practice, keeping up to date with educational thinking and giving critical deliberation with regard to education policy, with the emphasis on raising pupil achievement. Governments will introduce perspectives and policies that will make certain issues more or less fashionable. The emphasis on synthetic phonics as a way to encourage early reading and new methods of recognising and supporting children with special needs are two recent examples.

Due to the nature of schools you will have to be proactive in seeking out and taking responsibility for identifying and meeting professional development needs. You will need to be keen, to seek out appropriate opportunities, and to ensure that you are aware of the funding arrangements that go with these. CPD can take place in school, across schools, or through external agencies. The identification of professional development priorities as you continue your career after your induction year as a Newly Qualified Teacher is achieved through the appraisal system in schools.

Appraisal in schools

From September 2012 Performance Management was rebranded as Appraisal, and schools began to operate under new regulations. Appraisal in the school environment is carried out during each academic year, and will always follow the school's published Appraisal Policy. Appraisal policies are produced by a working party comprising a range of teaching staff, senior leaders, and in consultation with the recognised professional associations. Most are reviewed annually by the school's Governing Body. Appraisal policies aim to support the school ethos and help develop its ability to improve outcomes for pupils, whilst raising the morale of teachers by motivating them to update their skills and improve their performance.

All teaching staff will undergo an annual performance review. This can take different forms in each institution. One format is three separate reviews: one to set objectives for the year, an interim review, and then a final review to ensure completion of the original targets. In exceptional circumstances more reviews may be needed. Deadlines are imperative and each line manager is responsible for ensuring that appraisals take place within the required time-frame. The appraisal procedure will also be used to address any concerns raised about a teacher's performance. If concerns are such that these cannot be resolved through the appraisal process, there will be consideration of whether to commence the capability procedure.

Teaching staff who successfully complete their annual review and meet all the relevant standards are eligible to be considered for a pay award. It is the responsibility of the head teacher to review all documentation and make the appropriate recommendations to the school's Governing Body in respect of this.

Effectiveness of school appraisal procedures

The appraisal period runs for twelve months. Appraisers are always teachers and must be suitably trained to be able to undertake the role. The head teacher will be appraised by the Governing Body, supported by a suitably skilled and/or experienced external adviser appointed by the Governing Body.

Appraisers are selected by the head teacher, and will often hold line managerial responsibility for those they will appraise. Should there be an objection by either party in the pairing of appraiser and appraisee, then concerns will be carefully considered, and where possible an alternative appraiser will be offered. As part of the process, appraisers will ensure that objectives are set before, or as soon as practicable after, the start of each appraisal period. The objectives set will be Specific, Measurable, Achievable, Realistic and Time-related (SMART), and will be appropriate to the teacher's role and level of experience. In setting the objectives reviewers will have regard for what can reasonably be expected in the context of roles, responsibilities and experience, and will be consistent with the school's strategy for achieving a work/life balance for all staff.

Appraisal targets will vary amongst teaching staff depending on roles and responsibilities but will undoubtedly be in line with the school improvement priorities – this ensures all members of staff are working consistently towards the shared goals for school improvement. All teaching staff will have at least one or more teaching and learning targets, plus a professional development or subject specific target (three targets maximum). Teaching staff in receipt of a TLR (Teaching and Learning Responsibility) will normally have an objective set around their area of responsibility. Teachers will be also assessed against the appropriate set of Teachers' Standards.

Appraisal, to be effective, must include lesson observation. Outcomes must be reported confidentially and constructively within a climate of support and co-operation. They must also be carried out by qualified teachers who understand the need to act all times with professionalism, integrity and courtesy, with feedback provided as soon as possible after the event.

The number of observations required for appraisal purposes will be determined by each school; however that number must be appropriate and in accordance with the individual school's observation protocol. This is likely to include the provision of exceptional circumstances where concerns have been raised about a teacher's performance, or where a teacher may request additional observation visits to support and develop performance.

Training and development needs of staff

The continued development of teachers in any school is key to its progress. Appraisal gives individuals the opportunity to discuss personal targets and CPD requirements. This ensures the school's CPD programme is personalised to the needs of staff and school development plan. As part of the budgeting process the governing body will ensure that, as far as possible, resources are made available for training and development needs. Specific whole staff training needs should be identified prior to an appraisal period from the lesson observation review, staff quality assurance, and the school's development priorities. Many staff development programmes are organised to address key school improvement issues of Planning for Progress, Behaviour for Learning, Assessment for Learning, SEND, Literacy, Oracy and Marking. The head teacher will maintain an overview of staff development through the collation of a range of data, such as observations, external courses and INSET.

A thought

You may come across INSET activities (In-Service Training) or days on placements and in your first teaching post. These may lead to assessed outcomes, but often will not. However, even when not assessed, these are usually essential to your own professional development or competency and efficiency as a practitioner. INSET usually takes place at school, or maybe at an 'away-day' venue to enhance its value. CPD can take place in any context: at school, home, HEI, etc. All INSET therefore contributes to professional development, but not all professional development is INSET.

Tackling under-performance in the classroom

The capability procedure in schools will be applied to any employed member of staff whose performance has given rise to serious concerns regarding the completion of their duties. Dealing with a teacher who may be experiencing difficulties will need rapid identification of the issues they face, strong support, and appropriate development and coaching. At all times teachers must feel that they are being supported in order to improve their performance and resolve any issues. Where an employee may be under-performing, the head teacher or another line manager should investigate and collect evidence. Under-performance can be caused by a range of issues, such as a lack of understanding in respect of issues highlighted from observation, teaching and learning weaknesses, as highlighted in a parental complaint, illness, or personal circumstances. Regardless of the cause, support should be implemented as soon as possible.

If an appraiser has further concerns that the difficulties being experienced by a teacher are such that improvement may not be rapid or sustained, or if not rectified could lead to capability procedures, then the appraiser, the head teacher or a member of the leadership team will need to meet with the teacher and undertake the following:

- Assess the seriousness of the situation
- Explain the standards of performance required
- Outline the shortcomings in reaching those standards
- Explore the reasons for those shortcomings
- Give the employee an opportunity to respond
- Provide appropriate help and support (e.g. an opportunity to observe good practice, training)
- Provide an action plan
- Outline the time allowed for improvement.

The teacher's progress will be monitored as part of the appraisal process and a reasonable time given for their performance to improve. This will depend on the circumstances of the individual teacher and as outlined in the school's capability policy. The period of support provided should not last for too long (a typical school policy will allow six weeks). Feedback on the teacher's progress should be regular and clear instruction provided to help improve areas of concern. After the period of assessment is complete a clear and concise decision outcome must be reached and communicated.

If progress is clear and that improvement has been maintained then there is no longer a possibility of capability procedures being invoked and the teacher should be informed of this. If there is insufficient improvement made in the timescale, then it is likely that the teacher will be placed under formal capability proceedings.

A thought

Should teaching staff be required to keep evidence to support their annual appraisal or should this be the job of those appraising them? Surely teachers have enough to do?

Routes through the profession

As a trainee you will learn that your role is not just about teaching, as you become involved in pastoral duties such as acting as a form tutor. Schools will expect you to have a dual role – subject teacher and pastoral support. In terms of promotion, and routes to management, each generally follows a different path, so the one you choose to specialise in will be important. As a subject specialist you may initially aspire to Lead Practitioner (formerly Advanced Skills Teacher), head of a key stage within your subject, second in department, or head of department.

If the welfare of the child and social issues are more suited to your strengths then you may prefer to concentrate on the pastoral side. Pastoral care covers a range of job roles – from head/assistant head of year, learning mentor, attendance monitoring, and home school liaison officer, to head of year or key stage.

You can 'sample' both routes during your training to give you an idea of where your strengths and interests lie. For example, shadow staff currently in position and volunteer your time to support and help out with activities and events. This is the best way to get a feel for the job, the issues that may be faced, and the results that can be produced. Further support through CPD and training can provide the theory you will need to undertake a role, but nothing will prepare you better than first-hand experience.

INDIVIDUAL REFLECTION

Consider the following information and reflect on which of the following you do without thinking and which may need further development.

Professionalism:

- wear appropriate clothing for school
- don't bring your mobile phones into meetings
- students aren't your friends, so don't be over familiar.

(Continued)

(Continued)

Set your stall out:

- have high expectations of the students from the outset and make these explicit
- respect works both ways, so be firm but fair
- contact home and speak calmly and clearly with parents.

Know your subject:

- re-learn/revise your subject knowledge at each level you teach (KS3, 4 & 5)
- understand the difference in level of knowledge needed at each Key Stage
- know how to assess your subject at each level you teach.

Understand your students:

- learn names and key information about your students (understand their background)
- know the literacy, numeracy and communication levels of your students
- ensure your lessons are differentiated to cater for the range of abilities in your classroom.

Be clear about good/outstanding teaching:

- being Outstanding every lesson is difficult but you can be Good
- don't be an entertainer for a full lesson but do ensure you create an enthusiastic atmosphere
- plan for learning and progress every lesson
- control behaviour in the classroom
- greet every child at the door and be welcoming
- be aware of the atmosphere and potential situations arising (for instance, there may be issues following break or lunch)
- use humour and your personality to calm situations, but remember to be firm, fair and contact home when necessary.

Bring your subject to life:

- keep up to date with subject pedagogy and share your knowledge with students
- think about a subject-related activity/event/club where you can bring your subject to life and apply the theory to the real world/world of work
- have fun with your subject, run events, display work, market the subject at open evenings and encourage student ambassadors.

Regardless of your subject ensure you are a teacher of:

- literacy
- numeracy
- SMSC.

Be aware of the key policies, frameworks and policies that govern schools:

- know and understand Safeguarding, SEN, Inclusion, T&L, BFL
- read up on and familiarise yourself with Ofsted frameworks
- have a copy of the school's development priorities and know how your role will contribute.

Plan ahead:

- know your strengths and work with other colleagues to develop and improve areas of weakness
- volunteer some time to be involved in extra-curricular events, shadow staff in key areas of interest or research, and work on a area of pedagogy you want to develop
- request CPD/training in an area you want to master.

Later, experience in one or both routes will prepare you well for movement into 'Middle Management' – staff who are working at a higher level and being remunerated with a TLR (Teaching & Learning Responsibility). Middle managers are usually heads of larger departments (mathematics, English, science, MFL, humanities, technology), heads of Key Stages, or those who oversee key areas of school development such as literacy, CPD or behaviour.

From middle management, professional development moves into the realms of leadership. Different terminology/names are used for each level, but in general the structure is Assistant Head Teacher, Deputy Head Teacher, Head Teacher. Leadership staff move to a separate pay structure. It is normal at leadership level for extra qualifications to be required such as a Master's level and/or NPQH (National Professional Qualification for Headship).

Summary

- You are expected to develop into a 'reflective practitioner'.
- This means incorporating systematic reflection and self-evaluation into your practice in order to improve.
- To properly develop you will need to engage with the literature – to both read critically and learn to analyse and synthesise.

- Schools will help you develop through their own CPD programmes.
- Your progress will be supported by the appraisal process.
- There are different routes to promotion: use your school experience to choose the one that suits you.

Key reading

Burton, D. and Bartlett, S. (2005) *Practitioner research for teachers*. London: Sage.

Denby, N., Butroyd, R., Swift, H., Price, J. and Glazzard, J. (2008) *Master's level study in education*. Maidenhead: Open University Press.

Farrell, T.S.C. (2004) *Reflective practice in action: 80 reflection breaks for busy teachers*. London: Sage.

Mitchell, N. and Pearson, J. (eds) (2012) *Inquiring in the classroom*. London: Continuum.

Wallace, M. and Poulson, L. (eds) (2003) *Learning to read critically in teaching and learning*. London: Sage.

References and bibliography

Bell, B. and Gilbert, J. (1996) *Teacher development: a model from science education*. London: Falmer.

Blandford, S. (2001) 'Professional development in schools', in A. Banks and A.S. Mayers (eds), *Early professional development for teachers*. London: David Fulton.

Day, C. (2002) 'Revisiting the purposes of Continuing Professional Development', in G. Trorey and C. Cullingford (eds), *Professional development and institutional needs*. Aldershot: Ashgate.

DfE (2011) *Teachers' Standards*, July.

DfE (2012) *Teacher appraisal and capability: a model policy for schools*, May.

DfE (2014) School teachers' pay and conditions document. London: DfE.

Ghaye, T. and Ghaye, K. (1998) *Teaching and learning through critical reflective practice*. London: David Fulton.

Mansell, W. and James, M. (2009) *Assessment in schools. Fit for purpose?* The Assessment Reform Group. Available at www.tlrp.org/pub/documents/assessment.pdf

McEntee, G.H., Appleby, J., Dowd, J., Grant, J., Hole, S. and Silva, P. (2003) *At the heart of teaching: a guide to reflective practice*. New York and London: Teachers College Press.

Schön, D.A. (1983) *The reflective practitioner*. London: Temple Smith.

Visit https://study.sagepub.com/denby3e for extra resources related to this chapter.

Part II

STRATEGIES FOR TEACHING AND LEARNING

This section represents the art (and heart) of teaching. The key to excellent teaching is in the possession of excellent subject knowledge as a prerequisite, but this is only part of the story. Children and young people must be in a position where they are willing to learn and capable of learning, and this means good behaviour with minimal disruptions. Ofsted (2015) is clear on its expectations of behaviour, with key indicators being:

- pupils consistently display a thirst for knowledge and understanding and a love of learning, including when being taught as a whole class or working on their own or in small groups. This has a very strong impact on their progress in lessons.
- pupils' attitudes to learning are of an equally high standard across subjects, years and classes, and with different staff. Incidences of low-level disruption in lessons are extremely rare.

On outstanding teaching, Ofsted adds:

- all teachers have consistently high expectations of all pupils. They plan and teach lessons that enable pupils to learn exceptionally well across the curriculum.

- teachers systematically and effectively check pupils' understanding throughout lessons, anticipating where they may need to intervene and doing so with notable impact on the quality of learning.

This section therefore tackles the important area of behaviour management – without which good learning cannot take place. It also provides a brief 'Cook's tour' of the many theories of learning developed by educationalists and psychologists, along with practical advice to help you develop your own range of strategies.

CHAPTER 9

MANAGING YOUR CLASSROOM ENVIRONMENT

Jan Barnes

Standards linked to this chapter include...

1. Set high expectations which inspire, motivate and challenge pupils

   - establish a safe and stimulating environment for pupils, rooted in mutual respect
   - set goals that stretch and challenge pupils of all backgrounds, abilities and dispositions
   - demonstrate consistently the positive attitudes, values and behaviour that are expected of pupils.

(Continued)

(Continued)

7. Manage behaviour effectively to ensure a good and safe learning environment

- have clear rules and routines for behaviour in classrooms, and take responsibility for promoting good and courteous behaviour both in classrooms and around the school, in accordance with the school's behaviour policy
- have high expectations of behaviour, and establish a framework for discipline with a range of strategies, using praise, sanctions and rewards consistently and fairly
- manage classes effectively, using approaches that are appropriate to pupils' needs in order to involve and motivate them
- maintain good relationships with pupils, exercise appropriate authority, and act decisively when necessary.

Introduction

Classroom management is one of the most important tools to be found in a teacher's toolkit. It is effective management within the classroom that allows for the motivation of pupils learning. It is about creating a safe and secure environment where pupils are happy to respond and interact with the teacher' and within this environment pupils should feel free to both ask and answer questions and to engage with the lesson without fear of failure. Pianta and Hamre (2009) suggest three key parts to ensure effective classroom quality and a positive atmosphere. These are classroom organisation, instructional support, and emotional support. This chapter focuses on various ways of managing and organising classrooms and the pupils within them, and creating an environment where pupils are willing to learn. Classroom management is about leadership, and developing various tools and strategies for leading the class towards effective learning. Tools such as knowing the children within your class, and building relationships with them, where they are sure that you care about what happens to them and the learning you want them to achieve. It is as much about planning for behaviour as it is about the learning objectives and task outcomes you want to take place.

Classroom management and effective teaching

Classroom management brings about effective teaching: to understand what this means it is useful to define 'effective' in terms of teaching, and to do this you need to understand what underpins what teachers do. If you reflect upon teachers within your own experience who you found to be effective you will find that values such as respect and equal treatment are likely to be identified as a mark of effective teachers. Rogers (2006) identifies characteristics associated with effective teaching, noting that amongst characteristics such as self-confidence, patience, clear and organised teaching practice, they also minimise and manage distracting and disruptive behaviour and enable the continuation of learning within the classroom. They address any potential disruption to learning by employing classroom management techniques in a preventative manner. Rogers goes on to point out that the elements that affect teachers management include organisation within a classroom, materials and the way these are distributed to the class, engaging in maintaining pupil interest, time management, and ultimately planning to deal with typical disruptive behaviour.

Managing behaviour and promoting learning are interdependent. Powell and Tod (2004) suggest that teachers use the term 'learning behaviour' to emphasise this link. As a teacher you must teach positive learning behaviours just as you would teach the curriculum. Do not assume that pupils will understand what you expect 'being good' to mean in your lesson. Even with whole-school behavioural expectations, pupils and teachers will often interpret what those expectations look like in different ways. It is therefore imperative that when teaching a group for the first time you explicitly outline your expectations. This will also be a perfect opportunity for you to reflect upon (and even share) what a pupil can expect of you. Furthermore, just as you would briefly recap subject areas when teaching the curriculum, you will need to revisit aspects of your expectations throughout the year. Remember that this should often be proactive,

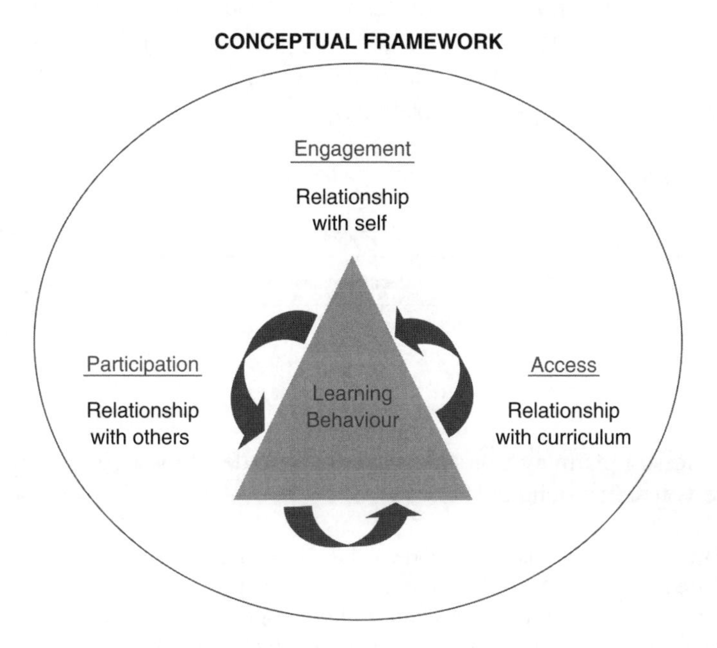

Figure 9.1 Model of learning behaviour (Powell and Tod, 2004)

not just a reaction to a current behavioural issue. Powell and Tod argue that learning behaviour arises from the learner's relationships – with the curriculum, with others (both adults and peers), and their 'relationship' with themselves. They offer the model in Figure 9.1 as a conceptual framework by which teachers can come to understand the determinates of learning behaviour.

Planning for classroom management

Good behaviour therefore doesn't just 'happen'. When you prepare your lesson plans you will also need to include planning for good behaviour. This form of planning is largely concerned with two crucial elements, that of preventing misbehaviour and that of reducing misbehaviour.

Preventative planning is about using strategies which prevent the recurrence of misbehaviour; these strategies help you with your effectiveness within the classroom environment. It is useful to develop your own set of ideas that will help you to bring this about.

A thought

In order to develop a set of resources to assist in preventing misbehaviour make an appropriate list of various tools you can use to help you build a preventative climate within your classroom. On a piece of paper or digital document draw a table with three headings (curriculum, organisation, and inter-personal), and under these make your lists as per the table below:

Table 9.1 Resources list to assist in preventing misbehaviour

Curriculum	Organisation	Inter-personal
Tasks matched to pupil need	Seating plans	Meeting and greeting

Preventative lesson planning is a skill that has to be developed. As a trainee it begins even before you start teaching:

> In your early visits to the classroom, you will be observing, which can feel uncomfortable, as pupils are inquisitive and will want to know all about you, weighing you up. You will want to settle in and learn the ropes, but do not be too friendly with the pupils, as you will eventually have to establish your authority with the whole class. (Chaplain, 2014: 189)

There are a number of things which are useful to think about when planning lessons and these include the following.

The tasks you are using to bring about learning. Ask yourself whether these are motivating to your pupils; are they engaging; will they challenge your pupils and yet allow them to succeed? If these tasks are motivating, engaging and challenging, your pupils will be interested in the work you are asking of them. If this is the case then they will be more interested in carrying out tasks than in thinking about challenging behaviour.

The timings and pace of your lesson. Are the sections or phases within your lesson too slow or too fast? Either can be detrimental to the atmosphere within the classroom.

The links between your lesson objectives, your task outcomes, and your plenary. These links should be logical, so that the pupils within your class understand what is expected of them and understand the purpose of the learning taking place. If these are related to real-life practice, then the pupils within your class are more likely to be responsive to the learning you wish to take place.

Lesson planning for classroom management to reduce misbehaviour. This is really concerned with behaviour management strategies rather than learning strategies and will be dealt with in the following chapter investigating challenging behaviour.

Other ways in which you can plan to reduce unwanted behaviour are concerned with the creation of a classroom which promotes good behaviour.

Safe classrooms – learning and feeling comfortable

Creating safe classrooms is about creating an environment which encourages learning, where pupils are safe to interact with the teacher without fear of ridicule or failure. Classrooms should be motivating with interesting and useful wall displays that will have an impact, motivate learners, and can be used to celebrate pupils' successes. We work best when we are comfortable – so think about the elements that make this so for pupils. The environment within a classroom hinges on many different aspects including the temperature of the room, the lighting, the layout, and the organisation of the room.

Temperature and lighting contribute to the ambience of the room. If the room is too hot or too cold it is likely to become uncomfortable and pupils are likely to become distracted and fidget, if the room is too dark its inhabitants can also become sleepy. It is important to get the ambience of the room correct in order to maximise the environment.

Room layout and organisation also contribute to the atmosphere and efficiency of the teaching space. When you are training to teach you are unlikely to be able to have much control over the layout of the room, however, the way in which tables are placed to facilitate for example group work can increase the efficacy of the room. In ICT suites there are often blind spots or if the computers are laid out around the room then you may often be interacting with the back of pupils' heads. Strategies need to be developed for specific parts of the lesson: for example, asking pupils to turn off screens and turn around if you need them to understand an instruction and for this interaction to be face-to-face. It is important when thinking about the layout of the room that you are conscious of being able to make eye contact with all your pupils. If this is not possible then it is advisable to make sure your movement around the room, either within your expositions or during the time they are on task, allows you to increase this interaction.

Movement is important. Learn not to teach from a fixed spot and remember that your influence and focus will change as you move around a room.

INDIVIDUAL REFLECTION

Think of a teaching space 'you will be using in your current training practice, then reflect about how you can use this space effectively:

1. Outline the layout of the room and prepare a seating plan for your pupils. This may take the form of boy, girl, boy, girl; or it may take the form of friendship groups or mixtures of ability. Ask the regular class teacher for advice.
2. What are the advantages and the limitations of the room? Does the layout support small group or pair working?
3. Consider the wall displays. What is the proportion of pupil work (and how recent is it)? Do particular year groups or forms have particular areas to display their work?

Reflect on how you might use this room, or how you might alter it should you be given the opportunity.

Deciding on classroom layout is likely to depend on the following:

- *The task/activity planned.* There is good evidence to suggest that some classroom layouts, such as rows, focus individuals on task behaviour, whilst others, such as groups, are better for developing a co-operative group-based approach to learning. Theory tells us that group work and dialogue are effective. See, for example, Vygotsky (1978), and his highlighting of the importance of both context and dialogue in 'enculturation'.
- *The chosen pedagogical tool, or teaching strategy or set of tasks* that comprise your overall teaching strategy.
- *The group* (including size of group, age, level of engagement, expected behaviour). Relating the layout and the seating plan to the group means that you will need to know the pupils within your class. You will also need to make a judgement as to how you will group or seat your pupils. For example, some pupils may not work well when seated next to certain other pupils. This central idea of 'knowing your class' is discussed further in Chapter 10.

- *The stage in the year.* This is not just to consider the changing seasons, but the way that pupil attitudes may change during an academic year. A dark dreary day, particularly if it has been raining and pupils have not had the opportunity to take their breaks outside, can have a very different impact from that on days when the weather is more clement. Enthusiasm for learning may also be high at the start of September, depressed by December, and renewed by holidays.

The legacy of Every Child Matters

Every Child Matters (2003) and The Children's Act (2004) were the response by the Labour government to Lord Laming's enquiry into the Victoria Climbie case in 2000. Victoria was a victim of cruelty who was perceived to have been let down by the lack of multi-agency coordination. Although modified by subsequent administrations, the principles laid down form the basis for much of the official administration considered helpful to children, notably bringing all local government functions of children's welfare and education under the statutory authority of local Directors of Children's Services. Fundamentally the act has five outcomes which are linked to human rights (UN Convention on the Rights of the Child, 1990) to ensure the wellbeing of children. The key outcomes to which children and young people are entitled are given as:

- be healthy
- stay safe
- enjoy and achieve
- make a positive contribution
- achieve economic wellbeing.

Application to primary and early years teaching

In Wales the Welsh government was even more emphatic, particularly with regard to the primary sector, stating that 'Educational provision for young children should be holistic with the child at the heart of any planned curriculum. It is about practitioners understanding, inspiring and challenging children's potential for learning.' In particular, the importance of children's play at this age (3–7 year olds) was emphasised, with teachers encouraged to be involved in play that involved 'open questioning, shared and sustained thinking' (DCELLS, 2008: 6). As a primary and EYFS specialist you should be aware of the importance of play and plan this into your lessons.

Thus all practitioners, including trainees, need to consider how the activities within their classroom and how they pay attention to good relationships brings about the development of a positive classroom climate and helps to secure the five outcomes. The following is an extract from the online Ofsted (2012) good practice database giving details regarding the five outcomes. Even though these no longer have statutory force, it is well worth taking this information into account when undertaking planning.

Table 9.2 The five outcomes

Outcome	Description
Being healthy	This outcome deals with the extent to which providers contribute to the development of healthy lifestyles in children. Evidence will include ways in which providers promote the following: physical, mental, emotional and sexual health; participation in sport and exercise; healthy eating and the drinking of water; the ability to recognise and combat personal stress; having self-esteem; and the avoidance of drug taking including smoking and alcohol. There should also be an assessment of the extent to which appropriate support is available for both pupils and staff to help achieve these positive outcomes.
Staying safe	This outcome is principally about the extent to which providers contribute to ensuring that 'children' stay safe from harm. Evidence includes complying with child protection legislation, undertaking CRB checks, protecting young people and vulnerable adults from bullying, harassment and other forms of maltreatment, discrimination, crime, anti-social behaviour, sexual exploitation, exposure to violence and other dangers. Ensuring that all relevant staff are appropriately trained.
Enjoying and achieving	This outcome includes attending and enjoying education and training, and the extent to which learners make progress with regard to their learning and personal development. Evidence to evaluate this includes arrangements to assess and monitor learners' progress, support learners with poor attendance and behaviour, and meet the needs of potentially underachieving groups. Also relevant will be the extent and effectiveness of the 'enrichment' of provision by promoting social, cultural, sporting and recreational activities. Learners' views about the degree to which they enjoy their 'learning life' are taken into account here.
Making a positive contribution	This outcome includes the development of self-confidence and enterprising behaviour in learners, together with their understanding of rights and responsibilities, and their active participation in community life. Evidence includes measures to ensure understanding of rights and responsibilities, the extent to which learners are consulted about key decisions, and the provision of opportunities for learners to develop and lead provider and community activities. There should also be a focus on enabling young people to develop appropriate independent behaviour and to avoid engaging in anti-social behaviour.
Achieving economic wellbeing	This outcome includes the effectiveness of the ways in which the provider prepares learners for the acquisition of the skills and knowledge needed for employment and for economically independent living. Evidence includes arrangements for developing self-confidence, enterprise and teamwork, the provision of good careers advice and training for financial competence, and the accessibility of opportunities for work experience and work-based learning.

Positive climate and routines – classroom rules

Bernstein (2000) considers classroom management from two distinct points of view: he distinguishes between these by those of a regulatory nature, one of 'order, relations, identity' (2000: 32), and those rules concerned with pupil behaviour within classrooms. Both are needed to create a positive climate within the classroom. Many authors (e.g. Cohen et al., 2004; Dillon and Maguire, 2011; Knight and Benson, 2013) suggest that the best way to create positive climate routines within the classroom is negotiating the classroom rules with the pupils within your class. These are likely to include school rules inasmuch as they will include the way a pupil dresses, for example the removal of coats and storing of bags as they settle at their desks or workstations. They are also likely to include the way in which the pupils answer questions, e.g. whether they use hands up or no hands up strategies within the classroom; the way they afford respect to their peers and the teacher within the room; and how this relates to their general behaviour within the classroom. However, for these rules to be effective they should be open, few in number, and agreed so that the pupils feel ownership. With this ownership rules become both realistic and achievable to maintain.

Effective classroom rules occur when those rules are modelled by the teacher and fully explained so that there is a clear understanding from pupils. Having done this it is useful to display the rules within the classroom in the form of a poster so there is a reminder of the agreement made between you and your pupils.

One of the key aspects in establishing classroom rules with pupils is linked to the presence of the teacher (Wubbels and Levy, 1993). Teachers need to be able to show their dominance within the classroom: this does not mean that they must be dictators within the classroom, but that they show a positive leadership style. Pupils should understand that the classroom is the teacher's domain into which they are invited in order to take part in the class. The development of this presence can be linked to teacher confidence; it is very much concerned with the way in which pupils perceive their teacher, and their confidence in adhering to the classroom's rules. To this end Robertson (1996) suggests that classroom management control is not just about the teachers' ability to show their dominance. Teachers also need to demonstrate that they are passionate about teaching their subject and to generate a similar motivation for the subject in their pupils, or it will quickly become apparent that any authority or respect the teacher may have is unfounded. It is in skills such as organising, presenting, communicating and monitoring that a teacher's actual authority rests. Robertson (1996) further suggests that to be effective in classroom control teachers need to show the following skills:

- Communicating their enthusiasm for the subject
- Continually engaging pupils using gestures, speech and eye contact
- Creating the right attitude in pupils to gain their interest, engagement and motivation for the subject and learning taking place

- Building positive and effective relationships with pupils in the class
- In developing this effectiveness within the classroom, it is also vital not to show negative attitudes towards pupils
- Maintaining attention: if you are bored with the subject how can you expect pupils to maintain their engagement?

Application to secondary teaching

How do you know that they have understood the nature of the task, and the expected outcomes? Simple, ask them to tell you, in their own words, what it is that they are expected to do, and how they will know that they have succeeded. This may feel to a beginning teacher like time wasted but is actually an essential and efficient use of time and a process that will pay dividends when they begin the task. Often this approach is embedded in primary classrooms but then receives less and less emphasis as pupils get older. Remember, children of any age group value clarity and certainty so secondary school teachers should take their cue from their primary colleagues.

Classroom behaviour plan

In considering how you want your classroom to be, it is worthwhile thinking about your approach to classroom management. Your reflection should include thoughts about how your pupils are going to move around and indeed how you are going to locate yourself within the classroom. You will need to take into account the learning that is going to take place in your classroom and how you can communicate this. How you can generate mutual respect, how you can maintain safety within your classroom, so that there is minimised risk, how you can manage safety so that pupils feel they are in secure environment. And finally, how you and your pupils can engage with the problem-solving aspects of your teaching and the tasks you wish them to complete. In doing this you are creating a classroom management or behaviour plan (Bosch, 2006).

Key rules – get them in, get on, get them out

Smith and Laslett (1993) outline four key rules of classroom management, which are still relevant today. These rules are as follows:

- **Get them in** – plan for the transition that is taking place to make it as smooth as possible. For example, pupils will need to move from one class to another and those classes will not always be in close proximity to one another. The way that pupils arrive at your classroom will depend on what has occurred to them previously. Their previous classroom may have been at the other end of the school, or if it is the end of break or lunch, they may be in a boisterous mood (also often true after PE or other inherently active lessons). Ideally you should be in your classroom waiting for your pupils to arrive, where you can employ your preferred greeting strategy. This may be greeting them at the door, or greeting them as they come in while giving them clear instructions regarding your expectations. It should be clear that you are welcoming them into *your* space.

- **Get on with it** – you want the start of the lesson to be smooth, prompt and focused. Starters enable pupils to find their place and prepare for the lesson, whilst engaging in an activity relevant to the forthcoming lesson. This also lets you take the register and possibly deal with any latecomers, all the while remembering that the key thing is to move the lesson on. You can deal with why some pupils are late and any catch-up they may require once everyone is on task. Proceeding with the lesson, maintain an appropriate but varied pace to ensure engagement from pupils, to employ stimulating tasks with varied content but appropriate to your pupils' needs. The differentiation of these tasks should be appropriate for both the less able and more able pupils, providing a challenge whilst maintaining opportunities for success.
- **Get on with them** – know your pupils and build a relationship with them. Make sure you know their names but always maintain your level of authority; you are not there to be their friend. Let them know that you care about what happens to them and be approachable, yet treat them all equally and justly. Find something out about each that can generate a conversation. Use of personal names is polite, it models respect, and if you do need to correct anything it is far easier to challenge any misdemeanour on an individual basis. Help them to succeed by attending to their varied needs, with clear rules concerning how they seek help. Do they need to put their hands up, or perhaps ask a peer first? Always acknowledge calls for help and offer that assistance discretely. Be aware of what is happening in the classroom and match your movements to the needs of the classroom.
- **Get them out** – this is about finishing your session and moving them on to their next location, be it another lesson, break, lunch, or even their trip home. Be aware of time so that you can start rounding off your lesson appropriately and pupils can be orderly in their exit. Recap the learning and give them a sense of what they have achieved as this helps them to leave the class on a positive note. Let them know what they will be doing the next time you teach them, and leave them enthused and wanting to return for their next lesson. Have clear exit routines – think about how you will collect any work carried out so that it can be marked and fed back promptly. It might be a pupil collects work, or that all pupils stack their work/books in a designated place, or indeed it may be that the work is to be uploaded to virtual learning environments (VLEs). Establish a routine, e.g. should pupils line up before exiting, or stand behind their chairs?

Use of voice and developing a presence

It is important to vary the quality and volume of your voice appropriate to the type of lesson and activity within it. The keyword here is 'variety'. There is nothing worse than listening or trying to listen to someone who uses the same tone throughout. You can adapt the pace, volume, modulation and pitch to convey different messages. The voice you use when reinforcing something will be very different from the voice you use to give instructions for a task. If your voice is too high pitched, it can sometimes sound desperate and apologetic, and seem as if you are asking pupils for permission when you are giving directions. Also consider the language you use – make sure it is positive and clear as this will help pupils understand what you require of them. Key to making the voice more interesting is to practise varying your pitch, volume and tone. Your voice is an essential tool in your teaching 'kit' so look after it! It is used constantly and can easily become tired, especially if you are talking too loudly for much of the time. In varying the tone, volume and pitch your voice will be more effective and less strained. Remember, a tired voice is rarely an interesting voice. Also develop a stern voice for when this is needed – it doesn't have to be loud, but it must carry authority. Never resort to shouting.

A thought

Next time you are observing the practice of your mentor, or that of another experienced teacher, listen for variations in the voice (pitch, tone, volume) that person uses. Think about the impact these variations are having on the lesson and reflect upon how these may assist you in your own practice.

Use of praise

Use of praise and recognition within the classroom can act not only as a way of motivating the pupils, it can also help to build a positive environment within the classroom. Research has shown that the use of praise can be very effective in managing the pupils in your care. Such use is one of the fundamental aspects of Behaviour for Learning (B4L, 2007). However, for praise to be truly effective it needs to have been earned and also appropriate: if the praise given by a teacher is purely cosmetic it will seem artificial and prove unsuccessful, and if used insincerely it is likely to undermine any relationships built with the class. Praise with some groups of older pupils may also be seen as 'un-cool' when given publicly. This does not mean that they will not respond to praise as younger pupils will, just that you will have to be careful about when and how you deliver praise. For example, it may be worth considering less public ways of showing your encouragement. When giving praise there are a number of fundamental aspects:

- **Personal**: praise should be given to individuals or groups in a personal manner. The easiest way of doing this is by using names. Praise does not have to be verbal; it can take the form of a smile or other non-verbal positive signals such as a thumbs-up.
- **Specific**: praise should be linked to a particular achievement. It could be a reaction to the correct answer, or to achieving particular aspects of a task or activity. The specificity may be different for different members of the class, perhaps due to different abilities. For example, one pupil may have praise for achieving a task that he or she found difficult, whereas other pupils may have found the task easy so praise may not be as appropriate. When dealing with younger pupils, or pupils with particular special needs, praise may be appropriate for sitting still, concentrating, or merely not disrupting the learning of the rest of the class.
- **Genuine**: praise should always be genuine. Praise for its own sake will be viewed by pupils as demeaning. Praise should always be given to pupils who have really achieved something. Overuse and careless repetitive praise which is not genuine can give praise which has been genuinely earned a diminished status.
- **Time**: praise which is given close to the achievement or attainment is usually the most effective for motivating pupils.

GROUP EXERCISE

You have two pupils, a boy and a girl, who have suddenly achieved exceptionally well in a lesson. Normally these pupils do not engage well in the classroom, but on this occasion they have made valuable contributions. You are pleased with this outcome and want to find a way to encourage them to repeat their engagement and quality of work. The class has a reputation for being difficult. Following the fundamental aspects of praise outlined above (i.e. making the praise personal, specific, genuine and timely) in your group discuss:

- whether it would it be counter-productive to praise the pupils in public
- how you could praise them if you chose to praise them in private
- whether you would praise them in different ways, due to their age or gender.

Summary

- Good classroom management is a prerequisite to good teaching.
- Planning and organising your classroom will reduce behaviour issues.
- Consider all the elements of the classroom (ambience, layout, TA support, time of year etc.).
- Establish a positive climate, with agreed rules and routines.
- Use your voice to create interest and variety.
- Praise is a powerful and positive tool to support good behaviour and good habits.

Key reading

Bosch, K. (2006) *Planning classroom management: A five-step process to creating a positive learning environment*. Thousand Oaks, CA: Corwin.

Galton, M., Steward, S., Hargreaves, L., Page, C. and Pell, A. (2009) *Motivating your secondary class*. London: Sage.

Knight, O. and Benson, D. (2013) *Creating outstanding classrooms: a whole-school approach*. London: Routledge.

Rogers, B. (2006) *Classroom behaviour: a practical guide to effective teaching, behaviour management and colleague support* (2nd edn). London: Sage.

Scrivener, J. (2012) *Classroom management techniques*. Cambridge: Cambridge University Press

References and bibliography

B4L (2007) Now in *The National Archives*. http://webarchive.nationalarchives.gov.uk/20101021152907/http:/www.behaviour4learning.ac.uk/ViewArticle2.aspx?ContentId=13206

Bernstein, B.B. (2000) *Pedagogy, symbolic control, and identity: theory, research, critique* (4th edn). Maryland: Rowman & Littlefield.

Bosch, K. (2006) *Planning classroom management: A five-step process to creating a positive learning environment*. Thousand Oaks, CA: Corwin.

Chaplain, R. (2014) 'Managing classroom behaviour', in T. Cremin and J. Arthur (eds), *Learning to teach in the primary school*. London: Routledge.

Cohen, L., Manion, L. and Morrison, K. (2004) *A Guide to Teaching Practice*. London: Routledge.

Department for Children, Education, Lifelong Learning and Skills (DCELLS) (2008) *Framework for children's learning (aged 3–7 years) in Wales*. Cardiff: Welsh Assembly Government.

Dillon, J. and Maguire, M. (2011) *Becoming a teacher: issues in secondary education*. Maidenhead: Open University Press.

Knight, O. and Benson, D. (2013) *Creating outstanding classrooms: a whole-school approach*. London: Routledge.

Ofsted (2012) *Ofsted Good Practice Database - Every Child Matters (ECM)*. Retrieved from The Excellence Gateway Treasury: http://archive.excellencegateway.org.uk/page.aspx?o=167914

Ofsted (2015) *School inspection handbook*, January, No. 120101.

Pianta, R.C. and Hamre, B.K. (2009) 'Classroom processes and positive youth development: conceptualising, measuring, and improving the capacity of interactions between teachers and pupils', *New Directions in Youth Development*, 121: 33–46.

Powell, S. and Tod, J. (2004) 'A systematic review of how theories explain learning behaviour in school context', in *Research Evidence in Education Library*. London: EPPI-Centre, Social Science Research Unit, Institute of Education.

Robertson, J. (1996) *Effective classroom control: understanding teacher–pupil relationships*. London: Hodder & Stoughton.

Rogers, B. (2006) *Classroom behaviour: a practical guide to effective teaching, behaviour management and colleague support* (2nd edn). London: Sage.

Smith, C. and Laslett, R. (1993) *Effective Classroom Management: A Teacher's Guide*. London: Routledge.

Vygotsky, L. S. (1978) *Mind and society: the development of higher mental processes*. Cambridge, MA: Harvard University Press.

Wubbels, T. and Levy, J. (1993) *Interpersonal relationships in education*. London: Falmer.

Useful websites 

www.behaviour2learn.co.uk

http://archive.excellencegateway.org.uk/page.aspx?o=167914

www.Ofsted.gov.uk

www.estyn.gov.uk

Visit https://study.sagepub.com/denby3e for extra resources related to this chapter.

CHAPTER 10

BEHAVIOUR STRATEGIES IN CHALLENGING CLASSROOMS

Ed Southall

Standards linked to this chapter include...

1. Set high expectations which inspire, motivate and challenge pupils

    - establish a safe and stimulating environment for pupils, rooted in mutual respect
    - set goals that stretch and challenge pupils of all backgrounds, abilities and dispositions
    - demonstrate consistently the positive attitudes, values and behaviour which are expected of pupils.

7. Manage behaviour effectively to ensure a good and safe learning environment

- have clear rules and routines for behaviour in classrooms, and take responsibility for promoting good and courteous behaviour both in classrooms and around the school, in accordance with the school's behaviour policy
- have high expectations of behaviour, and establish a framework for discipline with a range of strategies, using praise, sanctions and rewards consistently and fairly
- manage classes effectively, using approaches which are appropriate to pupils' needs in order to involve and motivate them
- maintain good relationships with pupils, exercise appropriate authority, and act decisively when necessary.

Introduction

Creating a positive classroom environment in which pupils are safe, secure and able to learn will underpin everything that you do as a teacher. In 2014, Ofsted reported that 'deeply worrying' persistent low-level disruption in classrooms frequently prevented learning, had a detrimental impact on the life chances of some pupils, and was a contributor to good teachers leaving the profession (Ofsted, 2014). Never has the behaviour of pupils received so much attention in the media and been so high on the agenda of Her Majesty's Inspectorate of Education. It is critical therefore not only that school leadership teams apply a robust behaviour management system, but also that teachers are well equipped to deal with all levels of pupil behaviour. Wherever you are on the 'continuum' that Rogers (2011) describes, you will need to develop a range of effective management skills for all situations. Rogers states that:

> There are a number of well-established theoretical positions addressing behaviour management and discipline in schools … ranging from 'explicit teacher control' (for example, particular forms of assertive discipline) to non-directive approaches (for example, teacher effectiveness-training). These 'positions' on a continuum, are in part philosophic, in part pedagogic and in part psychological – all have implications for one's values and practices as a teacher. (2011: 6)

Effective management of pupil behaviour is one of the most fundamental skills to develop as a teacher. From how you organise your classroom, through to the way in which you interact with pupils, outstanding teachers have both the confidence and the skill set to deal with the multitude of situations that require behaviour management. As a beginning teacher, this is something you will need to master early on. Identifying and defusing minor behavioural situations before they escalate will become one of the most valuable skills you possess as your experience and confidence grow. These skills, despite being used primarily to describe dealing with poor behaviour, also encompass the handling of positive behaviour, managing participation, and encouraging collaboration within the classroom. Often, how you deal with a well-behaved pupil can impact on how others in your lesson act and react in your learning environment.

Applying these skills in school situations that for a variety of reasons may be more challenging is equally important. Many of the issues that impact on behaviour are common to almost all classrooms. However, in a number of classrooms you will also face issues that are less common – children with particular needs, or who behave (or misbehave) in particular ways. This chapter first considers how you can plan for good behaviour, and then looks at how you can recognise and cope with challenging behaviour, along with gaining an understanding of some of its causes.

Managing behaviour through active learning

A key contributor to poor pupil behaviour is boredom. If pupils aren't encountering a range of learning experiences throughout a school day, they are increasingly likely to become distracted. This applies not only to children but adults as well. Ask yourself when you last sat through a lecture or meeting or even watched a film without wanting to check your phone. We live in a world full of easily accessible distractions. We need breaks, a cup of tea, a change of scenery, some music perhaps, just to give a little variety to a situation. Lessons are no different. Pupils are more likely to stay engaged if they are exposed to a variety of stimuli – film, teacher demonstrations, pictures, discussion, movement and ICT are just a few examples of how you can enhance pupil engagement and reduce the risk of their straying off task. There will never be a perfect combination of activities that works for every group. Some pupils will work best from a textbook or worksheet for part of a lesson whereas others may respond better to a role-play activity. Some may prefer a range of activities in your afternoon lesson, but respond better to a quieter more teacher-led environment in the morning. The key is to know your classes, and that takes time. You must also be clear about the *purpose* of each task you direct for pupils to complete and the *outcome* that will show them that they have completed it successfully. If the task is simply there to fill time, or to make things more active at the cost of deeper learning, then reconsider its fitness for purpose. Furthermore, consider the balance between your choice of active learning activities and your ability to control the class. If you are letting them move around the room for example, how confident are you that you will be able to get them back to their seats and listening later on?

Managing expectations

Before any task, it is vital you communicate your expectations to pupils. What does success look like? How will they know if they are doing well? Sometimes showing pupils 'what a good one looks like' (often abbreviated to WAGOLL) can avoid confusion (which often leads to distraction) and allow pupils to focus more on the expected outcomes rather than interpreting the task. How will the task end? What are you expecting pupils to do and how are they expected to conduct themselves? How much time do they have? An effective technique to refocus the class after an activity is the use of a visible timer (there are many versions available online). When the time runs out (with or without an audible alarm), pupils have a clear ending and new beginning to a part of the lesson. Don't be afraid to cut a task short. If pupils are losing interest, or have begun to complete the task before its expected end, adapting your lesson around this is essential. Allowing a task to dwindle can open the door to poor behaviour.

Managing accessibility: differentiation and challenge

Another considerable contributor to straying off task in lessons is a pupil who simply gives up. As soon as a pupil is off task, the likelihood of poor behaviour increases greatly. Pupils who are on task generally demonstrate predictable behaviours. However pupils who are off task are far less predictable. The reasons for straying off task can vary. As well as the dangers of repetitive tasks in lessons, pupils can also become bored through a lack of challenge. It is incumbent on you to deliver explanations of tasks concisely and with clarity, and develop differentiation strategies that will enable pupils of all abilities within a class to access the work and make appropriate progress (see Chapter 14).

But how is that achieved? There are a number of effective strategies available to you, many of which start at the planning stage of your lesson. Asking yourself simple questions such as 'what if they don't understand this?' and 'what if they grasp this very quickly?' will help you begin to create more scaffolding around a topic for weaker pupils, or a greater challenge for the more able. Consider the needs of your pupils when you are planning lessons. How well do you know each individual? For example, will your pupil with poor literacy be able to access the main activity? Once again we are pulled towards the fundamental expectation that you must *know your pupils*. You will have to know their needs, what they will respond to and how they will respond to it. You won't always get this right, but the more familiar you are with a class, the more you can reduce the risk of poor behaviour developing through inappropriate tasks.

Application to secondary teaching

It is easy to focus differentiation entirely on supporting weaker pupils in lessons. However it is just as important to give an appropriate challenge. This does not necessarily mean creating many different resources for the same activity. Be creative. You could have a range of questions that span from simple to extraordinarily difficult within one activity, or you could develop questions that allow for a range of answer depths – through the use of technical vocabulary, or the application of a concept to real life, or the projection of an idea arising from a pupil's own questions around a topic. It is important to allow all pupils access to more difficult questions and challenges. Never assume that a lower ability pupil will not want to attempt harder tasks. It is unfair to deny them that opportunity. On a similar note, don't underestimate how much challenge you will need to provide for some pupils. There will be those who will not have to struggle with anything you ask them if you stay within the boundaries of your provided curriculum. Don't be afraid of giving them access to material that will truly test their understanding beyond the needs of the curriculum. If they are not finding anything challenging, you run the risk of losing your most able pupils.

Managing reflection (and contrition)

When dealing with poor behaviour, there is a need not only for pupils to be punished in accordance with your school's behaviour policy, but also for them to *accept* that their behaviour was inappropriate. Often a pupil can be punished without reflecting upon their actions, and so the process itself is ineffective. For example, consider a girl who has sworn at another pupil during a lesson. She is given a detention for half an hour after school the next day. During the detention she sits in silence until the time is up, then goes home. At no point during this procedure has she reflected upon her behaviour, or taken any responsibility for her actions. She may have sat for thirty minutes thinking about what she is going to do that evening, or worse, grown increasingly frustrated at you for the injustice of the punishment as she believes she did nothing wrong. Is it reasonable to expect her to come to you after the lesson and talk through what she did without support and guidance from you? Be conscious of the need to restore broken relationships and to talk through serious behavioural incidents with any of the pupils involved. Again, it should be stressed that you are the adult. If you don't address and resolve the issue, there is every chance that the pupil involved will be coming into your next lesson bearing a grudge, or worse, over time may stop attending your lessons. Well structured questioning goes a long way in helping pupils to reflect on their actions. 'Why did you do that?' will most likely be met with 'I don't know'. 'You know that was inappropriate behaviour, don't you?' will also prompt an answer that does not require the pupil to think. Furthermore, demanding an apology will often result in a reactive, disingenuous response. Try instead to discuss who is affected by the pupil's actions. Delve deeper until they have realised that not only did the event affect the teacher and pupils involved, it also affected their parents, the rest of the class, the Teaching Assistant, the learning, and so on. Once you feel they have realised the true extent of the issue, any apology will at least be sincere, and the slate can be wiped clean for the next lesson. Following such discussions, mutually agreed targets are far more likely to be effective.

GROUP EXERCISE

Think back to your own time at school and think of the ways in which you or your friends were punished for bad behaviour. How constructive was this? Did it deter you? Would it deter everyone? Share these experiences in your group and discuss what you would define as a 'constructive' punishment. Make a list of punishments that do little to deal with the cause of the behaviour.

Acknowledging positive behaviour

All too often the focus on negative behaviour can be at the expense of those pupils who are modelling good behaviour, effort and attitude. Pupils who never cause a problem, and who can always be relied upon, do not deserve to be ignored. Be mindful of how much attention you give to good behaviour. Praise can be an excellent tool to encourage pupils to adopt the behaviours of others. Be aware that some pupils may not like being publicly praised – often it can cause embarrassment or anxiety about how other pupils will react to them. However there are other ways to recognise behaviours that meet or exceed your expectations. Letters, postcards or texts home, school-based rewards, written praise in books, a quiet word when others are on task – the key here is that in whatever way is most appropriate to the pupil, good behaviour is acknowledged and not taken for granted.

INDIVIDUAL REFLECTION

Make addressing positive behaviour a focus for your observations. Talk to teachers about how they have reinforced positive expectations as a way to prevent poor behaviour. Develop some routines that you can use in your own teaching for different age ranges. For example, you could develop a positive behaviour reward scheme, some good behaviour stickers, a weekly phone call home to a different pupil, or email a picture of the 'best looking' classwork to that particular pupil's parent.

Involving other stakeholders

When dealing with poor behaviour, it can be easy to lose focus on the wider options available to you. You do not have to tackle behaviour on your own. You have line managers, Heads of Department, form tutors, Heads of Year, Assistant Head Teachers in charge of behaviour and learning, and often the most effective stakeholders – parents. If a pupil is persistently disruptive, parental involvement can often prove very effective, and almost certainly necessary. Wouldn't you want to know if your child was getting into trouble at school? Of course some parents are more supportive than others, but you should never ignore the option by pre-empting the parental response. A note in their pupil planner or a phone call home will let the pupil know that their behaviour in school is not separate from their behaviour at home. The same approach should be taken for good behaviour too. Often a good phone call home for a pupil who has often been a problem, but in a particular lesson was exceptional, can really motivate that pupil to change their attitude towards your lessons. There will almost certainly be a wealth of behavioural strategies available to you through your school's behaviour policy and procedures as well. Subject reports, whole school reports, time-out cards for pupils displaying aggressive behaviour, and removal rooms are all likely to feature at your school.

Consistency

Being consistent is a key skill for teachers. From a pupil's perspective, consistency equates to fairness and fairness commands respect. If some pupils are seen to be 'getting away' with things, whilst others are punished for relatively little, this can create tension in the classroom and lead to confrontational behaviours. However consistency is not something that will come easily, and in truth, it is often more sensible to be *unfair*. Confused? Consider the pupil who is particularly rowdy or problematic when arriving at your door. Once in your lesson, they chat noisily to their neighbour – but you don't want them to. You speak to them about their behaviour, but a few minutes later they are doing it again, and despite further warnings they follow a similar pattern. If you strictly follow your behaviour system, that pupil will probably have a detention at this point. But you are only three minutes into the lesson. You now have no ammunition left, and that pupil is possibly going to be with you for the next fifty-seven minutes. Furthermore, they will most likely have become frustrated with you now too, as in their mind they haven't had a chance to settle and already find themselves in a detention. So now they might be thinking 'I can behave how I want, because I've already got a detention', and become confrontational. This may seem like an extreme example, and hopefully in your school it is. You may well have a system whereby pupils displaying this kind of behaviour are removed from your room, but be aware that there are pupils who will frequently display this kind of behaviour. They cannot be removed from your room three minutes after the start of *every* lesson. As a teacher therefore there will always have to be an element of common sense and flexibility when punishing a pupil. It may be that some pupils need a few more verbal warnings before you start to drill through the consequence system. You will know when enough is enough, and when lines have been crossed despite an appropriate warning – and that line may well sit slightly differently for each pupil. The enormous difficulty therefore is to be as consistent as you can, without appearing to tolerate misbehaviour in some pupils more than others.

A thought

Think back to when you were at school. Was there a child who had a bad reputation? A child who for some reason seemed to get away with more than the other pupils? What behaviour did he or she display? How did the teacher deal with it? Was it effective? What are your thoughts about how that child behaved now? Perhaps with hindsight you can see a clearer pattern to the behaviour, or the reasoning behind it, or you can think of strategies that the teacher used or should have used.

Always follow through

Whilst consistency in behaviour management may need to be constantly re-evaluated, often within a single lesson, one thing that must never be compromised is following through on both punishments and rewards. If you say you are going to send a letter home for good behaviour, then you must do so. If you say a pupil will be in detention, then there is no room for leniency. As soon as your sanctions and rewards are perceived as empty threats and promises, then you have lost one of your most valuable tools, as well as some of your credibility. Pupils will no longer strive to please you or meet your expectations if your promises of letters and phone calls home lead only to disappointment.

What if the behaviour becomes more challenging?

Regardless of your school, your experience and your consequence system, there will always be more challenging behavioural situations that occur. These will become less frequent as you become more experienced, and develop the ability to spot the signs that a situation is about to escalate, but it would be naive to assume they will go away forever. How you deal with those situations will very much depend on what caused them and who they involved. However here are some general guidelines that are applicable to most scenarios.

Stay calm

Behaviour spreads behaviour. If the most authoritative person in the room begins to panic, then pupils will inevitably reassess the situation and begin to panic themselves. Just like when a toddler grazes a knee and looks to the parent's expression before deciding how to react, children will look to you to gauge the severity of a situation. Your reaction to the pupil(s) who have caused the incident is also important. If they are causing disruption for example, and you panic, then the control you have, or even their perception of your control, will disappear. That control may have been the one thing preventing an escalation of the problem. Your judgment in these situations will be crucial. If you are panicking, or angry, or stressed, then you may not be of the right frame of mind to make the best decisions to diffuse a situation.

Avoid confrontation

Some pupils will want confrontation. As a professional you will need to remove as many opportunities for them to confront you as possible. Staying calm is of course a key factor. But consider how you will respond to a pupil in these situations. Shouting at them is likely to frustrate them further, or embarrass and humiliate them, to which they will of course respond negatively. Something as simple as engaging with them may be enough for them to confront you. Often the best strategy is to calmly tell a pupil their behaviour is inappropriate, and then immediately move on with the lesson – focusing your attention on other pupils who are promoting more positive behaviours. This essentially removes the pupil's audience and gives them no-one to focus on. Some pupils will try to draw you into an argument. Don't let them. Even if it means they have the 'last word' and you move on, this is better than running the risk of a full-blown argument with a child who in such circumstances will have no desire to negotiate or acknowledge what you have to say. You can always reprimand them in private after the lesson. This does not have to be on show to everyone.

A thought

When addressing poor behaviour, the tone with which you address pupils is something you will need to carefully consider. A good tip here is to imagine the parents of the pupil you are speaking to standing next to them. Would you berate the child in front of them in the same way as in front of the class? What is the most likely response from a child if you react to their behaviour by shouting at them and humiliating them in front of their peers? Of course they need to be punished with an appropriate (and proportionate) response, but consider when, where and how.

Often by shouting at a pupil, you are risking them shouting back at you. What would you do then? Shout louder? Where does it end? Use a more rational approach. You are the adult. Be firm, but do not risk losing control of the situation by getting (or acting) angry. Speak to the pupil privately or one-to-one whilst the rest of the class continue working.

Ignore selectively

Sometimes selective hearing can be the best approach. If a pupil has been difficult, and as you move on from their behavioural incident you hear them mutter under their breath something that you at best can only assume is insulting, remember that you do not have to be drawn straight back into the incident you were just moving away from. You can deal with it after the lesson, or when the rest of the pupils are on task. The pupil involved is most likely muttering under their breath for more attention – be it from the friend sat next to them, or in hopes that you will be drawn straight back into the incident all over again. Imagine how this would play out if you did confront them again:

- 'What did you say?'
- 'Nothing.'
- 'Yes you did, I heard you.'
- 'No you didn't.'

You're getting nowhere. And the lesson has stopped again. Remove the audience, reduce the problem.

Application to primary and early years teaching

It is less likely that you will become embroiled in a war of words with a much younger pupil, or find yourself being whispered about by them. However it is important to acknowledge that similar problems do occur:

- **Removing the audience** – in primary school and early years, the audience is more likely to be the pupils themselves rather than attempts to provoke the

(Continued)

(Continued)

teacher. It therefore may be necessary to move the problematic pupil away from their peers, or selectively move their peers away from them.

- **Selectively ignoring** – it may be that a pupil is becoming increasingly frustrating by asking the same questions over and over again, such as 'what do we do now?' or 'why?', or simply stating they 'can't do it / I don't know what I'm doing'. This may be their strategy for more attention, one-to-one help to avoid independent work etc. You could try selectively ignoring such calls if you are confident they are distractive tactics, or alternatively encourage more proactive language in your classroom such as getting pupils to ask themselves 'what parts of this task do I understand, and which parts can I start now?'.

De-escalation of confrontational behaviour

Sometimes a trigger may induce even more challenging behaviour or a lost temper. Learn to spot the signals that behaviour might be about to deteriorate – raised voices, a higher register of voice, unusual behaviour such as a refusal to participate from a normally compliant child. Learn to read body language as well – children will posture before a confrontation so look out for signs like shoulders back, directed stares and making fists.

Control your reactions to avoid escalation. Faced with a 'threat' your body will want to take you into a confrontation. Your adrenalin levels will rise, your emotional barriers will fall. You must, therefore, stay calm and in control. Model the behaviour that you expect from your pupils. Lowering your voice, for example, can often be much more effective than raising it. This in itself may be enough to defuse a situation. You will want to use the tools that work 90% of the time, so may resort to reasoned argument and an appeal to the pupil's sense of responsibility and community. So you could try saying 'you are stopping other children from learning' or make an appeal to their self-image, 'you're just making yourself look silly'. Consider that you are facing a young person who, for whatever reason, has lost his or her temper and read the above – will these really work?

There are three major families of techniques that are proven to defuse challenging situations. Each of these has variations and adaptations that you can develop for your own situation.

Model behaviour. Be excessively polite and make sure that you (and other pupils) are not in anyone's personal space. Remain calm and collected. Acknowledge the source of anger or frustration and empathise: 'I understand why you feel that way, but...' is a powerful opening.

Use the language of choice. Try not to close the door on a situation and allow children room to make their own choice. So, for example, saying 'either move away from Sean, Eddie or you get to eat lunch with me' is more effective than an instruction with no options. Also allow for exit strategies – some of these may be built into a system, such as time-out cards or 'cooling-off' areas.

Distract. This is especially effective if you spot the signs of a situation developing. 'Sean, that's a really excellent piece of work' or 'Fiona, I'd like you to explain how you did that' can have the effect of engaging the brain and disengaging the misbehaviour. This can also be linked to giving responsibility: 'Sean, could you start collecting the materials in, thank-you' effectively moves him away from Eddie and a burgeoning situation.

The behaviour iceberg

As a final thought on behaviour in the classroom, consider the behaviour iceberg. The behaviour you see from a pupil will rarely be based entirely on your lesson. Pupils are unpredictable, as we all are sometimes. Often as teachers we neglect to acknowledge that we are only seeing a snapshot of each child on each day. We don't know what happened the lesson before, at lunchtime, at home, or the night before on Facebook. All of these factors contribute towards pupils' behaviour in your lesson. You have very little, if any, control over that. Similarly, those pupils who perhaps display poor behaviour on a regular basis may in fact be displaying comparatively excellent behaviour considering their circumstances. It is a sad fact that some pupils do not have a good support network at home or with friends. In extreme cases, pupils may not be living with either parent, or may be victims of domestic abuse or worse. Some children may have suffered such circumstances that they will be considered to be 'children in crisis' – namely those pupils whose circumstances or experiences will place them outside normal parameters and thus will make your classroom even more challenging. Often the behaviour of such children may be difficult to deal with, ranging from extreme passivity (an unwillingness or inability to contribute) to attention-seeking episodes such as temper tantrums. Triggers for such behaviours could be illnesses, specialised medical conditions, or periods of crisis in a child's life. At an individual level these can range from family issues such as divorce, bereavement, sibling rivalry, and family illness (that could mean a child has carer responsibilities), to social issues such as domestic violence/abuse, peer or group pressure to commit crime, bullying, and alcohol- or drug-related issues, as well as sexual and biological issues such as developing sexuality and pregnancy. Issues could be as simple as children seeking attention because they are not loved to complex medical conditions that will require professional intervention. Children may have borne witness to events that have affected them, or be in communities whose standards may be at odds with those of their school. There are, for example, large groups such as refugees or asylum seekers who may carry horrific experiences with them. There may be children who do not share the usual mores of a classroom, often due to lack of experience (e.g. Roma children who have no background of education). If these conditions are the basis on which a pupil has learnt 'acceptable' behaviours, it is perhaps not surprising that their actions and reactions towards others are considered appropriate by them and inappropriate by us.

Conclusion

Unusual or trying circumstances don't make poor behaviour excusable, but may go some way to make it understandable. In such cases, the best advice is still 'know your class': it is important to be aware of children's circumstances so that you can show appropriate support and empathy. Remember, emotional support is one of the key pillars of the effective classroom (Pianta and Hamre, 2009). Jennings (2014: 6) also emphasises the key role of emotional support:

> Teachers who are skilled at providing emotional support respond to their students with warmth and sensitivity, and they recognize, understand and are responsive to their students' individual needs and perspectives.

Again, the school's own systems are likely to provide the best way to deal with such issues in an expert and professional manner.

Summary

- The prerequisite of positive learning behaviour is effective teaching that actively engages pupils in their learning.
- Negative behaviour can be minimised if you develop a positive classroom climate, with effective classroom routines, where the pupils feel safe and secure.
- Praise is the most powerful tool for building pupils' self-esteem in the classroom.
- One of your priorities, as a teacher new to the profession, must be to develop a range of strategies for dealing with low-level disruption and also for maintaining a professional approach to more challenging behaviour.

Key reading

Jennings, P.A. (2014) 'Early childhood teachers' well-being, mindfulness, and self-compassion in relation to classroom quality and attitudes towards challenging students', *Mindfulness*, 1–12.

Powell, S. and Tod, J. (2004) 'A systematic review of how theories explain learning behaviour in school context', in *Research Evidence in Education Library*. London: EPPI-Centre, Social Science Research Unit, Institute of Education.

Rogers, B. (2011) *Classroom behaviour: a practical guide to effective teaching, behaviour management and colleague support*. London: Sage.

References and bibliography

Bennett, T. (2010) *The behaviour guru: behaviour management solutions for teachers*. London: Continuum.

Jennings, P.A. (2014) 'Early childhood teachers' well-being, mindfulness, and self-compassion in relation to classroom quality and attitudes towards challenging students', *Mindfulness*, 1–12.

Ofsted (2014) 'Below the radar – low level disruption in the country's classrooms'. Available at www.gov.uk/government/publications/below-the-radar-low-level-disruption-in-the-countrys-classrooms

Pianta, R.C. and Hamre, B.K. (2009) 'Classroom processes and positive youth development: conceptualizing, measuring, and improving the capacity of interactions between teachers and students', *New Directions in Youth Development*, 121: 33–46.

Rogers, B. (2011) *Classroom behaviour: a practical guide to effective teaching, behaviour management and colleague support*. London: Sage.

Useful websites

Coe et al. (2014) 'What makes great teaching?', The Sutton Trust. Available at www.suttontrust.com/wp-content/uploads/2014/10/What-Makes-Great-Teaching-REPORT.pdf

Ofsted (2014) 'Below the radar – low level disruption in the country's classrooms'. Available at www.gov.uk/government/publications/below-the-radar-low-level-disruption-in-the-countrys-classrooms

Visit https://study.sagepub.com/denby3e for extra resources related to this chapter.

CHAPTER 11

BEGINNING TO UNDERSTAND HOW YOUNG PEOPLE LEARN

Neil Denby

Standards linked to this chapter include...

1. Set high expectations which inspire, motivate and challenge pupils
   - establish a safe and stimulating environment for pupils, rooted in mutual respect
   - set goals that stretch and challenge pupils of all backgrounds, abilities and dispositions.
2. Promote good progress and outcomes by pupils
   - demonstrate knowledge and understanding of how pupils learn and how this impacts on teaching
   - encourage pupils to take a responsible and conscientious attitude to their own work and study.

4. Plan and teach well structured lessons
   - impart knowledge and develop understanding through effective use of lesson time
   - promote a love of learning and children's intellectual curiosity.

Introduction

As a trainee or beginning teacher new to the profession, it is easy to think that teaching is pretty much one-way traffic. The teacher teaches, the children learn. But if you remember your own time at school, or draw on your experience as a parent, you will remember that the process of teaching and learning is very much a two-way one. Teaching and learning have to take place together as even though they are often separated as subject matter, they are intertwined and mutually dependent. What is learning? To say that learning has taken place, changes must occur in knowledge, skills, abilities – what may be called competencies – and/or behaviour (Woolfolk, 2010). Such changes should be permanent, and in many cases are measurable. Learning is impossible, however, if communication is not effective and clear. Communication itself is only effective if it is two-way and therefore involves feedback.

Communication

The traditional model of communication is shown in Figure 11.1. In this model there is any amount of coding and decoding taking place and therefore there are vast possibilities for misunderstanding. In the learning situation, a teacher has to first code the message – this means putting it into a form that can be understood, such as writing, pictures or images. Even at this stage, some codes may be better understood than others. The teacher then decides how the message will be transmitted, in what format, and through what medium. The child receives the message and first has to separate it from what communication theory refers to as 'noise'. This is all the other messages and distractions that are being dealt with. In the classroom these can include cultural influences, peer pressure, the outside world, interruptions from peers, and physical messages such as 'I'm too hot' or 'I'm hungry'. Only when the noise is dealt with can the receiver then concentrate on the message. They can only understand this if they understand the coding and have access to the medium; they can only demonstrate that they understand it by supplying the appropriate feedback – i.e. another transmission, in another medium, and also coded.

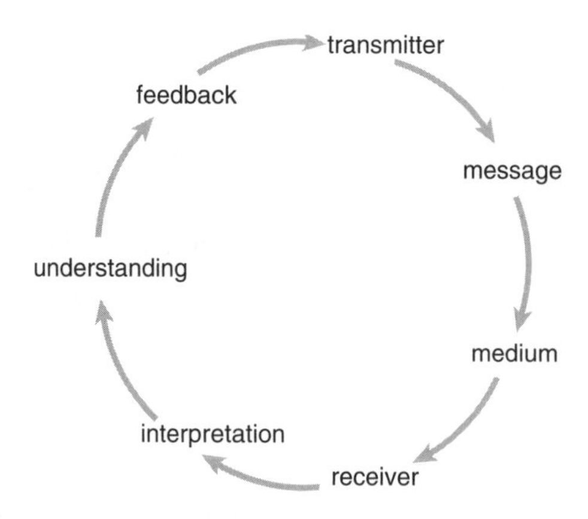

Figure 11.1 Traditional model of communication

A thought

Think about it. To ask the simple question 'What is 2 + 2?' and receive the answer '4' is a complex process. The questioner has coded this question in language and symbols. The '+' or the word 'plus' may not be within the child's understanding. There is an implied notion that this is a calculation, but no concrete instruction. The respondent has to deal with abstracts and respond with the appropriate symbol. Now think about some of the questions you have asked in class and you may realise why these did not meet with an instant response!

If we accept Mehrabian's (1971, 1981) model of communication then things become even more difficult. Mehrabian claims that communication has three clear facets, and that only one of these (and a minor one) is the actual words spoken. Just 7 per cent of meaning is in the words that are spoken, whereas 38 per cent of meaning is in the way that the words are said (called paralinguistics) and 55 per cent of meaning is in facial expression and body language. For a teacher's words to carry meaning, the message must be conveyed in a way that clarifies the meaning rather than obscures it. So, for example, a child who cannot properly see the teacher is at an immediate disadvantage. Vygotsky (1978) claimed that if we are to define a species by the tools that it uses, then communication is the main tool that defines *homo sapiens*.

A thought

A message can often be misunderstood because of cultural differences. For example, in certain African cultures to look straight at a superior (such as a teacher) is seen as an act of bravado or defiance. In a Western culture that insists that 'you look at me when I'm telling you off' this can therefore create a problem. A boy would show a culturally correct attitude by keeping his eyes downcast while his teacher would expect acknowledgement of the reprimand through eye contact.

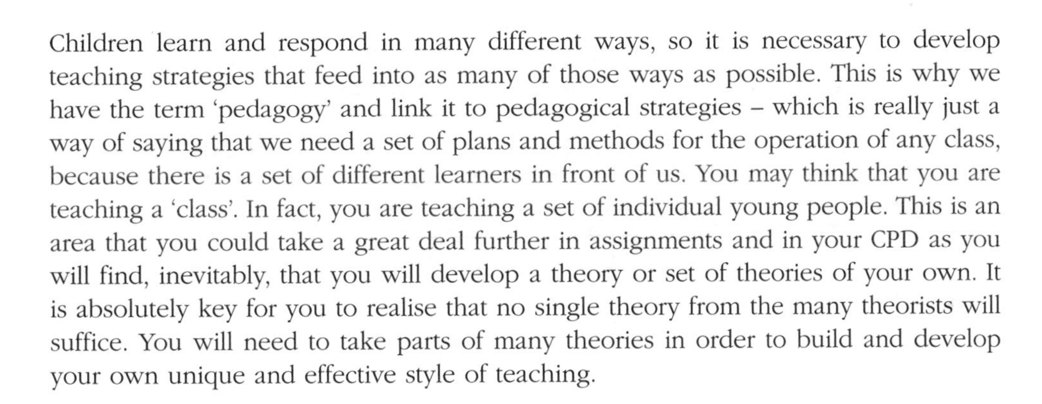

Children learn and respond in many different ways, so it is necessary to develop teaching strategies that feed into as many of those ways as possible. This is why we have the term 'pedagogy' and link it to pedagogical strategies – which is really just a way of saying that we need a set of plans and methods for the operation of any class, because there is a set of different learners in front of us. You may think that you are teaching a 'class'. In fact, you are teaching a set of individual young people. This is an area that you could take a great deal further in assignments and in your CPD as you will find, inevitably, that you will develop a theory or set of theories of your own. It is absolutely key for you to realise that no single theory from the many theorists will suffice. You will need to take parts of many theories in order to build and develop your own unique and effective style of teaching.

Why do children learn?

> One of the most deeply held beliefs about learning is that learning is undertaken 'for its own sake'... But the idea of learning as a marketable commodity and the idea of learning for its own sake both leave out the use that learning can be to the individual and to the quality of thought. Learning is never for its own sake in the sense of some higher reach of abstraction that enables each person to escape the realities of life. Learning continues to have a distinct purpose for the individual and for the individual's relationship to others. (Cullingford, 1990: 206–7)

Children and young people (and everyone else) learn because they want to. This may be triggered by a need that might be utilitarian – survival, a better job, an enjoyable skill – or by a desire to learn for more esoteric reasons (although Cullingford would see a more selfish purpose to such learning). If young people don't want to learn a specific concept, method or process, it will be because they don't see the need for it or its application to their lives. If we can introduce this need, the learning becomes imperative.

When people need to learn, they are much more efficient learners. Should you ever find yourself in a foreign country and not proficient in the language of that country, you will understand what is meant by the need to learn. Often this need is strongly linked to a survival instinct and may involve learning a skill. The first major steps in learning that a child takes are walking and talking – both extremely complex operations which carry some risk. Parents know instinctively what sort of progress their child should be making and may reintroduce a need if progress appears to be halted. For example, a child who can crawl effectively and efficiently may be slow to learn to walk. Parents therefore may move the furniture to reinforce that need. As Moylett (2006: 111) says: 'We are all competent learners from birth and it is usually our parents who give us the confidence to keep learning and stretch the boundaries of our understanding.'

Speech is learnt through copying, repetition and reward. A child needs to learn language if they are to be efficient at expressing needs – 'I am hungry, I want that, let me go' – in ways other than gesture and crying. A child is even proficient enough to learn much of the code that messages are couched in both verbally and non-verbally. They need to learn, so they do so efficiently and effectively. According to Tony Buzan (1995: 28):

> The young child's ability to learn language involves him in processes which include a subtle control of, and an inherent understanding of, rhythm, mathematics, music, physics, linguistics, spatial relations, memory, integration, creativity, logical reasoning and thinking …

Teachers may try to introduce a 'need' at various stages ('you need this examination result in order to …' is typical) but the focus should really be on the 'want'. What is it that can make a child or young person want to learn?

Wanting to learn

The word that we use for 'wanting' to do something is motivation. What motivates a person to work harder or do better? There are many external influences on the child (and much research into their effects) that are, in the main, beyond teacher control. The influence of culture or society, for example, may be extremely powerful. There may be cultural events or obligations taking place that serve as 'noise' as far as learning is concerned. There may also be mixed messages – with the home teaching one outlook or set of values, and the school another.

INDIVIDUAL REFLECTION

Are the 'British Values' included in the Teacher Standards (and made part of the Ofsted inspection framework) actually 'British' or really universal values that apply to all cultures? What would you add to or subtract from them to make them universal?

The influence of parents and the home is also paramount. How well educated are the parents? Are there books in the home? Is access to knowledge easy? Is there a quiet space to work? Is there access to technology? All of these will have an effect on a child's ability to study and learn. Social factors have a significant effect on learning. According to the Rowntree Foundation (Hirsch, 2007), 'Children growing up in poverty and disadvantage are less likely to do well at school. This feeds into disadvantage in later life and in turn affects their children.'

Peer group pressure is also influential. Is the child part of a social group where learning is applauded, or where it is seen as 'soft' or conformist and therefore to be avoided? This is the home territory for much bullying behaviour.

A thought

Praise is free and extremely powerful. Use praise as a tool in the classroom. Smile and give positive feedback. Even if a child has got it wrong, you should find some area to praise before putting them on the right lines. This builds self-esteem and creates feelings of security and social acceptance – the first steps before Maslow's higher order needs can be tackled and the basis for Herzberg's ideas (see below).

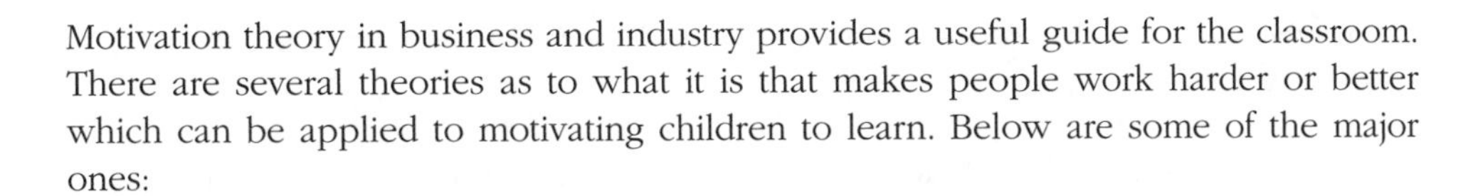

Motivation theory in business and industry provides a useful guide for the classroom. There are several theories as to what it is that makes people work harder or better which can be applied to motivating children to learn. Below are some of the major ones:

- **Frederick W. Taylor** (1856–1917) was an American who sought greater efficiency in engineering plants. He pioneered a 'carrot and stick' approach through Scientific Management Theory. This meant rewards for those who worked hard enough and penalties for those who didn't. Although now pretty much defunct in industry, this model does still find its way into the classroom.
- **A.H. Maslow** (1908–1970) is perhaps the best known motivational theorist. He said that people worked in order to climb a 'hierarchy of needs'. Starting with survival, people then sought safety and security, then social and family fulfilment, then status, and finally what Maslow called self-actualisation needs. We might think of this better as ambition or fulfilment, which implies that children must feel safe, secure and socially accepted before there is any real motivation to learn 'outside' of this structure.
- **Frederick Herzberg** (1923–2000) came to similar conclusions as those of Maslow. He asked workers what motivated them and found out that the main things were

a 'job well done', a feeling of being appreciated, trust, responsibility and promotion. One of the major factors which demotivated people was if a job was boring. Some conditions, which Herzberg called 'hygiene' factors, were also discovered to make people unhappy, and demotivate them, if they were missing or poor. In work terms these were good pay and working conditions. In learning terms these were the creation of an atmosphere for learning – a clean, bright, safe and attractive classroom space, for example, where children felt they had some ownership.

- **Victor Vroom** (b. 1932) introduced expectancy theory or the path–goal concept. His contention was that motivation could be linked to goals. If these goals were seen as attainable, workers would work towards them. If they were seen to be out of reach, workers were demotivated. This is important when you are thinking of setting targets – there must be intermediate targets, i.e. small incremental steps that can be attained by each individual on their way to the main goal.

One strong area of motivation comes in being able to succeed in producing the results required. This, known as efficacy, is essential to good teaching. Teaching is a challenge, and learners will present many different tests – of patience, knowledge and skills. Teachers who have succeeded in the past will see these as challenges, and rise to them, rather than perceiving them as problems. As Saylor (2010: 55) states:

> A strong sense of efficacy enhances individual accomplishment and personal wellbeing in many instances. People with strong perceived capabilities approach more difficult tasks and see them as challenges rather than threats.

From where does such a sense of efficacy stem? Generally from having proved oneself in some way:

> For teachers, it is being able to face a situation or problem and know that they can deal with it. 'Mastery experiences are the most effective source of beliefs in one's capabilities, as success builds a strong belief that one can be successful in the future.' (Saylor, 2010: 55)

For pupils, self-efficacy is the extent or strength of belief in their ability to complete tasks and reach goals. Bandura (1986) suggests that pupils with higher self-efficacy work harder, continue to try for longer, persevere when faced with a struggle, are more optimistic and less anxious, and achieve greater results. Ways in which self-efficacy may be increased include co-operative learning and progress comparisons with goals, not peers. Goals should be specific, short term and attainable, and pupils should share responsibility for their own progress (Schunk and Pajares, 2002): 'We decrease self-efficacy if instruction is inflexible and pupil involvement in planning is discouraged; also if we compare pupil's progress with each other, rather than an objective (and personalised) measurement.'

Ability to learn

You may think that one of the main factors that influences learning is the innate ability to learn carried by each child. But here the science becomes, at best, fuzzy. There is no accepted measure of intelligence. It has long been accepted that IQ tests are more to do with technique and repetition than any objective measurement. Neuroscientists (and their imitators) have discovered much more about the brain than was ever known before: it can grow; it can become more efficient; it can recover from serious trauma in unexpected ways; it responds to certain stimuli. The TED talk by Sarah-Jayne Blakemore on the development of the adolescent brain (at www.ted.com/talks/sarah_jayne_blakemore_the_mysterious_workings_of_the_adolescent_brain?language=en) explains some of the more recent advances. Everything from hydration to crossword and number puzzles is claimed to increase brain power, along with vitamin supplements, exercise and fish-oil.[1]

Learning theories

This is a necessarily brief round-up of some key learning theories. Never forget that there are many others, including the one you are just developing to cope with that particularly intransigent class or individual. Those listed below are recognised as the key theories and ideas on which many more variations have been built. Some are directly related to education, others to areas of science, psychology or even business: all can be adapted and adopted to improve learning in your classroom.

Piaget

Jean Piaget (1896–1980) was responsible for cognitive development theory. This is based on the notion that children construct 'cognitive structures' in order to understand and respond to their environment. The structure is a child's reality and it is within this structure that learning takes place. As children get older they move to more complex structures. The school age stages are 'concrete operations' (approximating to ages 7–11) and 'formal operations' (approximating to ages 11–16). In the first of these children can create structures to explain experiences. They gain the ability to see from other perspectives and can tackle a problem using several aspects of it. In the second of these children can 'conceptualise'. They can think in abstract terms and not need the experience in order to learn. This has implications for the stages in which we introduce learning (and therefore for curricular content), and for knowing how far we can step outside the construct. If the learning is sufficiently different, then a child re-forms the construct to take account of this. If it is too different, this lies outside the realm of possible learning (see Vygotsky).

Vygotsky

Lev Vygotsky (1896–1934) moved away from the notion of 'stages of development'. It was his contention that development was too complex to be divided into stages, but presented a continuum. His social constructivist theory examined the idea of a 'zone of proximal development' (ZPD). This required analysis of where a child is today and where a teacher wants them to be. The teacher then provides the 'scaffolding' to get them there. Vygotsky described this as follows: '… the distance between the actual development level as determined by independent problem solving and the level of potential development as determined through problem solving under adult guidance or in collaboration with more capable peers' (Vygotsky, 1978: 86). Vygotsky also emphasised the importance of social interaction in helping learning to take place, and therefore the central role of communication.

Learning outside the ZPD is not assimilated by the child (see Piaget) so it must be incremental, based on current knowledge and understanding. The notion of collaboration is also an important one. The implications for the classroom are that learning should take place in a spirit of teamwork and cooperation, desks should be grouped, and teachers should be supportive facilitators rather than instructors.

Skinner

B.F. Skinner (1904–1990) first aired his ideas on operant conditioning in the 1930s. His work was built on the classical conditioning work of Pavlov. Operant conditioning means that learning has taken place when there is an observable change in the behaviour of the learner as a result of teaching. Learning in operant conditioning occurs when 'a proper response is demonstrated following the presentation of a stimulus' (Ertmer and Newby, 1993: 55). There are three stages to the learning which may be looked at as a question and answer technique:

- a stimulus (the question)
- a response (the answer)
- reinforcement (praise for the right answer or correction).

The major criticism of behaviourism is that it gives learners only a passive role. There is no journey of discovery, just a response to what is being taught. It may be compared more to 'training' than 'education' as it does not require understanding or insight. Skinner refuted this and saw learners as active. In operant conditioning, in particular, the difference is that the learner is having an effect, i.e. acting on, rather than passively being acted on (Woolfolk, 2010). Skinner saw three necessary parts for learning – doing, experiencing and practising – which together would form a change in behaviour which would then be measurable. The implications for modern teaching lie in taking small steps, building learning and reinforcement.

INDIVIDUAL REFLECTION

Look at two or three of your lesson plans that form a sequence. State how each addressed different learning styles. Consider if you could have introduced other styles. Look at the progression of the lessons. Consider whether or not you are building in incremental steps, or making leaps from one level to another. What exercises or activities could you build in to ensure that learning is taking place and understanding is growing?

Bruner

Jerome Bruner (b. 1915) is another constructivist.[2] He maintains that learning is an active process. Learners build further knowledge on that which they already possess. There are appropriate classroom conditions to make this happen. The learning space and atmosphere must be conducive to learning, making learners ready to learn (readiness). Spiral organisation of knowledge should make this more accessible to learners; learning should be sequential, and a process of building. Learners should be encouraged to extrapolate or extend from knowledge to fill in the gaps for themselves in what has been termed a 'learning journey'. The implications of this for teaching are that the teacher should act as a facilitator to enable learners to discover for themselves. A question and answer technique creates a dialogue where discovery can take place. The curriculum should be designed as a spiral, so that learners are continually building on knowledge already gained. Bruner's final proposition is often overlooked – that there should be appropriate rewards and punishments (see motivation, above).

Bandura

Albert Bandura (b. 1925) – another pyschologist rather than an educationalist – developed social cognitive theory, which proposes that learning takes place when a learner observes others, particularly in social settings. He foresaw the central role of media in education, as this provides many different and unique examples of behaviour that can be observed. He also stated that learners who have self-efficacy – an individual belief in their power to learn – are more likely to succeed. Strategies to increase efficacy include achievable short-term goals, cooperative learning, positive and regular feedback, and student-centred approaches such as student-created learning plans and tasks rooted in student interests.

Kolb

Kolb's (b. 1941) experiential learning cycle draws on the work of Piaget and others. He sees a cycle of learning, which he represents diagrammatically as a circle (see Figure 11.2), emphasising that learning is a continual process rather than having a single measurable outcome. Its four stages are concrete experience, reflective observation, abstract conceptualisation, and active experimentation. It can be summarised as 'do, review, learn, apply'. The teacher provides pupils with a concrete experience. This should be active rather than passive, so the verbal 'I talk, you listen' instruction is weak. Role play, trying out, a demonstration or other stimulus close to 'doing' are needed. Students then review the experience and discuss what happened and why. Phase 3 sees learners asking why this happened, would it happen again and using 'what if ' questions to build general principles. Finally, they test or apply these principles, which feeds into another round of 'doing'. As a teacher, you would be encouraging pupils to learn from experience and then apply that learning in new situations. Honey and Mumford (1982) developed this further into learning styles for 'activists', 'reflectors', 'theorists' and 'pragmatists'. The mistake which many beginning teachers make is to think of these as absolutes, when any style might suit a child depending on the situation.

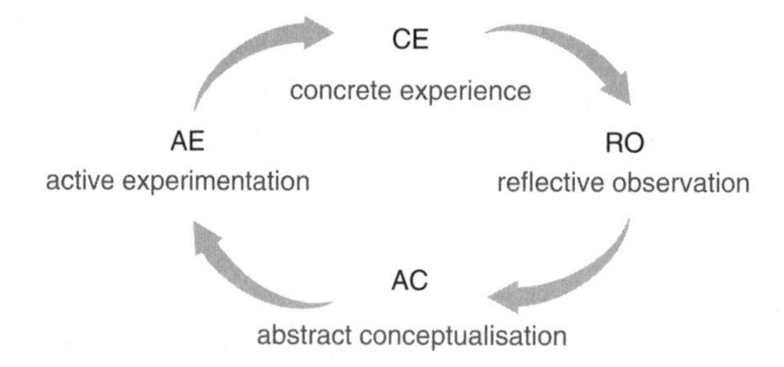

Figure 11.2 Kolb's experiential learning circle

(Source: Kolb, D. A. (©1984) *Experiential learning: Experience as a source of learning and development* (1st edn). Reprinted and electronically reproduced with the permission of Pearson Education Inc., New York, NY)

Gardner

Howard Gardner's (b. 1943)[3] concept of multiple intelligences was published in the book *Frames of mind* in 1983, and although not specific to education was immediately seized on by the educational community. He posited seven 'intelligences'. While these are not directly related to learning styles, nevertheless they suggest that each intelligence is closely linked to a particular way of learning. In more recent work Gardner has added three more (naturalist, linked to the natural environment; spiritual/existential, linked to religion; and moral or ethical).

The seven original intelligences (very briefly outlined) are:

- **Linguistic** – learning through words and language. Would typically be comfortable learning from or doing writing, reading, speaking out loud.
- **Logical-mathematical** – learning through logical thinking. Typically learns best when involved in analysis, measurement, logic, problem solving, incremental learning.

- **Musical** – learning through music. Happiest when performing, writing about music, detecting rhythm.
- **Bodily-kinaesthetic** – learning through bodily movement. Would typically be comfortable learning through role play, drama, construction activities.
- **Spatio-visual** – learning through pictures and images. Typically learns best when creating a picture or design or working with shapes.
- **Interpersonal** – learning through the ability to relate to others. Happiest when involved in human contact, empathising, working in teams or groups, relying on others.
- **Intrapersonal** – learning through understanding self, being adaptable, negotiating positive outcomes. Works best when working for self-improvement, or when a personal gain or reward can be seen from a learning activity.

Gardner's criticism was that schools and teaching focused too closely on linguistic and logical-mathematical intelligences, and insufficiently on the others, denying some children the opportunity to succeed. The theory of multiple intelligences gained the attention of the educational world and has led to some significant rethinking of styles of teaching.

GROUP EXERCISE

Discuss with other members of your cohort how each of you feels they learn best. Write three lesson plans in your subject area. Each should be attempting to teach the same content, but approaching it in a different style. Exchange lesson plans so that each is reviewed by a person who stated a preference for that style. How would they improve it? Now exchange plans so that each is reviewed by someone who preferred a different style. Discuss how the plan could be changed to incorporate both styles.

Buzan

Tony Buzan (b. 1942) has pioneered the 'two brain' theory of cognition and learning and is the inventor of mind-mapping. (You should note that this is a trade-protected name, whose creation is according to strict rules, and not the same as a bubble or spider diagram.) The left side of the brain (numbers, lists, words, logic, analysis, sequence, linearity) must be paired with the right side (rhythm, spatial, Gestalt, imagination, colour, creativity) to bring about true learning and begin to open up the potential of the brain. Learning activities which engage both sides of the brain result in 'synergy' – this may be stated as '1+1 is greater than 2' where the '1s' represent each side of the brain, meaning a greater gain than the addition alone would achieve. Mind-mapping helps learning through assisting study, recall and understanding.

Application to secondary teaching: case study

A beginning teacher in a science lesson planned (with a lower ability group) for them to understand how physicists know that the universe is expanding by teaching them the concept of 'red shift' in light waves. To do this, he began by teaching the 'Doppler effect' of sound waves. Pupils were questioned on how they heard trains or traffic approaching and leaving; on how they heard sirens on emergency vehicles; on what this told them about the direction of travel. They were able to identify what happened to the sound, and with the help of the teacher successfully conclude that the shape of the sound waves changed as the vehicle approached or left. From this they could deduce that if they knew how the sound wave was behaving, they could predict accurately the direction of travel. Some even realised that they could predict the speed of the vehicle. The last ten minutes of the lesson consisted of the teacher explaining that light waves behaved in the same way as sound waves, and that we could tell this by the way the colour of the light changed as the light wavelength increased, called 'red shift'. Looking at the light from further astronomical objects, such as distant stars, scientists could therefore conclude that the universe was expanding.

The pupils, who had enthusiastically grasped the concept of changing sound wavelengths, became confused and restless towards the end of the lesson, and conversations with them showed that not only had they not understood about red shift, but that it had undermined what they thought they had understood about sound waves.

What had happened and why? Can you link this experience to any of the theories outlined? How would you suggest that the lesson was planned and delivered differently?

VAK

The Visual-Auditory-Kinaesthetic or VAK model is probably most closely associated with Montessori schools in the Victorian era. Maria Montessori was the first woman to receive a medical degree from the University of Rome. Her research and innovations concentrated on early years education and the key developmental periods of the child. She, along with colleagues, used the scientific method to study ways to educate those with physical or mental problems that prevented them from learning. VAK was promoted as a way of reaching this group for whom conventional teaching could be a problem. It recognises that people have broadly different preferred learning styles. Learning may be preferred through pictures and images, sound and speech, or movement and touch. It is a feature of much good teaching that it builds opportunities to access each style into a lesson. VARK may be used to add an additional 'Read/Write' category to extend the accuracy of the original 'Visual/Auditory' one.

There are numerous free tests available on the internet for checking which is your (or a pupil's) preferred learning style. However, beware of nailing your colours to any one mast as learning styles will change with the subject, situation, mood, context – even the weather! The key to good teaching (and therefore good learning) is variation and variety in approach. VAK is not a cure-all, and the inclusion of it in lesson plans does not mean that you will necessarily reach everyone in a class. It should therefore be treated with some caution, as many see it as some kind of panacea. What VAK does do is ensure that you have a variety of approaches in a lesson, and this is something that is good practice anyway. Different approaches, changes in activities, transition activities – all of these contribute towards better learning by providing variety and maintaining interest.

Connectivism

Theories develop from each other, borrowing from here and there to form another way of operating. Psychology borrows from Buzan in claiming interconnectedness as a prerequisite for learning. This 'connectionism', based on nodes and links, is applied to education as connectivism – a learning theory that sits well with new technology in its dependency on communication channels, nodes and networks. Siemens (2005) calls it a 'learning theory for the digital age', with its clear reflection of how technology makes sense of a confused world as being something that human learners can adopt. Our learners now communicate via social networking sites, email and text, and these are aspects that we can include in our teaching. Indeed, the use of popular culture to enhance learning is not only proposed but also actively encouraged. Using social networks, video (such as YouTube) and music tracks in teaching and learning enhances the experience (and leads to yet more theories) (Gertrudix and Gertrudix, 2010). In connectivism, the strength of the communication channels connecting the nodes is implicitly important and can be enhanced through technology. Edward de Bono and his 'lateral thinking' ideas would support the idea of seeing connections as part of a whole as being vital, as would Tony Buzan, quoting the right-brain's ability to see the *Gestalt*, or whole picture. This organic growth and development of learning theories has always been the case, but may now move even more rapidly as discussion takes place via blogs and the internet rather than through learned journals.

Application to primary and early years teaching

Teachers in the primary classroom have to keep learners engaged and interested all of the time – this age group is unlikely to be sufficiently socialised to show patience, or to wait for further instructions before proceeding. This means that all parts of the lesson have to be active yet controlled. Even transitions can be used to reinforce learning. For example, when moving from one area to another, or from group work to pair work or individual work, the transition can be accomplished efficiently with a countdown (say 20 seconds to achieve it). This maintains pace and underlines the transition. In addition, this can be made into a learning activity: for example, how about carrying out the countdown in a different language each time? This also has the benefit of raising awareness of other languages and cultures.

Application to secondary teaching

One way to build in a variety of learning approaches, adaptable to any subject, is to introduce a topic in such a way that learners feel they have ownership. Separate the class into groups of four if this is possible. Each group is given a particular set of arguments or point of view. For example, in business education or economics (or PSHE) the groups could be looking at a proposed project from the viewpoints of different stakeholder groups. A new supermarket development, for example, may be welcomed by one part of the community for reasons of cheapness and ease of access, made unwelcome by local businesses, supported by a local authority that will gain revenue, opposed by conservationists, and supported by shareholders in hopes of increased profits. Each group is presented with just one point of view and has to develop an argument to support this viewpoint. This in turn should encourage collaboration and expression. Ownership will usually become so embedded that finding a solution will become difficult, and participants can empathise with similar real-world situations. This allows for group and team work, for participants to build on their own experiences, for different learning styles to be adopted by group members in a natural style, and for ownership of the learning. All of these are powerful influences on good learning.

Conclusion

There are many other theorists, some of whom you may feel should have been included. Is it fair, for example, to not explore de Bono and lateral thinking, or

Belbin and his discussion of the power and place of team roles applied to group learning? The answer is that you should construct your own theory, one that chimes with your own practice and experience, and remember that all those mentioned are just that – theories – and only valid if they work in your particular situation, with yourself and your learners. As teachers, we have to recognise that every child is good at something, that all children have areas where they can shine. Every child, every pupil, has immense potential which is often, sadly, not realised. At least part of our job as teachers is to remove any extraneous factors that may be preventing that potential being reached and to add any factors that we think might smooth the path. So there is no harm in making sure that learners are comfortable, feel safe, and are not put under undue pressure or tension. We can use music and movement, pictures and stories, role-play and drama, to reach as many learners and learning styles as possible. We can look at Maslow again – if a learner is hungry or thirsty, tired or threatened, uncomfortable or bullied, then learning will suffer. Use your common sense to develop your own theory that is unique to your situation and works.

Summary

- You should develop your own theory of learning, cherry picking from those outlined in the chapter the ones that work for you, in your classroom, at this time.
- Don't forget the common-sense notions about comfort, safety and security – creating an atmosphere where learning will take place.
- Use a variety of approaches and you will reach a variety of learners.
- Review lesson plans and units and schemes of work regularly to make sure that different styles are catered for.
- Individuals and small groups learn better than large groups. Giving individual attention, or facilitating group discussion, is still teaching – you don't have to stand at the front and expound!

Notes

1. Commercial concerns are not averse to skewing 'research' to try to make it look as if their product is effective. Read about the Durham fish-oil 'trials' at www.badscience.net/2007/09/ the-fishy-reckoning/
2. You can listen to Bruner being interviewed by visiting http://luria.ucsd.edu/Luria.mov
3. Gardner can be heard via podcast and seen via video on his own website at www.howard gardner.com/

Key reading

Ertmer, P.A. and Newby, T.J. (1993) 'Behaviorism, cognitivism, constructivism: comparing critical features from an instructional design perspective', *Performance Improvement Quarterly,* 6 (4): 50–72.

Hirsch, D. (2007) *Experiences of poverty and educational disadvantage.* Joseph Rowntree Foundation. Available at www.jrf.org.uk/knowledge/findings/socialpolicy/2123.asp

Moylett, H. (2006) 'Supporting children's development and learning', in T. Bruce (ed.), *Early childhood.* London: Sage. pp. 106–26.

Woolfolk, A. (2010) *Educational psychology* (11th edn). Upper Saddle River, NJ: Pearson Education.

References and bibliography

Bandura, A. (1986) *Social foundations of thought and action: a social cognitive theory.* Englewood Cliffs, NJ: Prentice-Hall.

Bruner, J. (1960) *The process of education.* Cambridge, MA: Harvard University Press.

Bruner, J. (1996) *The culture of education.* Cambridge, MA: Harvard University Press.

Buzan, T. (1995) *Use your head.* London: BBC Books.

Cullingford, C. (1990) *The nature of learning.* London: Cassell.

Ertmer, P.A. and Newby, T.J. (1993) 'Behaviorism, cognitivism, constructivism: comparing critical features from an instructional design perspective', *Performance Improvement Quarterly,* 6 (4): 50–72.

Gardner, H. (1993) *Frames of mind: the theory of multiple intelligences* (2nd edn). New York: Basic Books.

Gertrudix, M. and Gertrudix, F. (2010) 'La utilidad de los formatos de interacción músico-visual en la enseñanza' [The utility of musico-visual formats in teaching], *Comunicar,* 17 (34): 99–107.

Hirsch, D. (2007) *Experiences of poverty and educational disadvantage.* Joseph Rowntree Foundation. Available at www.jrf.org.uk/knowledge/findings/socialpolicy/2123.asp

Honey, P. and Mumford, A. (1982) *Manual of Learning Styles.* London: Peter Honey Publications.

Kolb, D.A. (1984) *Experiential learning: experience as the source of learning and development.* Englewood Cliffs, NJ: Prentice-Hall.

Mehrabian, A. (1971) *Silent messages.* Belmont, CA: Wadsworth.

Mehrabian, A. (1981) *Silent messages: implicit communication of emotions and attitudes* (2nd edn). Belmont, CA: Wadsworth.

Moylett, H. (2006) 'Supporting children's development and learning', in T. Bruce (ed.), *Early childhood.* London: Sage, pp. 106–26.

Saylor, C. (2010) 'Learning theories applied to curriculum development', in S. Keating (ed.), *Curriculum development and evaluation in nursing* (2nd edn). New York: Springer.

Schunk, D.H. and Pajares, F. (2002) 'The development of academic self-efficacy', in A. Wigfield and J.S. Eccles (eds), *Development of achievement motivation.* San Diego, CA: Academic Press, pp. 15–31.

Siemens, G. (2005) *International Journal of Instructional Technology and Distance Learning,* 2 (1) January.

Vygotsky, L.S. (1978) *Mind and society: the development of higher mental processes* (edited by M. Cole, V. John-Steiner, S. Scribner and E. Souberman). Cambridge, MA: Harvard University Press.

Woolfolk, A. (2010) *Educational psychology* (11th edn). Upper Saddle River, NJ: Pearson Education.

Visit https://study.sagepub.com/denby3e for extra resources related to this chapter.

CHAPTER 12

APPROACHES TO TEACHING AND LEARNING 1: DEVELOPING A RANGE

Joanne Pearson

Standards linked to this chapter include...

1. Set high expectations which inspire, motivate and challenge pupils
   - set goals that stretch and challenge pupils of all backgrounds, abilities and dispositions.
2. Promote good progress and outcomes by pupils
   - demonstrate knowledge and understanding of how pupils learn and how this impacts on teaching
   - encourage pupils to take a responsible and conscientious attitude to their own work and study.

4. Plan and teach well-structured lessons
   - impart knowledge and develop understanding through effective use of lesson time
   - promote a love of learning and children's intellectual curiosity.
5. Adapt teaching to respond to the strengths and needs of all pupils
   - know when and how to differentiate appropriately, using approaches which enable pupils to be taught effectively
   - have a secure understanding of how a range of factors can inhibit pupils' ability to learn, and how best to overcome these.

Introduction

You will not need to be very long in the teaching profession before you realise that it is impossible to separate teaching, learning and behaviour. These cannot be viewed in isolation – to do so is to reduce teaching to telling, learning to listening, and behaviour to sitting still and being quiet. It is perfectly possible to imagine a lesson in which a teacher talked, the pupils copied from a book and were quiet and stayed in their seats (you may even recall such lessons from your own schooldays), but was anything learned? This example is an exercise in the occupation of children rather than in their learning. The aim of teaching is to add to pupils' knowledge, skills and understanding, and so as a teacher you will need to be able to plan for lessons in which children learn rather than just behave.

Establishing effective relationships

The relationship between teaching and learning takes place within a personal relationship: that of the teacher and the pupil. Every pupil, and teacher, arrives at each lesson with a different set of needs and expectations. Managing these differing needs, adapting to the demands of 30 different people within one room, is one of the most challenging aspects of teaching. Some aspects of this are beyond the control of one teacher. For example, pupils' previous experiences will affect their attitude to school, to the teacher, and to the subject being taught. Within the classroom you will need to establish ways of creating positive relationships with pupils that will aid their learning rather than just their behaviour. This can be termed 'affective learning' – the learning of emotions or attitudes. As Shoffner (2008: 788) puts it, we should '... accept that teaching involves both head and heart, both reason and passion ...'. This affective learning supports the cognitive learning of knowledge and skills; indeed it is difficult to imagine how pupils can achieve their cognitive potential in a subject towards which they have very negative feelings. How then can you create positive and effective learning relationships with your pupils?

The art (and heart) of teaching

At the centre of the effective teacher/learner relationship is caring. Do you effectively communicate that you care about, and indeed are passionate about, what you teach? Do you communicate the importance, relevance and purpose of the subject you are teaching? Do the pupils have a sense of the potential, of the infinite possibilities of learning? Enthusiasm makes you a better teacher. Baumert et al. (2008) showed how the enthusiasm of mathematics teachers for teaching their subject led to higher quality instruction – as rated by both themselves and their students. As a teacher you should always remember the privilege and power the job holds; if you do not seem to believe in what you are teaching, if you cannot be enthusiastic, excited and engaged in the learning, then how can you expect your pupils to feel any different?

Caring also applies to the pupils. Are you interested in them? Do you believe that they can achieve? A passion for a subject will not be enough to establish a positive learning relationship if it is not matched with a passion and belief that all children can achieve and make progress. One of the common fears of beginning teachers is that they will fail, will not be able to 'control' a class or answer a child's question. Children have exactly the same fears in the classroom – they too are afraid of failing, of being labelled as unsuccessful (Cullingford, 2006). Just as trainee teachers need a mentor who believes in them, even when things sometimes go wrong, so pupils need teachers who believe in them, who support them and acknowledge that they have the potential to get better. This can be as simple as learning every child's name, but also encompasses a recognition of the differing needs and achievements of children. Every human enjoys being praised and having their achievements acknowledged and children are no different. As a teacher, it is your job to know and recognise individual pupil achievement. This requires:

- an understanding of what the pupil can already do/knows/understands
- a clear and realistic plan for each pupil's further progression
- an understanding of the specific and particular learning needs that some pupils may have.

Creating a positive learning relationship is the responsibility of the teacher. It can be characterised as the communication that the teacher enjoys their job, the subject they are teaching and the pupils themselves:

> Teaching is more than just a job, more than an intellectual challenge, more than a management task, for whom vocation and commitment are essential features of professionalism.

It is for teachers who are concerned through their work, with education in its broader sense, who acknowledge that emotional engagement and care are essential to good teaching, who are committed to service, and who are, have been or wish to be again, passionate. (Day, 2004: 10)

A thought

There will be some days when you do not want to be in the classroom, some aspects of a subject that you hate to teach, and some pupils that you groan at the thought of teaching. These are the days/lessons/pupils with which you will need to work the hardest. Sometimes this can be as simple as being honest with children: 'I know that iron and steel production is not as exciting as children working in coal mines, but if we do not understand this it means we will not be able to explain why so many children ended up working in coal mines.' On other occasions it is the determination to catch a difficult pupil doing something right and praise them for it. It is the building over time of small bridges like this that can change a pupil's attitude to learning or school.

Teaching strategies

Teaching has been around for a long time (the Ancient Greeks are still a useful starting point for educational philosophy and thought), but we are still in pursuit of 'what works' – that magic pedagogical tool which will allow us to meet the needs of all pupils. Many initiatives over the years have claimed to provide an answer but were based on little research or evidence: specific learning 'styles' (see Chapter 11) and 'Brain Gym' spring to mind. The truth is that defining effective teaching is hard but evidence is beginning to be gathered about practices that have a greater or lesser impact of pupils' performances. The Education Endowment Fund toolkit (http://educationendowmentfoundation.org.uk/toolkit/) and John Hattie's work (see http://visible-learning.org) are excellent starting points but still need to be thought of critically – will that approach work in this setting, and most importantly, *how will I know if it is or isn't working?*

Let's take a very specific example. There are many different approaches that can be adopted to teach a subject. Consider the Five Pillars of Islam as a topic. Pupils could be asked to:

- write a description of each of the Pillars
- draw an illustration to symbolise each of the Pillars

- interview a practising Muslim about the role of the Five Pillars in their life
- answer a series of questions testing their comprehension of the Five Pillars
- undertake a word search
- perform a role play exploring the practice of each of the Pillars.

The list could go on for much longer. There are three questions to be considered here. Of these teaching and learning strategies:

- which is most appropriate for the pupils in terms of supporting their learning (i.e. will allow them to meet the lesson objective)?
- which will challenge and stretch all pupils (i.e. will get pupils to do something more that they could already do)?
- which will enable pupils to make progress in RE (i.e. will be a step in a much bigger journey that fits together as a coherent whole)?

Teaching needs to meet all these needs. The above activities vary in their level of challenge and approach; it is for you as the teacher to consider the appropriateness of an activity for the class and the individual pupils within that class. It is up to you to decide which events or actions are significant, and which of less importance, and therefore which elements of a lesson should be altered or retained (Capel et al., 2009: 65–78). These elements also run alongside other aspects such as the quality of your subject knowledge, your ability to question effectively, the quality of the feedback you give to pupils before, during and after the lesson. A teacher's own subject knowledge has been shown to be a very consistent factor in effective teaching (Coe et al., 2014); if you, as a trainee, do not understand the Pillars of Islam fully prior to planning the lesson you will not be in a position to choose the objective that moves children's learning forward, nor the activity that will support it. If your explanation and questioning during the lesson are perfunctory the pupils may not be able to complete the activity no matter how 'good' it is, and if they cannot see what they have done well/ what they need to do better then how can they move on from this activity to the next step in their learning?

A thought

In any one teaching day you may adopt a variety of strategies as part of your planning. Nevertheless, you might use only a narrow range with each class. How can you monitor the impact each of these strategies has had on the class/ individual pupils so that you know which strategies are appropriate and when?

This is the fundamental job of a teacher and what teaching is – the choice of pedagogical approaches, that knitting together of activities into a scheme of work/ lesson to ensure all the children in your classroom make progress and learn. There is no one magic strategy that will do this, there is only the constant intellectual engagèment with reflection and evidence collection that will allow you to make reasoned judgements as to whether what you are doing is having the desired effect.

Personalised learning

Learning to teach can be divided into three phases (Leask, 2009):

- the first, in which you evaluate the experience you as a teacher have gone through
- the second, in which you start to focus on the experience of the class as a whole
- the third, in which you focus on pupils' individual learning. This can be termed personalised learning.

Personalised learning – namely the need to cater for all children in schools – may be a relatively recent term, but it has been part of the job of a teacher for much longer. It is important enough that we have devoted a whole chapter to it (see Chapter 14), but it is still worth exploring here. All children have different needs, not just those who may be identified in a formal way as having additional needs. A single lesson plan will illuminate the strategies you will adopt on a holistic level (and indeed may highlight specific strategies for some individuals within the class), but it is in the lesson itself that the interaction and support for the individuals within that class will be evidenced. What then might this look like?

One of the key indicators is the amount of time you as a teacher spend talking to individual pupils. Feedback has been suggested by the EEF (http://educationendowmentfoundation.org.uk/toolkit/feedback/) to have the most positive impact on pupil attainment for the least cost and not all feedback can be written. For example, what is the value in writing reams of feedback on Year 1 work if they cannot read or understand it? And who is this for? Oral feedback is still feedback and may be much more effective. This is not to say that direct instruction (talking from the front) is to be cut short, indeed research has shown it can be a more effective method of teaching than 'discovery learning' (Kirshner et al., 2006). Also clearly there are times within a planning cycle, for example at the start of a new topic or when explaining a new concept or skill, when you may need to have some didactic teacher talk. However, over a number of lessons your time with a class will need to be more equitably distributed so that more one-to-one time is developed. One of the ways a teacher can personalise a lesson is by talking, supporting, questioning and challenging individual pupils. This cannot always be done from the front of the room. It is also useful to ask the following questions as part of your reflection both during and after the lesson:

- How many of the pupils grasped the main points I was trying to get across?
- To which aspects might I need to return?
- How can I revisit areas of learning in a new way to support those who have struggled in this lesson?
- How can I, later on, reinforce and consolidate what they have learned successfully?

INDIVIDUAL REFLECTION

Observe two or three lessons and note down the movement of the teacher and his or her contact with individual pupils. How much of the lesson was spent talking to the whole class? How much time was spent working with individual pupils? What was the nature of the whole-class talk? Was it instructions, explanations, classroom management, praise? What was the nature of the individual teacher/pupil talk? Was it a clarification of the content or instruction, questioning, praise or chastisement? Who talked most in these exchanges – the teacher or the pupils? What evidence could you observe about the effect of the teacher/pupil talk?

Whole-class questioning and discussion can inform you about much of the understanding and learning in the room and of individual pupils, but it will not do this automatically and so you will need both to plan for it and monitor it.

Equally, productive interaction between teacher and pupil is not just conversations in which the teacher repeats instructions or clarifies concepts, it is also conversation that asks the pupils to talk, to clarify or explain their thinking, to reconsider their thoughts and answers in new ways with prompting and support from the teacher.

A thought

In some lessons pupils will be engaged and will enjoy themselves but will believe they have not 'worked' and therefore not 'learned'. Likewise they will think they have 'learned' where a lot of 'work' has taken place. By this, they will often mean a lot of listening or writing. Which type of lesson do you think is the most effective?

Application to secondary teaching

Teachers need to plan for productive interventions with individual pupils that will allow them to explore their understanding and support their further development. This means letting the pupils do much of the talking, listening to their answers and prompting/questioning them to allow them to make progress. Plan a lesson in which you will spend most of your time working with the pupils in the class and consider how you might talk to pupils about their work in a way that will demonstrate their understanding. Holt (1982) gives seven ways in which pupils might demonstrate their understanding. This occurs when:

- **They can state something in their own words.** This can be a discussion between the teacher and the pupil about the things they need to consider when producing a presentation, or a pupil retelling a story in their own words, or a conversation in lower school about why something is wrong to do.
- **They can give examples.** This might be when pupils are able to describe or perform various poses in order to demonstrate balance. It could also be a conversation or activity in which the pupils identify examples of franchised businesses.
- **They can state or identify the opposite.** This could be an exploration of a child's understanding of the mechanics of subtraction discussing what its opposite (i.e. addition) might look like. Younger children could identify the opposite of big or heavy. The same could apply to abstract concepts such as capitalism or democracy.
- **They can recognise something in other situations.** This may be recognising monotheism in religions other than Islam, or spotting quadrilateral objects in the classroom such as books or the board. In geography it may be asking a pupil to give you examples of natural disasters other than an earthquake.
- **They can make connections between one thing and other facts or concepts.** This could be asking pupils to make connections between the weapons the Romans used and those used in the Crimean War. It can also be asking them to explain the relationship between the music of Negro spirituals and rap music, or spot the similarities and differences in a range of houses.
- **They can make use of something in other ways.** This could be asking them how addition can help them tell the time. It can also be asking them to tell you how else they can use rhyme in a poem to change the meaning/tone etc.

(Continued)

(Continued)

- **They can foresee some of the consequences of something.** These are conversations along the lines of what would happen if ... you used a different material to make your hat ... you lowered the temperature of the water instead of raising it?

Strategies such as these not only enable a teacher to monitor pupil understanding and support individual progress, they can also act as useful language modelling for students who do not have English as their first language.

Application to primary and early years teaching

Even in the primary classroom, you should be seeking to establish a workable balance between yourself and pupils. If this balance means that you are talking, instructing, explaining for most of the time, to the whole class, this will quickly exhaust you. Encourage pupils to work on their own, or in pairs or groups on a task, and train them to recognise when you are available. For example, you could facilitate at the level of the child you are working with (physically – i.e. get right down there) by providing a visual cue that you are not available to others. Another technique is to use a traffic light system of coloured cards in red, amber and green. No hands or shouting out, but turn up red for immediate help, amber for support soon, and green for OK. A sea of green is a happy class: a sea of red indicates that a whole-class intervention is probably necessary.

Behaviour management strategies

Developing a variety of effective teaching and learning strategies is an essential prerequisite to the promotion of good behaviour. If children are interested, engaged and motivated, behaviour is unlikely to be an issue. But what if they aren't? What if a single child (or group of children) decides that this learning activity, this lesson, this teacher, or even this subject is not for them? Maybe this is due to the 'baggage' they are carrying with them – a dispute spilled over from another lesson, a row at home, or a problem in the community? Maybe it's a child who craves attention or needs to be noticed? Maybe a child is distracted or tired – just come in from the playground after break. Sometimes it will' just be the weather, a high wind, or a wasp at the window. Chapter 9 covers the ground of establishing the framework and environment for good behaviour, but what individual strategies might you develop? First you need to be very familiar with your school's policies for dealing with individual behaviour issues. For example, do they have an exit policy? Is there an on-call system? Then, consider the following:

- **Distraction techniques**. If a child is being very unwilling and difficult, are you able to divert them from the unwanted behaviour with a new stimulus? This might be doing a job for you in the classroom or a new task to complete.
- **Anticipating good behaviour**. Sometimes thanking children in anticipation that they will cooperate can be a useful management tool. 'Thank you for sitting down' instead of 'sit down now' can help to defuse an escalating or potential problem.
- **Make time for calm talk**. Rather than let a situation with an individual pupil escalate, create time after a difficulty for you to be able to talk calmly with the pupil about the behaviour and to explore any underlying issues behind that behaviour.

The place and purpose of homework

Teaching timetables are often pressured. It is important that as a teacher you recognise that learning does not always have to happen in a formal classroom situation with a teacher directing it. It is, however, also important to see homework, and learning outside the classroom, as a meaningful activity that is more than just filling up time for children. Does it move their learning forward from the lesson, or is it more of the same but to be done at home? If it is the latter consider why you have set it. If they have already understood and demonstrated their understanding in the lesson is this the right time to consolidate? If they have not understood in the lesson are they going to be able to do the work at home?

GROUP EXERCISE

As a group consider the last three homework tasks you have set for a class. Think about why you set them. Were they consolidating the learning? Moving it forward? Why was this the right time for that work to be set? Now consider ways in which the homework activities may be improved.

There are some questions to consider when planning homework:

- Have you left enough time in your lesson plan to be able to explain the demands of the homework adequately?
- Have you considered some of the barriers to the pupils completing the homework successfully? Not all children have access to paints/fabric/art materials in their home; not all have internet access. Some children do not have a room of their own or a quiet space in which to work. How can you manage this kind of task in these circumstances?
- Have you thought about how long the homework task will take to complete? Is it reasonable?
- Have you given the pupils the tools to be able to complete the homework? A typical example of this is a task that asks pupils to 'research' Peru or Florence Nightingale. Do pupils know what you mean by 'research'? If they do not they will copy and paste a page from a website or a book and may not even read it! Is this what you meant by research? If not then you will need to support their understanding of the true nature of research.
- What is the potential impact of the homework on their attitude and achievement in your subject? If they regularly get mechanistic tasks, or complete work at home that you then never look at or mark, how will this impact upon their motivation and engagement when they are back in the classroom?
- Are there support mechanisms in your school for pupil homework, e.g. homework clubs, and how can you help pupils to use them effectively? Are there resources in the community that you could make use of in out-of-school learning?

Out-of-school learning

Out-of-school learning can be seen as an opportunity to develop pupils' enthusiasms and interests and an opportunity to involve parents and carers more closely in the school life of their children. When parents are involved collaboratively in education, outcomes are positive (see Addi-Raccah and Ainhoren, 2009). For example, if the children have made a board game to explain the dangers to public health of living in a city in the nineteenth century, the homework could be to play the game with a parent or carer and ask them what they learned from playing it. Perhaps a child's engagement with reading might be more effectively developed if parents/carers are given the resources and support to read a book with their child rather than asking the pupils to undertake a comprehension exercise. This might involve communicating with parents and carers about the purpose of out-of-school learning and helping them to develop their own confidence that they can help their children not only to learn but also to enjoy learning.

Summary

- Effective learning environments are created when behaviour is connected to learning.
- Teachers must see their pupils as individuals who have different and changing needs.
- No one lesson strategy or teaching activity will work with pupils all the time. Pupils and teachers need variety.
- Learning can often be most effectively personalised when teachers plan for time to give pupils effective feedback.
- Homework should have a clear learning purpose and rationale. It should be realistic and achievable for pupils in differing circumstances.

Key reading

Coe, R., Aloisi, C., Higgins, S. and Elliot Major, L. (2014) *What makes great teaching?* Durham: The University of Durham.

Cullingford, C. (2006) 'Children's own vision of schooling', *Education 3–13,* 34 (3): 211–21.

Education Endowment Fund http://educationendowmentfoundation.org.uk/toolkit/

Hattie, J. (2008) *Visible learning: a synthesis of over 800 meta-analyses relating to achievement.* London: Routledge.

Shoffner, M. (2008) 'The place of the personal: exploring the affective domain through reflection in teacher preparation', *Teaching and Teacher Education,* 25 (6): 783–89.

References and bibliography

Addi-Raccah, A. and Ainhoren, R. (2009) 'School governance and teachers' attitudes to parents' involvement in schools', *Teaching and Teacher Education,* 25 (6): 805–13.

Baumert, J., Kunter, M., Brunner, M., Tsai, Y., Krauss, S. and Klusmann, U. (2008) 'Students' and mathematics teachers' perceptions of teacher enthusiasm and instruction', *Learning and Instruction* 18(5): 468–82.

Capel, S., Leask, M. and Turner, T. (eds) (2009), *Learning to teach in the secondary school* (5th edn). London: RoutledgeFalmer.

Cullingford, C. (2006) 'Children's own vision of schooling', *Education 3–13,* 34 (3): 211–21.

Day, C. (2004) *A passion for teaching.* London: RoutledgeFalmer.

DfES (2005) *Learning behaviour: the report of the practitioners' group on school behaviour and discipline.* London: HMSO.

Dix, P. (2010) *The essential guide to taking care of behaviour* (2nd edn). Harlow: Pearson Education.

Hattie, J. (2008) *Visible learning: a synthesis of over 800 meta-analyses relating to achievement.* London: Routledge.

Holt, J. (1982) *How children fail.* New York: Delacorte/Seymour Lawrence.

Kirschner, P. Sweller, J. and Clark, R. (2006) 'Why minimal guidance during instruction does not work: an analysis of the failure of constructivist, discovery, problem-based, experiential and inquiry-based teaching', *Educational Psychologist*, 41 (2): 75–86.

Leask, M. (2009) 'The student teacher's role and responsibilities', in S. Capel, M. Leask, and Turner (eds), *Learning to teach in the secondary school* (5th edn). London: RoutledgeFalmer, pp.18–28.

The 2020 Group (2006) *A vision for teaching and learning in 2020*. London: HMSO.

Shoffner, M. (2008) 'The place of the personal: exploring the affective domain through reflection in teacher preparation', *Teaching and Teacher Education*, 25 (6): 783–89.

Useful websites

Information on how to help parents and carers support learners in their homework and other out-of-class learning may be found at: http://webarchive.nationalarchives.gov.uk/20110202195947/ direct.gov.uk/en/parents/index/htm

Education Endowment Fund http://educationendowmentfoundation.org.uk/toolkit/ (last accessed 5 January 2015).

http://visible-learning.org – a website of Professor John Hattie.

Visit https://study.sagepub.com/denby3e for extra resources related to this chapter.

CHAPTER 13

APPROACHES TO TEACHING AND LEARNING 2: PLANNING, PROGRESSION AND SEQUENCE

Joanne Pearson

Standards linked to this chapter include...

2. Promote good progress and outcomes by pupils

- be accountable for pupils' attainment, progress and outcomes
- be aware of pupils' capabilities and their prior knowledge, and plan teaching to build on these
- guide pupils to reflect on the progress they have made and their emerging needs
- demonstrate knowledge and understanding of how pupils learn and how this impacts on teaching
- encourage pupils to take a responsible and conscientious attitude to their own work and study.

(Continued)

(Continued)

4. Plan and teach well structured lessons

   - impart knowledge and develop understanding through effective use of lesson time
   - promote a love of learning and children's intellectual curiosity
   - reflect systematically on the effectiveness of lessons and approaches to teaching.

Introduction

As teachers, we have a passion for our subject: we know intimately the content, the particular distinctive features, the methods and theories that underlie and support it. As teachers, we are already successful learners. This can make us forget key aspects of teaching and learning: we are not just teaching children more about phonics, the Second World War or quadratic equations, we are teaching them to become better writers, historians and mathematicians. This means not just teaching more content, but planning for progression. The problem is how to plan lessons that build together to allow children to become better at subjects as well as knowing more. How can we use what children are already able to do and what they already know to make them better at individual subjects? And what does 'being better' at a subject really mean? Woolfolk (2010) would want to see better competencies or skills, but is this enough?

A thought

What does it mean to get better at a subject? What does getting better at geography or music look like? Is it the acquisition of more facts – knowing the names of 12 rivers rather than five, or the compositions of three composers rather than two? This is a complicated area that provokes much discussion. Think about the nature of a particular subject, its features, unique and otherwise. Can you describe what it means to get better at these features? What progressive journey did you undertake to get better at the subject?

Starting points

There are several questions that must be answered when planning for progression:

- What does it mean to get better in a subject/area?
- What can the pupil already do (skills)?
- What does the pupil already know (knowledge)?
- What concepts and skills can the pupil apply (understanding)?
- What is the next step to progress them in their knowledge and understanding?
- How can we plan teaching and learning experiences that will allow the journey to take place?

Defining and describing progression

Until September 2014 there were national models for progression in a number of subjects in English schools and these were called 'level descriptors'. Since September 2014 these have been withdrawn, with the exception of P scales for pupils with Special Educational Needs which remain. There are still points within a child's education when they are compared against a national standard. These are in Early Years/ Foundation Stage, Key Stages 1 and 2, at GCSE and A level – but describing and capturing progression between these points is now the job of each school. (The mechanics of 'Progress 8' are explained in Chapter 23.) Content for National Curriculum subjects such as English, mathematics and science may be found in NC documents, but not indications of progress. Within these documents are the purpose, aims and content for each subject. For subjects that are not part of the National Curriculum (such as business studies, sociology and psychology) there are the national 14–19 subject criteria that describe the aims, assessment objectives and grade descriptions for each subject.

GROUP EXERCISE

In small groups of two or three download one of the following: a copy of the National Curriculum programme of study for a subject; the P scales; the early years/Foundation stage framework or the grading criteria for a subject at 14–19. Discuss the aims, concepts, processes and assessment objectives contained in these documents. To what extent do they match with your own definition of the subject? Examine the level/grade descriptions – how useful do these seem as a description of progress?

One reason for the abandonment of the NC levels was that they did not provide a definitive model of progression. They were designed to describe progress over a long period of time, whereas teachers needed to plan for progression over a much shorter time period, over a matter of weeks rather than years. An additional consideration is that children do not make progress evenly – individuals make progress in one concept or skill at different rates from one another, meaning that pupils in reality will reflect several levels in the same subject. However, this had been masked by a 'best fit' which did not help to inform future teaching and learning by highlighting what each child could do.

The task for the teacher is therefore to explore progression between national assessment points. This means thinking about how children learn (see Chapter 11), and exploring the levels of difficulty in the tasks that pupils are being asked to perform in lessons. One model for this is Bloom's taxonomy (Bloom, 1984). Bloom looked at the demands of different activities and categorised these into levels of challenge, creating a hierarchy of 'skills' ranging from 'knowledge' (lower level) to 'evaluation' (higher level). These are described as:

1. **Knowledge**. This can be the recall of information, for example dates or facts.
2. **Comprehension**. This is the understanding of facts, the interpretation of recalled data, for example comparing one fact with another.
3. **Application**. This is the ability to apply the information in other settings or solve problems using the knowledge and skills they have acquired.
4. **Analysis**. This is when pupils might begin to see patterns, to make connections and classifications.
5. **Synthesis**. Here pupils use old knowledge to create new knowledge. They pull together knowledge from several areas, they predict.
6. **Evaluation**. Here pupils make judgements about competing theories and beliefs. They formulate arguments and are able to support them.

This model has been further revised by Anderson and Krathwohl (2001), who came up with the following model:

1. Remembering
2. Understanding
3. Applying
4. Analysing
5. Evaluating
6. Creating.

Both these models are based upon what is called the 'cognitive domain' and have had their critics. For example, 'understanding' is a slippery word – what does it mean and what would it look like in the classroom? There is also no suggestion that these levels are chronologically based. For example, younger pupils cannot just remember, they can (and do) create or evaluate. Rather, the levels are a general model of how new knowledge may be processed and used at any age. These models, even with their flaws, are another tool by which teachers can explore progression and plan for pupils to improve within a particular subject. The exploration and categorisation of two other learning domains, the psycho-motor domain (physical skills and dexterity) and the affective domain (emotions and behaviour), never received the same attention but may be more important to you if, for example, you teach PE or dance, or encourage empathy in any subject.

Objectives and outcomes

Objectives are, and have always been, at the heart of teaching and are key to capturing progression for individual teachers and their pupils. An objective states the purpose of the lesson – today I am teaching X in order that the class can do Y. An individual lesson's objectives should be part of a medium-term objective from a scheme of work and a long-term objective from a year or key stage. The purpose of this unit is so that pupils can do what? The purpose of this Year 4 Physical Education curriculum is what? All teachers need to be able to answer these questions; this is planning for progression. An objective is not enough however, you will need objectives that can be seen, heard or read otherwise how will you know if they have been achieved? 'By the end of this unit pupils will recall number bonds to 10' is something you can see/hear or read in their books. 'Understand number bonds to 10' is much more slippery – what will that look like/sound like? Similarly, beware objectives that become a description of a task rather than an educational aim: 'finish the worksheet on number bonds' is not an objective, it is an activity. Learning objectives are therefore a tool for you as a teacher to articulate the purpose of this lesson/scheme of work/unit.

Learning outcomes are the means by which you collect evidence to see if the objectives have been met. If the objective is that pupils can 'recall number bonds to 10', then the outcome may be that by the end of the lesson pupils will successfully match pairs of numbers to make number bonds to 10. If your medium-term objective is to develop pupils' understanding of historical causation, then your outcome may be that by the end of the unit they are able to produce a piece of extended writing that describes and analyses the causes of the First World War.

These two key elements, the objective and outcome of a lesson, are always the starting point for planning: if you begin with an activity then fit the objective to it, you are not planning for progression you are filling time. Ask yourself, what am I trying to achieve this lesson and what evidence will I collect that will allow me and the pupils to see if we've achieved it? The next step can then be to consider what the success criteria for your outcomes will be – what will a really good essay on the causes of the First World War look like? Do the pupils have to be able to do the inversion of each of the number bonds to 10?

INDIVIDUAL REFLECTION

Look at two or three of your lesson plans that form a sequence. Use either Bloom's taxonomy or Anderson and Krathwohl's model and analyse the level of demand and difficulty in the objectives and outcomes the pupils undertook. To what extent was there any progression across the lessons? Go back to the National Curriculum document/subject specification to help with this. Finally, look at a piece of work produced by the pupils in one or more of the lessons. Have they made any progress as a result of the lesson (use both the taxonomy and the national guidance)?

Prior knowledge and understanding

Allowing pupils to get better at a subject means that we as teachers need to know what they *already* know and can do when they arrive at a particular lesson. There are several sources of information available to help us carry this out. These include the following:

- **The National Curriculum document for the key stage preceding the stage being taught.** For example, what content, skills and processes should children at Key Stage 2 have undertaken in geography? What are the expected numeracy levels of a pupil ending Key Stage 1?
- **The departmental scheme of work for the key stage being currently taught.** What content, skills and processes have the children already been taught during this key stage?
- **The individual assessment records for each pupil.** This may be in the form of Standard Attainment Test (SAT) results, internal school data, Early Years/Foundation Stage profile data, or departmental subject achievement descriptors.
- **Day-to-day observational assessment in lessons.** This is a powerful tool for planning subsequent lessons in the early years and beyond, as well as for scrutiny of outputs produced by the children in lessons.

While all of these sources are available and can be useful, in themselves they may be something of a blunt tool. Primary schools may have devoted very different amounts of time to subjects, especially those in the foundation rather than the core. You may be teaching a subject at GCSE or A Level that the pupils have never tackled before, such as business studies. How then can we as teachers plan for the progression of individual pupils?

A thought

Teaching a subject does not automatically mean that children have learned anything. The coverage of any content, skills or processes by a teacher does not always result in pupil learning. In fact it can result in the opposite. In 1993 Lightman and Sadler found that pupil understanding of a topic, in this case physics, could actually decrease as a result of being taught this in a lesson.

The most obvious starting point for this is the pupils themselves. As teachers, we should think about beginning new topics with an exploration of what they already know and can do rather than assuming no knowledge or assuming too much. The former results in no progress because if the pupils already know and can do things before coming to the lesson, then the lesson has added nothing. The latter results in no progress because if the teacher assumes pupils know and can do things they cannot, then the lesson will be beyond those pupils.

Application to secondary teaching

When planning a new unit of work consider the opening lesson as a means to assess pupil knowledge and understanding. This can be done in several ways:

- Undertake a baseline assessment – what is their knowledge and understanding at the beginning of the unit?
- Produce an overview map of the content, skills and processes that will be covered in the unit. The pupils can add to the headings, or colour the map in using a traffic light system – green for the areas they feel confident in already, orange for those they feel they are familiar with but lack full confidence, red for the unfamiliar. For example, in Key Stage 2 science: Plants is a unit they have already looked at in Key Stage 1; what can they recall? What looks like new knowledge, for example the parts of the plant? What could they have good guesses about? In Key Stage 3 French you want to develop their ability to take

(Continued)

(Continued)

part in a discussion about wider issues – pupils can traffic light their ability to use familiar language in a variety of new settings.

- Put the title of the unit on the board and ask the pupils to generate questions they would like to be able to answer about this topic by the end of the unit. Having done this, explore as a class any questions they have asked that they may already be able to answer in part or in total. For example, if the topic in history at Key Stage 3 is the First World War, pupils may ask: Why did it start? Why did it end? How was it fought? Who fought? Who won? Who were the soldiers? Some of these questions (e.g. who fought?) they may already as a class be able to answer (at least in part). Others, such as why the war began, they may have no understanding of. If the pupils are comparing their local area to somewhere unfamiliar in Key Stage 1 geography they may generate questions such as Is it hotter? Is it busier? Do the buildings look the same?
- Allow the pupils to generate their own mind maps. Put the title of the unit on the board and ask them to write down words, questions and/or images they think may be involved in this topic. What comes into their minds in music at Key Stage 2 when they are asked to think about Scotland? What do they associate with Marxism in A-'Level sociology?
- Try a 3-2-1 approach. Given a topic heading, ask the pupils to write down three things they already know/can do that will help them in this topic, two questions they would like to be able to answer at the end of the unit, and one target for their own progression during the unit.

Next steps

Once teachers feel confident about what pupils know and/or can do, the next challenge is to plan lessons that will allow all the pupils to move forward. This means thinking again about progression models and about how children learn. Take, for example, extended writing, where the level of challenge involved can depend on several variables:

- *Some questions may be harder than others* – describing events may be less challenging than explaining events (but it depends on the event!)
- *The level of support provided* – pupils may be given a rigid writing frame or may be given no supporting framework

- *The content may be more or less challenging* – concrete concepts such as a person or event may be easier to understand than abstract concepts such as capitalism or romanticism
- *The teaching strategies adopted can affect the challenge* – are pupils working together to discuss and draft ideas or are they working alone?

These examples are all factors which teachers must take into account when planning lessons to accommodate progression. Pupils may begin in Year 7 with extended writing about concrete concepts, in groups with writing frames, and by Year 9 may be writing individual pieces, unsupported, about abstract ideas, but this is unlikely to be a journey taken in one leap.

Implicit in all planning therefore are teacher knowledge and an understanding of what will be asked of the pupils at the end of the journey, i.e. what destination are we preparing them for? What are the final demands required of A-Level RE, Key Stage 1 teacher assessments, GCSE mathematics ...? Research (Van de Watering et al., 2008) has shown that students' preferences and perceptions of assessment have an effect on their performance depending on which cognitive processes are being assessed, and how this is done.

Application to primary and early years teaching

In the early years and primary stages there is likely to be a much more cross-curricular approach to planning and teaching than in the secondary phase. Nevertheless, lesson planning can still take the same sequential approach, and start from the point of finding out what children already know. If the topic is 'plant growth' for example, start from the seed and work through germination, leaves, buds, flowers, etc. in logical order, but only after finding out if anyone can 'help' the class by telling them, from their own knowledge or experience, how plants grow.

Teaching and learning

Knowledge of your pupils, of your subject, and of different and varied pedagogical approaches will precede the planning of sequences of lessons. The reality of this in the classroom means that you will never teach any lesson in exactly the same way twice. The content may be the same, but the pupils will not. They will have learned at different rates, made different mistakes, started with different prior knowledge. Planning needs to start with the pupils in front of you. Some factors that you may need to consider are as follows:

- **What learning experiences you have already given them**. Even if a class seem to respond very well to one particular teaching strategy, using it too often while ignoring others may result in boredom, disengagement and a lack of progress. It is useful to audit the teaching strategies you have used with each of your classes regularly to ensure variety. It is also useful to audit the knowledge and resources you employ in lessons: how inclusive is your subject content? For example, many primary school children will experience no Black history in their experiences at Key Stages 1 and 2 – how can you develop content that reflects a diverse society?
- **Being adversely affected by demands other than learning**. Do not avoid certain teaching strategies because of the age of the pupils or the demands of external assessment. If group work and discussion produce learning in Key Stage 2 English, then why should they not do the same in post-16 English? If role play aids the learning of a 5 year-old do not assume that it no longer aids learning at age 15. Try different techniques – success will increase your confidence, and prompt you to try even more methods (Saylor, 2010).
- **Explicitly thinking about the teaching 'style' you might adopt as part of the planning**. There will be times, for example when introducing a new concept, skill or area of content, that an 'expert' style may be most appropriate. This will involve you taking the role of the experienced learner and explaining to the pupils. When revisiting a concept, skill or content, it may be more appropriate for a 'facilitator' style of teaching. This involves very little teacher explanation and much more teacher support as the pupils work. Your style of teaching may also need to change as each lesson progresses and as you respond to pupils' needs and changing situations. If they are clearly demonstrating misconceptions at any point during a lesson think about pulling the class together and addressing these misconceptions; if individual pupils or groups need support, then facilitation at the appropriate level will be more effective than a whole-class approach. (There are several models of teaching styles – see e.g. Grasha's [1996] five styles.)
- **The role of language in teaching**. Your use of language in a lesson needs to be carefully considered. For example, when explaining a new concept how much subject-specific language are you going to use? Are there terms and phrases that pupils may misconceive? 'The Church' has a particular meaning in an RE or history lesson but it may have a different association for a pupil. Similarly in mathematics, 'product' has a particular meaning that differs from other uses of the word (for example, in business education). Questions need to be clearly planned. Will they be closed or open? Who will you ask? How will you ensure most children participate? How will you monitor/manage children's participation in the lesson? How demanding are your questions – are the class being challenged? Consider Bloom's taxonomy to support your question planning. For example, 'Who wrote Romeo and Juliet?' is 'recall of knowledge' and is at the bottom of the taxonomy,

while 'How good do you think it is?' is evaluative and of a much higher-order skill. It is often at the end of a lesson that teacher talk is less planned and so becomes less focused. Think about the purpose of the plenary – are you reviewing learning that has taken place or looking ahead to the next lesson's learning? Are you calming and settling or enthusing and exciting? Do you intend to review the lesson objectives or link the lesson to the bigger teaching objective? Are you dealing with misconceptions now or covering them next lesson? These are all decisions to be made both prior to a lesson and during a lesson as the pupils' learning becomes apparent.

- **The link between the activity you have chosen in a lesson and the learning**. Make sure this link is clear. How is note-taking going to develop learning and help achieve the lesson objective? If it is not then consider alternative activities. Be careful of finding a 'good' activity for a class and using it in a lesson without considering how it aids pupil' progress. The same applies to e-learning. This offers enormous opportunities for teaching and learning: it can give access to resources and images, create opportunities for independent learning, and supply pupils with the tools to revise and redraft work. E-learning is not just 'word processing', it encompasses podcasts, interactive learning, use of e-mail and the internet. However, it is not a panacea – as with any other activity it needs to meet the learning objective. It is a tool that should be used where appropriate – if listening to Martin Luther King's 'I have a dream' speech or seeing film of Gandhi's march to make salt aids learning and understanding, then the presence of these clips on the internet is priceless. Adding clipart to a document may not be quite so useful! The purpose of e-learning is to extend the subject learning – for example, to improve English, geography, design & technology. It is not an end in itself (see Chapter 21).
- **The role of language in learning**. This is twofold. It is the role that pupils' talk can play in their own learning and the role of talk between the teacher and an individual pupil in learning. Pupils talking to the whole class and one another about their learning is invaluable to teachers. For example, the Talk for Writing initiative encourages pupils to talk through their work before beginning to write. Like any other part of a lesson, talk needs to be planned with care. If an open-ended, challenging question has been planned as part of the lesson, give pupils the opportunity to consider their thoughts, and discuss and revise their opinions with a partner, before expecting an answer. The skills of discussion work – such as listening to others, articulating opinion along with supporting evidence and avoiding shouting out – do not happen naturally. They need to be explained and articulated. The potential of teacher/pupil talk is enormous. It is often when the most effective differentiation can occur. You decide to whom you will talk, how you will use this talk to support and challenge individual pupils, and how you will help to develop their ability to talk about their own learning.

- **Linking teaching and learning objectives**. Keep making links between the learning objectives in individual lessons and your overall teaching objectives. Teaching objectives are longer term – they are linked to progress. For example, as a PE or dance teacher, your teaching objective may be to develop pupils' control of whole-body skills: this will be achieved over a longer period of time than one lesson, and you will need to link your learning objectives for the children in each individual lesson to this overall teaching objective. This might be a lesson objective that states the children will be able to perform a balance. The lesson objective alone cannot achieve the overall teaching objective, rather it is one step towards it. Other lessons will need to be planned to support the medium-term teaching objective.

Planning a lesson can therefore never be carried out in isolation. Pupils have had many learning experiences before they arrive in our classrooms. We are not just giving them a single lesson. For teaching *and* learning to be meaningful we need to have a bigger plan in mind. Where have they come from and how did they get here? Where are you taking them and how will you get them there?

These are processes that will be reflected in your own learning 'journey' as a beginning teacher as you understand more about the process of learning (Buitink, 2008).

Summary

- Effective objectives with matching outcomes allow teachers to think about and plan for progression.
- Teachers need to have an understanding of what it means to improve at a subject.
- Progression is supported by planning that considers the learning journey of pupils.
- Lessons need to be linked together to support learning over the longer term.
- Each class and pupil will be at a different stage of learning and our planning needs to consider who it is we are planning for.

Key reading

Buitink, J. (2008) 'What and how do student teachers learn during school-based teacher education?', *Teaching and Teacher Education,* 25 (1): 118–27.

DfES (2004a) *Pedagogy and practice: teaching and learning in secondary schools.* London: HMSO.

DfES (2004b) *Excellence and enjoyment: learning and teaching in the primary years.* London: HMSO.

Van de Watering, G., Gijbels, D., Dochy, F. and Van der Rijt, J. (2008) 'Students' assessment preferences, perceptions of assessment and their relationships to study results', *Higher Education,* 56 (6): 645–58.

References and bibliography

Anderson, L. and Krathwohl, D. (eds) (2001) *A taxonomy for learning, teaching, and assessing: a revision of Bloom's taxonomy of educational objectives*. New York: Longman.

Bloom, B. (1984) *Taxonomy of educational objectives*. Boston, MA: Pearson.

Buitink, J. (2008) 'What and how do student teachers learn during school-based teacher education?', *Teaching and Teacher Education,* 25 (1): 118–27.

Grasha, A. (1996) *Teaching with style*. Pittsburgh, MD: Alliance.

Lightman, A. and Sadler, P. (1993) 'Teacher predictions versus actual student gains', *The Physics Teacher,* 31: 162–67.

Saylor, C. (2010) 'Learning theories applied to curriculum development', in S. Keating (ed.), *Curriculum development and evaluation in nursing* (2nd edn). New York: Springer.

Van de Watering, G., Gijbels, D., Dochy, F. and Van der Rijt, J. (2008) 'Students' assessment preferences, perceptions of assessment and their relationships to study results', *Higher Education,* 56 (6): 645–58.

Woolfolk, A. (2010) *Educational psychology* (11th edn). Upper Saddle River, NJ: Pearson Education.

Visit https://study.sagepub.com/denby3e for extra resources related to this chapter.

CHAPTER 14

APPROACHES TO TEACHING AND LEARNING 3: DIFFERENTIATION AND PERSONALISING PROVISION

Neil Denby

Standards linked to this chapter include...

5. Adapt teaching to respond to the strengths and needs of all pupils

- know when and how to differentiate appropriately, using approaches which enable pupils to be taught effectively
- have a secure understanding of how a range of factors can inhibit pupils' ability to learn, and how best to overcome these
- demonstrate an awareness of the physical, social and intellectual development of children, and know how to adapt teaching to support pupils' education at different stages of development

- have a clear understanding of the needs of all pupils, including those with special educational needs; those of high ability; those with English as an additional language; those with disabilities; and be able to use and evaluate distinctive teaching approaches to engage and support them.

Introduction

Sitting in front of you in a classroom is not a 'class' of children, much as you may think it is! It is a collection of individuals who, on any day of the week, or at any time of day, will have different priorities in their lives, including the ways in which they might learn. All pupils are different. They have different backgrounds, different needs and different ways of learning. Some of these differences may be physical, some more learning orientated, some more culturally or socially embedded. If the needs are specific, or are seen as a particular cause for concern, or of specialist intervention, then they will gain a category description of their own. Not having English as a first language can obviously be a barrier to learning in an English classroom, so there are special provisions for English as an additional language (EAL) learners. Similarly, special arrangements may be made for those with physical difficulties such as speech, sight, hearing and mobility. Special educational needs of all types are generally put under the heading of Special Educational Needs (SEN) or Learning Difficulties and Disorders (LDD). The first encompasses both ends of the spectrum, from those who have difficulty learning to those considered to be 'gifted and talented'; the second covers a whole range of physical and mental problems.

A thought

How many of the children in an average- sized class do you think have special needs? Think about all the possibilities – physical, mental, emotional, learning styles preferences, learning ability, skills possessed ... Who do you think is in the best position to assess these needs – parents and carers, bureaucratic bodies, or you, their teacher?

In your local authority there will be special schools for those for whom mainstream education is not possible. Many parents, however, would like their children to be educated with their peers, so will opt for normal school with special arrangements. Certain schools in the authority will therefore be designated as having special arrangements for certain groups and will receive appropriate funding for this. These are referred to as 'resourced schools' and will be adapted or specialised to cater for specific groups: for example, hearing, visual or communication impairment; or specific disabilities, such as pupils who are wheelchair users.

As well as these specific groups and individuals, you will be faced with a range of diverse needs. Every class that you teach will, to a greater or lesser extent, be of mixed ability. You must therefore develop an 'inclusive' approach to ensure that all those children are reaching their potential. The school will have collected a wide range of statistics and information regarding pupils and you should use this information to help plan lessons. Expert colleagues will help you identify the needs of specific groups for which they have responsibility. Accessing and understanding data, and how to make best use of support colleagues, are detailed in Chapters 23 and 7, while the focus on diversity occasioned by the Ajegbo Report and other research is discussed in Chapters 18 and 20.

INDIVIDUAL REFLECTION

Consider a class you are teaching and draw a Venn diagram to show in how many ways differentiation might be needed. Your circles could include, for example, language, culture, gender, learning style or preference and behaviour, as well as ability in its many layers.

Having a range of activities or routes through a lesson is called differentiation. Taking differentiation to its logical conclusion would mean creating a different learning plan or route for each pupil, which is called personalisation. Each is a step on the road to providing an excellent education by meeting children's individual needs.

To ensure children are confident, happy and engaged in learning, their individual needs must be met. This may sound simple but it is a highly complex task, requiring practitioners to be constantly alert and responsive (Hutchin, 2006: 30). Indeed Goepel (2009: 127) takes this a step further and also involves parents and carers:

> Personalised learning should also involve parents in their child's development and learning and should take into account the well-being of the child, including how the child learns. In this way the teaching and learning offered to all children takes into account difference and individualised planning.

'Fashionable' learning styles

The idea of learning styles is as old as the ancient Greeks. Plato taught through dialogues and analogies, for example. Socrates, his pupil, through inquiry and discovery, with the interplay of question and answer and conversations between pupil and teacher at its heart. You will read about the difference between learning styles and strategies; about whether 'learning' or 'cognition' is key to good education ('cognitive' styles and strategies are seen as different from their 'learning' cousins), about whether pupils learn better individually or collectively, in cooperation or competition, through seeing the Gestalt or the component parts of a problem. The key word may be said to be 'preferences', as these change over time and over situation, so you must be prepared to be flexible. What worked on one day, for one topic, may be anathema to the same pupil on another day, or for another topic.

Whilst it may be true that (Worm and Buch, 2014) 'Overall, students learn better when subjects are presented to them in a way that matches their preferred learning style', it will often be difficult for you as a teacher to pin down the style that suits each pupil and when, as there will be so many factors to take into account when an individual is deciding on the learning style or preference for a particular task.

There are numerous 'learning styles' theories. These theories, some of which are discussed in Chapter 11, move in and out of fashion, so beware of becoming a 'fashion victim'! Theories can be so popular for a time that they become embedded in official paperwork – so you may well have lesson planning or evaluation documentation that asks you, for example, where you have included 'VAK' or how your questions take pupils through Bloom's taxonomy; how you are using experiential learning (Kolb) or teamwork (Belbin); how your learning is scaffolded (Vygotsky) or promotes self-efficacy (Bandura). You can even have pupils try learning styles questionnaires (many are available online) to discover their 'primary' learning preference.

To take one example: the inclusion of VAK (Visual, Aural and Kinaesthetic) approaches means that there is some variety in a lesson – it does not, however, ensure that that lesson is reaching every individual at a level where each can succeed. It is just one approach among many: Hall and Moseley (2006) reviewed and critiqued more than a dozen individual and popular learning styles.

It is better, therefore, to plan thinking about the outputs that will allow pupils to succeed, in conjunction with a variety of approaches, rather than just the inputs you will control. So, for example, make sure that pupils can demonstrate their learning in different ways – perhaps visually, verbally or kinaesthetically – but also think about how these can be broken down. Visually, for example, could include: a diagram, a picture, an IT-produced wordcloud, a strip cartoon, a spider diagram. Verbally could be a bulleted list, a poem, a rap, a set of lyrics, a crossword or wordsquare, a script – and it does not have to be always written down: some pupils will be more confident speaking to demonstrate learning outcomes. Kinaesthetically could include modelling, a piece of music, a role play, a demonstration ... Gardner's (born 1943) multiple intelligences (see page 164) may be a useful way to think about how outputs might be categorised in order to reach the majority of pupils.

Differentiation

Differentiation means creating a variety of learning experiences and routes for pupils. Materials and methods in the classroom should be adapted to each different level of learning and each different learning style. At its most extreme, this creates a personal curriculum for each child – hence its inevitable link with the concept of personalisation. Joyce et al. (1997: 15) concluded that different experiences helped pupils to develop: 'Increasing the range of learning experiences provided in our schools increases the likelihood of more students becoming more adept learners.' The use of group work, for example, or the introduction of competitive elements, can lead to different requirements and emphases, all enhancing the learning experience and feeding into differing learning styles. In all cases, though, there needs to be variety and balance. As Worm and Buch (2014) state:

> A balanced approach with both cooperation and competition could be beneficial in many cases, but obviously, learning styles are individual preferences and tendencies that can influence the learning process.

Differentiation may be achieved through any number of routes – it does not just mean preparing work at different levels for different individuals, or having easier materials for part of your class. Differentiation by outcome (i.e. in a set situation like a test or class exercise each pupil will perform differently) is not really differentiation at all, but can be useful as a way of ranking young people by ability. You should aim to assess learning regularly, both in formal ways and through formative assessment for learning (see Chapter 19). Assessing learners' progress allows you to provide timely interventions, issue tasks of greater or less complexity, and/or arrange appropriate support. Self-assessment – encouraging pupils to think about their own learning – is also appropriate.

For any learner it is useful to create a five-phase 'map' so that you can set appropriate personalised targets. These phases are:

- Where are they now?
- How do you know this?
- Where do you want them to be?
- How will they get there?
- How will you know that they have arrived?

Application to primary and early years teaching

In primary classrooms in particular, but also in some secondary classrooms, the idea of the five phases is not something that occurs throughout the lesson, but at various points in the lesson. A primary lesson may well be 'chunked' so that there are individual parts or stages, each with its own mini-plenary at the end of each chunk. The five questions may then be asked at several points in the lesson, and strategies developed to personalise learning for those who are not able to move to the next chunk until learning is properly embedded.

Planning for differentiation

In what might be termed the 'traditional' teacher-centred lesson, the lesson is designed for the whole class with class learning outcomes and pupils set the same tasks to complete. Differentiation is by 'outcome', i.e. how well each pupil performs. In the differentiated lesson, targets and outcomes are set for individuals, pupils are set different tasks, and there is less teacher talk and more facilitation. The first has the advantage of being easier to prepare and manage, but for many of the pupils the level will not be right (whether too high or too low is equally problematic). The second makes whole-class interaction a lot harder and takes more preparation, but as a pupil-centred approach is better for learners. Your differentiated learning objectives become key signposts of learning within the lesson and within sequences of lessons. From a practical point of view, you may be able to aim for a lesson that falls part way between these two: one, for example, where different groups have different learning objectives with separate targets set for a few individuals. In this way you may only be monitoring and facilitating four or five pathways rather than 20 or more. For each lesson or series of lessons you will need to decide what the underlying essential learning is going to be for each group or individual, how they can best achieve this, and how (i.e. through what outcomes) they can demonstrate success. In addition, you will need further targets for the more able and possibly more complex tasks, and to plan appropriate support and interventions for weaker pupils. A good general rule is to work to objectives that state by the end of the lesson:

- All pupils will ...
- Most pupils will ...
- Some pupils will ...

It is then easier, within these broad groupings, to set individual targets. In practice, some whole-class teaching will take place and you will need to find a balance that allows all pupils to progress at a satisfactory rate. Differentiated approaches to learning include people, methods and materials.

People

The most vital element in the room is you, the teacher. It is your subject knowledge; your passion for your subject and your planning that determine whether learning is effective. David Sousa, in his '*How the Brain Learns …*' series writes about the latest research in neuroscience, education and psychology and how it can change our perceptions of what and how to teach. The focus is clearly on the teacher (Sousa, 2012: 4):

> Every day teachers enter their classrooms with lesson plans, experience and the hope that what they are about to present will be understood, remembered and useful to their students. The extent that this hope is realized depends largely on the knowledge base that these teachers use in designing those plans and, perhaps more important, on the instructional techniques they select during the lessons.

Apart from you, however, there are often many other people involved in a lesson. These include not just designated support teachers such as TLAs, but also technicians, librarians, parents and even other pupils. Mentoring – from a parent, a member of a community, or even an older student – can be an effective way of personalising a curriculum. It is a particularly useful way of ensuring that EAL pupils or those from diverse backgrounds understand concepts and ideas. Collaborative work within a group can also help learning. A more able pupil may learn a concept better by explaining it to a less able one (the motto of a good teacher should be *docendo discimus* – 'we learn by teaching'), creating better and more individualised learning for both. Similarly, group work can allow pupils to follow different paths and use different skills within the group.

Methods

Many of the methods of differentiation involve encouraging children and young people to think more deeply. Challenging pupils' assumptions and values, for example, will provoke a response coloured by diverse backgrounds and cultures and promote thinking. Questions should be cognitively demanding and in question sessions you must leave time for thought processes to take place. Open questions of course encourage more differentiated responses than closed questions. You should also make room for young people to respond in different ways – there is no reason for a response to always be written down. Encourage pupils to pace themselves, manage their own time, and work at a rate they find comfortable but within parameters where they can achieve.

Tasks should be set that require solutions to be thought out and measured. This can be encouraged by setting tasks or problems with no single solution, and crucially, requiring pupils to justify their choices and decisions. These skills of analysis and evaluation are often thought to be difficult, but are actually inherent in the human psyche. (Think about the thought processes involved in crossing a busy road, or ask any 14 year-old why such-and-such a team lost a match or so-and-so didn't win *The X Factor* or *American Idol*, and you will see how good people are at analysis and evaluation.) These skills can be further honed by using homework to extend the range or depth of a project. Bloom's taxonomy can provide a useful way to categorise levels of learning. Remember, however, that Bloom only succeeded in studying one of three taxonomies in detail – the cognitive domain i.e. thinking skills (see page 188). The other two domains demonstrate how alternative outcomes might be appropriate for other learning or types of learner. The psycho-motor domain reflects on manipulative skills ranging from imitation through manipulation and precision and on to articulation and naturalisation whilst the affective domain looks at how individuals receive, respond and value information before organising and characterising it.

Application to secondary teaching

An adolescent is defined as 'a young person in the process of developing from a child into an adult' (OED). This is someone who has entered puberty and will eventually become an independent adult member of society. The cognitive development of adolescents includes advanced problem-solving skills, an ability to see alternative viewpoints, an ability to think about thinking (metacognition), which includes considering how others think of you, and an ability to empathise. Not all of these will be immediately apparent! Watch the TED talk on 'The mysterious workings of the adolescent brain' by Sarah-Jayne Blakemore (2012) and consider how this knowledge of how the teenage brain develops might change your planning.

Materials

Materials can be prepared with different levels of support within them. A crossword, for example, could have cryptic clues, easy clues, first letters given, or partial answers given. Tasks or activities can be graded by difficulty, with pupils moving on to more demanding work as they succeed. Be careful that once a concept is understood and practised it is not unnecessarily repeated. It is easy to think that you are providing harder work when actually it is more of the same. You can also differentiate by making more information available at different levels and in different formats. Pupils can then access the information they need in a form with which they are comfortable and at a level they understand. Don't use too many curriculum materials to support your teaching. Research has found that beginning teachers tend to spend an inordinate amount of time on finding and developing curriculum materials, when they would do better to use the ones they have at hand and adapt and adjust them (Grossman and Thompson, 2008).

Some or all of these strategies can be used to differentiate both within lessons and across series of lessons. Using a single approach has problems so you will need to combine several techniques to ensure inclusive teaching. For example, differentiating by providing increasingly difficult tasks within a lesson is likely to bore higher ability pupils at the start of the lesson and leave weaker ones frustrated at the end. To reach all pupils and thus qualify as inclusive, the approach would need the addition of, for example, extra support, group collaboration and targeted intervention. The combination of people, tasks and materials will lead to pupils being able to take different routes through lessons, heading for individualised or personalised learning targets.

GROUP EXERCISE

Consider the range of outside influences that are going to have an effect on how willing or able an adolescent pupil is to learn. (For the purposes of this exercise we have excluded other, physical influences, such as hunger, thirst and comfort, but these are also important.) These could include issues of family, culture, emotion, social and peer life, morality and ethics, search for identity, sexuality ... Choose a small number of particular individuals that you teach and discuss how important you think each of these factors is to them. Then look at how you could plan to ameliorate negative factors or build on positive ones.

Personalisation

The idea of personalised learning in an educational context is not a new one, as Ken Boston, when Chief Executive of the Qualifications and Curriculum Authority (QCA), explained:

> The learning theory on which personalised learning is based goes back 30 years: that for each individual in each domain of learning there is a zone of proximal development – or achievable challenge – in which learning can occur. Teaching is effective only when it is sufficiently precise and focused to build directly on what the individual pupil knows, and

> takes him or her to the next level of attainment. If the learning task is beyond the zone of achievable challenge, no learning will occur and the child will be frustrated and disaffected. If the learning task is too easy and does not extend the child, again no learning will occur, and the child will be bored. (Boston, 2006)

It is, however, a concept that has been readily adopted by politicians in recent years. David Miliband, the Minister for School Standards in 2004, said the government's aim at the time was to make personalised learning a key feature of the education system. He claimed that:

> ... decisive progress in educational standards occurs where every child matters; careful attention is paid to their individual learning styles, motivations, and needs; there is rigorous use of pupil target setting linked to high-quality assessment; lessons are well placed and enjoyable; and pupils are supported by partnership with others well beyond the classroom. (Miliband, 2004)

Christine Gilbert, Her Majesty's Chief Inspector (HMCI), produced a report (Gilbert, 2006) that underlined the skills required for and the benefits to be gained from personalised learning. Those skills are:

- analysing and using data, with a specific focus on assessment for learning
- understanding how children learn and develop
- working with other adults (including parents and other children's service professionals)
- engaging pupils as active participants in learning.

She adds that personalised learning is learner centred, knowledge centred and assessment centred, and: 'Put simply, personalising learning and teaching means taking a highly structured and responsive approach to each child's and young person's learning, in order that all are able to progress, achieve and participate' (Gilbert, 2006: 6). This is an idea that has resonance in all public services where the 'person' is at the centre of service provision, particularly with multi-agency services. The concept of personalisation recognises that each learner is different, and that the 'hydra curriculum' (Lewis, 2007), where as each subject is cut another one or more takes its place, is no longer sustainable. Learners are more central and are expected to develop their own skill sets within descriptors that include teamwork, creativity and reflection on their own learning. Mick Waters, when Director of Curriculum at QCA, said that this means that:

> Curriculum subjects need to emphasise the possible routes through schooling and the application of specific learning in the world ... [This means] ... rejuvenating content within the curriculum to use subject disciplines to develop skills and personal qualities in context, and demonstrate links between the traditional and emerging subjects. (Waters 2007)

A thought

How possible is choice within an already overcrowded curriculum?

Charlie Brown: I learned something in school today. I signed up for folk guitar, computer programming, stained glass art, shoe-making and natural foods workshop. I got spelling, history, arithmetic and two study periods.

Lucy: What did you learn?

Charlie Brown: I learned that what you sign up for and what you get are two different things.

(Charles Schultz, quoted in Reimer, 1971)

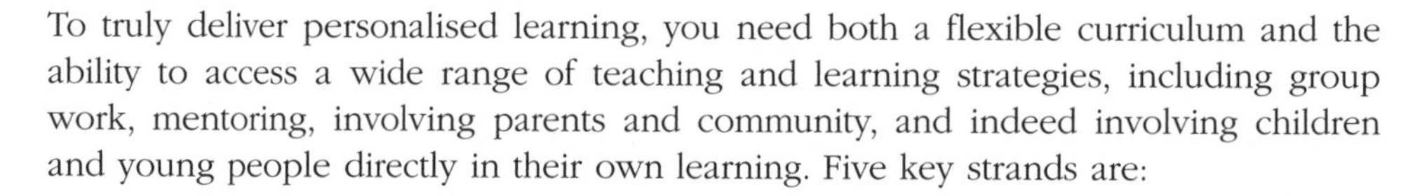

To truly deliver personalised learning, you need both a flexible curriculum and the ability to access a wide range of teaching and learning strategies, including group work, mentoring, involving parents and community, and indeed involving children and young people directly in their own learning. Five key strands are:

- the use of assessment for learning (Black and Wiliam, 1998, 2001) to establish where pupils are and how to move them on
- teaching for learning – planning teaching to be motivating and transferable
- creating choice within the curriculum
- engaging parents and communities so that learners perceive themselves as members of a wider social body
- listening to the student voice.

The importance of listening to the pupil' voice is vital. MacGilchrist et al. (2005: 65) believe that pupils have much to teach us: 'Particularly, we learn how articulate and in touch even the youngest pupils can be when they are given time to talk about their learning and their experience of it at school.'

Gray et al. (1999) agree that schools which combine paying heed to pupils' views with any of the suggested approaches to school improvement will achieve a more speedy improvement, while Hannam (1998: 3) is of the opinion that '*The views of pupils/students represent the single most neglected source of potential data for school improvement.*'

Pupil voice has become one of the cornerstones of the Every Child Matters agenda, and although agendas are changing the power of the pupil voice has been recognised and harnessed in school evaluation and improvement. Listening to, and benefiting from, the pupil voice is discussed in detail in Rita Cheminais' book *Engaging pupil voice to ensure that every child matters* (2008).

The future

The 2011 Education Act did not propose any changes that would remove the need for differentiation, or take away the benefits of personalisation. Indeed, the schools that find themselves, as Academies or 'Free' schools, outside the remit of the Local Authority or the strictures of the National Curriculum, may be the ones that are in a position to move away from the structures and systems that stand in the way of individualised learning (as suggested in the 2007 Children's Plan). These schools are able to teach pupils according to their 'stage not age', and on the whole 'test when ready' rather than at pre-set times. Some schools are already experimenting with early GCSE examinations, or taking key parts of what might be perceived as the 14–19 curriculum into the lower years at secondary. In 2014 changes were made to the way that success was recorded, in terms of school 'league tables', and so not all level 2 tests (e.g. BTECs) are now included, although a core of GCSEs must be present. In addition, Ofqual rules have changed, so that only a first attempt at a GCSE subject may be counted (to discourage early and repeated entry) and testing via modules is phased out. This means less personalisation is possible in testing, and this may have a negative knock-on effect on personalised teaching per se.

Conclusion

Of course, there is an obvious and dangerous conflict between the target-driven statistics, testing and ordering demanded by the government and Ofsted, and encouraged via school league tables and a subject-based curriculum and the idea of a curriculum geared to individual learning needs using individual learning preferences. Governments, parents and statisticians need the measurements to be able to chart progress and make comparisons. Individuals also need to be able to see and reflect on their own progress. Good learning is not always clearly linked to a subject, or to a level of progress within a subject, so it may be that, on occasion, you begin to think 'why am I doing this if it will not contribute to pupil grades?' The answer is that you are doing it because it is good learning, and because it is effective. This is a tension that you, in the classroom, will need to manage. You must take cognisance of figures and forecasts, but also plan and deliver a curriculum aimed at individual learners and their ability to succeed and to demonstrate that success.

Summary

- All pupils are different and every class is to some extent mixed ability.
- Differences include learning, language, and social and cultural backgrounds.
- You will need to take account of these differences in your planning and teaching.
- There are many types of learning style or preference – you will need to be flexible in your approach.
- Differentiation can be achieved using a combination of people, methods and materials.
- Personalisation is the concept that, where services are involved, the 'person' should be at the centre.
- Its application to education puts the learner at the centre and involves them directly in their own learning.

Key reading

Black, P. and Wiliam, D. (1998) 'Assessment and classroom learning', *Assessment in Education,* March: 7–74.

Black, P. and Wiliam, D. (2001) 'BERA final draft', in *Inside the black box: raising standards through classroom assessment.* Available at www.setda.org/toolkit/nlitoolkit2006/data/Data_InsideBlackBox.pdf

Gilbert, C. (2006) *2020 vision: report of the teaching and learning in 2020 review group.* London: DfES. Available at www.education.gov.uk/publications/eOrderingDownload/6856-DfES-Teaching%20and%20Learning.pdf

Goepel, J. (2009) 'Constructing the individual education plan: confusion or collaboration?', *Support for Learning,* 24 (3): 126–32.

Hall, E. and Moseley, D. (2006) 'Is there a role for learning styles in personalised education and training?', *International Journal of Lifelong Education,* 24 (3): 243–55.

Hutchin, V. (2006) 'Meeting individual needs', in T. Bruce (ed.), *Early childhood: a guide for students.* London: Sage. Chapter 4.

References and bibliography

Black, P. and Wiliam, D. (1998) 'Assessment and classroom learning', *Assessment in Education,* March: 7–74.

Black, P. and Wiliam, D. (2001) 'BERA final draft', in *Inside the black box: raising standards through classroom assessment.* Available at www.setda.org/toolkit/nlitoolkit2006/data/Data_InsideBlackBox.pdf

Boston, K. (2006) 'Tipping points in education and skills', speech to QCA Annual Review 2006. Available online at http://webarchive.nationalarchives.gov.uk/20081117153621/qca.org.uk/qca_11250. aspx

Cheminais, R. (2008) *Engaging pupil voice to ensure that every child matters: a practical guide.* London: David Fulton.

Gilbert, C. (2006) *2020 vision: report of the teaching and learning in 2020 review group.* London: DfES. Available at www.education.gov.uk/publications/eOrderingDownload/6856-DfES-Teaching%20and%20Learning.pdf

Goepel, J. (2009) 'Constructing the individual education plan: confusion or collaboration?'. *Support for Learning* 24(3): 126–132.

Gray, J., Hopkins, D., Reynolds, D., Wilcox, B., Farrell, S. and Jesson, D. (1999) *Improving schools: performance and potential.* Buckingham: Open University Press.

Grossman, P. and Thompson, C. (2008) 'Learning from curriculum materials: scaffolds for new teachers?' *Teaching and Teacher Education* 24(8): 2014–2026.

Hall, E. and Moseley, D. (2006) 'Is there a role for learning styles in personalised education and training?', *International Journal of Lifelong Education,* 24 (3): 243–55.

Hannam, A. (1998) cited in Ruddock, J. and Flutter, J. (2000) 'Pupil participation and pupil perspective: "carving a new order of experience"' *Cambridge Journal of Education,* 30 (1): 75–89.

Hutchin, V. (2006) 'Meeting individual needs', in T. Bruce (ed.) *Early childhood: a guide for students.* London: Sage. Chapter 4.

Joyce, B., Calhoun, E. and Hopkins, D. (1997) *Models of learning – tools for teaching.* Buckingham: Open University Press.

Lewis, P. (2007) *How we think but not in school.* Rotterdam: Sense.

MacGilchrist, B., Myers, K. and Reed, J. (2005) *The intelligent school* (2nd edn). London: Sage.

Miliband, D. (2004) 'Personalised learning: building a new relationship with schools', speech delivered at the North of England Education Conference, 8 January.

Perkins, D. (1993) 'Teaching for understanding', *Journal of the American Federation of Teachers,* 17 (3): 28–35.

Reimer, E. (1971) 'Peanuts', quoted in 'School is dead: an essay on alternatives to education', *Interchange,* 2 (1).

Sousa, D.A. (2012) *How the brain learns* (4th edn). London: Sage.

Waters, M. (2007) 'New curriculum, exciting learning'. Comment, *Guardian*, 5 February.

Welding, J. (1998) 'The identification of able children in a secondary school: a study of the issues involved and their practical implications', *Educating Able Children,* 2.

Worm B.S. and Buch S.V. (2014) 'Does competition work as a motivating factor in e-learning? A randomized controlled trial", *PLoS ONE,* 9 (1): e85434 (doi: 10.1371/journal.pone).

Visit https://study.sagepub.com/denby3e for extra resources related to this chapter.

CHAPTER 15

USING DIGITAL TECHNOLOGIES IN TEACHING STRATEGIES

Jan Barnes

Standards linked to this chapter include...

2. Promote good progress and outcomes by pupils
    - be accountable for pupils' attainment, progress and outcomes
    - be aware of pupils' capabilities and their prior knowledge, and plan teaching to build on these.
4. Plan and teach well structured lessons
    - impart knowledge and develop understanding through effective use of lesson time
    - promote a love of learning and children's intellectual curiosity
    - contribute to the design and provision of an engaging curriculum within the relevant subject area(s).

QTS standards in Wales are even more specific; trainees must

- know and understand the most recent national guidance on developing thinking, communication, ICT and number skills.

Introduction

Information communication technologies (ICT) or digital literacies have grown exponentially in recent times and the use of social media and mobile technology is now ubiquitous. It is with this in mind that as a trainee teacher you will need to think about how this technology can best support your practice. As a qualified teacher you will be expected to be able to use ICT effectively and appropriately to support your own teaching and also to support the learning of your pupils. The two key words here are effectively and appropriately.

Even though there has been a recent focus on the use of ICT and digital literacy to enhance teaching and learning, the availability of IT equipment such as tablets or the use of mobile phones in classrooms is not universal. Access will largely be dependent upon the ethos of the schools in which you are situated. Those schools where digital technologies or ICTs are integrated within all the curricula and used innovatively employ teaching strategies very different from those used in more traditional classrooms (Leask and Pachler, 2014). Pupils have an entitlement to be able to leave schools fully able to interact with technology and also be able to use digital technologies effectively and appropriately in their everyday lives.

A thought

Whilst the national curriculum and associated programmes of study state that ICT is to be used within subjects, this has gone far beyond the use of word processing and presentational software. The use of other, appropriate, software needs to be well thought out, and to be truly effective must enhance the learning process. Consider your own use of digital technologies over the last few days. Which of these do you think you could adapt to enhance either your planning or your teaching?

Digital literacy

What is digital literacy? Is it different from ICT as a skill? In 2012 The Royal Society in conjunction with Computing at Schools launched the report '"Shut down or Restart"'

(The Royal Society, 2012). This was an in-depth analysis of the teaching of ICT in England; one of the findings and recommendations was a rebranding of the subject and the inclusion of aspects of Computer Science into Information and Communication Technology (ICT). A further impact has been that in many instances ICT as a cross curricular skill is now referred to as Digital Literacy.

Digital Literacy consists of a number of metacognitive thinking skills which users of digital technologies employ when accessing digital information (Jones and Flannigan, 2006). Digital Literacy usually refers to the ability users have in effectively and appropriately accessing information in a digital environment. This skills-set is using not only ICT or a particular application, but also the ability to understand the outcomes of such use. This may include being able to understand the relationship between the use of variables when modelling a spreadsheet, or the ability to be able to communicate with different audiences for different purposes. Summey (2013) suggests that digital literacies are methods for managing information and communication in a variety of contexts, and further categorises these in the following manner:

- **Locating and filtering** which is concerned with finding, searching and identifying resources and at the same time being able to identify which of those resources are relevant to the task in hand. Examples of using this literacy may be internet searching; digital research; understanding how different search engines work; tagging.
- **Sharing and collaborating** which recognises the impact that social media have had on the global environment. However, it is also important at this point to recognise that it is interaction and collaboration which supports communication, recognising that effective communication can only exist between two or more entities. Examples of this literacy may include the use of social bookmarking; online document productivity; use of wikis, blogs, and collaborative use of the cloud (e.g. Dropbox, SharePoint).
- **Organising and curating** which is the recursive process of making sense of resources. This aspect of digital literacy may best be explained by regarding the conceptual background to databases and the storage of data, the definition of a database being a structured and organised set of data held on a computer. This aspect will also involve the ability to store, organise and search for that digital information. Examples may include E-portfolios; social bookmarking; microblogging; and VLEs.
- **Creating and generating** which is literacy not just being about creating new resources but also about the responsibility digital citizens have in that creation, whether via a presentation or a Wiki or a blog, or indeed a post on a social media site. Examples may include Open Educational Resources (OERs) and creative commons licence; podcasts; massive Open Online courses (MOOCs); and virtual

Learning Environments (VLEs). All of these allow opportunities for creating and generating material.

- **Reusing and repurposing** which is with the availability of resources via the web, particularly with the emergence of Open Educational Resources (OERs) and open licences, there has been a rise in the ability to recognise appropriate material which can be adapted for different use. Examples may include digital remix; mash-ups; OERs; and creative commons.

A thought

In examining the use of digital technology within your subject, and the subsequent development of digital literacy, it is useful to consider how comfortable you are with your personal digital literacy. For example, are you confident that you understand the examples associated with the various digital literacies?

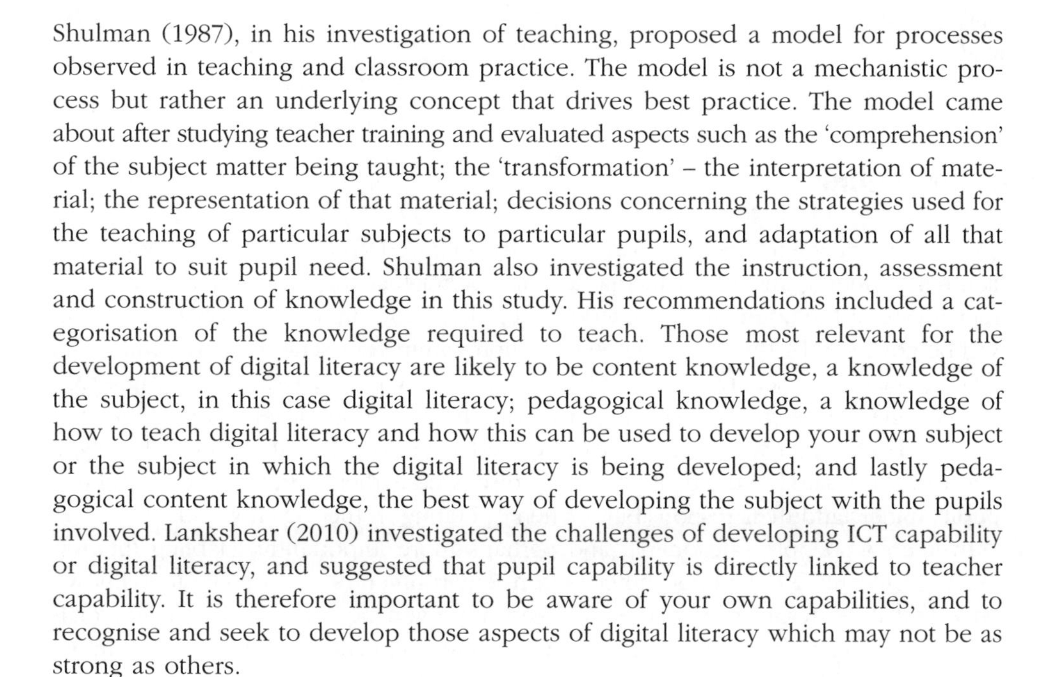

Shulman (1987), in his investigation of teaching, proposed a model for processes observed in teaching and classroom practice. The model is not a mechanistic process but rather an underlying concept that drives best practice. The model came about after studying teacher training and evaluated aspects such as the 'comprehension' of the subject matter being taught; the 'transformation' – the interpretation of material; the representation of that material; decisions concerning the strategies used for the teaching of particular subjects to particular pupils, and adaptation of all that material to suit pupil need. Shulman also investigated the instruction, assessment and construction of knowledge in this study. His recommendations included a categorisation of the knowledge required to teach. Those most relevant for the development of digital literacy are likely to be content knowledge, a knowledge of the subject, in this case digital literacy; pedagogical knowledge, a knowledge of how to teach digital literacy and how this can be used to develop your own subject or the subject in which the digital literacy is being developed; and lastly pedagogical content knowledge, the best way of developing the subject with the pupils involved. Lankshear (2010) investigated the challenges of developing ICT capability or digital literacy, and suggested that pupil capability is directly linked to teacher capability. It is therefore important to be aware of your own capabilities, and to recognise and seek to develop those aspects of digital literacy which may not be as strong as others.

INDIVIDUAL REFLECTION

How digitally literate are you? What are your ICT skills? Carry out an audit of your own skills: it may be useful to reflect on your skills when relating to the more traditional uses of software applications like word processing; spreadsheets; databases; presentation; electronic mail and the internet; and ultimately file storage. Once you are certain of how capable you are with these reflect on your use of the following:

- Videos
- Videocasts
- Video-blogging
- YouTube
- Podcasts
- Blogs
- Wikis
- VLE's
- Cloud storage
- OERs
- Mobile technology
- Mobile phones
- Tablets

Staying safe online

When using digital technology, particularly cloud-based applications and any form of internet searching and social media, it is important that the pupils in your care are fully aware of the boundaries needed to keep them safe on line (see Chapter 4). This will be governed by the ICT policy in operation within your school and it is important that you make yourself aware of how this impacts on your practice and on pupils' ICT use. Staying safe online is also concerned with the reduction of online threats such as viruses, Trojans and worms which can be hidden in downloadable media. Finally, if this aspect is related to the digital literacies discussed earlier, then it is also critical that pupils understand their responsibility when operating in the digital world.

In keeping people safe online, and perhaps more importantly enabling them to remain safe online outside of the classroom environment, it is essential to acknowledge that the internet has changed dramatically over the last decade. No longer is internet surfing restricted to the research of interesting material or facts, but with the evolution of Web 2.0 technologies the internet has moved from a medium of transmitting information to one where the expectation is of interaction with that medium. Web 2.0 technologies allow users to directly interface with whatever application they are using on the internet and has brought about the widespread growth of social media, blogs and wikis. People (including pupils) access these as both consumers and creators. With the ability to create comes responsibility; pupils should be taught the responsibility of their actions in their use of social media. Many pupils do not understand the possible consequences of the material they are publishing through these media, and should appreciate the impact their digital footprint (i.e. what they have created and published now) may have in the future.

A thought

Look at some of the learning resources available on the web concerned with internet safety (for example, the CEOP website). Register on the thinkuknow website at www.thinkuknow.co.uk/Teachers/Register/ How can you ensure internet safety in your subject area?

Key factors

When using ICT to support your teaching, there are a number of key factors that you may wish to consider when thinking about how its use will add to the planned learning experience and enhance learning in your subject. Developing digital literacy can aid skills development such as the ability to collaborate and share material, to assist in developing creative thought, and to aid problem solving. Use of complex searches, whether this is via the internet or through databases, develops the literacies linked to locating and filtering, which are skills integral to any form of research into an aspect or topic. The use of ICT, employing visual, sound bite, text and the ability to return to the resources, can help different learning types. Its use in support of the topic you are teaching may also make it more motivating and attractive to your pupils. ICT can be a motivational factor for some pupils, helping them in their writing. Other examples could be:

- the use of photo manipulation to support contemporary art in an art and design lesson
- the use of Google Earth within a geography lesson; the ability to zoom in and out of live pictures and then compare to the more traditional ordnance survey maps may bring the concept alive for some pupils
- the use of recorded speeches in a history lesson (such as Martin Luther King's 'I have a dream' speech).

Finally, the pedagogy associated with teaching a topic may call for the use of ICT or digital technology. Remember, the use of digital technology is only positive if it supports and adds to the learning experience and is designed to achieve better learning outcomes, so you will need to decide whether it will add to your pupils' learning experience. Using it 'for the sake of using it' is counterproductive – it is just another tool in your teaching toolkit.

Fixed or mobile?

Having decided that you are going to employ digital technology, and that the use of it is going to add positively to the outcome of your lesson, the next decision will be what form such technologies are likely to take?

Are you going to employ more traditional ICT strategies, such as the use of an computer laboratory with desktop PCs and possibly peripheral printers, or are you going to utilise mobile technology,such as tablets, mobile phones, cameras and other recording devices? The use of ICT, whether it is mobile or more traditional, requires careful planning.

Use of mobile learning has been present within education for over a decade, and in that time the technology has grown from the use of basic mobile phones to incorporating tablet technology, smart phones and MP3 players such as iPods. There are a number of different definitions for mobile learning, some of which have become synonymous with the use of iPads and apps within education. Seipold et al. (2014) are very clear that any ultimate definition of mobile learning should be inclusive, incorporating many facets of mobile learning rather than limiting the definition to the use of iPads and apps. One of the key aspects in the use of mobile learning is to be able to interact between learners and their own experience. Mobile learning allows a teacher to access learners' everyday experiences, such as the use of social media, surfing, and the collaborative dialogic skills with which users of mobile technology are comfortable. Good teachers are adept at turning these experiences into learning contexts.

With the use of traditional ICT the key factors which will need to be considered are as follows:

- Which aspect of ICT are you going to incorporate into your teaching?
- Which software application is best suited to support the learning you wish to take place?
- Do you have the correct access to ICT for this lesson?
- Is it logistically feasible?
- Is your ICT capability with the use of this software application sufficient to be able to support your learners?
- Will you need to teach your learners how to use the software application before you can utilise that software to support your learning outcomes?
- How do you assess pupil' learning; will you be assessing their use of ICT as part of this process? If so you will need to make sure that your learners are clear about their success criteria.

When using mobile learning there are further considerations which need to be reflected upon, including:

- How are you going to integrate the formal learning with mobility?
- How are you going to use mobile technology to construct the contexts in which learning can take place?
- If you are using apps to support the learning process how familiar are the pupils (and how expert are you) with their use?

The effective use of mobile technology is also dependent upon the IT network and the IT infra-structure; for example, there is a need for powerful Wi-Fi access throughout the establishment. Whilst these extra considerations may at first appear daunting, this is no different from when you are planning the incorporation of opportunities for literacy and numeracy within your teaching, and as such should not be off-putting but considered worthwhile when employing ICT within lessons.

The schools where mobile devices are used successfully in education are often establishments where the departmental heads and senior leadership teams have made conscious decisions about the use of mobile technology. They have considered how the mobile technology will fit into the ethos of the school and how the pedagogy of the subjects will accept the use of mobile learning. They will have also considered what training staff may need in order to comfortably and seamlessly embed the use of mobile technology into their practice.

GROUP EXERCISE

Rather than supplying mobile devices, some schools will plan for pupils to bring their own devices (BYOD). If you are thinking about employing a BYOD system:

- Will the pedagogy be suitable for all devices, Android, Apple, Windows or indeed laptops and phones?
- Are the apps/software you are thinking about using available for all devices and are the children able to download them?
- Are there any security issues either with the network or the internet which you may need to include in your planning?

In small groups map how these considerations could be solved.

Trainees' access to ICT

The use of ICT is also relevant in the support of your own teaching: it can help you plan, record pupil progress, and communicate and collaborate with colleagues. It can also assist in resourcing your lessons, for example, accessing online material. To enable you to do this you will need easy access to ICT. It is worth checking with your mentor or head of departments what ICT provisions are in place for you. For example, if you take your own tablet/laptop to the school will you be able to access either the Wi-Fi system or indeed the network? Many schools have computers in the staffroom or wireless networks which staff can access, and teachers often have their own computers. But remember – computers are complex and different computers are likely to have different hardware specifications and may be running different versions of software which may not be compatible. As a result, what works on, for example, your laptop, may not work in the classroom ... so you need to carefully check this out beforehand. It is essential that any use of ICT in teaching or learning you are planning is tried out in the specific classroom where this will be used.

The 'Cloud'

The nature of ICT is that it is in a state of constant development and with that development new innovations and adaptations frequently occur. The 'Cloud' and Web 2.0 technology are two such innovations, both of which were triggered by need. The 'Cloud' has been triggered by a need to combat the problem of storage and ever-increasing capacity needs. As applications become more and more complex, more and more user-friendly, and more and more able to have the flexibility to be operated by novices, the application size has grown. There is more capacity in even the most basic mobile phone than was present in desktop computers a few years ago. The result for combating the need for greater storage has been cloud storage. The 'Cloud' is a network of devices connected throughout the internet, offering storage through apps such as Dropbox, SharePoint and Google docs, with even social media employing this form of data storage. The key point to remember here is that the application is still using storage, just not storage over which the user has security control. For this reason everyone is well advised to use secure back-up procedures.

E-learning and blended learning

'If someone is learning in a way that uses information and communication technologies (ICTs) they are using e-learning' (Department for Education and Skills, 2003): this would imply that if you are using a computer, portable device tablet or mobile phone which has ICT capability then you are employing E- learning. The use of virtual learning environments (VLEs) within many secondary schools would indicate that e-learning has been embedded in education, particularly within the secondary sector. With advances in internet technology, in particular social media, blogs and wikis, use of the internet is changing, with an emphasis on communication rather than just information gathering. Pupils' use of the internet is based on interaction such as using social media or accessing chat sites. This change in perception of the internet has resulted in virtual learning environments becoming more widely used. These can be used as repositories for learning activities, or as repositories to which pupils may upload their work for teachers to evaluate, or as interactive discussion sites where pupils may upload and download podcasts, video blogs, images and generally engage with learning objects (Conole et al,, 2007).

If e-learning is about learning technology, then blended learning is a combination of the use of technology to support learning and traditional classroom teaching strategies. The important thing to remember when incorporating e-learning into teaching strategies is to ensure engagement. As with the use of any teaching strategy the key point is engagement with the learner; in the classroom this can be brought about through a number of strategies. These may include a dialogic approach, namely the generation of discussion or tasks employing a learner's metacognitive skills. Each of these strategies or activities requires a resulting change in perception of the subject being investigated. Hence learning is an active process, and the same active process takes place when employing e-learning. However, because the learner is distant from the teacher activities need to be devised which are going to ensure a two-way communication system to provide engagement. Examples of these e-activities can include learning objects to which the learner needs to respond in the form of discussion, or in the form of question-and-answer, or in using metacognitive skills to engage with a text and extract key information in order to engage with another activity. The important aspect when designing activities for e-learning is that each of these requires a self-motivated engagement.

Application to secondary teaching

Older pupils can make their learning deeper and more effective by using ICT to teach younger pupils. A group of Year 10 or 11 pupils could, for instance, post a video or podcast explaining a difficult concept in science, economics or mathematics, or demonstrating the pronounciation of a language. They could show how to use a tool in design technology or demonstrate a process. To be effective, pupils must learn the skill of aiming material at the right audience. This can then be archived as permanent resources within a department.

As explained previously in this chapter the use of ICT to support learning is changing rapidly. Games are emerging as credible learning objects, mobile learning is being incorporated in all classrooms, and there is the ability to use ICT in multiple forms with differing devices. Pupils use ICT automatically as part of their life outside of the school environment, via social media, smart phones and tablets. Utilising ICT in a lesson should no longer be a rarity but perhaps considered an expectation. Regardless of subject specialism there are apps and tools designed specifically to assist teachers in learning and teaching. Some of these tools may be generic whilst others have been designed specifically for the educational market. When selecting and evaluating any tool or app you may wish to use to support teaching, consider the following points:

- Pupils learn by doing, learning is an active process and pupils learn best when actively engaged in their own learning. Technology has the ability to make this learning more relevant.
- Pupils today are not only adept at using Web 2.0 technology such as social media, blogs and wikis, there is almost an expectation that technology in one of these formats will support the learning.
- Not only is there more software, but there are also interfaces allowing pupils to be creators of content and interact with that software increasing interactive learning.
- There are far greater opportunities for the use of voice and video and digital collaboration within the classrooms.

Application to primary and early years teaching

The four themes of EYFS are the unique child, positive relationships, enabling environments, and learning and development. These can all be underpinned by good practice in digital learning. It is important that the technologies used at primary and EYFS are appropriate to both age and stage of learning. Simple control technologies, for example, can both teach skills and allow children to learn through play. From 2014 in England the National Curriculum changed, and now includes an introduction to Computer Science from Key Stage 1: this encompasses programming using graphic interfaces such as Alice and Scratch. There are also many learning games that develop ICT skills at the same time as teaching numeracy or literacy. Play and exploration, safely and with appropriate technology, are key considerations. Primary and EYFS teachers should also consider involving parents, so they can 'catch up' with their children and understand how and why they are engaging with technology in learning. Pinterest, an image-posting site, has some interesting ideas (www.pinterest.com/tishylishy/early-years-ict/).

Due to the growth in the production of digital tools, apps and learning objects are available to teachers in all subjects. Development of these is constant so you will need to seek out your own specific examples for particular subject specialisms. The categories of such resources, from which you can choose the most suitable, include:

- **Web-based resources** are any resources found on the internet which can be directly or indirectly used to support pupils' learning. These may include websites, articles, web-based research, or games and activities. The internet allows opportunities to access material in a variety of formats (textual, graphical or multimedia). If using open educational resources, allowing collaboration with other teachers, you may re-use or repurpose under a Creative Commons licence. Web-based resources also include virtual learning environments such as Moodle, Edmodo, or Blackboard, and Web 2.0 resources such as blogs and wikis and social media. There are also bookmarking and tagging sites available such as 'Delicious' which allows you to collect the web-based resources in one area and tag them according to need.
- **Interactive whiteboards** and resources designed through interactive whiteboard software can be adapted to your needs. Interactive whiteboard software such as SMART and Activ allows the different media to be effectively drawn together within one learning object for use within the classroom. It also allows you to record work carried out within the lesson which can then be returned to at a later date to reinforce learning. Interactive software can also include the use of voting devices, which can be used to reinforce learning or generate discussion within the classroom. The use of voting technologies can ensure engagement and involvement, and at the same time give opportunities for forms of assessment for the teacher.
- **Multimodal resources** are large databases of images, sounds and videos which are stored electronically in a digital format for easy searching and use. An example may be the combination of videos, images and sounds to evoke particular atmospheres and environments to aid teaching, for example in history, English or geography.
- **Geographical Information Systems** are the use of technology such as Google maps and Google Earth together with GPS systems which allows for support in teaching geography and other humanities such as economics. Geographical Information Systems also allow the investigation of global statistics, coastal erosion, and the design and use of maps and geographical infrastructures.
- **Games** can be designed to simulate real-life situations that can be tested as part of the learning process. These may be of particular use when real-life situations are impossible to experience in any other way than through the virtual environment. Interactive games where the learners are making implicit and explicit decisions can also be used to promote logical thought and problem-solving skills.

- **Blogs and wikis** are effective self-publication tools that allow pupils to reflect on the learning, situations, or activities which supported their learning. They allow pupils to access the higher levels of Bloom's taxonomy, by reflecting on their learning, applying it to situations, analysing and evaluating. This can be further enhanced by the use of wikis to allow collaboration in the learning process. Wikis can be used to support team projects and group work that may be carried out over a period of time.
- **Podcasts and video casts** A podcast is a distributable audio programme, and these can be uploaded to, or downloaded from, VLEs. They can be particularly useful in language teaching, with podcasts made for students learning a second language enabling correct pronunciation. They may also be used to support pupils where English is an Additional Language. Podcasts and video casts may also be popular for form groups doing assemblies on particular aspects of their experience (a form group producing a video investigating cyber-bullying for example).

Summary

- ICT or digital literacy has become an integral part of education. There is an expectation of its use to support learning and teaching, but also from pupils who increasingly interact with ICT and digital technology on a daily basis.
- There are a number of extra considerations to be made when incorporating the use of ICT and digital literacy into teaching: the key consideration is to ensure that the use of ICT enhances the learning process.
- ICT and digital literacy can be used directly within classrooms, or can be used as a support mechanism in planning lessons, assessment, recording of people progression and production, and the use of resources.
- The use of ICT and digital literacy is growing through a vast array of tools and applications that are available both commercially and non-commercially through open educational resources to support teaching and learning.

Key reading

Seipold, J., Pachler, N., Bachmair, B. and Honegger, B.D. (2014) 'Mobile learning: strategies for planning and implementing learning with mobile devices in secondary school contexts', in M. Leask and N. Pachler (eds), *Learning to teach using ICT in the secondary school*. Abingdon: Routledge. pp. 185–204.

Summey, D.C. (2013) *Developing digital literacies: a framework for professional learning*. London: Sage.

The Royal Society (2012) *Shut Down or Restart? The way forward for computing in UK schools*. London: The Royal Society.

References and bibliography

Conole, G., Oliver, M., Falconer, I., Littlejohn, C. and Harvey, J. (2007) *Designing for learning: contemporary perspectives in e-learning research: themes, methods and impact on practice.* London: RoutledgeFalmer.

Department for Education and Skills (DfES) (2003) *Towards a unified e-learning strategy.* London: DfES.

Jones, B. and Flannigan, S. (2006) 'Connecting the digital dots: literacy of the 21st century', *Educause Quarterly*, 1–35.

Kennewell, S. (2013) *Meeting the standards in using ICT for secondary teaching: a guide to the ITTNC.* Abingdon: Routledge.

Lankshear, C. (2010) 'The challenge of digital epistemologies', *Education, Communication & Information*, 3 (2): 167–86.

Leask, M. and Pachler, N. (2014) *Learning to teach using ICT in the secondary school* (3rd edn). Abingdon: Routledge.

Miller, C. and Doering, A. (eds) (2014) *The new landscape of mobile learning: redesigning education in an app-based world.* Abingdon: Routledge.

Monteith, M. (ed.) (2004) *ICT for curriculum enhancement.* Bristol: Intellect Books.

Seipold, J., Pachler, N., Bachmair, B. and Honegger, B.D. (2014) 'Mobile learning: strategies for planning and implementing learning with mobile devices in secondary school contexts', in M. Leask and N. Pachler (eds), *Learning to teach using ICT in the secondary school.* Abingdon: Routledge, pp. 185–204.

Shulman, L.S. (1987) 'Knowledge and teaching: foundation of the New Reform', *Harvard Educational Review*, 59 (1): 1–22.

Useful websites 

ICT in education in depth: www.ictineducation.org
Educational games and simulations: http://nobelprize.org/educational/
Educational games and other resources: www.teachers-direct.co.uk
Tesconnect: www.tes.co.uk/ict-secondary-teaching-resources
Nearpod: www.nearpod.com
Google apps for education: www.google.com/edu/products/productivity-tools/
iPad Apps: www.google.com/edu/products/productivity-tools/
BBC: www.bbc.co.uk/education
Promethean interactive whiteboard resources: www.prometheanplanet.com

Visit https://study.sagepub.com/denby3e for extra resources related to this chapter.

CHAPTER 16

CREATIVITY

Sue Cronin and Sandra Hiett

Standards linked to this chapter include...

2. Promote good progress and outcomes by pupils
   - guide pupils to reflect on the progress they have made and their emerging needs
   - encourage pupils to take a responsible and conscientious attitude to their own work and study.
4. Plan and teach well structured lessons
   - impart knowledge and develop understanding through effective use of lesson time
   - promote a love of learning and children's intellectual curiosity

- reflect systematically on the effectiveness of lessons and approaches to teaching
- contribute to the design and provision of an engaging curriculum within the relevant subject area(s).

Introduction

What emotions does the term 'creativity' evoke in you as a beginning teacher? If someone asked you to do something creative would it excite you or scare you? Many teachers find the idea of being creative in their teaching a challenging concept. It is difficult enough to become an effective classroom practitioner so why put yourself under greater pressure to do something that may be risky or take you outside of your comfort zone? In this chapter we are going to consider the value of developing a creative mindset – that is a practitioner who sees the significance in developing a creative approach to teaching and learning. We will look at how you can develop skills and strategies and habits of mind that will support you as a teacher to develop your own creative capacities and most importantly those of your pupils.

A creative mindset

A starting place is to consider how we think and feel about being creative. Carol Dweck (2007) has undertaken seminal research into the importance of mindsets in learners and teachers. Her research has centred around the differences between growth and fixed mindsets held by learners and teachers and the impact this belief can have on learning outcomes. Dweck argues that some people believe that intellectual abilities are basically fixed, i.e. that people have different levels of ability and nothing can change that. In contrast, others believe that intellectual abilities can be cultivated and developed through application and effort. Her research suggests that it is crucial that teachers not only have growth mindsets but also work to develop them in their learners to ensure everyone grows traits of perseverance, resilience and hard work. These are the critical skills and attitudes needed by leaners to develop their full potential. It is the fixed mindset in the teacher and learner that creates a powerful invisible barrier to achievement. We can build on Dweck's notion of mindsets and the importance of removing invisible barriers to achievement to the idea of creativity. If we have a fixed mindset in relation to creativity we would not believe it is possible for a person to develop their creative capacities, whereas if we adopt a growth mindset we would believe that everyone has the capacity to become more creative in their thinking and actions.

A thought

Figure 16.1 shows the two ends of a continuum. In reality most people will lie somewhere in between and may move forwards and backwards depending on changing circumstances. Where do you think you stand?

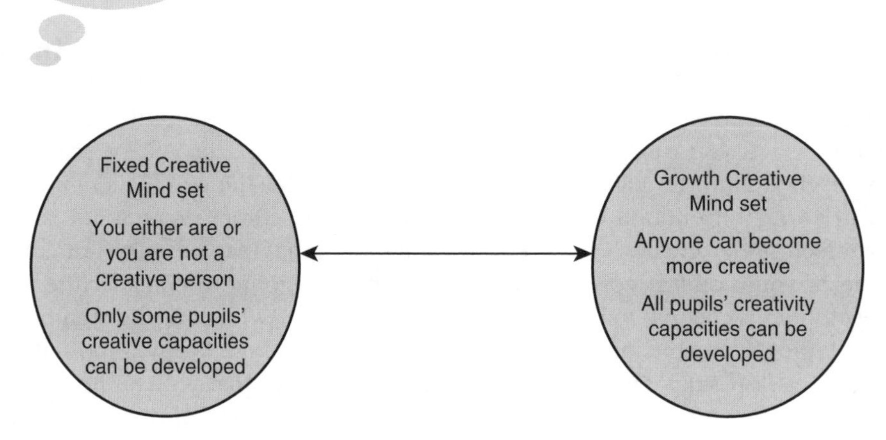

Figure 16.1 The creative mindset continuum

Subject knowledge

There is a link to confidence and subject knowledge in terms of where we may sit on this continuum. Teachers who are secure in their subject knowledge are more likely to have the confidence to take risks and to adopt more creative strategies for their learners. Teachers who are not secure may be much more likely to lock down the learning, avoiding open-ended approaches which could expose their own limitations. Thus depending on the familiarity with the topic or subject area you are teaching you may be more or less likely to teach it in a creative way. This is not inevitable – some teachers do not fall into this trap and take the opportunity to teach something new as an opportunity to innovate. It is important to be aware of the need to continually develop your own subject knowledge, because not only is there always more to learn but it will also support more confident and creative teaching.

Closely linked to the depth of subject knowledge is the potential to view some subjects as naturally more creative than others. The terms 'creative subjects' or 'creative arts' are frequently used to describe subjects such as music, art and drama: the natural inference is that other subjects such as the sciences and mathematics are not creative subjects. A danger of such an interpretation is that teachers may fall into the trap of developing less creative approaches in some subjects. You must be careful not to reinforce this false polarity and recognise the creative potential for teaching and learning in all subjects.

It is not only the subject content and the nature of the topic which may affect your creative confidence, it may also be your particular group of learners. For example, some teachers develop more creative approaches when working with lower attaining pupils, thinking they will require more varied learning strategies to maintain engagement and support understanding. There is a danger in both primary and secondary teaching in what are high stakes examination years, such as Year 6 and Y11, that lessons become limited to a restricted range of teaching and learning strategies. This is particularly the case with high attaining groups where expectations and assessment pressures can be particularly acute.

A thought

Thinking of a class you know, which children do you anticipate will embrace creative learning activities and who will resist? How could you use this insight to inform your planning and teaching?

Defining creativity

In deciding how to view creativity and if you have a creative growth mindset it is necessary to consider and clarify what is meant by the term. This is not easy as there are many different interpretations. There are many writers and theories surrounding the concept of creativity and creative teaching and learning (Craft, 2001, 2003; Perkins 1993; Robinson, 2001). In its introduction the NACCE (National Advisory Committee on Creative and Cultural Education) report 'All Our Futures: Creativity, Culture and Education' (NACCE, 1999) noted how elusive the term is to define and how different contexts give rise to different interpretations. It provides a democratic description which it argues recognises everyone's ability to be creative. It defines creativity as 'Imaginative activity fashioned so as to produce outcomes that are both original and of value' (NACCE, 1999: 30).

This statement is followed by a more in-depth explanation of the different elements. The meaning of imaginative activity is explained in terms of generative activity, namely thinking outside of the box and coming up with new approaches and alternative ways from the usual routines. This aspect is certainly achievable for beginning teachers as you will not have had the time to establish well-worn routines! Bringing fresh approaches to the teaching of topics will be a natural consequence of teaching many topics for the first time. This does not mean that you will not benefit from asking more experienced teachers for their ideas and strategies – very often existing approaches can be the inspiration for new creative insights. As the NACCE report notes, originality is relative to the person and their own previous work and output. It is not always possible or desirable to create something that is completely unique, but it is always possible to be novel and innovative. The final characteristic of value is an interesting aspect to defining creative activity, and the NACCE report sets out why this facet is essential. It is linked to the notion that creative acts stem not only from generative thought processes but also from evaluative thinking. Not every original idea can be of value – it may be a dead end, too bizarre or flawed. For the imaginative activity to qualify as a creative idea, the outcome must have some value in relation to the purpose of the task undertaken. Judging the value is not necessarily straightforward and there are many different criteria which could be applied: for instance aesthetic appeal, ability to satisfy, an ability to be enjoyable, as well as the degree of usefulness and effectiveness. Sometimes, the report notes, the value is not immediately recognised. Although this aspect is difficult it is an important aspect for teachers to remember. Developing evaluative skills is a key aspect of creative education, and guiding learners to understand and manage the interplay of the two aspects of generative and evaluative activity is a fundamental role for the teacher.

A thought

Think about how often you intervene when groups of pupils are working together. By being too keen to do this, you can stifle the creative process. Instead, stand back and, if it is necessary to take part, do so by asking open-ended questions; why do you think that will work ... what makes you say that ... what if ... ?

Creative endeavour

The democratic notion of creative endeavour being within the reach of all is echoed by Anna Craft's research (Craft, 2001; Jeffrey and Craft, 2004; Craft and Jeffrey, 2008) which differentiates between big C and little c creativity. Big or high C creativity is that which is the extraordinary work of a few elite creative geniuses, but little c creativity is the everyday creativity required to navigate through the changing social and economic times of an increasingly technologically demanding world. This definition acknowledges the creative powers of everyone and sets a challenge for you to be aware of, and take account of, this latent ability in all of your pupils. As teachers we must all create the conditions to harness these creative capabilities. This challenge has two aspects: you need to be creative in your teaching, but most importantly you must teach with the aim of developing pupils' creative powers. These two dimensions are linked but there are different considerations to both aspects.

Application to secondary teaching: case study 1

St Ambrose Barlow Roman Catholic High School in Salford, England, has been described as 'one of the top ten creative schools in the world' (Kelly, 2012). Arguing that 'creativity is what makes us outstanding', head teacher Marie Garside was awarded a CBE in December 2014 for leading this outstanding school. Since establishing a holistic approach to creative education, teachers at the school report that children are more engaged in their learning, are enjoying learning, and that they are making better progress. The increase in attainment is not just evident in those subjects traditionally considered 'creative' but is also evident in the rise in mathematics and English scores at Key Stage 4, with a significant increase from 59% A–C in 2008 to 82.5% in 2014.

What started with one teacher providing a catalyst for change has now resulted in the evolution over twelve years of a highly creative school with a whole-school approach supported by the entire staff. As an active participant in the national Creative Partnerships programme, Bernie Furey (Assistant Head) was aware of the potential benefits of creative teaching and learning for young people's education. Inspired by the pioneering work of Linda Nathan in Boston, Bernie and her head teacher visited the Boston Arts Academy, MIT and Harvard to investigate different models of creative education in the USA. This visit informed the creative school that St Ambrose Barlow RCHS is today. The creative school took time to develop in incremental stages, allowing teachers to embrace new ways of working over time. There are now six key elements that underpin the school's approach:

- **Personal commitment of the teaching team** to creativity is considered a most important element in the school's current success. This is a key aspect within the recruitment of all new teachers at the school, regardless of their subject discipline or years of experience, and features in every job specification.
- **Developing the curriculum** with a vision for growth over time.
- **Continuing professional development for all staff** is generated through yearly projects. Staff work in collaborative research groups to initiate and develop a project that must have a creative focus to last the academic year.

(Continued)

(Continued)

Each year new groups are formed to allow new teams to form. Beginning teachers at the school have training sessions every week and benefit from a school culture of developing creative pedagogy.

- **The school council** is given a significant status in school and student voice drives change. For example, the school council was asked to create a poster on 'what makes good teaching and learning' that has informed teachers' practice and the agenda for staff appraisal.
- **Working with outside partners** has become a core part of the curriculum. £20k is set aside each year to fund collaborative teaching and learning with external creatives. These collaborations provide experiences for staff and pupils that are aspirational, providing unique opportunities that bridge the world of school and cutting edge practices in the wider world.
- **The learning environment** is a key component in the learning experience and it is teachers' responsibility to make creative use of potential spaces to inspire learning.

This school requires everyone to have a commitment to the value of creativity. At an outstanding school such as Ambrose Barlow you could be asked questions such as the ones below. What would your answers be?

- Can you give an example of a creative lesson you have taught?
- Can you outline the advantages of a creative curriculum?
- How would you contribute to developing creative learners?

Teaching creatively

Teachers who teach creatively are more likely to provide the environment which allows creativity to flourish in their learners. This may seem an obvious statement but it is easy to forget the power of teacher modelling. In your classroom how you choose to operate will have a huge impact on how learners think and act. The opportunities you create can explicitly support creative learning, but how you act and engage will have an implicit influence on your learners. Cremin (2006) argues that in order for teachers to support the creative development of their pupils they themselves should be engaged in creative endeavours. Her research working with primary teachers showed benefits for those teachers who were given extended opportunities to engage artistically and creatively as writers themselves. By engaging in some degree of risk taking and experiencing what Boler (1999) termed a 'pedagogy of discomfort', the teachers developed personally in terms of their own creative outcomes and became better placed to support their pupils. Enacting a creative process, in this case through engagement with developing their own writing, allowed the teachers to empathise with their pupils' creative enterprise. They could recognise the difficulties and hurdles in undertaking creative activity and support and encourage risk taking. Learners will model their own practices on those they see demonstrated in their classrooms. As Jeffrey and Craft (2004: 84) note, 'Teaching for creativity is more likely to emerge from contexts in which teachers are teaching creatively.'

INDIVIDUAL REFLECTION

Recognise your practices in relation to creativity and in particular reflect on your questioning and 'thinking out loud' strategies. These are important elements of the modelling habits you want to develop in your learners. The use of skilful questioning to establish a creative learning environment is a key aspect of being a successful beginning teacher.

Practical steps to developing creative teaching

- **Develop an environment of enquiry in your classroom.** Creativity requires a questioning stance, and possibility thinking. As a beginning teacher you will need to establish a habit not only of questioning your pupils but also of questioning by your pupils. You will need to engender the 'what if?' question, ensuring your pupils know that not only is it okay to ask questions but it is actually important to do so. A safe environment where risk taking and thinking out loud are encouraged is an important nurturing space for creative activity. Together with your learners you can establish an environment in which ideas are generated from imaginative thinking considering all the possible answers to unexpected questions.
- **Vary teaching activities.** There are many great resources available to support good and outstanding teaching. Many websites offer free resources and materials to spark your own ideas. A danger is that there are just too many, and it is easy to be lured by a great looking activity which looks as if it will engage your pupils but which is not actually relevant to the learning objective you have set. Always stay focused on what you are expecting the learning outcomes to be for the lesson and look to use resources which will help you achieve these in novel and creative ways. The pupils can provide their own creative 'resource' through using their imagination, for example, tackling a mathematical investigation or a scientific experiment using their own designs. The key element is that you are clear about

what you are aiming to achieve, and then look for supporting stimulus rather than an attractive looking resource leading the learning.

- **Identify a creative coach and buddy**. Everyone needs encouragement and inspiration, particularly when starting in the teaching profession. Hopefully you will be lucky in finding plenty of support and encouragement from colleagues, but this does not always happen without some proactive help. There will always be cynics in the staffroom who have done and seen it all before and will tell you not to bother. Avoid these people! Creativity feeds off enthusiasm, passion and energy, so you will need to look for other teachers who have this and talk to them. They may not be someone you work with closely in your year group or department, but they will be positive and encouraging of your ideas and can act as a sounding board. Actively search for a creative buddy, someone who will get excited about trying out a new idea or approach with a class, maybe even undertaking a joint project. If this proves difficult look to the internet – there are many great blogs and sites to join and discuss latest education thinking which can inspire some innovative teaching.
- **Model risk taking.** Claxton (1997) identified a common trait of creative teachers as their 'confident uncertainty', i.e. they were sufficiently confident in their subject and pedagogical knowledge to allow space for the unknown. As your confidence as a teacher increases you should increase the space for uncertainty; allow space for your learners to surprise you and for you to surprise yourself. Taking risks with an idea you are not certain will work is an exhilarating experience. However it is important to be prepared for the inevitable fact that it will not always work – even though it will always be a valuable learning experience. This can prove particularly vital during your training. If you don't try new approaches, how will you ever find out which will work?

GROUP ACTIVITY

Work with a small group of fellow trainees to generate positive creative learning opportunities. Map the skills that you have already developed that could be helpful in developing a creative curriculum using a creative tool like a mind-map. Discuss what further skills you need to develop and add them on.

Teaching for creativity

- **Scaffold learner-centred activities**. Part of teaching creatively will be to include strategies that engage learners to think and act in autonomous ways. A key tool to nurture creative thinking is the use of 'what if?' questions. Your pupils need to become active agents in the learning process; considering different possibilities and explanations will support the development of those problem-solving skills that are needed to think creatively. This process aspect of creativity is as important as the creative product. Providing learning experiences in which there are choices and lines of enquiry open to allow the learner opportunities to make decisions is an important feature to build in to your teaching repertoire. Pupils need opportunities to take ownership of their learning, thus increasing their autonomy and engagement.

- **Create opportunities for peer interactions and group work.** Learners need to be able to play with ideas in increasingly skilful ways and this is helped by social interactions. Csikszentmihalyi (1996) argues that creativity does not happen inside the head of the individual alone but when these thoughts interact with others on a socio-cultural context. Thinking out loud and bouncing ideas off others can help the generative processes and the evaluative aspects of creativity. Make sure that you scaffold opportunities for these interactions and that this, in turn, scaffolds and supports the development of reflective and evaluative skills in learners.

Application to primary and early years teaching: case study 2

A three-year longitudinal research project in the North West of England investigated the understanding and implementation of creativity in education by beginning and newly qualified teachers from 2009–2012. Over 1,200 beginning teachers took part in a survey from five universities, including primary teacher training and secondary education students. Following the survey, 36 volunteered for an extended participation to track their teaching experience of creative education from their final training year through to the end of their second year of teaching. The aims of this research project were as follows:

- To investigate what trainees, NQTs and recently qualified teachers (RQTs) understand by national policy on guidelines on creativity.
- To understand if perceptions change over time, and if so in what ways.
- To know how trainees, NQTs and RQTs enact creative practices in the classroom.
- To identify the institutional (schools and training providers) conditions necessary to ensure beginning teachers can be creative in their classroom teaching.
- To know which steps schools and training colleges need to take to ensure creative practices are sustained.

(Continued)

(Continued)

The research showed that many trainees and RQTs initially lacked confidence in their own abilities to be creative, and what helped them to improve was a good mentor or colleague who could inspire and encourage. Interestingly, being observed was also useful in developing creative confidence. One primary NQT in the research project noted:

> The assistant head [teacher] came to observe me teach the other day because I am an NQT ... and at the end of the lesson she said, 'You do so many things that I don't think you really realise ... you were saying "I wonder what the artist was thinking when he made that", "I wonder what was going through his head", "I wonder how that is going to affect what you draw."' And she could see the [children] just kind of tilting and scratching their heads thinking.

In this case the NQT had not been aware of the impact of her 'thinking out loud' strategies on the pupils and on the atmosphere this helped to form in her classroom. The assistant head teacher had helped her start to see that she was beginning to establish a creative learning environment by encouraging possibility thinking and giving her pupils lots of opportunities to participate and share ideas.

Not every beginning teacher found their placement school was supportive of developing creative approaches to learning, and one beginning teacher discovered difficulties when she did not negotiate her intended approach with the class teacher first. This student teacher commented:

> When I used creative thinking techniques such as mind-mapping on placement the class teacher took them off the wall and threw them away as she thought they were scruffy.

In contrast another student teacher had found a creativity week placement had been a particularly 'valuable experience' that 'allowed my capabilities to grow'. Misunderstandings are more likely to occur where there is a lack of communication and agreement between all those investing in children's education. Team planning was a regular feature of NQTs' practice that reduced the chances of misunderstandings like those reported by the trainee teacher above, but often there was a need to compromise within.

Many of the NQTs participating in this research reported that their interest in teaching for creativity was informed by their life experiences before becoming a teacher. Common features included a love of learning new things, being engaged in interests and hobbies outside of education, and an ability to draw upon these experiences to enrich children's learning.

Children's attitudes towards creative education was a strong theme in this research and beginning teachers consistently recorded that high attaining children were often the most reluctant to try unfamiliar creative learning activities. They found the children who most often exceeded expectations through creative learning opportunities were those who underachieved or were considered less able within more conventional teaching methods.

It is important that children in primary and early years settings can learn through play. Describe how you could harness types of play to make learning more creative and more effective.

The TED talk by Sir Ken Robinson (2006) on the importance of creativity (www.ted.com/talks/ken_robinson_says_schools_kill_creativity?language=en) is an interesting discussion of the state of creativity in education. His conclusion is that 'creativity is as important now in education as literacy and we should treat it with the same status'.

Conclusion

If the purpose of education is to prepare young people for adult life, to develop their ability to shape their world, and to overcome the challenges that face them in order to be fully functioning members of the wider community, then teachers need to develop resourceful and autonomous learners. One of the legacies of objectives-led teaching over the past two decades in the UK has been the tendency to limit children's opportunities to develop creative thinking in what is often called a 'spoon feeding' approach to teaching. As a beginning teacher you may have experienced a rich educational experience where your creative potential was fostered. On the other hand, you may find that in order to embrace creativity in your teaching practice you will need to challenge the pedagogy that is familiar to you before you can foster creativity in your classroom. Developing opportunities for open-ended learning, child-centred engagement and teamwork (see Chapter 5) is part of any outstanding teacher's toolkit and essential for all creative teachers. Understanding the difference between open-ended learning and simply unplanned teaching is dependent on the teacher's grasp of what is meant by creativity in education. As a beginning teacher the key to success will be careful preparation, but planning and allowing opportunities for pupils to contribute to learning and surprise you will lead to exciting and creative teaching.

Summary

- Developing a creative mindset is important in overcoming the barriers to achieving creativity in teachers and learners. Don't assume that all teachers and learners have an innate creative mindset, and be prepared to nurture this in yourself and your pupils.
- There are multiple definitions of creativity. The way you conceptualise creativity will influence the values and attitudes that inform your practice.
- Teaching creatively should not be confused with teaching for creativity. These are related by not synonymous.
- Practical steps to developing creative teaching include: the development of a flexible and evolving teaching repertoire; establishing a coach or buddy to support you as you develop a creative pedagogy; and modelling risk taking for your students.
- Scaffold learning – creative education does not mean that it is unstructured or unsupported.
- Develop opportunities for peer interaction and group work and be prepared to develop children's social interaction skills over time.
- Communication and collaboration are key to developing positive working relationships in every context, and even more important where there is an element of unpredictable outcomes (for teachers and learners).

Key reading

Craft, A. (2001) 'Little c Creativity', in A. Craft, B. Jeffrey and M. Leibling (eds), *Creativity in Education*. London: Continuum.

Craft, A. (2003) 'The limits to creativity in education: dilemmas for the educator', *British Journal of Education Studies*, 51 (2): 113–27.

Cremin, T. (2006) 'Creativity, uncertainty and discomfort', *Cambridge Journal of Education*, 36 (3): 415–33.

References and bibliography

Boler, M. (1999) *Feeling power: Emotions and education*. New York: Psychology Press.

Claxton, G. (1997) *Hare brain, tortoise mind: Why intelligence increases when you think less*. London: Fourth Estate.

Craft, A. (2001) 'Little c Creativity', in A. Craft, B. Jeffrey and M. Leibling (eds), *Creativity in Education*. London: Continuum.

Craft, A. (2003) 'The limits to creativity in education: dilemmas for the educator', *British Journal of Education Studies*, 51 (2): 113–27.

Craft, A. and Jeffrey, B. (2008) 'Creativity and performativity in teaching and learning: tensions, dilemmas, constraints, accommodations and synthesis', *British Education Journal*, 334 (5): 577–84.

Cremin, T. (2006) 'Creativity, uncertainty and discomfort', *Cambridge Journal of Education*, 36 (3): 415–33.

Csikszentmihalyi, M. (1996) *Creativity: flow and the psychology of discovery and intervention*. New York: Harper.

Dweck, C.S. (2007) *Mindset: The new psychology of success*. New York: Ballantine.

Jeffrey, B. and Craft, A. (2004) 'Teaching creatively and teaching for creativity: distinctions and relationships', *Educational Studies*, 30 (1): 77–87.

Kelly, R. (2012) *Educating for creativity: a global conversation*. Calgary: Brush Education Inc.

National Advisory Committee on Creativity and Cultural Education (NACCE) (1999) *All our futures: Creativity, culture and education*. London: Department for Education and Employment & Department for Culture, Media and Sport.

Perkins, D. (1993) 'Teaching for understanding', *Journal of the American Federation of Teachers*, 17 (3): 28–35.

Robinson, K. (2001) *Out of our minds*. London: Capstone.

Visit https://study.sagepub.com/denby3e for extra resources related to this chapter.

Part III

IMPORTANT ISSUES AND SKILLS

This section brings together important elements of the framework in which you will teach. These may not fit comfortably within the 'Strategies for Teaching and Learning' section but are nevertheless vital for effective teaching and learning. The section includes discussions of issues that you will encounter sooner or later in your career, such as inclusion and the teaching of children for whom English is not their first language. Some issues are central to a successful classroom, such as the use of assessment and a clear knowledge of the rights of the child.

As a teacher you will inevitably be asked to teach issues and areas other than your own subject specialism, some of which will require understanding and empathy (such as PHSE) or to co-operate with other colleagues in delivering themes or priorities as decided by the government of the day. Cross-curricular and extra-curricular planning and teaching issues are therefore included.

There is also a wealth of information collected by schools that will give you an insight into how progress is measured both in schools and between schools, and the tools that can therefore be used to encourage such progress.

The final chapter is placed here in the hope that you will have now qualified, and will find this a useful guide to the unique teacher interview experience and the process of induction in your first teaching post.

CHAPTER 17

INCLUSION

Jonathan Glazzard

Standards linked to this chapter include...

5. Adapt teaching to respond to the strengths and needs of all pupils

    - know when and how to differentiate appropriately, using approaches which enable pupils to be taught effectively
    - have a secure understanding of how a range of factors can inhibit pupils' ability to learn, and how best to overcome these
    - have a clear understanding of the needs of all pupils, including those with special educational needs; those of high ability; those with English as an additional language; those with disabilities; and be able to use and evaluate distinctive teaching approaches to engage and support them.

Introduction

What is inclusion? As a trainee or beginning teacher it is important that you understand what it is supposed to be as well as what, in many cases, it actually is. It often means different things to different people and their varying vested interests inevitably influence how they conceptualise and interpret it (Dunne, 2009). It is not easy to get this right. Educators should not dismiss inclusion because it takes time to get it right or because they make inevitable mistakes along the way (Cole, 2005). Instead, they might consider using inclusion as a vehicle for experimenting with creative, innovative approaches in a bid to reach out to all learners. Arguably inclusion has become 'a risky business' (Cole, 2005: 342) for children, schools and governments, due to the current limited notions of school effectiveness: 'While social policy is dominated by the rhetoric of inclusion, the reality for many remains one of exclusion and the panacea of "inclusion" masks many sins' (Armstrong et al., 2011: 30). This chapter first looks at your responsibilities as a teacher in terms of inclusion, and then explores current debates regarding inclusion and the tensions associated with its implementation. It also introduces you to the Code of Practice for Special Educational Needs (DfE, 2014) and considers some practical strategies for meeting the diverse needs of learners.

Equality legislation

Inclusion presupposes a lack of discrimination, but this is reinforced by legislation. Your school, academy or college must comply with the Equality Act 2010 which outlaws both direct and indirect forms of discrimination for people with protected characteristics. These characteristics are listed in the legislation and include age; disability; gender reassignment; marriage and civil partnership; pregnancy and maternity; race; religion or belief; sex; sexual orientation. Individuals with these characteristics are protected under the legislation, and schools will need to be able to demonstrate that these individuals have not been subject to forms of discrimination including, but not limited to school admissions, bullying, harassment, or a lack of access to educational opportunities. Ofsted inspections focus sharply on a school's compliance with this legislation, and the penalties are severe in cases where inspectors find evidence of non-compliance. Schools will need to be able to demonstrate that reasonable adjustments have been made to enable children and young people to have equality of educational opportunity.

A thought

Think about a time when you have felt included. How did you feel? Then think about a time when you felt excluded. Again reflect on how you felt. Based on these experiences what does inclusion mean to you?

Your duties as a teacher

The Code of Practice for Special Educational Needs (DfE, 2014) emphasises teachers' duty to have the highest expectations of SEN pupils. It stresses that the quality of teaching is critical in raising outcomes for all learners, and that teachers must not use the label of special educational needs as an excuse for weak teaching.

Within current educational policy there is a clear assumption that providing children with the right kind of high quality teaching will, in the vast majority of cases, mean that they are not identified as having special educational needs. The Green Paper for special educational needs (DfE, 2011) identified a need to reverse the culture of low expectations that had prevailed in education towards SEN pupils. It challenged the over-identification of children being labelled as having special needs when in some cases pupils had not been provided with the right kind of teaching to meet their needs. It also highlighted that the special educational needs system in England was too complex, too bureaucratic, and picked up issues too late. Many parents did not understand the system and there was an insufficient focus on outcomes for children and young people (DfE, 2011).

The revised Code of Practice (DfE, 2014) attempted to address these issues by the introduction of a single phase of school-based assessment known as SEN Support. This replaced the previous two-phased assessment processes of School Action and School Action Plus. Statements of special educational needs have been replaced by Education Health Care Plans. These are multi-agency plans designed to reduce the need for different agencies to produce their own assessments. There is a greater focus on pupil and parent partnership in the revised Code than was the case in its predecessor (DfES, 2001), and there is a greater focus on outcomes for children and young people. The Code covers children and young people from birth to the age of 25, and there is a significant emphasis on educational institutions supporting young people with SEND into further and higher education, employment and housing, thus focusing on outcomes for young people.

Key principles of the revised Code of Practice

- Participation of children, their parents and young people in decision making.
- Early identification of children's and young people's needs and early intervention to support them.
- Greater choice and control for young people and parents over support.
- Collaboration between education, health and social care services to provide support.
- High quality provision to meet the needs of children and young people with SEN.
- Focus on inclusive practice and removing barriers to learning.
- Successful preparation for adulthood, including independent living and employment. (DfE, 2014)

The formal definition of special needs is unchanged and is stated as follows:

> A child and young person has SEN if they have learning difficulty or disability which calls for special educational provision to be made.
>
> A child of compulsory school age or a young person has a learning difficulty or disability if they have significantly greater difficulty in learning than the majority of others of the same age or has a disability which prevents or hinders them from making use of facilities of a kind generally provided for others of the same age in mainstream schools. (DfE, 2014)

Classroom teachers' responsibilities

Within the revised Code of Practice (DfE, 2014) there is a clear expectation that all teachers, including trainees, must:

- **focus on outcomes for the child:** be clear about the outcome wanted from any SEN support
- **be responsible for meeting special educational needs:** use the SENCO strategically to support the quality of teaching, evaluate the quality of support, and contribute to school improvement
- **have high aspirations for every pupil:** set clear progress targets for pupils and be clear about how the full range of resources are going to help reach these
- **involve parents and pupils in planning and reviewing progress:** seek their views and provide regular updates on that progress
- **teaching assistants can be part of a package of support for the individual child:** but should never be a substitute for the teacher's involvement with that child.

There is a clear emphasis within the inclusion statement that teachers must set suitable challenges for all pupils and respond to pupils' needs, overcoming potential barriers for individuals and groups of pupils.

The National Curriculum

Within the revised National Curriculum (DfE, 2013: 8) there is a statutory framework for inclusion which covers all national curriculum subjects.

Teachers should set high expectations for every pupil. They should plan stretching work for pupils whose attainment is significantly above the expected standard. They have an even greater obligation to plan lessons for pupils who have low levels of prior attainment or come from disadvantaged backgrounds. Teachers should use appropriate assessment to set targets which are deliberately ambitious.

Lessons should be planned to ensure that there are no barriers to every pupil achieving. In many cases, such planning will mean that these pupils will be able to study the full national curriculum.

A minority of pupils will need access to specialist equipment and different approaches.

With the right teaching, that recognises their individual needs, many disabled pupils may have little need for additional resources beyond the aids which they use as part of their daily life. Teachers must plan lessons so that these pupils can study every national curriculum subject. Potential areas of difficulty should be identified and addressed at the outset of work.

Unpacking the notion of inclusion

Hodkinson (2012) raises the question of whether inclusion, with its associated notions of equality and social justice, can co-exist within an education system based on neo-liberalist principles of marketisation and competition. His critique emphasises that inclusion has operated merely as an extension to the discourse of integration by placing responsibility for its success or failure on the learners rather than focusing on the quality of the learning experiences made available to them. A focus on presence and blame rather than a radical transformation of schooling demonstrates a lack of critical questioning about the nature of the curriculum and leads to the marginalisation of those learners who cannot compete in normative terms (Hodkinson, 2012). Wedell (2008: 128) has argued that schools which effectively include do so 'in spite of the system' rather than because of the system and this could explain why progress towards inclusion has been slow (Ainscow et al., 2006). Inclusion therefore needs to be unpacked, critically interrogated and problematised on both a theoretical and a practical level in order to develop a clearer sense of what it means and how it might be applied in educational contexts.

Levels of inclusion

Inclusion can exist in varying degrees from surface level to a level where it is deeply embedded into the value systems, rituals, routines and culture of schools and other institutions (Corbett and Slee, 2000). Inclusion cannot be divorced from personal values, and for inclusion to be successful within educational contexts, there needs to be a collective inclusive ethos based on shared values which are committed to the principles of social justice, equity (Erten and Savage, 2012) and democracy. However, this is problematic because people's values vary enormously (Hansen, 2012) and these will inevitably lead to variations in the way inclusion is defined, interpreted and enacted in practice (Sikes et al., 2007).

What do we mean by inclusion?

Current educational policy in England is focused on closing educational gaps between different groups of learners, thus ensuring equality of educational opportunity. The term 'inclusion' has dominated the educational global landscape since the Salamanca Agreement in 1994 when 92 governments agreed to 'adopt as a matter of law or policy the principle of inclusive education, enrolling all children in regular schools, unless there are compelling reasons for doing otherwise' (UNESCO, 1994, para 3: ix). However, the act of merely enrolling learners with diverse needs into mainstream schools does not do justice to the concept of inclusion.

Inclusion is a word which means different things to different people (Clough, 2000) with different vested interests. This is complicated further by the fact that social, political and cultural contexts shape interpretations of inclusion. Inclusion has a multiplicity of meanings (Graham and Slee, 2008), and so to pin inclusion down to a single entity would fail to do it justice (Nind et al., 2003). Inclusion 'is not a simple, unambiguous concept' (Lindsay, 2003: 6), not least because it cannot be disassociated from values, which are neither shared nor stable.

Avramidis et al. (2002: 158) have noted that inclusion 'is a bewildering concept which can have a variety of interpretations and applications'. It has become an elusive and empty term (Gabel, 2010) and Cole makes a useful point in arguing that it is better to explore meanings rather than the meaning of inclusion (Cole, 2005).

Inclusion has been reflected metaphorically in the literature as a journey (Ainscow, 2000; Allan, 2000; Nind, 2005; Azzopardi, 2010). Julie Allan's humorous reference to the term 'inconclusive education' (Allan, 2000: 43) serves as a reminder that inclusion is always in process and never complete. Thus inclusion challenges schools to continually develop their capacities to reach out to all learners (Ainscow, 2000) by developing pedagogies which connect individual learners with their own ways of learning (Corbett, 2001). Inclusion necessitates a deep cultural change within schools to make schools more able to respond to difference. It places an onus upon them to examine the environmental, curricular and pedagogical factors which limit achievement (Erten and Savage, 2012), resulting in a radical reform of pedagogy and value systems (Mittler, 2000). Such an approach represents a perspective which challenges educators to examine factors in the school environment which limit achievement rather than focusing on deficits within individual learners.

Emphasis on traditional discourses

Hodkinson and Vickerman (2009) have argued that government definitions of inclusion have continued to emphasise the traditional discourses of special educational needs. In fact inclusion is not just concerned with this group of learners. Inclusion reaches out to all learners and celebrates all forms of diversity. Rather than inclusion transforming the existing structures, policies and practices of schooling and challenging deeply engrained injustices, inclusion has sustained inequalities by creating subtle forms of segregation (Slee, 2011). Through its connection with special needs, inclusion has served to protect the status quo in schools (Graham and Slee, 2008; Slee, 2011). As a concept inclusion has continued to focus on notions of assimilation and presence rather than representing a struggle for equality, social justice (Hodkinson, 2012) and rights. Inclusive education must be disassociated from special educational needs so that it is able, as a policy discourse, to articulate its distinct values (Slee, 2011) based on social justice, democracy and equity. This necessitates a departure from processes which label, segregate and stigmatise to enable schools to embrace diversity.

GROUP EXERCISE

Work together as a group to share behaviour strategies that you have used or observed in school. Compare your strategies with those of Helen on page 254. Produce an information leaflet for your peers to provide them with guidance on how to manage challenging behaviour.

Exploring interpretations

Cole's narratives (Cole, 2005) are helpful in exploring interpretations of inclusion. They explore the collective voices of six women who were both mothers and teachers of children with special educational needs and disabilities. Within these narratives the mother-teachers emphasised the need for educators to embrace humanitarian values (Armstrong, 2005) by developing a pedagogy which emphasises care, dignity and respect. The emphasis on 'careful teaching' is also prominent in the early writing of Jenny Corbett (Corbett, 1992). The experience of becoming parents had a substantially positive impact on the professional identities of these teachers (Cole, 2005) and this theme has been identified in previous research (Sikes, 1997). The mother-teachers embraced the language of 'normality' by viewing difference as normal rather than special. In doing so they rejected the deficit pathologising language of special educational needs.

Christine Lloyd's call for a reconceptualisation of achievement and the 'denormalisation of institutions, systems and rules which comprise education and schooling' (Lloyd, 2008: 228) is central to understanding inclusion as a radical transformation of both policy and practice. Such a transformation demands major changes to the education system (Nilholm, 2006) by disrupting the current structures of schooling (the curriculum and assessment structures) which result in segregation and systemic failure. Inclusion raises critical questions about the purposes of education and challenges politicians to reconceptualise current limited notions of achievement. Transformation at a pedagogic level alone is insufficient to facilitate social justice. In order to develop inclusive schools, the curriculum and assessment processes need to be radically overhauled to enable education to respond to diversity. However, changing schools and school systems is problematic because 'there is not a perfect system awaiting us on the shelf' (Nind et al., 2003) and various models rather than one model will be required. The notion of inclusion as a radical transformation is a well-established theme within the literature (Mittler, 2000; Farrell, 2001; Nind, 2005), with some scholars emphasising teachers' role as change agents (Skidmore, 2004; Nind, 2005). Additionally, the emphasis on ensuring the maximal participation of all learners (Nutbrown and Clough, 2006) has also been emphasised.

Hegarty (2001) warned that inclusion would have a case to answer if it diverted attention away from a school's core function of promoting learning towards a focus of promoting values of equity and social justice. Whilst these critiques are conceptually sound they do not sufficiently articulate how the current structures of schooling (curricula, assessment processes, limited notions of achievement) create barriers to participation and achievement which subsequently result in exclusion. Inclusion is crucially about the politics of difference and identity (Slee, 2001b) which interrogates the structures, policies and practices of schooling (Slee, 2011). It demands a process of educational reconstruction and revisioning (Slee, 2001a) rather than a process of assimilation into an unchanged system.

A thought

Do you think that the education system meets the needs of all learners? What alternative models (curriculum and assessment) might be adopted to create a more inclusive education system? How could these be applied in your placement school?

Inclusion and standards: exploring some tensions

The term performativity was coined by Lyotard in his thesis entitled 'The Postmodern Condition' (Lyotard, 1984). It refers to the emphasis on the use of outcome-related performance indicators. These are frequently expressed as quantitative measures of performance which drive the modern education system through the use of narrow performance indicators which are then used to evaluate school effectiveness. School performance is evaluated in quantitative terms and made public via league tables and the publishing of inspection ratings. According to Ball (2003: 216) '... performativity is a technology, a culture and a mode of regulation that employs judgements, comparisons and displays as means of incentive, control, attrition and change ...' .

The Education Reform Act (1988) gave birth to a National Curriculum which provided an entitlement for all children to both a common curriculum and assessment process. Although the introduction of a common curriculum 'legitimated entitlement and extended notions of educability' (Bines, 2000: 23), such a move was problematic in that it failed to recognise the diverse nature of pupils' abilities. Additionally it perceived deviations from normal patterns of development as difficulties (Bines, 2000). Paradoxically, the National Curriculum, whilst claiming to offer a breadth of experience, failed to address the breadth of education necessary to meet learners' diverse needs (Wedell, 2008). The machinery of performativity was established by the Conservative government in the late 1980s and early 1990s through the introduction of high stakes assessment processes, school inspections and national performance indicators. Subsequent neo-liberal policies of governance have continued to base education on a functionalist model which uncritically assumes that the norms and values being inculcated are beneficial to all (Roulstone and Prideaux, 2008). This model emphasises academic success as a necessity for employment in an industrial society. Within this policy framework, inclusion has become a disciplinary force which has been used to regulate individuals and communities by emphasising individual responsibility for individual achievement (Armstrong, 2005). However, neoliberalist policies are problematic for children with disabilities who may never be able to lead an entrepreneurial life (Goodley, 2007; Goodley and Runswick-Cole, 2011).

Application to secondary teaching

The following quotes from students have been taken from my own research (Glazzard, 2010), and provide guidance to teachers on how to support learners with dyslexia:

> I think teachers should make lessons more exciting cos I get bored and distracted. If I'm not interested or think the teacher is droning on I just doze off into my own little world. I have to be excited, have to want to learn the subject. It's really important with dyslexic people because I think we have a short attention span.

> Well the person I think has done the most and really supported me is Mrs S. She has done the most out of the school ... She knows how I feel. She's qualified to work with dyslexic people ... She's always been there if I've needed someone to talk to or needed help. If I'm feeling down I'll go and talk to her and she has always sorted it out for me ... She's the only teacher in the school that's really done wonders for me. She has really helped me.

(Continued)

(Continued)

Some of them have written for me in lessons and they have given me encouragement and stuff and help with spelling. Yeah they have been generally supportive.

My history teacher at the moment, Miss K. She is very supportive. My special needs teachers have been supportive obviously ... They have told my teachers that I have got dyslexia so some of my teachers now realise that I need to be treated slightly differently, like not expecting me to write as much. All of them in fact have changed things like my history teacher. Like when they do lots of writing, I don't have to do it. She prints it off. My science teachers ... print the work off for me. I still do the questions and stuff. I'm not lazy. I still do all the work that they have to do ... I just don't have to write as much. That's the main example. It's just a lot easier to work in the lesson.

INDIVIDUAL REFLECTION

How do you think it feels like to have dyslexia? Arrange to talk to another trainee teacher who has a diagnosis of dyslexia. Find out which strategies they find helpful in supporting their learning; which are least helpful; what advice they can offer you in relation to supporting learners with dyslexia in school.

Quantifying success

Over the last two decades the language of performativity has been internalised by institutional leaders, teachers, learners and parents. Teacher and school effectiveness are evaluated both internally and externally on the basis of measurable quantitative outcomes. This pervasive discourse can have devastating consequences for those children (and their schools and teachers) who '... might never be capable of (nor interested in) such achievements' (Goodley, 2007: 322).

Inclusive values don't hit performance targets

Ball (2003) argues that the performative discourse has resulted in increased competition, devolved accountability, incentives, and the introduction of new forms of surveillance and monitoring processes designed to ensure that outcomes continually improve.

Within performative regimes Ball suggests that 'value replaces values' (2003: 217) as new performance-related values replace previous values of care, cooperation and commitment. Thus Corbett's commitment to 'careful teaching' (Corbett, 1992) leads to limited rewards in an education system which privileges outputs. Within this 'labyrinth of performativity' (Ball, 2003: 230) there is a high degree of instability, resulting in anxiety and insecurity. Teachers learn to focus their energies on maximising performance, often displacing their own professional beliefs about education for social justice (Ball, 2003). In turn 'the heart of the educational project is gouged out and left empty. Those who threaten performance (teachers and learners who do not fit the required marketised subject construction) are made to conform or excluded' (Roulstone and Prideaux, 2008). Thus, within a marketised education system, inclusive values are unlikely to be rewarded and education for moral and socially just purposes is displaced.

Whilst Ball's critical deconstruction of educational policy perceptively identifies the damaging effects of performativity, arguably the costs are greater for children with special educational needs and disabilities. Additionally, the costs of teaching learners who are unlikely to achieve national performance indicators are extensive, especially for teachers who work in schools with pupils with diverse needs. Despite this, teachers can make a positive difference to the lives of such learners and provide them with developmentally appropriate and relevant learning experiences, in spite of policy rhetoric which emphasises the importance of closing educational gaps and raising standards. Cole (2005) argues that inclusion presents itself as a risk on different levels when performance indicators are the overriding concern:

> Policies of inclusion have to exist within the context of the broader, general education policy but this is not going to be an easy relationship and it is one that many argue is incompatible ... In such a relationship there will be winners and losers and it is suggested that the losers will be the children who are deemed as having special educational needs. (Cole, 2005: 334)

Within regimes of performativity the use of compensatory and deficit approaches (Lloyd, 2008) seeks to maximise student performance. This inevitably creates tensions for children for whom the standards are unattainable or irrelevant. Surveillance mechanisms 'create subjects which are known and marked in particular ways' (Allan, 2008: 87), and continual pressure to attain socially constructed performance outcomes results in constant reinforcement of a sense of failure (Benjamin, 2002b; Lloyd, 2008).

Special Educational Needs?

Within official policy scripts (DfE, 2011; DfE, 2014) those learners with special educational needs are labelled as vulnerable and their teachers and schools are held to account for having low expectations. However, policy texts present over-simplistic notions of inclusion (Lloyd, 2008), fail to offer a radical transformation of the curriculum or the assessment process, and uncritically assume that one size fits all. As long as teachers continue to be 'assessed in ways that celebrate high-achievement over the valuing of difference' (Goodley, 2007: 319) inclusion may be too great a risk for teachers and schools to take, and children with special educational needs will become casualties within a policy framework that actively promotes exclusion. Limited notions of school effectiveness based on narrow performance indicators fail to engender inclusive cultures within schools. Schools and teachers which embrace inclusion ultimately risk developing reputations for being good at inclusion but ineffective in maximising educational performance, and for many schools this becomes a risk not worth taking.

Application to primary and early years teaching

Case study: challenging behaviour

James was an able 4 year-old who was perceived as presenting challenging behaviour. He had been permanently excluded from two nurseries prior to joining the nursery at school. This nursery was in a separate building to that of the mainstream school.

When James entered the nursery at school, he was deemed to be a danger to other pupils. He was regularly excluded on a temporary basis. He regularly kicked and punched the other pupils and threw equipment around the room when he was not able to get his own way. After a term it was time for James to transfer to the reception class, which was part of the mainstream school. A review meeting was held prior to the transfer to discuss his difficulties. The meeting was attended by professionals from the educational psychology team, the behaviour support team, teachers, and James's mother. At the meeting his mother attributed his behaviour to his diet by arguing that it was a response to certain additives. She explained that she was carefully controlling his diet and that this had led to an improvement in his behaviour.

Prior to James entering the reception class, he undertook a series of visits accompanied by his mother. The teacher (Helen) observed James closely and noted the triggers for his 'outbursts'. On one visit James opened the draw which held Helen's compact disks. He took a compact disk out of the draw and started playing with it. Helen asked him for it back. James refused. Helen explained that if he did not give it to her, she would take it off him. He still refused and so she removed it from his hand. James responded to this by picking up the box of disks and throwing them around the room. He then picked up a scanner which was next to a computer and threw it across the room. It narrowly missed another child.

When James came into the reception class on a full-time basis he demonstrated a range of behaviours. He would strum the radiators whilst Helen was talking, he constantly shouted out, and he often refused to cooperate with teacher expectations. He regularly hit other children and refused to sit down during whole-class sessions. James was particularly challenging towards the supply teachers by refusing to cooperate with their expectations. His behaviour at lunchtime was a cause for concern. He ignored requests from lunchtime supervisors and threw cutlery at other children.

James did not respond well to sanctions. On one occasion he was made to stay in the classroom at playtime and he reacted by kicking the chairs around the room and pulling the displays down from the wall. On another occasion when James was withdrawn from the classroom for disruptive behaviour, he responded by scratching Helen's hands.

Helen developed a variety of strategies for dealing with James. These strategies worked well. This was measured by a reduction in the number of fixed-term exclusions that had to be made. The strategies were:

- **Time out.** This strategy was applied when James refused to comply with Helen's requests. The request was repeated a second time to give James the opportunity to rectify his mistake. If he still refused to do as he was asked he was taken out of the classroom to sit in a set place. He was accompanied by his teaching assistant. A sand timer was used and set into operation from the moment he sat down. The teaching assistant sat with her back to James during the entire time pretending to be busy with a task. This was deliberate so that James did not gain attention. If he was sitting calmly by the time the sand had travelled through the timer he was then allowed to return to class. If he continued to be disruptive the sand timer was turned without warning and the process started again. During the whole process there was no communication between James and the teaching assistant. It was only necessary to turn the sand timer a second time on one occasion.
- **Positive reinforcement.** This strategy was used when James was deliberately being slow at changing his shoes in the cloakroom. Instead of asking him to hurry up, Helen would go to James and emphasise to him that she was really pleased with the way he was trying. James would then work faster to please Helen even more. This strategy was simple but very effective.
- This strategy was also applied when James was taken off a group activity to do one-to-one reading. James often pretended that he could not say his sounds or

(Continued)

(Continued)

read his words. Helen started to praise him as soon as he sat down by telling him that he was a good reader and she really enjoyed listening to him. This strategy worked well as James worked hard to please Helen. Another effective strategy was to carry out individual sessions with James five minutes before playtime. He soon realised that he had to complete the task or he would miss some of his break.

- **Working with all the adults in the setting.** Initially James only responded to requests from Helen. He was particularly difficult when working with other adults in the setting. Helen shared useful strategies with the support staff and ensured that James spent several weeks working with each adult other than herself. All the adults had equal responsibility for managing his behaviour and they all had the authority to put the strategies into operation. James started to then see the adults as having equal status.

James's behaviour in the classroom really improved. However, he continued to present challenging behaviours to other adults in school such as lunchtime supervisors (when James was in the dining room and on the playground), the head teacher (when James was in assembly) and other teachers (when they were carrying out playground supervision). The head teacher frequently had to send him out of assembly and back to Helen. Other teachers on duty at playtime sent for her if he presented inappropriate behaviour and lunchtime supervisors also referred problems back to her. The consequences of these actions were that James felt that the only adults who were able to manage his behaviour were those in his classroom and he refused to cooperate with any other adult in the school.

Practical strategies to support inclusion

The following strategies may support you in implementing your duty to include pupils. However, this is not an exhaustive list:

Pre-teaching skills and knowledge before lessons

Promoting diversity through events

Providing access to different resources (physical or human) to enable pupils to access the lesson

Visual timetables to provide clarity of routine

Technological adaptations including specialist software and hardware such as laptops, tablets and spell-checkers

Using a range of visual, auditory, and kinaesthetic teaching and learning strategies

Using writing frames or other planning templates to support students to structure written tasks

Providing pupils with written/pictorial instructions to enable them to complete a task

Providing short, focused tasks rather than one long task

Printing handouts on coloured paper

Providing students with notes rather than expecting them to write in lessons

Making the learning active and practical

Finding alternative ways of recording learning rather than writing in lessons, e.g. making a film/poster/presentation

Teaching children explicitly about specific impairments and providing them with strategies to support their peers.

Summary

- Inclusion is a broad term and is not limited to pupils with special educational needs.
- You need to have high expectations of every child that you teach.
- You need to plan to remove barriers to learning, participation and achievement.
- View learning difficulties as challenges for your teaching rather than difficulties within the child.
- Have a positive attitude towards all learners and encourage them to achieve their best.
- Challenge discrimination directly.
- Promote diversity in your teaching.

Key reading

Ainscow, M., Booth, T. and Dyson, A. (2006) 'Inclusion and the standards agenda: negotiating policy pressures in England', *International Journal of Inclusive Education*, 10 (4/5): 295–308.

Dunne, L. (2009) 'Discourses of inclusion: a critique', *Power and Education*, 1 (1): 42–56.

Glazzard, J., Hughes, A., Netherwood, A., Neve, L. and Stokoe, J. (2015) *Teaching and supporting children with special educational needs and disabilities in primary schools*. London: Sage.

References and bibliography

Ainscow, M. (2000) 'Profile', in P. Clough and J. Corbett (eds), *Theories of inclusive education: a students' guide*. London: Paul Chapman.

Ainscow, M., Booth, T. and Dyson, A. (2006) 'Inclusion and the standards agenda: negotiating policy pressures in England', *International Journal of Inclusive Education*, 10 (4/5): 295–308.

Allan, J. (2000) 'Reflection: inconclusive education? Towards settled uncertainty', in P. Clough and J. Corbett (eds), *Theories of inclusive education: a students' guide*. London: Paul Chapman.

Allan, J. (2006) 'The repetition of exclusion', *International Journal of Inclusive Education*, 10 (2/3): 121–33.

Allan, J. (2008) *Rethinking inclusion: the philosophers of difference in practice*. Dordrecht: Springer.

Armstrong, D. (2005) 'Reinventing "'inclusion"': New Labour and the cultural politics of special education', *Oxford Review of Education*, 31 (1): 135–51.

Armstrong, D., Armstrong, A.C. and Spandagou, I. (2011) 'Inclusion: by choice or chance?', *International Journal of Inclusive Education*, 15 (1): 29–39.

Avramidis, E., Bayliss, P. and Burden, R. (2002) 'Inclusion in action: an in-depth case study of an effective inclusive secondary school in the south-west of England', *International Journal of Inclusive Education*, 6 (2): 143–63.

Azzopardi, A. (2010) *Making sense of inclusive education: where everyone belongs*. Saarbrucken: VDM.

Ball, S.J. (2003) 'The teacher's soul and the terrors of performativity', *Journal of Education Policy*, 18 (2): 215–28.

Benjamin, S. (2002a) 'Valuing diversity: a cliché for the 21st century?', *International Journal of Inclusive Education*, 6 (4): 309–23.

Benjamin, S. (2002b) *The micropolitics of inclusive education*. Buckingham: Open University Press.

Bines, H. (2000) 'Inclusive standards: current developments in policy for special educational needs in England and Wales', *Oxford Review of Education*, 26 (1): 21–33.

Black-Hawkins, K., Florian, L. and Rouse, M. (2007) *Achievement and inclusion in schools*. London: Routledge.

Clough, P. (2000) 'Routes to inclusion', in P. Clough and J. Corbett (eds), *Theories of inclusive education: a students' guide*. London: Paul Chapman.

Cole, B. (2005) 'Good faith and effort? Perspectives on educational inclusion', *Disability and Society*, 20 (3): 331–44.

Corbett, J. (1992) 'Careful teaching: researching a special career', *British Educational Research Journal*, 18 (3): 235–43.

Corbett, J. (2000) 'Profile', in P. Clough and J. Corbett (eds), *Theories of inclusive education*. London: Sage, pp. 69–73.

Corbett, J. (2001) 'Teaching approaches which support inclusive education: a connective pedagogy', *British Journal of Special Education*, 28 (2): 55–9.

Corbett, J. and Slee, R. (2000) 'An international conversation on inclusive education', in F. Armstrong, D. Armstrong and L. Barton (eds) *Inclusive education: policy, contexts and comparative perspectives*. London: Fulton.

Department for Education (DfE) (2011) *Support and aspiration: a new approach to special educational needs and disability: a consultation*. London: DfE.

Department for Education (DfE) (2013) *The National Curriculum in England: Key Stages 1 and 2 Framework Document*. London: DfE.

Department for Education (DfE) (2014) Special educational needs and disability code of practice: 0 to 25 years: Statutory guidance for organisations who work with and support children and young people with special educational needs and disabilities. London: DfE.

Department for Education and Skills (DfES) (2001) *Special educational needs code of practice*. London: DfES.

Dunne, L. (2009) 'Discourses of inclusion: a critique', *Power and Education*, 1 (1): 42–56.

Dyson, A. (2001) 'Special needs education as the way to equity: an alternative approach?', *Support for Learning*, 16 (3): 99–104.

Erten, O. and Savage, R.S. (2012) 'Moving forward in inclusive education research', *International Journal of Inclusive Education*, 16 (2): 221–33.

Farrell, P. (2001) 'Special education in the last twenty years: have things really got better?', *British Journal of Special Education*, 28 (1): 3–9.

Gabel, S.L. (2010) 'Foreward: disability and equity in education and special education', in A. Azzopardi (ed.), *Making sense of inclusive education: where everyone belongs*. Saarbrucken, VDM, pp. 9–10.

Giroux, H.A. (2003) 'Public pedagogy and the politics of resistance: notes on a critical theory of educational struggle', *Educational Philosophy and Theory*, 35 (1): 5–16.

Glazzard, J. (2010) 'he impact of dyslexia on pupils' self-esteem', *Support for Learning*, 25 (2): 63–9.

Goodley, D. (2007) 'Towards socially just pedagogies: Deleuzoguattarian critical disability studies', *International Journal of Inclusive Education*, 11 (3): 317–34.

Goodley, D. and Runswick-Cole, K. (2010) 'Len Barton, inclusion and critical disability studies: theorizing disabled childhoods', *International Studies in Sociology of Education*, 20 (4): 273–90.

Graham, L.J. and Slee, R. (2008) 'An illusory interiority: interrogating the discourse/s of inclusion', *Educational Philosophy and Theory*, 40 (2): 247–60.

Hansen, J.H. (2012) 'Limits to inclusion', *International Journal of Inclusive Education*, 16 (1): 89–98.

Hegarty, S. (2001) 'Inclusive education – a case to answer', *Journal of Moral Education*, 30 (3): 243–9.

Hodkinson, A. (2012) '"All present and correct?": exclusionary inclusion within the English education system', *Disability and Society*, 27 (5): 675–88.

Hodkinson, A. and Vickerman, P. (2009) *Key issues in special educational needs and inclusion*. London: Sage.

Lindsay, G. (2003) 'Inclusive education: a critical perspective', *British Journal of Special Education*, 30 (1): 3–12.

Lloyd, C. (2008) 'Removing barriers to achievement: a strategy for inclusion or exclusion?', *International Journal of Inclusive Education*, 12 (2): 221–36.

Lyotard, J.F. (1984) *The postmodern condition: a report on knowledge*, Vol. 10. Manchester: Manchester University Press.

Mittler, P. (2000) *Working towards inclusive education: social contexts*. London: David Fulton.

Nilholm, C. (2006) 'Special education, inclusion and democracy', *European Journal of Special Needs Education*, 21 (4): 431–45.

Nind, M. (2005) 'Inclusive education: discourse and action', *British Educational Research Journal*, 31 (2): 269–75.

Nind, M., Rix, J., Sheehy, K. and Simmons, K. (2003) *Inclusive education: diverse perspectives*. London: David Fulton.

Nutbrown, C. and Clough, P. (2006) *Inclusion in the early years*. London: Sage.

O'Hanlon, C. (2003) *Educational inclusion as action research*. Maidenhead: McGraw-Hill Education.

Roulstone, A. and Prideaux, S. (2008) 'More policies, greater inclusion? Exploring the contradictions of New Labour Inclusive Education Policy', *International Studies in Sociology of Education*, 18 (1): 15–29.

Sikes, P. (1997) *Parents who teach: stories from home and from school*. London: Cassell.

Sikes, P., Lawson, H. and Parker, M. (2007) 'Voices on: teachers and teaching assistants talk about inclusion', *International Journal of Inclusive Education*, 11(3): 355–70.

Skidmore, D. (2004) *Inclusion: the dynamic of school development*. Berkshire: Open University Press.

Slee, R. (2001a) 'Social justice and the changing directions in educational research: the case of inclusive education', *International Journal of Inclusive Education*, 5 (2/3): 167–77.

Slee, R. (2001b) 'Inclusion in practice: does practice make perfect?', *Educational Review*, 53 (2): 113–23.

Slee, R. (2011) *The irregular school: exclusion, schooling and inclusive education*. London: Routledge.

Slee, R. and Allan, J. (2001) 'Excluding the included: a reconsideration of inclusive education', *International Studies in Sociology of Education*, 11 (2): 173–91.

UNESCO (1994) *The Salamanca Statement and framework for Action on Special needs Education,* World Conference on Special Needs Education Access and Quality, Available at www.unesco.org/education/pdf/SALAMA_E.PDF (last accessed 01.08.13).

Wedell, K. (2008) 'Confusion about inclusion: patching up or system change?', *British Journal of Special Education*, 35 (3): 127–35.

Wilson, J. (2000) 'Doing justice to inclusion', *European Journal of Special Needs Education*, 15 (3): 297–304.

Visit https://study.sagepub.com/denby3e for extra resources related to this chapter.

CHAPTER 18

TEACHING PUPILS WITH ENGLISH AS AN ADDITIONAL LANGUAGE

Ian Quigley

Standards linked to this chapter include...

1. Set high expectations which inspire, motivate and challenge pupils
    - set goals that stretch and challenge pupils of all backgrounds, abilities and dispositions.
2. Promote good progress and outcomes by pupils
    - be aware of pupils' capabilities and their prior knowledge, and plan teaching to build on these.

(Continued)

(Continued)

5. Adapt teaching to respond to the strengths and needs of all pupils

   - know when and how to differentiate appropriately, using approaches which enable pupils to be taught effectively
   - have a secure understanding of how a range of factors can inhibit pupils' ability to learn, and how best to overcome these
   - have a clear understanding of the needs of all pupils, including those with special educational needs; those of high ability; those with English as an additional language; those with disabilities; and be able to use and evaluate distinctive teaching approaches to engage and support them.

Introduction

The School Census data for 2012 indicated that there were 8.2 million children in English schools: 4.2 million students were educated in state-funded primary schools, 3.2 million in state-funded secondary schools, with the remainder in fee-paying independent institutions. Within the state sector, over one quarter of the 7.4 million pupils had an ethnicity other than *White British*. Of course, many of these children were from families who have lived in this country for several generations, yet 18 per cent of primary pupils and 13 per cent of secondary students were classified in national statistics as having a first language other than English (NALDIC, 2012).

It is these children who must learn English whilst frequently speaking and being regularly exposed to another language. We refer to these pupils as having English as an 'additional language', and they are therefore known as *EAL students*. DfE statistics showed that in 2012 the number of EAL learners in English state schools exceeded one million for the first time. With average class sizes of 27 in the primary phase and 21 in the secondary sector, it is not unreasonable to expect two, three or four EAL students in any English classroom. Whilst this number will vary between schools in rural or urban environments, all newly qualified teachers should be aware of the issues faced by these pupils and also of the teaching strategies that can be used to maximise their learning.

A thought

How plurilingual are you? How many languages can you use to say hello or goodbye?

Glossary

Teachers undertaking work in this area can find a range of terms that, at first, seem interchangeable but in fact are subtly different. A glossary is useful in providing clarity of meaning. Franson (2009) provides the best.

Bilingual

The term describes a learner who uses two languages to communicate.

Plurilingual

This term is used to describe individuals who speak more than two languages.

Multilingual

This term does not refer to individuals but groups or institutions. You may live in a multilingual community or work in a multilingual school. Some of the people within it, however, may be bilingual or plurilingual.

Native Speaker

An individual who uses a language, other than English, as their first language.

Community Languages

This term refers to the languages, other than English, that are spoken within a geographic area. For example, Punjabi is one of the predominant community languages in Bradford.

Home Language

The language most frequently used within an individual's home. A pupil, for example, may have Polish as their home language, but live in a neighbourhood where Bengali is the predominant community language spoken in local shops, and attend a primary school where she is taught in English.

Mother Tongue

This term refers to the learner's first language and will usually be the language of the home. As a student progresses through the educational system, it may, however, not be the language they speak most frequently.

Who are EAL students?

The backgrounds and circumstances of EAL students are as wide and varied as with any other group of students. It is, however, useful to delineate them into two groups:

1. Students who have recently arrived in this country.
2. Students whose families may have lived in this country for many years but do not speak English at home.

'New arrivals'

A child from a family who has recently arrived in this country will be accessing the British education system for the first time. These students face a number of challenges. Not only do they have to learn English, they will also have to learn a curriculum in this new language. In the classroom and the playground, they will have to socialise in a language they are unfamiliar with and assimilate the social and cultural expectations of their new environment (South, 1999). The ability of a 'new arrival' to meet these challenges will depend on a variety of factors, including:

- their previous educational experiences
- their levels of literacy and oracy in their first language
- their familiarity with the Roman script
- their social, economic, and even political circumstances.

The potential spectrum of experiences is illustrated by the case studies below.

Student 1

Lukas is 12 and recently arrived in this country from Germany. His father, who speaks English fluently, has been promoted to a senior position at the local car factory. Lukas attended kindergarten and the local *Hauptschule* (elementary school) until the age of 11. He spent two terms at the town *Gymnasium* where he studied English as part of the curriculum. Lukas is very 'sporty' and is hoping to play football for the school. He has previously visited England on a family holiday, but all he remembers was the rain!

Student 2

Amina is 9 and arrived in England six months ago from Somalia. The family has recently been granted refugee status. The circumstances in her home country are such that she has received little formal education. Amina has knowledge of some

English words and phrases that she learnt at the Short Term Holding Facility. The family has been housed in an area of town with a predominantly Muslim population. Despite her African name meaning 'peaceful and secure', Amina appears nervous and withdrawn.

GROUP EXERCISE

As a teacher, what information would you require for a 'new arrival' EAL student joining your class? In groups of three, devise a checklist of appropriate questions. Share these with your cohort. Discuss what assistance you might need in gaining answers to these questions.

'British bilingual'

Large numbers of ethnic minority students have spent all of their lives living in Britain and readily use 'everyday colloquial English' (Franson, 2009). They speak a minority language at home and in their community, but speak English at school.

For these pupils, their ability to communicate with a level of competence can lead to an assumption that their understanding of English and their progress as learners are much greater than they actually are (South, 1999). Many of these children may have reached a 'plateau' in their understanding of English and often find it difficult to make further progress (Franson, 2009). Consider these case studies.

Student 3

Ceyda is 8 years-old and was born in the UK of Turkish parents. Her mother only speaks Turkish, but her father works locally and is competent at conversational English. When Ceyda joined the reception class she spoke her home language almost exclusively. She initially made good progress but has not yet developed an understanding of tense – 'Miss, I am hungry for I am not eating this morning'. When questioned at a parents' evening, Ceyda and her father are more concerned with her progress in mathematics than in English.

Student 4

Juniad is a high achieving Year 10 student studying nine GCSE subjects. He lives in a predominantly Muslim community and attends a multicultural school. His mother and father speak conversational English and he has a brother and a sister who both attended university. In recent examinations Juniad's results have been disappointing. An analysis of the scripts shows that he has not understood the rubric of the questions. For example, he *described* the difference between an acid and an alkali when the question required him to *explain* the differences.

The way language is used in schools is often different from the way it is used in the 'outside' world. Basic oral competence in a language enables you to communicate effectively, but it often will not meet the language demands of 'English' as a school subject or other disciplines within the National Curriculum (Safford, 2005).

INDIVIDUAL REFLECTION

Think about how you use your native language (which may, of course, not be English). What phrases or constructions do you use that would single you out as a native speaker? Do you use colloquialisms and slang? Can you access 'new language' in your mother tongue (text speak, for example)? Use this reflection to think about how you can make accessing a new language less complex and easier for pupils like those in the case studies here.

As the case of Ceyda illustrates, the level at which English is used by bilingual students can reach a plateau that 'gets the message across' but is technically incorrect. Unless this is addressed, the lack of precision in language use will impact on her progress. Issues like this, of course, need to be approached sensitively, particularly if, as in the case of Ceyda and her father, they are satisfied with their standard of English.

Juniad's case also highlights a common problem for bilingual pupils. Many subjects have a specialist language content that is rarely used in everyday speech. Similarly, textbooks and examination papers, particularly in the latter years of secondary school, use instructional words with a specific meaning that may be used interchangeably in general conversation. Whilst this difficulty may not be a problem exclusive to EAL students, bilingual pupils who use English less frequently in their home or community have less opportunity to develop the breadth of vocabulary or the subtlety of meaning required in public examinations.

BICS and CALP

Ceyda and Juniad are both part-way on a journey from Basic Interpersonal Communication Skills (BICS) to Cognitive Academic Language Proficiency (CALP). These are terms coined by Professor Jim Cummins at the University of Toronto.

Having good, or even passable, social English, does not mean that a pupil is proficient enough to understand and respond to subject or examination specific technical language. BICS enables pupils to interact with their peers, often in situations where the context, and in particular the social context, makes meaning or shades of meaning much clearer. Situations such as when playing or supporting sport, waiting in the dinner queue, shopping or eating with friends, talking or texting on mobile phones, already have helpful scaffolding in terms of context in place to enable new language learners to both acquire and understand vocabulary and expression. By contrast, CALP takes much longer to acquire. CALP does not just refer to subject specific knowledge but to generic skills that, for most pupils, are part of a teacher's expectations. Pupils need to be able to actively listen and understand, to put across a point of view orally and in writing, to access the higher levels of Bloom's taxonomy – applying, synthesising, analysing, and evaluating. CALP also includes an understanding and ability to respond to specific instructions. What, for example, does an examiner mean by 'explain' or 'demonstrate' or 'calculate, showing your workings'? Cummins estimates that CALP acquisition can take from five to seven years (so an older child may never have the chance to acquire such skills in an educational context), whilst BICS may take only a couple of years of immersion in the target language.

Pupils will approach the acquisition of CALP from two distinct perspectives, and teachers working with such students need to realise that both exist and are dependent on language learners' level of education. Pupils who have CALP in their own language will acquire it in a new language much faster than those who do not. For the former, it is a transfer of understood concepts into a new medium; for the latter, it is the much more difficult task of learning new concepts in a new medium. Cummins (2000: 39) concludes that 'Conceptual knowledge developed in one language helps to make input in the other language comprehensible.'

A thought

Attempt the the following questions.

1. Xyat noyouk do you lzt qf you uix yellox and blue?

   a. Blak
   b. Greend
   c. Purpley
   d. Broun.

(Continued)

(Continued)

2. Xyat ws qhz napitul of Fransse?

   a. Lundon
   b. Munick
   c. Lyon
   d. Pariz.

3. Xyat ws ghz lighezt jumqer you saz qake using rach gf these digidz 6, 9, 1 and 3 wqly wnce?

   a. 3196
   b. 9613
   c. 9631
   d. 1369.

Could you make a good attempt at finding the correct answers? Sometimes 'a little knowledge can go a long way' and disguise our lack of complete understanding.

Teaching EAL students

Occasionally, you might hear the argument that EAL students should be 'taught English' before they access the curriculum.

This argument is flawed on (at least) two counts:

1. As we have seen in our case studies, EAL students are not a homogeneous group. They are children and young adults with a wide range of experiences and needs. They may range from 'new arrivals' with no grasp of English or knowledge of the Roman script, to 'British bilinguals' with developed and competent language skills that may be beyond those of some native English speakers. When has a child been 'taught enough English' to join your class?
2. Research has shown that EAL students can take as long as seven years to acquire a level of English comparable to their native English-speaking peers (Collier and Thomas, 1989). Ensuring that these pupils receive the broad and balanced education they deserve demands teaching the full curriculum at the same time as acquiring the language.

Your strategies for teaching EAL students will, of course, vary with your circumstances. You may be working in a large urban multicultural comprehensive with a specialist EAL base and a team of support staff, or in a small rural primary preparing for their first 'new arrival'.

Within this section we will look at a broad range of approaches that will be useful whatever your environment.

Strategies for 'new arrivals'

In the first weeks of a 'new arrival' joining your class you should undertake the following:

- Always personally greet the student using their name.
- Try to learn a few simple words or phrases in the pupil's home language.
- Use translation programs (e.g. Babel fish) to produce translations of key words and instructional phrases. You might want to print your work on cards and laminate them. Always ensure that you include the phrase in English and an illustrative picture as well as in the home language.
- For older children, purchase a bilingual dictionary for yourself and the student.
- If the pupil has difficulty reading their home language you can use a 'text to speech' translation program or website. Most of these devices will allow you to take the phrase and embed it into an audiovisual presentation. You can therefore create a 'PowerPoint' of key phrases where each slide illustrates a phrase in English but the instruction is spoken in the child's home language.
- Try to use mime when in conversation with the child – however embarrassing this may feel!
- Until the pupil develops the ability to form letters and construct words, modify assessment tasks to accommodate the use of drawing and cartoons, and cut and paste images when conveying answers and ideas.
- In the beginning, allow the child to use their home language when attempting to communicate with you – this may also require mime! Always reinforce and repeat the English word or phrase when you have understood.
- After an appropriate period, however, you should slowly begin to encourage the use of English – '... now in English please' – as you move on to the next phase.

Strategies for the development of language competence

As language begins to embed you will want to develop vocabulary, comprehension and grammar. The following strategies are therefore more appropriate for 'new arrivals' who are beginning to communicate in English, and 'British Bilinguals' who are relatively new to the school and usually communicate in their home language.

- Begin by determining the language content of a new topic. Identify:
  - new vocabulary
  - new or rarely used instructional phrases
  - key concepts and their sequence in an argument or debate.

- Use illustrations for new vocabulary (e.g. the names of scientific equipment, cooking apparatus, etc.). You can purchase excellent commercially produced posters that can be displayed during the teaching of the topic. The age of their target audience, however, means that they can appear rather 'childish' to older EAL students, and so it may be advisable to produce your own.
- To ensure the understanding of new instructions, you may continue to use translation software. It may be more discreet, at this stage, to include these phrases on personalised worksheets.
- To convey difficult concepts and the sequencing of ideas, try to make the lessons as visual as possible. You can explain the concept by telling a story through linked pictures and diagrams in addition to the key English words and phrases. You could use clipart, for example, to show images that match the words, along with a table of key words, as in Figure 18.1.
- To develop spoken English, begin to increase the complexity of your questioning. Move from closed questions ('What is … ?'; 'How many … ?'; 'What did … ?') to more open and demanding questions ('Why did … ?'; 'What would happen if ... ?'; 'How does ...?').
- Similarly, expose the student to paired and small group work with competent speakers of English, and if possible, the pupil's home language.

Tell the story of how to stay healthy through images of: healthy food; unhealthy food; overweight person; person exercising; normal weight person.

Key Words	كلمات السر التي اهل
Food	الغذاء
Health	صحية
Unhealthy	غير صحي
Eating	الكأل
Exercise	ممارسة

Figure 18.1 Language development writing frame

- On a one-to-one basis, rectify the student's errors in pronunciation and grammar. Approach this gradually and sensitively once the pupil is confident in using English. Never correct the pupil in front of the class.

Application to primary and early years teaching

Select a topic with which you are familiar and list the inherent key words and concepts. Use translation software and images to illustrate and explain these words and ideas in a language (other than English, but spoken by one of your pupils) of your choice. Let the pupil, using the vocabulary provided, explain the topic to a small group (one table). These pupils then explain it to other tables. Check understanding in both the target language and English.

This helps to develop both language skills and confidence. It also gives the non-English speaker more status. (If you have several non-English speakers, adapt the exercise so that it is inclusive for all.)

Strategies for 'British bilinguals'

There will come a time for many 'British bilingual' students when their progress is limited by reaching the plateau in language usage that we have previously discussed. For many of these students, the strategies you use may be a continuation of those we have just outlined or similar to the teaching methodologies you would use with native English speakers who are not making progress.

However, very able bilingual students – particularly those in the later secondary years – will need to develop the complexity of language required to achieve the highest grades in public examinations. This needs to be approached sensitively without implying that their English skills are somehow inadequate or underdeveloped.

Three particularly useful strategies are:

- Using drama and role play to communicate in a variety of roles. For example:
  - using language to solicit information or opinions from others
  - using language to give information or opinions to others
  - using language to argue a point of view, etc.
- Providing opportunities to discuss and reflect upon appropriate use of key words and the reasons we select certain phrases over others.
- Modifying worksheets, tests and homework to include explanations and examples of the meaning of common words and phrases used in the rubric of examinations (e.g. outline, describe, discuss, contrast, explain, compare, etc.).

Application to secondary teaching

Devise a role-play scenario to illustrate the key dilemmas in a topic of your choice, creating roles to facilitate the use of language. An example is given below.

A class of Year 11 students were required by their subject specification to not only understand the causes of global warming but also be able to discuss the difficulties inherent in finding solutions to the problem. By studying past papers the class teacher noticed that candidates were required to *describe* and *explain* the causes of global warming and then *compare*, *contrast* and *justify* the different opinions of those trying to find a solution.

She began, through the use of text, video and class discussion, to identify the increasing use of fossil fuels and deforestation as the principal causes. When concluding the lesson, the class were asked to make notes on a worksheet devised by the teacher. The secondary focus of the worksheet (in addition to the facts) was to delineate between *describing* a cause and *explaining* its effect on the climate. This was achieved by discussing different text boxes in small student groups to decide if each contained a description of a cause or its explanation.

In the next lesson, students were asked to research the different roles they may be selected to play for the 'United Nations Global Warming Action Committee'. The teacher provided 'character cards' that outlined each role and suggested appropriate references for additional research.

Examples of some these roles were:

A Minister for Energy – who argues that he cannot meet his country's energy needs without the use of cheap fossil fuels.

A representative for a European farming consortium – who describes the increases in crop failure due to climate change.

A Brazilian government official – who explains that her country needs to cut down areas of forest to provide farmland for the rapidly increasing population.

A UN scientist – who illustrates the consequences of continued global warming.

In the next lesson, some students were selected to play the roles and others were required to question the committee to *solicit* their opinions and points of view.

At the end of the role play, the students were asked to write a newspaper report describing the discussions of the 'committee'. In this report they were asked to *compare and contrast* the positions of the committee members by grouping them into those in favour of action and those against. They were then asked to *justify* the position taken by each committee member. The teacher provided a help sheet for some students that enabled them to match the justifications to individual roles.

Celebrating diversity

Language is not just about communicating information. Language can also express shared social and cultural beliefs. By learning English, EAL students are not only acquiring another language, they are also learning about another culture and developing another identity (Franson, 2009).

If we are not careful, the social and political issues surrounding multiculturalism and diversity in the UK can complicate the task of learning English. Olsen (2000), cited in Pellino (2010: 1), says some EAL students

> ... often come to realise that in order to be fully accepted, they must abandon their native language, surrendering an aspect of their identity. They are caused to feel they must either speak English or nothing at all. Thus, they become caught in a painful power struggle over the use of English and their native language.

The Ofsted Inspection Framework of 2014 expects all schools to actively promote 'British Values', these being defined as a belief in democracy, individual liberty, and a mutual respect and tolerance of those of different faiths and beliefs. Similarly, the Race Relations (Amendment) Act 2000 places a duty on schools to:

- eliminate racial discrimination
- promote equality of opportunity
- promote good relations between people of different racial groups.

As the population of English classrooms becomes increasingly culturally diverse, we can meet these expectations and improve the experiences of EAL students by celebrating this diversity, and if necessary, combating racist attitudes within schools. All schools will have equality policies and strategies to deal firmly with racist incidents. As teachers we must also look to our own behaviours to avoid unintended consequences from our actions, for example:

- We must be careful not to misinterpret the body language of EAL students – in some cultures, for example, looking away whilst an authority figure is speaking is a sign of respect.
- We must accept that many EAL students will be silent for long periods of time as they adjust to hearing a new language and try to assimilate the social etiquette of the classroom.
- We must expand our use of exemplars and illustrative stories to include as wide a range of material from other countries and cultures as possible – not all scientific discoveries were made by white European men with beards!
- We must be swift to act to tackle any occurrences of discrimination or racism that may occur in our classrooms – 'we do not use language like that in this school'.

Ignoring such incidents, however minor, only condones those opinions in the minds of the perpetrator and the abused.

- When appropriate, we must allow groups of EAL students to speak together in their community language, even if we feel excluded. Not to do so, implies that we are automatically suspicious of the content and nature of their conversations.

There are many simple strategies that you can use within the classroom to promote diversity and interaction, for example:

- Ensure that new arrivals are assigned trustworthy students as 'buddies' who will accompany the child at break and lunchtimes and support you in explaining school systems and expectations.
- Ensure that your seating plan results in students of different ethnicities regularly working together.
- Similarly, ensure that you provide regular opportunities for group work and discussion with a constantly changing mix of students.
- Ensure that all pupils in your class are exposed to novels and films that tell stories from a wide variety of cultures.
- Use the many excellent class-based exercises that promote diversity during form periods, wet lunchtimes, etc. There are suggestions for sources of these materials at the end of this chapter.

Multilingual schools with a varied ethnic mix are usually well versed in celebrating diversity. As a trainee or newly qualified teacher, becoming involved in these 'whole-school' activities can be an interesting and enlightening experience. Examples of such activities are:

- The celebration of religious holidays and key dates. For example Eid, Yom Hashoah, the International Day of Tolerance, etc.
- Constructing large-scale displays that promote the message that the school regards its multicultural population as a positive attribute.
- Ensuring that the canteen regularly provides food from different cultures and the school uses a variety of restaurants for out-of-school celebrations.
- Organising 'collapsed timetable' events where all years take part in activities that will inform the students about the different cultures within the school; for example, United Colours Days.
- Entering the school for the British Council Specialist Schools Academy Trust Cultural Diversity Award to gain recognition for the positive promotion of different cultures with an institution.

As Britain becomes an increasingly multicultural society, it is the hope of the majority that this country adapts to become a place where different cultures can retain their individual identities but work together for the common good. This is less likely to happen if those cultures do not have opportunities to meet, discuss and better understand each other. Similarly, ethnic minorities in any country may never be as valued as the indigenous population until their standard of education and resulting qualifications allow them to occupy positions of importance and influence. Teachers and the institutions in which they work have a vital role to play in this process. Only by ensuring that all students, including those with language barriers to learning, reach their full potential, and by valuing and celebrating the differences that exist between us, can the goal of equality be achieved.

Summary

- More than one in 10 pupils in UK classrooms speak English as an additional language.
- The demography of this group of students is, however, wide and varied. Some EAL students will be 'new arrivals' to this country and have no knowledge of Roman script, whilst others will have lived in this country all of their lives but speak a language other than English within their home and local community.
- As teachers we need to be aware of the range of strategies we may be required to employ – from introducing 'new arrivals' to the English language, to moving bilingual students from a basic level of language competence to the complexity of use required of them in public examinations.
- As teachers we must support these students by providing an atmosphere within the classroom and the school that values their native language and culture.

Key reading

Collier, V.P. and Thomas, W.P. (1989) 'How quickly can immigrants become proficient in school English?', *Educational Issues of Language Minority Students,* 5.

Cummins, J. (2000) *Language, power, and pedagogy: bilingual children in the crossfire.* Multilingual Matters.

Franson, C. (2009) *Bilingualism and second language acquisition.* Available at www.naldic. org.uk/ITTSEAL2/teaching/bilingualism.cfm

Pellino, K. (2010) *Effective strategies for teaching English language learners.* Available at www.teach-nology.com/tutorials/teaching/esl

References and bibliography

Collier, V.P. and Thomas, W.P. (1989) 'How quickly can immigrants become proficient in school English?', *Educational Issues of Language Minority Students,* 5.

Cummins, J. (2000) *Language, power, and pedagogy: bilingual children in the crossfire.* Multilingual Matters.

Department for Education (DfE) (2012) *School Census Data 2012.* London: DfE.

Franson, C. (2009) *Bilingualism and second language acquisition*. Available at www.naldic. org. uk/ITTSEAL2/teaching/ bilingualism.cfm

NALDIC (2012) www.naldic.org.uk/eal-advocacy/eal-news-summary/210612.

Olsen, L. (2000) 'Learning English and learning America: immigrants in the centre of a storm', *Theory into Practice*, 39 (4): 196–202.

Pellino, K. (2010) *Effective strategies for teaching English language learners*. Available at www. teach-nology.com/tutorials/teaching/esl

Race Relations (Amendment) Act (2000) TSO.

Safford, K. (2005) *Teaching language and curriculum*. Available at www.naldic.org.uk/ ITTSEAL2/teaching/Teachingapproaches.cfm

South, H. (1999) *Working paper 5: The distinctiveness of EAL: a cross-curriculum discipline*. Watford: NALDIC.

Useful websites

For EAL background, advice and guidance

Department for Education (DfE) (2010) *Schools, pupils and their characteristics*. Available at www.education.gov.uk/rsgateway/DB/SFR/s000925/index.shtml

Milton Keynes Ethnic Minority Achievement Support Service (2004) *Supporting pupils learning English as an additional language*. Available at www.mkweb.co.uk/emass/documents/ Website_EAL_Artwork.pdf

National Association for Language Development in the Curriculum (NALDIC): www.naldic.org.uk/

SFE (2009) The EAL resource file. Search www.sfe.co.uk using EAL as the search term to reach resources.

For EAL resources and ideas

EMA (online support for ethnic minority attainment): www.emaonline.org.uk/

For language translation

Google translate: translate.google.com/

To celebrate diversity and combat racism

British Council Schools Online. Available at https://schoolsonline.britishcouncil.org/content/uk

Central Council For Europe Youth Directorate (1995) *All equal all different*. Available at www. iwtc.org/ideas/24_equal.pdf

Specialist Schools Academy Trust Cultural Diversity Award. Available at www.ssatuk.co.uk/cpd/ accountability-and-data/cultural-diversity/

Teaching and Learning in Scotland (2011) *Race equality*. Available at www.antiracisttoolkit.org.uk

Visit https://study.sagepub.com/denby3e for extra resources related to this chapter.

CHAPTER 19

UNDERSTANDING AND USING ASSESSMENT AND FEEDBACK

Angela Gault

Standards linked to this chapter include...

2. Promote good progress and outcomes by pupils

    - be accountable for pupils' attainment, progress and outcomes
    - be aware of pupils' capabilities and their prior knowledge, and plan teaching to build on these.

6. Make accurate and productive use of assessment

    - know and understand how to assess the relevant subject and curriculum areas, including statutory assessment requirements
    - make use of formative and summative assessment to secure pupils' progress

(Continued)

(Continued)

- use relevant data to monitor progress, set targets, and plan subsequent lessons
- give pupils regular feedback, both orally and through accurate marking, and encourage pupils to respond to the feedback.

Introduction

Assessment has a key role to play in teaching and learning. As a teacher you will be expected to assess pupils' learning and provide feedback to encourage learning, but it doesn't end there. You will also need to be able to use assessment developmentally, to help pupils to make progress in their learning. So, as a trainee teacher, how can you begin to understand how to use assessment effectively for these various purposes?

Your starting point depends very much upon what you understand already about assessment. The good news is that you know a tremendous amount about certain types of assessment, so will be building on an existing knowledge base. Assessment is common in all walks of life: driving tests and job interviews are just two common examples; and of course, as a beginning teacher, you will be particularly interested in educational assessment such as external examinations. You will have taken many of these and achieved various qualifications at key points in your education, each enabling you to progress from one stage of learning to the next. In fact, you have become an expert in passing formal examinations and can appreciate that as a teacher you will be supporting your pupils to take examinations and ultimately to gain their own qualifications.

A thought.....

If your schooling was in England it is likely that you will have progressed from GCSEs at 16 to GCE Advanced Levels (A Levels) at 18 and then to an honours degree, in order to be eligible to embark upon a teacher training course. Even if you have not followed this particular academic pathway, you will have achieved equivalent qualifications. You will understand that qualifications are often age specific, certainly during the years of compulsory education, and are categorised according to 'difficulty'. You will also understand that in order to move on to the next level of challenge, you will have to undergo an assessment and achieve at least at a specified minimum level in order to 'pass'. Do you think this is an effective way to measure progress? Why? Why not?

Assessment of Learning (AoL)

Summative assessments sum up, or provide a measure of, learning at the end of a course or phase. Successful learners are awarded a mark, level or grade, even a certificate, to validate their achievements and to give them access to the next level or phase of learning.

External summative assessments, controlled by organisations outside the educational institution attended by the pupil, are established features of our education system. There are examples at all levels: Early Years Foundation Stage profiles are moderated by external examiners; National Curriculum end of Key Stage 2 tests, GCSEs and A Level examinations are all set by awarding bodies, such as the three main examination boards in England – AQA, Edexcel and OCR. (For more information on awarding bodies, their examination specifications and the support they offer to teachers, browse their websites, given at the end of this chapter.)

A school's external examination results, for example KS2 test scores or GCSEs, are monitored at regional level by Local Authorities and at national level by the DfE and Ofsted. Schools use national software packages, such as SIMS (School Information Management System), to manage and store school assessment data, as well as to serve other school management functions. They use RAISEonline, originally commissioned by the then DCSF and Ofsted, to manage and analyse their pupils' progress and attainment as part of their self-evaluation processes. The data generated through RAISEonline also provide external organisations with common sets of comparable school-level information. Summative assessments managed by examination boards both provide pupils with certificates and qualifications and data about school performance that generate headlines about national educational standards. This dual purpose is problematic, and discussed later in the chapter.

AoL also takes place within schools whenever a teacher assesses a pupil's work or practical activity, and produces a summative grade or level. Schools track pupils' progress against predicted targets and produce summative assessments at least once a year, reporting these outcomes to parents/carers. Records of summative assessment are also key when a pupil moves from one class to another, or from one school to another.

Application to primary and early years teaching

In a primary setting, spend some time with children in the top 'leavers' class and make a list of the sort of assessment information you think would be useful to the secondary teachers receiving them. Once you have completed your list, under various headings, check out with a secondary colleague whether this really is the sort of information they would want, and the format in which it would be most useful. A similar activity can be undertaken for transfer between early years settings and primary schools.

Planning for progress

Your use of assessment is not limited to summary outcomes; you will use assessment for an even more fundamental educational purpose, namely to help you support pupils' progress in learning. This kind of assessment lies at the heart of teaching and learning and will become a major focus of your professional development.

Put simply, you need to know, at the point of teaching, how well pupils are learning. You are responsible for ensuring that pupils continue to make good progress. It is too late to wait until an end of course test to find out that pupils have learned little or nothing, or that they have misunderstood important concepts. If pupils are not learning effectively, then you need to modify your teaching. When you start to teach a new class, you need to know where your pupils are, in terms of their learning, in order to plan their next steps and your teaching. You must assess their learning during the lesson, so that you can support their progress, and again at the end of the lesson, so that you can plan the following sequence of lessons.

A thought

Your own professional learning is just as important as that of your pupils, and these learning journeys intersect. Just as you will be assessing your pupils' learning, so you will start to assess or evaluate your own efficacy and progress as a teacher. These evaluative and formative reflections lie at the centre of your professional learning journey.

Assessment for Learning (AfL)

Assessments of pupils' learning during the lesson, or the diagnosis of pupils' learning outcomes, with the purpose of modifying or designing teaching to improve pupils' next steps in learning, is called formative assessment or assessment for learning. It is formative because it informs your understanding of where learners are in their learning and helps you to identify what they need to learn next in order to make progress. Only when you know this, can you provide effective, timely feedback and plan the best ways for your pupils to build upon their learning. Research has shown that effective, timely feedback supports future learning (Black and Wiliam, 1998b; Hattie and Timperley, 2007; Shute, 2008).

The more skilled you become at formative assessment, and the more you understand learning progression in the subject or topic, the more proficient you will become at planning and tailoring your pupils' opportunities to learn. Ultimately, you want to support your pupils to be able to inform, or assess, themselves, so that they can take ownership of and responsibility for their own learning. You need to be able to model this process for them, and exemplify it through your own professional learning and development.

How to begin

There are several key strands to assessment for learning. First you will need to consider your pupils: what they know already, what they need to learn next, and how they learn best. Also, you will need a deep understanding of your subject, or the topic to be learned, and what progression in learning that subject or topic looks like. You will need to draw from learning theories and apply your understanding of how pupils learn. In addition, you will need an understanding of various assessment strategies and tools, how best to use them, and when. Last but not least, you will need to develop the teaching skills to pull these strands together into a coherent, cohesive learning experience for your pupils.

The best place to begin is always with your pupils, and the most fundamental starting place is not their grades on a spreadsheet or tracking system, but their personalities – specifically their emotional responses to learning.

How do your pupils feel about learning?

There are some children for whom learning seems to be part of their character; they have an insatiable curiosity and want to learn anything and everything. Others have not found learning to be an easy, enjoyable, or worthwhile experience. They can equate learning with feelings of failure or embarrassment and so they have become reluctant to engage. Learning has become too much of a personal risk. Most children fall somewhere along this spectrum, so most need to be motivated and supported to learn to varying degrees.

This is one of your key responsibilities as their teacher. Ultimately you hope that your pupils will be motivated and will learn independently of you, but again most will need to be taught these independent learning skills, and even the most enthusiastic will also need to be taught how to learn most effectively. Knowing where your pupils are on this 'motivated to learn' continuum is important if you are to plan effectively for their success in learning (see Chapter 11). In skilful hands, assessment for learning strategies can be used to motivate even the most reluctant learners. Used without awareness, or regard, for pupils' emotional responses to learning, assessment can deter even the most enthusiastic of learners.

What have your pupils learnt already and how do you know?

The next key strand of AfL is knowledge of what your pupils already know, understand, appreciate, or can do. This is often called 'prior learning'. As a beginning teacher, just like any teacher new to a class, you should be provided with assessment data about your pupils. Pupils' marks, levels or grades, usually derived from summative assessments at key points during the year, show what and how well they have learned so far. You should also be given pupils' target levels or grades for each year, or even each half-term. From this you can see how well your students are progressing towards their targets. Remember that model trajectories of progression are idealised and pupils progress at different rates, for a whole host of reasons. These data provide you with an assessment profile for each of your pupils. In addition, there is still no substitute for looking at pupils' work and talking to them about their learning. Fundamentally you need to understand where your pupils are in terms of their learning, before you can plan to move that learning forward.

What do marks, levels or grades mean?

You must understand not only what knowledge and skills have been assessed, but also the performance criteria used in awarding a mark, level, grade, or teacher comment on a piece of work.

Marks, levels or grades are just useful shorthand for the performance/learning criteria or grade descriptors that sit behind each measurement of pupil attainment. An understanding of these descriptors helps you drill down into what pupils know, understand and can do – and thus what they need to learn next to attain the next tier of criteria descriptors. The wording of these descriptors can help you compose the next, most appropriate, learning objectives and how best to assess these, in other words how the pupils will show what they have learned (usually termed 'learning outcomes'). Your lesson plan will provide an outline of the teaching and learning activities that will help pupils towards achieving those learning outcomes.

What does learning in your subject 'look like'?

Learning goes on inside pupils' heads. For teachers to be able to check that learning has occurred, and certainly for teachers to be able to make judgements about the nature and quality of that learning, then learning needs to be made 'visible' (Hattie, 2012). For you to be able to make those judgements, you will need to create opportunities for pupils to show what they have learned, so that any 'visible' learning can be matched against performance descriptors i.e. pupil learning outcomes. Put very simply, these are a list of 'can dos'. So your pupils will need to evidence, through speech, writing, actions, or a combination of these elements, what they have learned.

Learning is about experiencing changes in understanding, appreciation or skills (see Chapter 11). For you to recognise these changes in a learner you need to know what those changes are likely to be and what they might look like. A sequence of performance descriptors, or indicators, acts as a guide to change or progress and can help you to recognise progress or development in learning. Particularly for non-core curriculum subjects, or integrated subject/topic areas, some schools will use terminology such as 'emerging', 'developing', 'secure' or 'exceeding' to indicate pupils' levels of attainment against a particular set of expected subject- or topic-based learning descriptors.

A thorough understanding of performance criteria in a subject or topic gives you a framework of learning progression that you can draw upon in your planning and teaching. This framework also provides reference points when assessing pupils' learning.

The relationship between curriculum subjects and performance criteria

Learning can be described in terms of performance criteria or grade descriptors, presented in a hierarchy of challenge. But where do these performance criteria come from? This question takes us into considering the very distinctive nature of each curriculum subject.

Each subject has its own body of knowledge and this knowledge is organised or structured in a specific way. The organisation of knowledge into disciplines or subjects goes back to the time of Aristotle and has been modified and developed over time and across cultures (Young, 1971; Biglan, 1973; Hirst, 1974). In addition, each subject has its own meanings and characteristic terminology. To acquire, and also demonstrate, subject knowledge is to engage in very subject-specific ways of organised thinking and communicating.

Increasing your subject knowledge involves a deepening appreciation of the relationships between those facts, procedures and skills that are central to it, and an understanding of how to investigate and present knowledge in that subject. All subject disciplines have key concepts or 'big ideas', and it is important to know what these are and to acquire an understanding of the relationships between them. This subject structure not only enables the learner to organise or categorise new knowledge, it also provides distinctive signposts to help that learner explore and acquire new knowledge.

Application to secondary teaching

In secondary schools, teachers belong to subject departments and closely identify with their particular group of subject specialist professionals (Lave and Wenger, 1991). Whilst you are training to teach, you will not only develop your teacher identity you will also become a subject specialist immersed in the content and language of your subject.

During professional learning conversations with your subject colleagues, explore effective ways of teaching specific aspects of subject content, or agree how best to address pupils' common misconceptions in a given topic.

Subject-specific performance descriptors or assessment criteria contain expressions of subject knowledge, using the specific language characteristics of the subject. They are organised to show the hierarchical relationships between key facts, concepts, skills and procedures, and how subject knowledge 'builds' or is progressive. However, this presupposes that subject knowledge is organised in a linear or layered, systematic fashion, with each aspect of knowledge building on from the last.

'Linear' subject structures can be considered to be an over-simplified view. Many theorists prefer a spiral (Bruner, 1960) rather than a linear model, which conveys the idea of revisiting existing knowledge in order to build upon it. A framework of progressive descriptors, which is itself progressive, supports a systematic approach to teaching and learning. This can be a useful starting point and practical tool for teachers and learners, especially when learning itself is seldom straightforward, easy to recognise and verify. However, it is very important to view such a framework as a support or scaffold to learning and assessment, and not see it as a straightjacket or the *only* expression of knowledge and potential learning in that subject.

Core curriculum subjects such as English, mathematics and the sciences have well-established assessment frameworks aligned to curriculum content. These may be in the form of assessment level grids, examination grade specifications, or schools may have developed their own equivalent 'pupil-friendly' versions for everyday use, for example in the form of learning or skills ladders, inch pebbles, milestones, mastery statements, or other forms of progression indicators.

For non-core curriculum subjects and inter-disciplinary topics you may turn to more generic frameworks or taxonomies, such as Bloom's Taxonomy (1956), or variations on it, such as Anderson and Krathwohl (2001) or the structure of observed learning outcome model (SOLO) developed by Biggs and Collis (1982) and adapted by Hook and Mills (2011) and McNeill and Hook (2012). Such frameworks are based upon a hierarchy of the demands on the thinking skills and understanding of the learner.

In these cases the subject content is a variable factor, and is added by the teacher. One key challenge for teachers is to recognise and select appropriate subject specific content. Another challenge is for all teachers to have an appreciation of the significance of pupils' literacy skills, which are universal learning tools, when deploying any model of learning (Dewey, 1938; Bruner, 1960; Piaget, 2000)

Peer and self-assessment

Assessment for learning strategies resonate with several key learning theories, particularly those presented by Vygotsky (1986), Bruner (1974) and Kolb (1984) (see Chapter 11). This can be seen if we explore one important aspect of AoL – peer and self-assessment – through the lens of social constructivist learning theory.

Peer assessment and self-assessment require pupils to understand what is being learned and to engage with the evidence of learning as expressed in the assessment criteria, in order to make accurate assessments of each other's and their own work. From this assessment, they can provide appropriate targets for improvement and future learning. In this way, learners are actively involved in taking their learning forward. When peer and self-assessment are designed as a classroom-based activity, with opportunities for dialogic feedback interaction between pupils, then pupils are actively engaged in constructing meaning or understanding about their learning. Conversational theory (Laurillard, 1993) focuses on this process of learning through conversations or dialogue, specifically the interaction between teachers and learners.

Self-assessment helps pupils develop their ability to learn and it is 'necessary for effective learning' (Boud, 1995: 14): 'Pupils are more likely to make rapid progress in their learning if they understand what they are aiming for' (DfES, 2004: 10), and learning becomes more effective when learners are able to identify for themselves what they understand and what they do not, as this enables them to learn independently without feedback from the teacher. If pupils are not engaged in self-assessment, the effect 'is to remove them from participation in the core processes of learning' (Boud, 1995: 12), and 'This can lead to disengagement with the learning process and sometimes to poor behaviour' (DfES, 2004: 1). Peer assessment helps pupils increase their understanding of the assessment process and improve their self-assessment. It is difficult to assess one's own work accurately; however, in order to make progress with learning, it is important to learn to do this (Boud, 1995). Robust discussion with other pupils can help learners discover the strengths and weaknesses of their own work. Assessing others' work helps pupils view their own work more objectively and assess its worth more accurately.

Therefore, working together on tasks, feeding back to each other, and then revising work in response to that feedback, is a powerful learning model grounded in the principles of AfL.

GROUP EXERCISE

Whatever style of assessment is being used, in practice there are some common issues that should be considered and some questions you will need to ask when planning assessment.

What? Is it clear what is being assessed? Both pupils and teachers should know before and during the assessment exactly what will be assessed. Look at your lesson plan and decide whether the assessment is relevant and valid. Assessment should focus on the intended topics.

How? Is the assessment feasible? The precise details of how the assessment will be carried out should be decided in advance. This will help ensure that all the tasks can be done, completed in the time, and the assessment is fair and consistent.

When? When will assessment take place? It should be clear in your planning at what points pupils will be assessed. Lesson plans should include explicit planning for AfL, and pupils given ample warning of important AoL events, such as end-of-unit tests.

Look at a series of four lesson plans in your group and see where they have included assessment opportunities. Suggest other places where you could have included assessment. Make sure that you are planning both opportunities for assessment and opportunities for feeding back the results. In addition, your lesson evaluation should indicate how you will feed the information forward into future lesson plans.

AfL strategies and formative feedback

There are a wide variety of AfL strategies that you can use to analyse learning and generate formative feedback for your pupils (DfES, 2004). These strategies will vary considerably in the general applicability of the information they yield and in their formality. Informal dialogue with individual pupils and formal end-of-unit written tests are the extremes on a continuum of assessment strategies. For example, informal dialogue with a pupil enables the teacher to uncover misunderstandings or uncertainties at the point of learning, and provide the learner with additional explanations or strategic advice on how to tackle a problem. End-of-unit test results provide pupils with information about the correctness of their responses. The extent to which test results can be formative depends on whether and how the assessment criteria are shared with pupils before and after the actual test or used by the teacher to plan future learning.

Research shows that 'good feedback can significantly improve learning processes and outcomes, if delivered correctly' (Shute, 2007: 2). Also feedback that incorporates encouragement and praise with references to effort and learning outcomes can support pupils' confidence and motivation to learn (Dweck, 2006).

Finally, it is important to state that there is no best type of strategy or feedback. The challenge for you as a teacher is, in each case, to select the most appropriate AfL strategy and the type, extent and timing of formative feedback. This decision will be based upon the nature and demands of the learning task, the desired learning outcomes, and the cognitive and affective characteristics of the pupils (Shute, 2007: 30–3).

The wider importance of assessment

When discussing external summative assessment, you will not be the only person who is concerned with how well your pupils are learning or achieving. Apart from the pupils themselves, there are their parents or carers, your teacher colleagues, and your school senior management and governors. Outside the school, Local Authority/Trust/Academy leaders will be monitoring the progress and attainment of your pupils, and through these results, teachers' performance. The Department for Education also monitors school assessment data. Ofsted inspectors visit schools and make judgements upon the quality of teaching, learning and leadership based, to a great extent, upon pupil learning outcomes.

External examination results, particularly at the end of KS2 (national tests) and KS4 (GCSE), but also at post-16 level, are used to make judgements about the quality of schools, and by association, the quality of the teaching and teachers in each school. This correlation between pupils' results and teacher effectiveness is easy to assert but has been more difficult to understand fully and verify (Barber, 1996; Koedel and Betts, 2007; Aaronson et al., 2007; Murphy et al., 2013). Nevertheless, it is a correlation that continues to be the focus of research (Coe et al., 2014a).

League tables

External assessment results are accessible via league tables on the DfE website, on the Ofsted website through its Data Dashboard pages, and published in the national and local press. Results that are deemed to be very favourable give a school high status and kudos. Less than favourable results, and a low position in the league tables, can impact upon the size and nature of pupil intakes (with financial implications for schools) and the quality and quantity of applications for teaching vacancies at those schools. Very low results can generate an Oftsed inspection, a notice to improve, the loss of senior management jobs and school closure, or a fresh start under a different management structure such as that provided by an Academy trust. In short, the league tables support a quasi-market education system, i.e. a market system that is funded from the public purse.

Benchmarks

GCSE league tables record those percentages of a school's pupils who have achieved above the national benchmark score across a range of five approved subjects, including English and mathematics. The government exercises its power to raise this benchmark score, a strategy which it is claimed raises school standards. The government also determines which subjects are important enough for inclusion, and more significantly therefore, which subjects are not. These league tables have been extended in recent years to include a second core group of subjects known collectively as 'E-Bacc' subjects. These subjects are considered to be 'passport' subjects deemed necessary for admission to Russell group universities. Progress 8 measures are the latest addition to the league tables. These focus on students' progress in their learning from the end of primary school to the end of key stage 4 (KS4) across eight approved subjects. The eight subjects include the five EBacc subjects and allow three other approved 'high value' arts, academic or vocational subjects. Pupils' point scores from their Progress 8 examination subjects at the end of KS4 are compared against an estimated Attainment 8 score. (For a detailed explanation of this process, see Chapter 23.) A pupil's Progress 8 result will show either a positive or negative value added score and will be used to calculate a school Progress 8 score. The school will be expected to exceed a pre-determined floor standard score if it is to avoid inspection.

A world-class education system: international comparisons

The government evaluates the quality of pupils' attainment across the country through its own national assessments, but is also interested in making comparisons with pupil attainment in other countries. A different set of assessments is used for this purpose. The Programme for International Student Assessment (PISA) project, launched by the Organisation for Economic Cooperation and Development (OECD), provides international tests and comparative data on 15 year-olds' competencies in reading, mathematics and science. These results have been used to inform national education policy since 2000, predominantly to fuel policy arguments for improving pupils' test scores, which in turn are equated to a measure of national educational standards. In 2012 another assessment tool, the PISA-based Test for Schools, was developed. This test provides school-level results and is voluntary. It is promoted as an international benchmarking tool and the means by which schools can improve student outcomes. The outcome of these comparisons will be reported with great fanfares in the press but need to be studied carefully to see if they have any meaning for your subject.

INDIVIDUAL REFLECTION

League tables are so potent that teachers are under significant pressure to ensure that their pupils attain the highest possible results. This can be seen as encouraging a 'teaching to the test' approach to education. Given that not all desired educational outcomes can be assessed reliably through external summative assessments, then important areas of experience can be neglected in schools, resulting in a narrow curriculum comprised of content that can be easily assessed. Do you agree with this comment? What evidence can you find in your school to support it?

Conclusion

As a teacher you will be concerned with assessing your pupils' learning to help them make progress and as a mark of their attainment. Whether we agree or not, external assessments are also used to measure the effectiveness of teaching, teachers and schools, i.e. for national education accountability purposes (Newton, 2007). Assessment is not a stand-alone item but neither is it 'neutral'. There are many stakeholders, much complexity, and many opportunities for interference, confusion and incoherence – all of which can be used to support different agendas.

Tensions arise when there is a mismatch between the forms and purposes of assessment – specifically when one form of assessment is designed and used for one particular purpose, yet its assessment outcomes are used for another.

The assessment purposes of education ministers, who are interested in measuring the impact of national education funding and justifying new education reform initiatives, are different from the assessment purposes of teachers who are engaged in the actual teaching, learning and assessment process in the classroom (Stobart, 2008; Elwood, 2013). Yet the same assessment framework is used to serve both purposes. The concern is such that some schools, mainly in the independent sector, have opted out of the national system and use international awards instead, for example the International Baccalaureate, claiming that these awards provide a greater breadth and challenge for pupils.

The national drive to improve pupil attainment and to increase school accountability has resulted in a plethora of national education policies. National assessment has been deployed as a tool of enforcement for these policies. Concerns about the negative effects of external assessments and league tables upon the nature and quality of learning in schools are leading to a re-think about how assessment can be used more effectively to support quality and independent learning. The demise of the Assessing Pupil Progress (APP) programme is one example of such revisions. However, the space left by APP must be taken up by teachers who, through the development of their practice and a professional consensus regarding the validity and reliability of teacher assessment, can re-claim and develop assessment of and for learning. After all, 'Assessments in themselves are not inherently formative or summative – it is the process and how the information is used that is important' (DfES, 2004). This is the challenge for you, as one of the next generation of teachers.

Summary

- Assessment for learning (AfL) or formative assessment helps teachers judge pupils' progress and improve the focus and pace of teaching and learning.
- Every interaction with a pupil is an opportunity for AfL.
- Feedback to pupils should let them know what is understood and what is not so that they gain confidence and can concentrate their efforts to improve.
- Self-assessment helps pupils develop the ability to learn independently, and learn more quickly and efficiently.
- Peer-assessment helps pupils increase their understanding of the assessment process and improve their self-assessment; dialogue helps this learning process.
- External assessments and national benchmarks are used to inform different agendas, so teachers need to take care how they interpret these.

Key Reading

Black, P. and Wiliam, D. (1998) *Inside the black box: raising standards through classroom assessment*. London: King's College.

Black, P., Harrison, C., Lee, C., Marshall, B. and Wiliam, D. (2004) 'Working inside the black box: assessment for learning in the classroom', *Phi Delta Kappan*, 86 (1): 8–21.

Glazzard, J., Chadwick, D., Webster, A. and Percival, J. (2010) *Assessment for learning in the Early Years Foundation Stage*. London: Sage.

References and bibliography

Aaronson, D., Barrow, L. and Sander, W. (2007) 'Teachers and student achievement in the Chicago public high schools', *Journal of Labor Economics*, 25 (1): 95–135.

Anderson, L.W., and Krathwohl, D.R. (eds) (2001) *A taxonomy for learning, teaching, and Assessing: A revision of Bloom's Taxonomy of Educational Objectives*. New York: Longman.

Barber, M. (1996) *The learning game*. London: Gollancz.

Biggs, J. and Collis, K. (1982) *Evaluating the quality of learning: the SOLO taxonomy*. New York: Academic Press.

Biglan, A. (1973) 'The characteristics of subject matters in different academic areas', *Journal of Applied Psychology*, 57: 195–203.

Black, P. and Wiliam, D. (1998b) *Inside the black box: raising standards through classroom assessment*. London: King's College.

Bloom, B.S. (ed.) (1956) *Taxonomy of educational objectives, the classification of educational goals – Handbook I: Cognitive domain*. New York: McKay.

Boud, D. (1995) *Enhancing learning through self-assessment*. London: Kogan Page.

Bruner, J. (1974) *The process of education*. Cambridge, MA: The President and Fellows of Harvard College.

Clarke, S. (2014) *Outstanding formative assessment: culture and practice*. London: Hodder Education.

Coe, R. et al. (2014a) 'What makes great teaching?', The Sutton Trust at www.suttontrust.com/wp-content/uploads/2014/10/What-Makes-Great-Teaching-REPORT.pdf

DfES (2004) *Pedagogy and practice: unit 12: assessment for learning*. London: DfES.

Dewey, J. (1938) *Experience and education*. New York: Macmillan.

Dweck, C.S. (2006) *Mindset: the new psychology of success*. New York: Random House.

Elwood, J. (2013) 'Educational assessment policy and practice: a matter of ethics', *Assessment in Education: Principles, Policy & Practice,* 20 (2): 205–20.

Hattie, J. (2012) *Visible learning for teachers*. New York and London: Routledge.

Hattie, J. and Timperley, H. (2007) 'The power of feedback', *Review of Educational Research*, 77 (1): 81–112.

Hirst, P.H. (1974) *Knowledge and the curriculum*. London: Routledge and Kegan Paul.

Hook, P. and Mills, J. (2011) *SOLO taxonomy: A guide for schools. Book 1. A common language of learning*. New Zealand: Essential Resources Educational Publishers Limited.

Koedel, C. and Betts, J.R. (2007) 'Re-examining the role of teacher quality in the educational production function'. Working Paper 07-08. Columbia: University of Missouri.

Kolb, D. (1984) *Experiential learning*. Englewood Cliffs, NJ: Prentice-Hall.

Krathwohl, D. (2002) 'A revision of Bloom's Taxonomy: an overview, theory into practice', *Theory into Practice*, 41 (4): 212–18.

Laurillard, D. (1993) *Rethinking university teaching: A framework for the effective use of educational technology*. London: Routledge.

Lave, J. and Wenger, E. (1991) *Situated learning: legitimate peripheral participation*. Cambridge: Cambridge University Press.

McNeill, L. and Hook, P. (2012) *SOLO Taxonomy and Making Meaning. Books 1, 2, 3. Text purposes, audiences and ideas*. New Zealand: Essential Resources Educational Publishers Limited.

Murphy, J.F., Hallinger, P. and Heck, R.H. (2013) 'Leading via teacher evaluation: the case of missing clothes?', *Educational Researcher,* 42 (6): 349–54.

Newton, P. (2007) 'Clarifying the purposes of educational assessment', *Assessment in Education: Principles, Policy and Practice*, 14 (2): 149–70.

Ofsted (2011) *The impact of the 'Assessing pupils' progress' initiative*. Available online at www.ofsted.gov.uk/publications/100226

Piaget, J. (2000) The language and thought of the child (3rd edn). London and New York: Routledge Classics.

Qualifications and Curriculum Authority (2009) *Get to grips with assessing pupils' progress.* London: Department for Children, Schools and Families.
Shute, V.J. (2007) *Focus on formative feedback Research Report.* Princeton, NJ: Educational Testing Service. Available at www.ets.org/Media/Research/pdf/RR-07-11.pdf
Shute, V.J. (2008) 'Focus on formative feedback', *Review of Educational Research*, 78 (1): 153–89.
Stobart, G. (2008) *Testing times: the uses and abuses of assessment.* London: Routledge.
Vygotsky, L.S. (1986) *Thought and language.* Revised and edited by Alex Kozulin. Cambridge, MA: The Massachusetts Institute of Technology Press.
Young, M. (1971) *Knowledge and control.* London: Collier Macmillan.

Useful websites

The content and assessment of the National Curriculum is available online via the DfE website. Previous versions are available in the national archive (www.nationalarchives.gov.uk/).
Information about National Curriculum tests is available at www.gov.uk/government/collections/national-curriculum-assessments-test-frameworks
Awarding body websites:
AQA – www.aqa.org.uk
Pearson Qualifications - http://qualifications.pearson.com/en/home.html
OCR – www.ocr.org.uk
WJEC – www.wjec.co.uk
CCEA – www.rewardinglearning.org.uk
Several key publications by the Assessment Reform group are now available from the website of The Association for Achievement and Improvement through Assessment: www.aaia.org.uk/
For further information about SOLO taxonomy see: http://pamhook.com/solo-taxonomy/
To find out more about the OECD and PISA tests see: www.oecd.org/pisa/keyfindings/pisa-2012-results.htm
Find out about RAISEonline at: www.raiseonline.org/about.aspx
Access school data from the Ofsted Dashboard http://dashboard.ofsted.gov.uk/

Visit https://study.sagepub.com/denby3e for extra resources related to this chapter.

CHAPTER 20

THE RIGHTS OF THE CHILD

Jonathan Glazzard

Standards linked to this chapter include...

1. Set high expectations which inspire, motivate and challenge pupils

   - establish a safe and stimulating environment for pupils, rooted in mutual respect.

2. Promote good progress and outcomes by pupils

   - encourage pupils to take a responsible and conscientious attitude to their own work and study.

(Continued)

(Continued)

Teachers' Standards Part 2: Personal and Professional Conduct

Teachers uphold public trust in the profession and maintain high standards of ethics and behaviour, within and outside school, by:

- treating pupils with dignity, building relationships rooted in mutual respect, and at all times observing proper boundaries appropriate to a teacher's professional position
- showing tolerance of and respect for the rights of others.

Introduction

This chapter focuses on the UN Convention on the Rights of the Child. The Convention, otherwise known as the CRC, is a comprehensive list of children's rights, and one that has been accepted and ratified by every country in the world except the United States of America, Somalia and South Sudan. In many cases there are caveats included in the ratification (such as the supremacy of Sharia law in countries with Islam as the state religion), but it nevertheless represents a triumph of agreement on how children should be viewed. Children – particularly in schools – are used to finding themselves in a disadvantageous power situation; they are used to having rules imposed and being passive recipients rather than proactive instigators. Often, they are not used to being asked for an opinion, so may be unsure as to what is expected of them if they are asked. The Convention seeks to change this 'passive' view of children as recipients of care and support and replace it with a view of children as human beings – people – with a clear and appropriate set of rights. Unicef outlines these as rights that describe 'what a child needs to survive, grow, and live up to their potential in the world. They apply equally to every child, no matter who they are or where they come from'. Children are defined in the CRC as any person under the age of 18. There are 54 Articles in this legislation and each one focuses on an aspect of children's rights with the 'best interests' of the child at their core. They enshrine parental rights and responsibilities and rights to health, identity, liberty, privacy and family life. They give freedom to practise religion, to meet with and associate with other children, and to be protected from violence. Specific articles give rights to refugees, disabled children and children in care. Children should be protected from all forms of exploitation including abduction, child labour, drug and sexual exploitation.

GROUP EXERCISE

Each person in your group should choose one or two of Articles 12, 27, 28, 34 and 36 of the *UN Convention on the Rights of the Child* to research into, and then present the information about these aspects of the legislation to your peers.

You can access a summary of the complete list of Articles at www.unicef.org.uk/Documents/Publication-pdfs/UNCRC_summary.pdf.

Whilst it is impossible to say that one Article is of more importance than another, as a trainee or beginning teacher there are some that will be of more significance to you in your practice. These are Article 28 and Article 29, which detail the child's right to education and that 'education must develop every child's personality, talents and abilities to the full', and Article 12 which places a duty on schools to allow children to express their opinions, to listen to those opinions, and to take them seriously. This chapter explores the benefits of child (and pupil) voice and additionally it offers a critical perspective. Examples of school practices are interwoven throughout the chapter.

A useful starting point is to be clear on what is meant by children's rights. This chapter adopts the following perspective:

> Children's rights are about treating children with the equality, respect and dignity to which they are entitled, not because they are the 'adults of tomorrow', but because they are human beings today.
>
> (Child Rights International Network Website)

Promoting children's participation: giving children a voice

According to the *United Nations Convention on the Rights of the Child* (1989):

> State parties shall assure to the child who is capable of forming his/her own views the right to express those views freely in all matters affecting the child, the views of the child being given due weight in accordance with the age and maturity of the child.

Article 12 states that children and young people have a right to express an opinion and to have their opinion taken into account. The Ofsted framework for school inspections now requires inspectors to make judgements on the extent to which schools involve pupils in the development of policies and practices and the extent to which schools seek, value and act upon children's views. Therefore schools have a duty to ensure that pupils' views are sought, heard, valued and acted upon. In excellent schools regular consultation with pupils is valued and pupils are agents of change.

Giving children a voice in their education is critical to a democratic and socially just education system. The assumptions which underpin child voice are that children are confident, capable individuals who are able to make informed decisions about matters which affect them. In other words, children are now viewed as social actors or social agents; their contribution is valued because they are the key stakeholders within the education system and they have a right to voice their opinions, and for these opinions to be listened to, considered and acted upon where appropriate.

Viewing children as social actors is significantly different from historical perspectives on childhood. Throughout history children have been marginalised and exploited. They were treated as inferior to adults and punished when they did not conform. Throughout the twentieth century children were passive recipients of education and it was only in the latter part of that century that the child voice agenda gained momentum. It was also only in the last decade of the twentieth century that literature appeared that began to look at the child as more than a cipher or an 'incompetent respondent' (Robinson and Kellett, 2004). Children needed to be under adult supervision or the protection of (in particular in schools) *in loco parentis* teachers. That children could have thoughts and opinions that could help to shape research and policy was seldom considered. Since the mid-1990s, however, there has been 'a marked epistemological shift from research which objectifies children, placing their needs under the auspices of the family, to research conducted with children' (Weller, 2006: 304).

Maintaining the balance of power

The notion of pupil participation can affect the balance of power in schools and staff may feel threatened if pupils are given, or appear to be given, increased levels of power. Shier (2001) offers a model of participation which allows schools to develop pupil participation progressively through giving pupils increasing levels of empowerment and responsibility. Schools can initially develop participation by listening to children, encouraging them to express their views, and then taking these into account. He suggests a model for schools to follow that grows participation almost organically, giving pupils incremental increases in power and responsibility. This starts by schools listening to pupils, then allowing them to participate in decision making, and finally encouraging them to take a hand in policy making. Some commentators, such as Wood (2003: 365) are still of the opinion that there is a long way to go, stating that 'while pupils are often considered the key stakeholders in education, rarely are their voices seriously taken into account in polices devised to improve teaching, learning and achievement'.

At the end of the process, schools can start to involve children in decision-making processes, eventually allowing pupils to share power and responsibility for more strategic decision making. There are, however, caveats. If the empowered pupil proposes a radical shift in the curriculum (for example, the abandonment of Friday afternoons as being unproductive) would teachers not feel that they were entitled to resist? This perhaps gives some idea of the limitations of pupil empowerment. Cremin et al. (2011: 587) make the point that children should be aware that they do not have the power to make major changes, but are in fact participating in a partnership in which they are merely one of the players. It has also long been accepted (Bernstein, 1981; Bourdieu, 1989) that the way in which opinions are expressed will influence their relative power. Those, therefore, with skills of language or argument (perhaps linked to background, culture or home life) will have a greater (and disproportionate) influence than those who struggle to make themselves heard. This has implications for power within groups, across ethnic groups, and across class divides.

A thought

Many schools have pupil/student councils to provide pupils with a forum for expressing their views. However, often the learners who are selected to sit on these councils are able, articulate, and very capable of expressing their perspectives. What steps could schools take to make school councils more representative of all learners?

Managing opportunities for pupil voice

All children have a right to be heard and the real challenge for some schools will be the issue of how to provide meaningful opportunities for learners with communication difficulties and other severe impairments to express their views. Schools need to develop a broad range of inclusive strategies which help pupils with special educational needs and/or disabilities to express their views. Strategies could include the use of objects, pictures, signs or symbols which enable pupils to make simple choices.

Moves to increase levels of pupil participation are likely to challenge the current value systems in some schools. Mutual respect between pupils, their peers and their teachers is central to this process. Pupil participation helps to foster awareness that children have rights as citizens to express their views and this raises their self-esteem. Rudduck and Flutter (2000: 1) write that educators can learn much from pupils 'from their observations about what helps them to learn, what switches them off and what kind of support and recognition they value', but that this will only be effective if pupils are 'sure that teachers are really interested in what they have to say [and] that their views will be given careful consideration … ' (ibid: 2).

Application to secondary teaching

In some secondary schools subject teachers are asked to formally collect pupils' views each half term through the use of a survey (perhaps online) and focus groups of pupils. The subject teacher considers the feedback from the students and issues the students with a 'you said/we did' response. This provides pupils with information on how their feedback has been acted upon, thus closing the loop on their suggestions. In cases where students' suggestions cannot be acted on subject teachers write a brief commentary to explain the reasons why their comments have not been addressed. It is important that methods such as this are seen as open and transparent and that responses are honest. Although it may be difficult, responses (including those from focus groups) should be properly analysed and also reported to governors.

Benefits of pupil voice

Seminal literature on pupil voice has emphasised the importance of empowering learners to be active agents in their own education (Pollard and Triggs, 2000; Rudduck and Flutter, 2000, 2004; Flutter and Rudduck, 2004). Empowering learners to express their views and effect positive change can reduce learner disengagement and enhance pupils' self-esteem (MacBeath et al., 2003). Consultation with learners can lead to positive improvements in teaching and learning (Flutter and Rudduck, 2004) because students have a unique insight into the teaching and learning strategies that engage or disengage them. Research suggests that increasing levels of pupil participation and engagement in their own education enables learners to become agents of change (Fielding and Bragg, 2003) and this can be empowering for students when they recognise the influence they have had on their own education. Smith et al. (2005: 9), in 'a systematic review of what pupils, aged 11–16, believe impacts on their motivation to learn in the classroom', see pupils' views as 'an important prerequisite for informing teaching practices in schools'. Rudduck returns to this theme time and again, for example Rudduck and McIntyre (2007) emphasise the importance of not just letting pupils have a voice, but also of actively listening to them. Deuchar (2009: 35) however, warns that pupils may not automatically take to commenting on their own experiences; they may instead find it 'difficult to adjust to the idea of being given more say in what and how they learn'.

Despite the benefits of a commitment to pupil voice, the literature has also identified and explored teacher apprehension with regard to the apparent erosion of their power as increasing power is transferred onto learners (Robson and Fielding, 2010). Some teachers may feel their professional authority has been eroded or they have less control over their students. In spite of these concerns teachers who view their learners as partners in their education rather than as passive recipients of their education generally develop effective relationships with their students. Students rarely want to revolt against their teachers and they understand that sometimes certain decisions need to be made in their best interests by those in more powerful positions. Transferring some power to learners enables pupils to feel they are part of a democratic education system and enabling them to effect positive change in their own education prepares them for living in a democratic society and for becoming citizens of their communities who are able to influence change. Students rarely want to revolt! They simply want to feel that they have been consulted.

INDIVIDUAL REFLECTION

Find out the strategies that your school uses to 'listen to the pupil voice'. How obvious are these (and their outcomes) to both pupils and staff? Is there more that could be done to make sure that pupils both gave their views and that these were heeded? What further practical strategies can you suggest?

Strategies for implementing the pupil voice agenda

Your school will have developed a range of strategies for listening to the pupil voice. These should have been designed to diminish some of the power differential between 'school' and its pupils, but may also limit the actual influence a pupil might have. Strategies might include ideas to help pupils to make their views known and keep these confidential, such as pupil questionnaires to collect their views each term and pupil voice boxes in classrooms to enable pupils to post anonymous comments; this may also be set up so that views can be expressed electronically such as through a website or blog. Pupils may be encouraged to take more responsibility for their own learning through guided learning conversations to assess their own learning and learner needs and set targets for themselves. Those who are allowed to participate in setting their own rules – at a classroom or school level – are more likely to uphold such rules.

A thought

Student councils often provide opportunities for pupils to make changes to aspects of daily school life, such as the design of the school playground or the content of school lunches. How might schools build on these practices so that learners have a more strategic influence on their education?

More formally (and publicly), there may be class or school councils, pupils involved in recruitment processes through interview panels, and specific named pupils elected to become student voice advocates whom other students can approach. At an even greater level of pupil involvement, pupils may be encouraged to take part in lesson observations or learning walks; to help formulate the school ethos and vision; to evaluate the school provision for Ofsted; or to be part of school improvement planning.

Application to primary and early years teaching

For younger pupils, the idea of expressing an opinion (and having it acted upon) may be difficult, so easier routes must be created. For example, some primary schools now include a pupil comments box in each classroom. This provides an opportunity for pupils to make anonymous suggestions for improving the quality of their education. The process is made more accessible through the use of paper slips with the headings 'start, stop and continue'.

Start: Things they want to be introduced in the classroom accompanied by a reason for their introduction

Stop: Things they no longer want to continue in the classroom accompanied by a reason for ceasing them

Continue: Things that are working well and therefore need to be continued.

Pupils select a slip and record their ideas on it before posting it in the box.

In an early years setting accessibility requires even more scaffolding. For example, at the start of each half-term the children are included in the planning process by helping to make decisions about the resources (enhancements) they would like to see in the environment of the classroom (areas of continuous provision). This includes opportunities for children to make decisions about how to develop specific areas such as the sand and water areas and the role-play areas.

A critical perspective

The notion of child rights can be problematic because different communities, societies and cultures do not necessarily interpret rights in the same way. Children's rights discourses often emphasise children's rights to protection (from harm, hunger or thirst), provision (such as education and shelter), and participation (Franklin, 2002).

However, in some societies it is necessary to put a child's right to protection (i.e. welfare rights) above their right to participation and provision. In war-torn countries for example it might not be possible for children to access education because the provision may have been destroyed. In some societies, illness, homelessness and poverty mean that welfare rights have to be given higher priorities than liberty rights and rights to provision. Additional rights above the basic rights of protection, food and water are difficult to justify in these contexts where the right to survival must be the priority.

Additionally, in some societies and cultures children are not recognised as having rights outside their immediate group. Their responsibility is towards their community or cultural group and they are not seen as having individual rights beyond this. Furthermore, in some cultural groups, societies or communities children have a duty to respect their elders, and therefore viewing children as social agents is particularly problematic because it may cause relationships within families to break down.

A thought

Should teachers always implement learner suggestions? When might this be appropriate and when might it be inappropriate?

Within the UK the commitment to child voice or 'listening to the pupil voice' is evident in the way that education initiatives have been designed to place the child at the centre of those policies. Children's perspectives are considered as they are stakeholders in their education and therefore should be able to influence it. For example, within the revised *Code of Practice for Special Educational Needs* (DfE, 2014) there is a clear policy commitment to the principle that children and young people should be able to influence their own education by reviewing their own progress, contributing to decision-making processes and taking increasing levels of involvement in setting targets and goals for their future educational development and aspirations.

Conclusion

Children are no longer seen as 'passive recipients' of education, but as 'active participants' who should be encouraged to have views, to express those views, and to have them listened to and acted upon. As a trainee or beginning teacher you need to be aware that listening to the pupil voice is a key part of your development.

Summary

- Children are human beings – they have rights as human beings, not just as children.
- Familiarise yourself with the *UN Declaration of the Rights of the Child.*
- Be aware of how pupil voice is encouraged in your setting, and how you can add to this encouragement.
- A commitment to the principle of children's rights can be problematic in some cultures and societies.
- School inspections in England focus sharply on the extent to which learners have been able to influence their own education.

Key reading

Cremin, H., Mason, C., and Busher, H. (2011) 'Problematising pupil voice using visual methods: findings from a study of engaged and disaffected pupils in an urban secondary school. *British Educational Research Journal*, 37 (4): 585–603.

Jones, P. and Welch, S. (2010) *Rethinking children's rights: attitudes in contemporary society.* London: Continuum.

Shier, H. (2001) 'Pathways to participation: openings, opportunities and obligations', *Children and Society,* 15 (2): 107–17.

United Nations (1989) *United Nations Convention on the Rights of the Child.* Geneva: UN.

Wood, E. (2003) 'The power of pupil perspectives in evidence-based practice: the case of gender and underachievement', *Research Papers in Education,* 18 (4): 365–83.

References and bibliography

Bernstein, B. (1981) 'Codes, modalities, and the process of cultural reproduction: a model', *Language in Society,* 10: 327–63.

Bourdieu, P. (1989) 'Social space and symbolic power', *Sociological Theory,* 7 (1): 14–25.

Cremin, H., Mason, C. and Busher, H. (2011) 'Problematising pupil voice using visual methods: findings from a study of engaged and disaffected pupils in an urban secondary school'. *British Educational Research Journal*, 37 (4): 585–603.

Deuchar, R. (2009) 'Seen and heard, and then not heard: Scottish pupils' experience of democratic educational practice during the transition from primary to secondary school', *Oxford Review of Education,* 35 (1): 23–40.

Fielding, M. and Bragg, S. (2003) *Students as researchers: making a difference.* Cambridge: Pearson.

Flutter, J. and Rudduck, J. (2004*) Consulting pupils: what's in it for schools?* London: RoutledgeFalmer.

Franklin, B. (2002) *The new handbook of children's rights.* London: Routledge.

MacBeath, J., Demetriou, H., Rudduck, J. and Myers, K. (2003) *Consulting pupils: a toolkit for teachers.* Cambridge, Pearson.

Pollard, A., Triggs, P., with Broadfoot, P., McNess, E. and Osborn, M. (2000) *What pupils say: changing policy and practice in primary education*. London and New York: Continuum.

Robinson, C. and Kellett, M. (2004) in S. Fraser (ed.), *Doing research with children and young people*. London: Sage.

Robson, C. and Fielding, M. (2010) 'Children and their primary schools: pupils' voices', in R. Alexander (ed.), *The Cambridge Primary Review Research Surveys*. London: Routledge. pp.17–48.

Rudduck, J. and Flutter, J. (2000) 'Pupil participation and pupil perspective: carving a new order of experience', *Cambridge Journal of Education*, 30 (1): 75–89.

Rudduck, J. and Flutter, J. (2004) *How to improve your school*. London: Continuum.

Rudduck, J. and McIntyre, D. (2007) *Improving learning through consulting pupils*. Abingdon: Routledge.

Shier, H. (2001) 'Pathways to participation: openings, opportunities and obligations', *Children and Society*, 15 (2): 107–17.

Smith, C., Dakers, J., Dow, W., Head, G., Sutherland, M. and Irwin, R. (2005) 'A systematic review of what pupils, aged 11–16, believe impacts on their motivation to learn in the classroom', in *Research Evidence in Education Library*. London: EPPI-Centre, Social Science Research Unit, Institute of Education, University of London.

Weller, S. (2006) 'Tuning-in to teenagers! Using radio phone-in discussions in research with young people', *Social Research Methodology,*. 9 (4): 303–15.

Wood, E. (2003) 'The power of pupil perspectives in evidence-based practice: the case of gender and underachievement', *Research Papers in Education*, 18 (4): 365–83.

Useful websites

Child Rights International Network: www.bettercarenetwork.org/themes/ViewTheme.asp?id=2

DfE (2014) Special educational needs and disability code of practice: 0 to 25 years: Statutory guidance for organisations who work with and support children and young people with special educational needs and disabilities, DFE.

United Nations (1989) *United Nations Convention on the Rights of the Child*: www.unicef.org.uk/Documents/Publication-pdfs/UNCRC_summary.pdf.

Visit https://study.sagepub.com/denby3e for extra resources related to this chapter.

CHAPTER 21

CROSS-CURRICULAR PLANNING ISSUES

Neil Denby

Standards linked to this chapter include...

1. Set high expectations which inspire, motivate and challenge pupils
   - establish a safe and stimulating environment for pupils, rooted in mutual respect
   - set goals that stretch and challenge pupils of all backgrounds, abilities and dispositions.
2. Promote good progress and outcomes by pupils
   - demonstrate knowledge and understanding of how pupils learn and how this impacts on teaching
   - encourage pupils to take a responsible and conscientious attitude to their own work and study.

4. Plan and teach well-structured lessons

   - impart knowledge and develop understanding through effective use of lesson time.

Introduction

A number of subjects, concepts, and methods may be fairly considered to be cross-curricular in nature. This means that they cross traditional curriculum boundaries either as concepts or methods which appear in more than one area, or as themes that run through various subjects. Take, for example, environmental or green issues – these will arise in geography, design technology, business and economics, science, and others, and should not be presented in each case as something entirely new.

Major cross-curricular skills such as literacy and numeracy are discussed in the next chapter. The use of ICT and digital technologies is discussed in Chapter 19. These areas are highlighted in the National Curriculum document (2014; paragraphs 5.2 and 6.1) as being inherently cross-curricular, and the responsibility of all teachers in terms of delivery. There are, however, other areas where cooperation within and between subjects is desirable and can reap dividends.

It is worth first looking, briefly, at the development of the National Curriculum which, to many people's surprise, has been around for less than thirty years. Before this, there was some commonality of approach in terms of core subjects such as English and mathematics, but a wide range of examination boards and little idea of how to make genuine comparisons between one school and another.

History of the National Curriculum

The National Curriculum was first introduced in the Education Reform Act 1988 with ten subjects and a plethora of attainment targets. Since then it has tended to see-saw between an 'all things to all men' approach, where it was virtually impossible to fit in all of the content, to a narrow, often ideologically or politically tinged, tight 'core' curriculum. The original National Curriculum was always seen as containing too much content (teachers complained that there was not enough time to teach all of it) so it was reduced in size in 1995. This reduction, however, tended to 'over-correct' in terms of content and produced a very narrow curriculum. Curriculum 2000, the revisited version rolled out at the millennium, had much less proscription and more room for individual interpretation and routes of delivery. The 2005 Rose Review proposed freeing it up even further, with an emphasis on creativity and cross-curricular skills, but this was abandoned by the coalition government that took office in 2010 in favour of a much narrower and more restrictive, knowledge-based curriculum.

The 2014 National Curriculum is thus neither progressive nor developmental, but instead is based on what might be considered sterile ideas of knowledge transference, retention and regurgitation rather than the dynamism of creativity, active learning and transferable skills. It is predicated on American ideas of a knowledge-based core curriculum (Hirsch, 1996) and as such removes the need for teachers to be able to teach methods, concepts and skills. Hirsch has published long lists of knowledge which he considers 'appropriate' for each age and stage in America. In the UK this has even led to the development of American-type teacher training routes, based on the idea that, as long as the teacher has knowledge (as demonstrated by a good university degree), they will be a good teacher of their subject. Thus 'Teach First' is based on 'Teach for America', whose mission since 1990 has been to encourage high-achieving college graduates to teach in low-income communities for two years. Troops to Teachers is based on the American model of the same name (run by the Department of Defense, not Education) and designed to bring ex-servicemen into the classroom. As a trainee or beginning teacher, however, you will need to be very wary of such knowledge-based approaches as you will quickly realise that it is the skills that you teach and by which you teach that really make the difference in education. Even the National Curriculum documentation itself is clear that teaching should not be limited to just those elements that form its core, and that understanding and skills rank as highly as knowledge. As it says at paragraph 3.2:

> There is time and space in the school day and in each week, term and year to range beyond the national curriculum specifications. The national curriculum provides an outline of core knowledge around which teachers can develop exciting and stimulating lessons to promote the development of pupils' knowledge, understanding and skills as part of the wider school curriculum. (National Curriculum Document, 2014)

In addition, Ofsted are now clear that:

> Inspectors must not advocate a particular method of planning, teaching or assessment. They will not look for a preferred methodology but must record aspects of teaching and learning that they consider are effective, and identify ways in which teaching and learning can be improved.(Ofsted, 2015 para. 39)

Application of the National Curriculum

The National Curriculum applies to all maintained schools in England (i.e. those under Local Authority control) but not to academies and 'free' schools who may deliver their own curriculum, providing it is 'broad and balanced'. In practice, these schools will deliver similar curricula to maintained schools, if only so that they can be judged by the same criteria in terms of progress and GCSE and post-16 outcomes. The 2014 changes to the National Curriculum included new programmes of study and how they will be phased in. For example, in secondary schools new KS4 programmes of study for mathematics and English are to be introduced in 2015 to Year 10 whilst the new science programme is not due in Year 10 until 2016.

Cross-curriculum dimensions

The old National Curriculum also contained 'Cross-curriculum dimensions', included as useful vehicles to help schools to plan a more integrated curriculum. Many schools recognised, and continue to recognise, that building such themes into the curriculum helps to provide richness and depth.

These 'dimensions' should be embedded in your teaching wherever possible. You should not be attempting to teach them in isolation, as often they are inextricably bound up with each other. They include the idea of children's rights and the pupil voice, of 'green' initiatives and the global village, of responsibility and rights as embodied in citizenship, of a young person's place in their community. Whilst there will be no statutory duty to deliver any of these dimensions, schools will clearly still have them embedded into their teaching and learning strategies.

A thought

None of the cross-curricular 'dimensions' is a subject in its own right. Consider these more as part of the scaffolding or framework for all subjects.

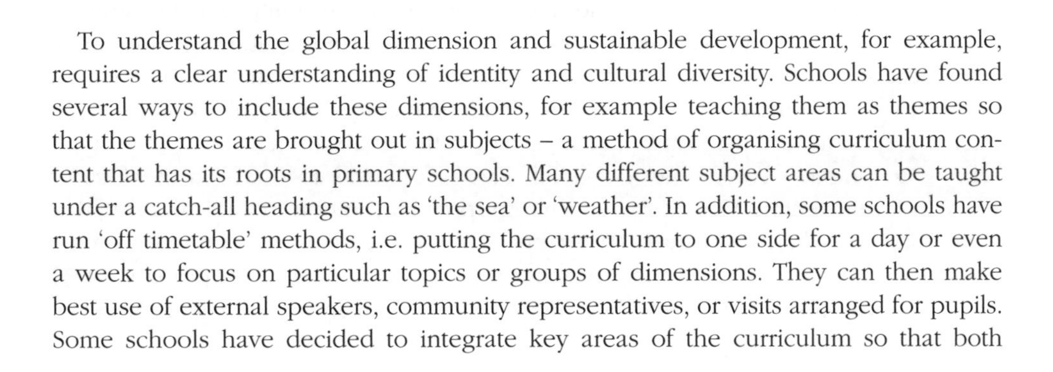

To understand the global dimension and sustainable development, for example, requires a clear understanding of identity and cultural diversity. Schools have found several ways to include these dimensions, for example teaching them as themes so that the themes are brought out in subjects – a method of organising curriculum content that has its roots in primary schools. Many different subject areas can be taught under a catch-all heading such as 'the sea' or 'weather'. In addition, some schools have run 'off timetable' methods, i.e. putting the curriculum to one side for a day or even a week to focus on particular topics or groups of dimensions. They can then make best use of external speakers, community representatives, or visits arranged for pupils. Some schools have decided to integrate key areas of the curriculum so that both subject and dimension are given equal opportunities. You can see that many of these strategies presuppose teachers working across departments, integrating knowledge and sharing planning. According to Mick Waters, Director of Curriculum at QCA at the time, 'The cross-curriculum dimensions are essential tools to help young people make sense of the wider world. They should permeate the curriculum and the life of a school' (QCA, 2009). The seven dimensions, which 'reflect some of the major ideas and challenges that face individuals and society, and can help provide links for learning across the whole curriculum' (QCA, 2009) were as follows:

- identity and cultural diversity
- healthy lifestyles
- community participation
- enterprise education
- global dimension and sustainable development
- technology and the media
- creativity and critical thinking.

Planning guides to each dimension were published in 2009 and schools created systems and methods to deal with the requirements. If these were seen as adding value to the curriculum they will still be in place in many schools, so you could well find them in the schools where you train or begin your teaching career. The paragraphs below outline the expectations under each heading.

Identity and cultural diversity

Identity and cultural diversity promotes understanding of the diverse society of both the UK and the world. It includes ideas regarding tolerance, the origins of diversity and ethnicity, and how and why, historically, different cultures, values and beliefs have developed. It encourages young people to think about who they are, where they have come from, and their contextual place in the society in which they live. This was strengthened through the recommendations in Keith Ajegbo's report (Ajegbo et al., 2007) into the idea of 'Britishness' and how multiculturalism should be introduced to the curriculum. The report, entitled 'Diversity and citizenship', was part of the drive to promote what has been called 'community cohesion'. Commissioned after the London terrorist bomb attacks it led to the establishment of a duty on all schools to promote community cohesion. Part of this was to establish the idea of PREVENT – Preventing Violent Extremism. An Ipsos Mori report in 2011 reported that almost all the schools surveyed (95%) knew about the statutory duty to promote community cohesion, with secondary schools (54%) more likely than primary (46%) or special schools (44%) to say they knew a great deal. In addition, the executive summary states:

- primary, secondary and special schools all often view 'community cohesion' in terms of citizenship, multiculturalism, faith and race/ethnicity: more than three quarters mention each of these
- secondary schools also view cohesion in terms of socio-economic status (85%), deprivation (75%) and anti-social behaviour (76%): over three quarters mention these
- almost all primary (89%), secondary (93%) and special (89%) schools say their understanding of community cohesion is better since the introduction of the duty to promote community cohesion: well over half say it is a lot better (Phillips et al., 2011: 8).

However, the overall conclusion was that whilst schools may understand the duty better, this was not being matched by actions. A key part of Ajegbo's review is the emphasis on how Citizenship was taught, and how it could contribute to a better understanding within and between communities. Good citizenship education – when it actually delivers the social and moral elements – could combat intolerance, bigotry and religious extremism.

Community cohesion is no longer a specific part of rating schools, but still falls under the general heading of promoting the spiritual, moral, social and cultural development (SMSC) contained in the Education Act 2002 (Section 78).

Trojan horses and British values

In November 2014 non-statutory advice entitled 'Promoting fundamental British values as part of SMSC in schools' was published by the DfE as a result of the 'Trojan Horse' inquiry, which revealed practices in certain Birmingham schools that were contrary to the Education Act. These included evidence of the imposition of a conservative religious view, a narrow curriculum, intolerance of difference, restrictions in learning languages, contraception removed from sex and relationships education, segregation of the sexes, homophobia, extremist assemblies, music and drama banned, and only Islam being taught in RE. In total, this was seen as the development of 'a culture of fear and intimidation'. As a result of these investigations, certain changes were made to definitions of SMSC and new Ofsted terminology introduced. You will realise, when you read the paragraphs below about citizenship, that many of these values should already be part of the curriculum. Pupils are to 'reflect about their own beliefs', 'respect the civil and criminal law of England', and 'appreciate the viewpoints of others'. Social development includes accepting and promoting 'fundamental British values' such as democracy, the rule of law, respect and tolerance. Cultural development includes showing understanding and tolerance towards a range of 'diverse faiths and cultures'. There is specific mention of being tolerant of disability, homosexuality and other races, and awareness-raising of cultural issues such as forced marriage, female genital mutilation, radicalisation and extremism, and gang culture.

Ofsted guidance says that the teaching of SMSC is 'inadequate' if pupils are 'intolerant of others and/or reject any of the core values fundamental to life in modern Britain'.

Healthy lifestyles

Healthy lifestyles include eating healthily, taking exercise, and enjoying play. Pupils need to meet and be comfortable with a range of professionals who can offer advice, and be educated to make informed and sensible choices regarding their lifestyles. Physical education has remained a compulsory part of the NC, but has a less detailed programme of study, implemented from 2013. It encourages pupils to play competitive sport, and it is the intention for all to learn to swim.

Community participation

Community participation was already built into the Citizenship curriculum, but is reiterated here as understanding the community in which pupils live and developing a positive role within it, acting as responsible citizens. This encourages pupils to make an effort not only to be a part of their local community, but also to support it. GCSE specifications in Citizenship are also written to promote such participation.

Enterprise education

Enterprise education encourages children and young people to 'be enterprising', i.e. to take risks, tackle problems and innovate. It has been built into various parts of the curriculum, such as work-related learning and 'Personal Learning and Thinking Skills' (PLTS). Pupils have run mini-enterprises and been encouraged to enter competitions such as Young Enterprise. This is a leading business charity reaching a third of a million pupils a year with the support of over 350,000 businesses. The Young Enterprise Company Programme encourages 15 to 19 year-olds to set up and run their own real company from school or college and every year over 30,000 do so (www.young-enterprise. org.uk). They raise their own starting capital, make their own product, and devise their own advertising and promotion with the help of a local business adviser. Pupils learn about keeping accounts, financial common sense, dealing with people, working in teams, and other important and transferable skills. There are regional heats with the 12 winners from each region competing in the national HSBC Young Enterprise Innovation Awards in London to become the UK's Young Enterprise Company of the Year. Interestingly, winners do not have to have a successful product but do have to show that they understand the hows and whys of their company's performance. Young Enterprise also provides curriculum materials and classroom support through their development programmes.

Global dimension and sustainable development

Young people should be aware of global issues and their own responsibilities within this context. They should know what is meant by sustainability and aim to develop sustainable and environmentally friendly lifestyles as responsible and aware citizens. Again, this is an idea that is included in the citizenship curriculum, but one which has more resonance in schools than merely in citizenship lessons.

Technology and the media

Young people should be able to treat technology and the media in a critical way. They should have the skills to take advantage of new technology, but the awareness not to fall foul of any of the dangers. These include not only the obvious areas of cyberbullying and identity theft (see Chapter 4), but also thinking about how much time they spend on a computer, for example, and what is appropriate. The development of computing skills is linked to the idea of digital literacy – pupils should be able to operate computers so they can express themselves and their ideas and develop skills that are transferable to the working world.

Creativity and critical thinking

Children and young people should learn to use their imagination to develop ideas and to seek creative solutions to problems and issues (See Chapter 16). They should have the capacity to learn from others and to hold and support an opinion on their own or others' work or viewpoints. The human being is a naturally creative animal, so this should be encouraged in pupils. The DfE says 'In order to bring the curriculum to life, teachers need the space to create lessons which engage their pupils, and children need the time to develop their ability to understand, retain and apply what they have learnt' (DfE, 2011).

Critical thinking includes being able to take a critical view of the way that the media work. Pupils should be able to detect media bias, for example, and not be easily misled by such things as advertising and marketing claims.

INDIVIDUAL REFLECTION

There are many more cross-curricular issues than those specifics outlined here. Look back at a series of your lesson plans and decide which cross-curricular strands, dimensions or ideas are already present and which others could be added in to enhance learning.

GROUP EXERCISE

In your group, consider and share ways in which you could introduce a concept or idea in your subject that could be used in another subject. Suggest which other subject and how it could be taught. Some examples of cross-curricular links provided by QCA in the past include the following:

- Mathematics concepts are taught in art, geography, history, biology, business and science
- Literacy is an integral part of all written and spoken learning
- In art, learners need to understand the history of art
- In history, learners need to have an understanding of the borders between different countries or the consequence of a geographical structure
- In literature, history is integral.

PSHE

PSHE (Personal, Social, Health and Economic Education) is a non-compulsory part of the National Curriculum which nevertheless contains some compulsory elements. You may find this confusing: you may find the way that different schools treat PSHE equally confusing. Schools have the freedom to choose how they provide PSHE. Sometimes it has its own timetable slot, sometimes it is part of form or tutor time; sometimes it provides an excellent underpinning to the rest of the curriculum by being taught by a team of experts. Thus for some schools PSHE has a central timetable place, is well-staffed and resourced, and carries a positive status. In others it is very much a 'poor relation', often underfunded and quite possibly taught by a wide variety of staff who ended up with 'spare' time on their timetables. At some point in your teaching career, whatever your specialist subject, you are likely to be asked to teach some part of the PSHE curriculum. This is usually because, although there is an expert PSHE teacher or team of teachers who organise the PSHE curriculum, resources are often stretched for its delivery. You therefore need to be familiar with the guidance relevant to your chosen age range. PSHE now has no programmes of study or frameworks, as apparently for this subject 'Teachers are best placed to understand the needs of their pupils and do not need additional central prescription' (DfE guidance, 2013). The statutory parts of the programme are those linked to drug education, financial education, sex and relationship education (SRE), and health education.

- **Drug and alcohol** education is supported by an evidence-based information service called 'Mentor-ADEPIS' (Alcohol and Drug Education and Prevention Information Service), accessed at http://mentor-adepis.org
- **Financial education** is included in the mathematics programmes of study and is also now part of citizenship education (see page 307)
- **SRE** is statutory in maintained secondary schools for which there is guidance that has been in place since 2000 (DfEE 0116/2000)
- **Health education** – diet, healthy eating and the importance of physical exercise – is a key part of the physical education curriculum.

Key Stage outcomes

There are now no Key Stage outcomes published for pupils and there were never any assessments or tests for PSHE, but to help you indicate how pupils are expected to make progress it is worth revisiting the pre-2014 Key Stage outcomes. These give a good idea of where you should expect a pupil to be at the end of each Key Stage:

- **End of Key Stage 1.** Children can identify some feelings and be able to manage them in themselves and others. They can make simple choices about some parts of their life and know, for example, how to keep clean, eat well, and the importance of exercise and rest. They can tell right from wrong, especially in cases that could be specific to them such as bullying.
- **End of Key Stage 2.** Children have developed a sense of their own worth and that of others. They can begin to look to the future and the development of appropriate skills to manage change or for jobs. Healthy lifestyle understanding includes that related to emotional issues. Pupils have some understanding of drugs and the harm they can do. They understand how actions have consequences and can recognise and challenge negative behaviour.
- **End of Key Stage 3.** Young people have developed the capacity to evaluate their own achievements. They can plan targets for the future and manage money competently. They know how to stay physically and mentally healthy and have the capacity to counter negative pressure. They recognise difference and diversity and develop the skills to challenge prejudice.
- **End of Key Stage 4.** Young people are self-aware, can set goals for the future, and can respond positively to both praise and criticism. They are competent to manage their personal finances. In terms of health, they can judge the relative merits of different lifestyle choices, assess risks and benefits, and know where to go for professional advice on such issues. They understand and can discuss relationships. They are aware of diversity and challenge offensive behaviour in this context.

Application to primary and early years teaching

In primary it is normal for a teacher to take a class for much of its timetable, and to thus – as both an academic and pastoral teacher – become more attuned to the needs and skills of that class than might be the case for a secondary form tutor. Construct a table that lists the expected outcomes for the appropriate Key Stage against your class members for a chosen class so that you can see who has reached particular 'life skills'. Key Stage 1 and 2 may be listed as follows:

End of Key Stage 1 children:

1. Can identify some feelings
2. Can manage feelings in themselves and others
3. Can make simple choices
4. Know how to keep clean
5. Know to eat well, take exercise and rest
6. Can tell right from wrong.

End of Key Stage 2 children:

1. Have developed a sense of their own worth and that of others
2. Can begin to look to the future to manage change or for jobs
3. Can relate emotional issues to healthy living
4. Have some understanding of drugs and the harm they can do
5. Understand how actions have consequences
6. Can recognise and challenge negative behaviour.

For example:

Class 2B.

Key Stage 1						
Name	**1**	**2**	**3**	**4**	**5**	**6**
Dean	✓	✓	✓			✓
William		✓	✓	✓	✓	
Jared			✓	✓	✓	

You may want to put a simple tick, as in the example, or devise a scale, perhaps shading boxes as competency develops. Remember these are expectations by the end of the Key Stage, so at ages 7 and 11. Once you have an overall picture, and can identify particular areas of concern, develop ways to address these as part of your normal lesson planning.

Citizenship: a retrospective

The following paragraphs review how the place of citizenship in the curriculum has changed since being introduced as a compulsory subject of the National Curriculum in 2002, and describe how it has been treated in the 2013 curriculum review for the 2014 National Curriculum.

Citizenship: 2002

Citizenship became a compulsory subject in the secondary curriculum in 2002, following the recommendations of the Crick Report (Crick, 1998). This was set up as a result of the Labour Party's 1997 White Paper *Excellence in schools*, in which Secretary of State David Blunkett pledged to 'Strengthen education for Citizenship and the teaching of democracy in schools' (quoted in Crick, 1998: 3).

It became part of the PSHE curriculum at Key Stages 1 and 2 and a National Curriculum subject in its own right at Key Stages 3 and 4. There were non-statutory guidelines for Key Stages 1 and 2 and Programmes of Study for Key Stages 3 and 4. Crick fought for the content of the Citizenship orders to be minimal, and to allow schools to build their own frameworks for teaching it. The Citizenship NC document was therefore the shortest of all the NC subjects, and the requirements for Citizenship at KS3 or KS4 fitted onto a single page.

The three central strands of Citizenship education were recognised as:

- **Social and moral responsibility.** Pupils learn, from the beginning, self-confidence and socially and morally responsible behaviour, both in and beyond the classroom, towards those in authority and each other.
- **Community involvement.** Pupils learn how to become helpfully involved in the life and concerns of their neighbourhood and communities, including learning through community involvement and service.
- **Political literacy.** Pupils learn about the institutions, issues, problems and practices of our democracy and how citizens can make themselves effective in public life, locally, regionally and nationally, through skills as well as knowledge.

Delivery

For each of these strands, a school could decide on its own method of delivery. In general, these were either as a discrete subject, through cross-curricular audit plus enhancement, or by whole-school (or year group) events or activities – a citizenship 'week', for example. The reality was that, while some schools were very good at teaching citizenship, many were less than adequate. Of the three strands, the easiest to teach – involving institutions, processes and procedures – was political literacy. However, many teachers also saw this as 'dry'. Community involvement was more difficult as it involved taking children and young people out of school confines and into the community (or organising visitors and speakers to come in). Of greatest difficulty was the teaching of social and moral responsibility. By 2005, Ofsted's initial inspections of Citizenship led them to conclude:

> Increasingly, schools are taking National Curriculum citizenship seriously and establishing comprehensive programmes. As yet, however, pupils' achievement and the quality of teaching compare unfavourably with established subjects and there is little that is graded very good. In one in four schools, provision is unsatisfactory. (HMI, 2005: 3)

In certain subject areas, teachers found there was a natural affinity to Citizenship. It was often taught by historians, or as part of the RE department's brief. Much of the NC content was native to business and economics education. The skills of citizenship, as given in the central strands, are skills that all subjects should be encouraging and developing, and this is part of the argument for removing Citizenship as a separate subject. Others can see the opposing view that, if these skills are not compulsorily embedded in the curriculum, they are likely to be treated as less than essential, and will fail to be delivered or developed at all. In 2009 it was reported that schools favoured various delivery models as follows:

> Assemblies – used in over three-quarters of schools (81 per cent of schools, up from 67 per cent in 2004).
>
> Extra-curricular activities – used in just under a half of schools (49 per cent of schools, up from 37 per cent in 2004).
>
> Special events – used in 44 per cent of schools (up from 37 per cent in 2004).
>
> Specific subjects – used in around two-fifths of schools (41 per cent, up from 35 per cent in 2004), with the most common subjects used as a vehicle for CE being PSHE, RE, History, and Geography (in 80, 73, 62 and 55 per cent of schools, respectively).
>
> Tutorials – used in 37 per cent of schools (up from 30 per cent in 2004). (Keating et al., 2009:12)

2007 National Curriculum

The 2007 National Curriculum revisited the core requirements but included attainment targets up to Level 9 (exceptional performance), where pupils could demonstrate mastery through analysis, evaluation and synthesis 'to present coherent, perceptive and compelling arguments on a wide range of citizenship issues' (QCA Citizenship, 2007). Its content carried much more detail and a different focus from that of the pre-2007 curriculum, with an emphasis on individual participation in the political process and in living in harmony with others (particularly diverse others) whilst developing the skills of 'critical thinking and enquiry', 'advocacy and representation', and 'taking informed and responsible action'. Subject content was defined under the headings of 'democracy and justice', 'rights and responsibilities', and 'identities and diversity – living together in the UK'. This echoes the areas which pupils were reported as seeming to be being most relevant:

> Student comments [related to] ... a perceived relevance of four main topic areas: government and politics; rights and responsibilities; community; and religious and ethnic groups. (Kerr et al., 2007: 38)

A thought

Do you know which concepts that might be applicable to your subject or age range are taught in other subjects or ranges? You should make a point of observing lessons in other subjects, or in the age range before or after yours, with this question as a particular focus of the observation.

2014 National Curriculum

Citizenship remains a statutory part of the National Curriculum in England with programmes of study and attainment targets for Key Stages 3 and 4. There are, however, subtle differences from the 2007 to 2013 curriculum. There is, as you would expect, an emphasis on democracy, government and the creation of laws, with rights referred to as 'precious liberties', but in addition there is the assumption that pupils are gaining such knowledge to help them to participate in processes and 'play a full and active part in society' (Citizenship Programmes of Study 2014) as responsible citizens. There is a presumption in favour of some sort of volunteering or community-based service, with a suggestion that this is school based in Key Stage 3 but includes 'the opportunity to participate actively in community volunteering' in Key Stage 4. In addition, the curriculum promotes the development of critical thinking skills and the ability 'to weigh evidence, debate and make reasoned arguments'. An additional element is that of personal financial management skills, with pupils taught to 'manage their money well and make sound financial decisions'. The attainment targets for the demonstration of learning are vague and no indication as to how they are to be demonstrated is given: 'By the end of each key stage, pupils are expected to know, apply and understand the matters, skills and processes specified in the relevant programme of study' (ibid.).

Application to secondary teaching

The RSA (Royal Society of Arts) Opening Minds curriculum (currently used by around 200 secondary schools) is based on five competence categories. Each category contains a number of individual strands, expressed in terms of student progress and outcomes. These include:

- **Competences for Learning** – taking account of their own learning style and managing learning; being creative, being able to handle and use ICT
- **Competences for Citizenship** – developing an understanding of ethics and values and their own place and role in society along with an understanding and respect for cultural diversity: included in this competency are also personal financial management and the social implications of technology
- **Competences for Relating to People** – understanding how to relate to other people in varying contexts, how to operate in teams, how to develop other people, how to communicate effectively, and how to manage relationships, stress and conflict
- **Competences for Managing Situations** – such as managing their own time, managing change, managing risk and uncertainty, and being entrepreneurial and initiative-taking
- **Competences for Managing Information** – developing techniques for accessing, evaluating, differentiating, analysing and synthesising information, and developing reflection and critical judgement.

Consider these five areas and use them in planning a short series of lessons. How do they change the style or direction of your teaching? Do they improve learning?

Summary

- There are numerous cross-curricular skills and aptitudes that pervade the curriculum.
- These include English skills (such as literacy and oracy), numeracy and ICT skills.
- PSHE promotes life skills and is a compulsory part of the NC.
- Citizenship promotes political literacy, participation and tolerance.
- There is a requirement to promote spiritual, moral and cultural development, including the promotion of fundamental British values.
- Many skills and methods learnt are transferable, and therefore relevant to the real world.

Key reading

The Ajegbo Report (2007) 'Diversity and citizenship' can be downloaded from the DfE archive at www.education.gov.uk/publications/standard/publicationdetail/page1/DFES-00045-2007

Information on Key Skills and Functional Skills – and their future – can be accessed at www.apprenticeships.org.uk/Partners/KeySkillsExtension.aspx

References and bibliography

Ajegbo, K. et al. (2007) *Diversity and citizenship: curriculum review*. London: Department for Education.

Crick, B. (1998) *Education for citizenship and the teaching of democracy in schools: final report of the Advisory Group on Citizenship*. London: QCA.

DfE (2010) *The importance of teaching schools*. White Paper. London: DfE.

DfE (2011) *Review of the National Curriculum in England: remit*. Available at www.education.gov.uk/b0073043/remit-for-review-of-the-national-curriculum-in-england/rationale-for-the-national-curriculum-review

Hirsch, E.D. (1996) *The schools we need and why we don't have them*. New York: Anchor Books (Random House).

HMI (2005) *Citizenship in secondary schools: evidence from Ofsted inspections (2003/04)*, HMI 2335.

Keating, A., Kerr, D., Lopes, J., Featherstone, G. and Benton, T. (2009) *Embedding Citizenship education in secondary schools in England (2002-08): Citizenship education longitudinal study seventh annual report*. National Foundation for Educational Research, DCSF RR172.

Kerr, D., Lopes, J., Nelson, J., White, K., Cleaver, E. and Benton, T. (2007) *Vision versus pragmatism: Citizenship in the secondary school curriculum in England: Citizenship education longitudinal study: fifth annual report*. National Foundation for Educational Research, DfE RR845.

Ofsted (2015) *School Inspection Handbook*, January 2015. Available at www.gov.uk

Phillips, C., Tse, D. and Johnson, F. (2011) *Community cohesion and PREVENT: how have schools responded?*, Research Report DFE-RR085 2011.

QCA (2009) 'Guidance on cross-curriculum dimensions'. News release, 12 March. Available at www.qcda.gov.uk/news/1024.aspx

RSA (2008) *Opening Minds impact update: Autumn 2008*. Available at http://.thersa.org/-data/assets/pdf-file/0003/139764/Microsoft-word...Opening-Minds-impact-update-Autumn-2008-v.2.pdf

Secretary of State for Education and Employment (1997) *Excellence in Schools,* CM368. London: TSO.

Useful websites

RSA Opening Minds: www.RSAopeningminds.org.uk/
Young Enterprise: www.young-enterprise.org.uk/

Visit https://study.sagepub.com/denby3e for extra resources related to this chapter.

CHAPTER 22

CROSS-CURRICULAR TEACHING ISSUES

Jayne Price and Fiona Woodhouse

Standards linked to this chapter include...

1. Set high expectations which inspire, motivate and challenge pupils

   - establish a safe and stimulating environment for pupils, rooted in mutual respect
   - set goals that stretch and challenge pupils of all backgrounds, abilities and dispositions.

(Continued)

(Continued)

2. Promote good progress and outcomes by pupils

   - demonstrate knowledge and understanding of how pupils learn and how this impacts on teaching
   - encourage pupils to take a responsible and conscientious attitude to their own work and study.

4. Plan and teach well structured lessons

   - impart knowledge and develop understanding through effective use of lesson time.

Introduction

Cross-curricular teaching is an area which teachers may think they are achieving just by using theme-based approaches. However, there is a lot more than this to good cross-curricular lesson planning and delivery. This chapter seeks to clarify some of the issues around teaching across subjects and to inspire you to begin to explore how you can develop your own teaching in this way.

The context for cross-curricular teaching

Cross-curricular teaching was an aspect that was emphasised in the National Curriculum issued in 2007. In the primary and early years stages the curriculum was divided into subject areas but with many cross-curricular links emphasised. For example, at Key Stage 1 the geography target 1b which was to 'observe and record' was linked to the mathematics target Ma2 Number 5a, to 'solve a relevant problem by using simple lists, tables and charts to sort, classify and organise information'. Historically primary schools have gone beyond this simple linking of subjects via their targets and instead planned teaching via themes. In the recent past, the requirements for literacy and numeracy hours have squeezed curriculum time and many schools have therefore moved away from this themed approach. The Rose Report (Rose, 2009) and the Cambridge Review of Primary Education (Alexander, 2009) imply that there should be more encouragement for schools to consider cross-curricular approaches. The Rose Report tried to encourage cross-curricular teaching by suggesting that subjects were not discrete but instead became 'areas of learning', for example an area called 'scientific and technological understanding'.

Barnes (2011: 12) discusses the history of cross-curricular teaching and suggests that 'educators ... have been conscious that combined perspectives were required in order to understand aspects of the physical, social or personal world'. He goes on to infer that a particular set of values and attitudes, such as liberal, inclusive, constructivist, relativist and intercultural, are embedded in cross-curricular pedagogies.

In secondary schools there is still a subject-based approach to teaching with whole-school initiatives of a cross-curricular nature being much rarer, although as with the primary curriculum there was some highlighting of areas which could have been developed across subject areas.

The new National Curriculum (DfE, 2014) phased in from September 2014 carries no explicit mention of cross-curricular teaching. This curriculum has a very different 'feel' to it with more prescribed subject content at all key stages. (Remember, only state maintained schools must follow the prescribed National Curriculum: academies, independent and 'free' schools do not have to do so.)

There will be one valid argument from many subject areas that it will be challenging to work through the curriculum content within their own subject without building in additional activities that touch on other curriculum areas. It is therefore worth asking whether segregating subjects into discrete areas – when they have often drawn on each other to understand concepts or develop skills – is a positive move. Will pupils begin to make the links between subjects if we are unable to model these processes in classrooms?

A thought

Should you treat the National Curriculum as a blueprint or as more of a general guide as to what should be taught? How much do you think that government policies such as the National Curriculum shape how we teach in the classroom?

Cross-curricular teaching; what it is and what it is not

Savage (2011: 8) has produced a good working definition of cross-curricular teaching:

> A cross curriculum approach to teaching is characterised by sensitivity towards, and a synthesis of knowledge, skills and understanding from various subject areas. These inform an enriched pedagogy that promotes an approach to learning which embraces and explores this wider sensitivity through various methods.

This suggests that a good cross-curricular approach brings together knowledge as well as the skills and processes from different subject areas to further enrich and develop pupils' understanding. The emphasis here is on developing the cross-curricular learning experience from within a subject perspective.

Cross-curricular teaching should be more than certain subject skills being used as teaching and learning activities in another subject area. A classic example could be a science lesson on the planets opened by the playing of the Planet Suite by Holst, and the result being labelled as a cross-curricular activity. What learning linked to the music curriculum are the pupils gaining from this and what does it really tell them about the nature of the planets in science? Likewise, using drama to enact historical events may help pupils understand the history, but what is the learning in terms of the drama curriculum in this situation? Moreover, as technology develops using tools such as the internet and iPads are not cross-curricular teaching with ICT, they are using a teaching resource to enhance learning. These are useful teaching resources and strategies but not truly cross-curricular teaching.

A thought

During your observations of other teachers look to see if any cross-curricular approaches or links are being used/made and then judge how genuine these are, in terms of subject specialisms, and therefore how useful.

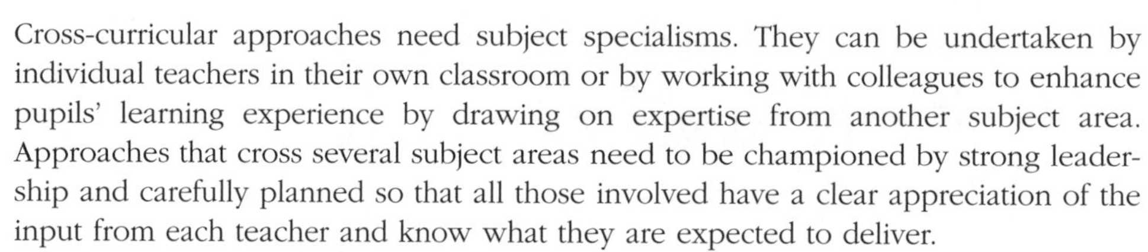

Cross-curricular approaches need subject specialisms. They can be undertaken by individual teachers in their own classroom or by working with colleagues to enhance pupils' learning experience by drawing on expertise from another subject area. Approaches that cross several subject areas need to be championed by strong leadership and carefully planned so that all those involved have a clear appreciation of the input from each teacher and know what they are expected to deliver.

Savage (2011) argues that there are two prerequisites for effective cross-curricular working. First of all, teachers need to show sensitivity towards the subject discipline and pedagogy. Each subject is underpinned with its own unique set of values, philosophies and pedagogy, and the maintenance of these while cross-curricular working is essential if the learning is to be meaningful and pupils are to make progress within the subject.

Secondly teachers will need to be willing to embrace and explore subject knowledge beyond the confines of their own subject areas, so that not only are they prepared to learn about pedagogy outside their own subject but can also acquire the knowledge necessary to be able to understand the concepts fully in order not to water down or give false information to pupils.

Effective cross-curricular working is about making genuine links between subjects in terms of key concepts, curriculum content, and learning processes, or it is about exploring a dimension or a theme across different subjects when this would greatly enhance pupils' understanding by looking at these from different subject perspectives. An essential component is that the process builds on existing knowledge and enhances progression in each subject by embracing good subject pedagogy at all levels.

When successful, cross-curricular working has the potential to inspire and engage pupils by contextualising their learning in real-life situations and experiences, while at the same time providing teachers with an opportunity to be creative and innovative with curriculum planning and development.

STEM collaborations

One initiative which has been introduced into schools is the STEM agenda, still championed by several organisations. This recommends collaborative work between the teachers of science, technology, engineering and mathematics (STEM). There are examples of how schools have addressed this initiative, including the development of after school STEM clubs. The aim of STEM is to increase young people's choices and chances through these subjects, and one of the key purposes is to ensure '… that all young people, regardless of background, are encouraged to understand the excitement and importance of science, technology, engineering and mathematics in their lives, and the career opportunities to which the STEM subjects can lead' (STEMNET, 2011).

These STEM clubs are examples of teachers working together to provide enrichment activities and many are based around the design of a particular object. To ensure that these activities focus in a cross-curricular way it is important that teachers from each area consider how an activity will develop understanding in their own subject.

Application to secondary teaching

A group of PGCE students were asked to design an activity for an after school event that linked key learning across mathematics, technology and science. The ideas that came from their collaboration were exciting, from designing a 'car' propelled by an elastic band to producing mini rockets using bicarbonate of soda. More importantly, they linked the activities with key learning outcomes from the relevant National Curriculum documents, and went on to explain how one activity could enable the pupils to synthesise skills from different subject areas to produce focused learning.

(Continued)

(Continued)

Select two other subjects that you think could be used to support cross-curricular teaching in your own subject area and then develop a lesson plan (or series of lesson plans) that utilises skills and knowledge from each area to benefit the teaching of all of the areas. If possible, work with other trainees or teachers in your school and make use of their expertise.

Developing cross-curricular pedagogy

One way of organising cross-curricular learning in both primary and secondary schools traditionally has been a 'topic' or 'theme' approach. This is sometimes based around current events and world affairs. The real danger with this approach is that it can be characterised by a lack of focus on what learning will take place and can have little coherence in terms of which subjects are involved. For example, a topic on China, inspired by the Beijing Olympics, was organised for Year 8 pupils with a collapsed timetable for the day. The overall aim was to develop the cross-curriculum dimension of cultural understanding. Subjects were involved by virtue of the fact that they were the subject specialisms of the Year 8 pastoral staff who were working with the pupils throughout the day. The pupils made fireworks in science and Chinese food in design and technology; they composed a song for the Olympic opening ceremony in music; they learned some Chinese phrases in MFL and made shadow puppets in art. Although the pupils no doubt enjoyed the day, it is open to question how much that day really developed pupils' cultural understanding of China and how much it really succeeded in reinforcing stereotypes. The development of cultural understanding requires deep learning rather than surface learning. This approach exemplifies some of the weaknesses of the 'topic' approach where activities are chosen because of their relationship to the title or theme rather than because they support coherence and progression in learning in the subjects or the development of Key Skills or dimensions (Laurie, 2011).

A thought

Recall the 'themed' approaches to your own learning at primary level. Can you remember the subject knowledge or skills gained when you studied 'the sea' or 'weather'? Why is this?

The first part of developing any shared experience is to identify the learning objectives. A key question is: How do you want pupils to be different at the end of the experience? Focusing on what you want pupils to 'learn' rather than what you want them to 'do' can often broaden the scope in terms of cross-curricular learning. Using a key question approach to focus pupils' learning can help to identify subjects and activities that can make the biggest contribution to that learning. Rather than 'doing' activities associated with China, a key question such as 'What should be included in the London 2012 Olympic opening ceremony?' has more potential for developing cultural understanding, and is more coherent in terms of helping to decide which subjects could make the most contribution. It is much better to limit the number of subjects involved rather than try to include everything that has a tenuous link to the theme.

Another more legitimate starting point for a cross-curricular experience would be to identify places in the curriculum where the same content is taught by different subjects. For example, the Blues is a topic commonly taught in the music curriculum, and the Slave Trade is taught in history. Surely there is a link here? These types of links occur more naturally, and the driving force is that there are gains for both subjects by teachers working together to enhance pupils' understanding.

Darwin, evolution and religion

Contrast the China example with the following case study.

This cross-curricular experience stemmed from the 200th anniversary of Darwin's birth and the 150th anniversary of the publication of his book *On the Origin of Species*. Two teachers decided to celebrate this event by using it as a teaching opportunity within science and religious education. Evolution falls within the science curriculum so pupils do need to understand the basic theory of evolution; religious education investigates the different religious understandings of creation. Both subjects were aware of embedding the aims of the previous curriculum (would this be still possible with the new curriculum?) and the Personal, Learning and Thinking Skills (PLTS), particularly 'exploring issues from different perspectives'. A key question here could be 'Can you understand a scientific theory whilst holding a religious view?' Within the science lessons during the week the pupils undertook several activities to understand the key theory of evolution and the evidence to support this theory. Within religious education at the same time they considered the different religious views on creation. Following this the group then explored the impact Darwin's theory had on Victorian society and how religious teachings are similar and dissimilar to the theory of evolution. One outcome of this activity was to be able to give an overview of the theory from different religious perspectives. By carrying out what was effectively an investigation across two subject areas the pupils not only developed subject-specific skills, but also learning was enhanced by being supported in the work in the other subject area.

The pupils were made aware that the cross-curricular teaching was intentional and careful planning between the two teachers ensured that they were able to make several links at appropriate times so that ideas from one subject were brought into the discussions and activities in the other. The teaching of these two related areas was enhanced by the cross-curricular planning and teaching.

Application to primary and early years teaching

Think of a 'key question' that would be interesting and useful to the age range that you teach. Some ideas could be:

- What goes into making their favourite TV programme?
- What goes into making a birthday cake?
- How does a plant grow?

Break down the topic into the various subject areas that could be addressed. For example, for the 'how does a plant grow?' example pupils could plant the seed, check on its health, measure its growth, chart that growth, draw the plant, and describe the process. Consult the subject specialists for each task or outcome to find out what pupils should be learning. Build all of this into one or more lessons.

Planning for cross-curricular working

Some key principles emerge from this discussion:

- Subjects should only be included in a cross-curricular experience when the connections made will genuinely enhance pupils' understanding by looking at a topic through different perspectives.
- Clear objectives for the cross-curricular experience should be established and focused on pupils' learning, for which each subject involved makes a unique contribution. A key question approach can focus thinking in this area.
- The foundation of successful cross-curricular experiences is good subject teaching and learning, where pupils make progress in subject specific skills, knowledge and understanding. Coherence and progression need to be considered in terms of the rest of the subject curriculum. At primary level, the subject coordinator should be able to ensure these links are appropriate.

Organising cross-curricular teaching

How then can cross-curricular teaching be organised? For cross-curricular working to be successful, it needs support from the senior leadership team to provide the resources and timetable flexibility that can make it happen. There is a balance to be made here – timetables which facilitate teachers and pupils working together can end up being a straitjacket just as much as those that have no flexibility, forcing cross-curricular working in the ways that this chapter has advocated against.

Schools are approaching this in different ways: collapsing timetables for one day every half term; having a whole week away from the normal timetable; or setting aside a period a week for flexible teaching approaches. Cross-curricular approaches also sometimes need different physical spaces, both with specialist subject equipment and larger group spaces, so this also needs to be taken into account. In addition to the timetable issues, time needs to be set aside to allow teachers to plan collaboratively.

Planning lesson content

Once curriculum and planning issues have been resolved and the key question, learning objectives and appropriate subject involvement have been decided, the next consideration is planning the lesson content. Obviously the aim is for pupils to be completely engaged in their learning throughout the project. Creative approaches which require pupils to work collaboratively with a range of stimuli, and enquiry-based tasks which allow them to make connections, develop hypotheses and work practically and independently, are more likely to engage them in this way. Starting the project with some sort of shared stimulus such as a visit out of school, a public event, a performance, a visiting speaker, or an exhibition, can really inspire pupils and spark their interest in the theme chosen. It is important that teachers ensure that pupils have the skills to match the challenges set. It would be appropriate for teachers to allow some time to develop subject specific skills during the project if necessary, before returning to the theme to allow pupils to use them in context.

The next planning consideration is how pupils will demonstrate their learning. It is useful when planning shared objectives to plan shared outcomes as well. These need to be as broad as possible to enable pupils to demonstrate their learning across the range of subjects. An example of this can be found in a collaborative unit of work based on the Holocaust involving RE, history and music. The key question was 'How should the Holocaust be remembered in Yorkshire?' The outcome directly reflected the key question with pupils producing an appropriate memorial to be shared. Possible responses included: a documentary film including pictures and original music; a poem or song suitable for an act of remembrance; a recorded 'radio' documentary on the experiences of a local survivor or witness; a small exhibition suitable for a museum or gallery; a presentation suitable for Holocaust Memorial Day in an assembly; a textbook double spread appropriate for pupils a year younger.

A final consideration here is how we can show pupils that their learning is transferable. It is appropriate to plan a lesson towards the end of the unit which makes the connections between the subjects explicit and also outlines the discrete learning that has taken place within the individual subjects.

Assessing cross-curricular learning

If careful planning, as described, is carried out, subject specific statements of attainment can be used to make assessments to measure pupil progress during collaborative working. (See Chapter 17 for an appropriate 'assessment for learning approach' that would work efficiently and effectively.) It is vital to consider process and progress as well as the final outcome. Teachers can ensure progression during the unit by sharing the learning objectives and making the success criteria clear; by building in review time and giving appropriate feedback; by allowing opportunities for pupils to seek peer feedback when they feel this is appropriate; by intervening appropriately in group tasks, asking key questions and making suggestions; and by continually revising learning activities to ensure pupils are challenged appropriately.

Cross-curricular teaching in the present curriculum context

In the present curriculum rather than explicit links being made there are some underlying ideas that can help support cross-curricular teaching. All state schools must promote the spiritual, moral, cultural, mental and physical development of pupils at the school, and of society prepare pupils at the school for the opportunities, responsibilities and experiences of later life.

This alludes to a holistic approach to pupil development. Aim 3.1 of the curriculum also implies a curriculum that rather than disaggregating the learning should pull together the curriculum to give it some coherence to:

> ... provide pupils with an introduction to the essential knowledge they need to be educated citizens. It introduces pupils to the best that has been thought and said, and helps engender an appreciation of human creativity and achievement.

What the curriculum does is highlight key areas that need to be embedded into all subject areas and these could be a stimulus for considering developing some cross-curricular links and activities. There are two key areas that are mentioned: Numeracy and Mathematics and Language and Literacy.

For numeracy and mathematics it is clear that all teachers, regardless of subject, should:

> ...use every relevant subject to develop pupils' mathematical fluency. Confidence in numeracy and other mathematical skills is a precondition of success across the national curriculum.

It does go on to explicitly identify aspects of numeracy and mathematics that need to be included so that pupils can understand the importance of mathematics and can then:

- apply arithmetic fluently to problems
- understand and use measures
- make estimates and sense check their work
- apply their geometric and algebraic understanding, and relate their understanding of probability to the notions of risk and uncertainty
- understand the cycle of collecting, presenting and analysing data.

Many areas of the curriculum use these skills, from measuring ingredients for science practicals or food technology to presenting evidence in history and English, from graphing trends in economics and business to constructing bar charts in geography. The challenge however is seeing how these can be truly cross-curricular activities rather than a set of skills that happen to be used in a number of areas of the curriculum.

INDIVIDUAL REFLECTION

Explore the statutory and non-statutory guidance for cross-curricular aspects of the curriculum for your own age group and/or subject specialism. Discuss this with your school-based mentor and identify how cross-curricular opportunities are provided in your placement school. Compare your findings with those of other trainees and begin to explore the philosophical and practical approaches that make cross-curricular working successful.

For the language and literacy area, the curriculum states that:

> 6.1 Teachers should develop pupils' spoken language, reading, writing and vocabulary as integral aspects of the teaching of every subject. English is both a subject in its own right and the medium for teaching; for pupils, understanding the language provides access to the whole curriculum. Fluency in the English language is an essential foundation for success in all subjects.

Again, as with numeracy there are specific skills that are encouraged in all subjects and are broken down into spoken language: reading and writing and vocabulary development. These are detailed below.

Pupils should be taught to:

- speak clearly
- convey ideas confidently using standard English
- learn to justify ideas with reasons
- ask questions to check understanding
- develop vocabulary and build knowledge
- negotiate, evaluate and build on the ideas of others
- select the appropriate register for effective communication
- give well-structured descriptions and explanations and develop their understanding through speculating, hypothesising and exploring ideas
- read fluently
- understand extended prose (both fiction and non-fiction) and be encouraged to read for pleasure
- develop the stamina and skills to write at length, with accurate spelling and punctuation
- know the correct use of grammar
- write to include narratives, explanations, descriptions, comparisons, summaries and evaluations: such writing supports them in rehearsing, understanding and consolidating what they have heard or read.

Teachers should:

- develop pupils' vocabulary actively, building systematically on pupils' current knowledge
- increase pupils' store of words in general and the links between known and new vocabulary, and discuss the shades of meaning in similar words
- should be taught the meaning of instruction verbs that they may meet in examination questions
- should induct pupils into the language which defines each subject in its own right, such as accurate mathematical and scientific language.

Even though the present National Curriculum fails to clearly advocate developing cross-curricular links it is apparent that building some cross curricular activities into our teaching is beneficial to pupils and can make learning more meaningful. We need to think about how we package the learning that we plan to ensure we have a good climate for deep learning.

> By making connections between subjects, events and activities, teachers will be able to design coherent learning experiences that are relevant and meaningful to learners. They will be able to use more dynamic and innovative teaching and learning approaches, choosing how learning is organised, where it takes place and who should lead it. (QCA, 2007: 5)

Again, making learning more meaningful is about developing independence of learning. Cooke (2011) suggests that we can do this in three ways: by allowing pupils more opportunities to consider what they will learn by providing opportunities for them to ask key questions which can be investigated during the unit; by allowing pupils to determine how they will learn by offering a choice of tasks and ways of responding; and by giving pupils more ownership of their assessment by encouraging them to ask for formative feedback when they need it rather than waiting for a formal opportunity. This may then result in more cross-curricular activities.

GROUP EXERCISE

Form a group of three either at your placement or your learning institution. If possible, make sure you have different subject specialisms. If this is not possible with fellow trainees, involve a couple of teachers. Choose an appropriate 'key question' that uses all the subject expertise and plan a cross-curricular project suitable for a class of pupils you are teaching on school placement. Consider the key issues outlined throughout this chapter.

Summary

- At the heart of successful cross-curricular teaching is careful planning which ensures coherence and progression within individual subjects as well as transferable skills and understanding.
- A prerequisite for the inclusion of particular subjects in cross-curricular projects is that the connections made will genuinely enhance pupils' understanding by considering the topic through different perspectives.
- The overall aim of a cross-curricular approach is to develop coherence across the curriculum, making the natural connections between different subject specialisms explicit. This has the potential to make learning more relevant by setting specific knowledge and skills in their context.

Key reading

Laurie, J. (2011) 'Curriculum planning and preparation for cross-curricular teaching', in T. Kerry (ed.), *Cross-curricular teaching in the primary school*. Abingdon: Routledge.

Savage, J. (2011) *Cross curricular teaching and learning in the secondary school*. Abingdon: Routledge.

References

Alexander, R. (ed.) (2009) *Children, their world, their education: final report and recommendations of the Cambridge Primary Review*. London: Routledge.

Barnes, J. (2011) *Cross-curricular learning 3–14* (2nd edn). London: Sage.

Cooke, C. (2011) 'Personal, learning and thinking skills and functional skills', in J. Price and M. Savage (eds), *Teaching secondary music*. London: Sage.

Department for Education (DfE) (2014) *The National Curriculum in England: framework for key stages 1 to 4*. Available at www.gov.uk/government/publications/national-curriculum-in-england-framework-for-key-stages-1-to-4

Laurie, J. (2011) 'Curriculum planning and preparation for cross-curricular teaching', in T. Kerry (ed.), *Cross-curricular teaching in the primary school*. Abingdon: Routledge.

Qualifications and Curriculum Authority (QCA) (2007) *The new secondary curriculum: what has changed and why?* London: QCA.

Rose, J. (2009) *Independent review of the primary curriculum: final report*. London: DCSF.

Savage, J. (2011) *Cross curricular teaching and learning in the secondary school*. Abingdon: Routledge.

STEMNET (2011) *Vision and purpose*. Available at www.stemnet.org.uk/content/vision (last accessed 27 April 2011).

Visit https://study.sagepub.com/denby3e for extra resources related to this chapter.

CHAPTER 23

ACCESSING AND USING STATISTICAL INFORMATION

Ian Quigley

Standards linked to this chapter include...

1. Set high expectations which inspire, motivate and challenge pupils

    - set goals that stretch and challenge pupils of all backgrounds, abilities and dispositions.

2. Promote good progress and outcomes by pupils

    - be accountable for pupils' attainment, progress and outcomes
    - be aware of pupils' capabilities and their prior knowledge, and plan teaching to build on these.

(Continued)

(Continued)

6. Make accurate and productive use of assessment

   - know and understand how to assess the relevant subject and curriculum areas, including statutory assessment requirements
   - make use of formative and summative assessment to secure pupils' progress
   - use relevant data to monitor progress, set targets, and plan subsequent lessons.

Introduction

In the distant past when schools largely followed their own curricula, the comparison of one school with another, or of one performance with another, was at best ad hoc and at worst biased and ill-informed. Now that clear statistics do exist, you are expected to know how schools make use of them and how you can use these to improve your own effectiveness.

The Education Reform Act of 1988 introduced a National Curriculum to the state schools of England, Wales and Northern Ireland. For the first time, the content of the curriculum in primary and secondary schools would be decided by central government and specified in detail. A central feature of the Act was the introduction of National Tests in the core subjects of English, mathematics and science. These Standard Attainment Tests, or 'SATs' as they became known, would be attempted by the vast majority of pupils at the ages of 7, 11 and 14.

Running concurrently with reform of the curriculum, came rationalisation of the public examination system. The dozens of examination boards that existed in the early 1980s were eventually reduced to just three major boards by 1997 (AQA, OCR and Edexcel). These institutions were overseen by the Qualifications and Curriculum Authority, an '*executive non-departmental public body*', whose core function was to ensure a consistency of standards between the qualifications offered.

With a common curriculum, standardised assessments at selected key stages and comparability between public examinations (especially GCSE), the performance of individual schools could now be compared. The first *School and College Performance Tables for Secondary Schools* were published in 1994, with primary 'league tables' following two years later. These have been a source of information (and controversy) ever since.

A thought

Acronyms abound in the education sector. These apply to the discussion of statistical information contained in this chapter so it would be useful to be familiar with them:

- CATs = Cognitive Ability Tests
- DfE = Department for Education
- FFT = Fischer Family Trust
- MTG = Minimum Target Grade
- NFER = National Foundation for Educational Research
- Ofsted = Office for Standards in Education
- RAISE = Reporting and Analysis of Improvement through school Self-Evaluation
- VA = Value Added

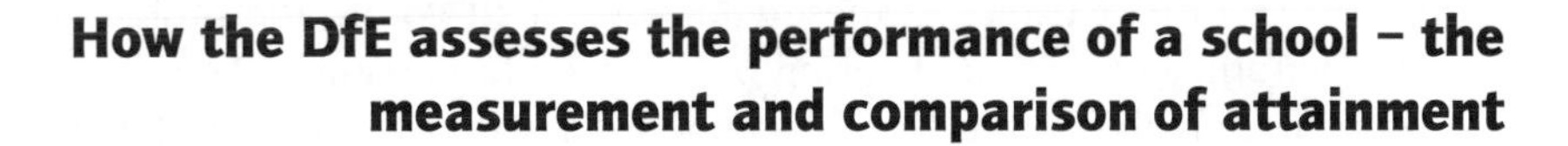

How the DfE assesses the performance of a school – the measurement and comparison of attainment

Every year the performance of a primary school is measured by an analysis of its National Test scores. In the case of a secondary school, its results at GCSE (and where appropriate its post-16 achievements) are scrutinised.

The resulting document, known as 'RAISEonline', forms the basis for all Ofsted inspections. There is, therefore, an expectation that the governors and managers of a school will be able to interpret the data it contains and act on this information by formulating plans to improve the achievements of the school.

A school's performance can be judged using three methods of analysis – threshold measures, value-added measures and progress measures.

Threshold measures

From their inception, school performance data have contained *threshold measures*. These are simply numbers expressing the percentage of students achieving a type of result at the end of a key stage. For example, the percentage of primary pupils achieving the *expected standard* in mathematics or the percentage of students achieving five or more *good* grades at GCSE.

The number of threshold measures has increased and decreased over the years, often to monitor (and perhaps influence) the type of curricula offered.

Tables 23.1 (a) and (b) illustrate the range of threshold measures for contrasting primary and secondary schools.

A thought

Study the data shown in Tables 23.1(a) and (b). What does this information tell you about these schools? Is it possible to judge which is the most successful primary and secondary school? What factors may influence the results these schools achieve? As a parent, which schools would you choose?

Problems

Even a quick glance at these tables will alert you to the problems of comparing the performance of schools using only threshold measures. Raw data such as these measure only the output of an institution. They do not consider the ability of its intake or pupils' social and economic circumstances.

Table 23.1(a) Exemplar threshold measures: primary

Threshold Measure	Primary School A	Primary School B
Percentage of students achieving at least the *expected standard* in English	82	44
Percentage of students achieving above the *expected standard* in English	56	38
Percentage of students achieving at least the *expected standard* in mathematics	78	40
Percentage of students achieving above the *expected standard* in mathematics	54	32
Percentage of students eligible for free school meals	4	28
Percentage of SEN students	3	16

Analysis based only on results cannot assess the 'value' that a school adds. Pupils who attend a secondary school whose intake includes a significant number of low achieving children may in fact make greater progress than those in a neighbouring school which selects the most able pupils in the district. Similarly, though many may assume that the children entering the reception classes of primary schools are 'blank canvases',

Table 23.1 (b) Exemplar threshold measures: secondary

Threshold Measure	Secondary School A	Secondary School B
Percentage of students achieving five or more *good* GCSE grades	94	52
Percentage of students achieving five or more *good* GCSE grades including English and maths	62	38
Percentage of students achieving at least one *good* GCSE grade	99	85
Percentage of students eligible for free school meals	8	35
Percentage of SEN students	6	29

those within the profession recognise that the early experiences of a child impact on their primary school years. Such experiences are influenced by home circumstances and the education of their parents (Douglas, 1964).

Value-added measures

Value-added measures try to take account of differences in prior attainment and social demography. With over twenty years of statistical data to draw on, *National Progression Lines* have been created to predict the attainment of students as they pass from the primary to the secondary phase. These progression lines have been created by comparing the National Test scores achieved by thousands of students in Year 6 to the GCSE grades they achieved at the end of Year 11. By using these graphs, a student's results at the end of Key Stage 2 can be used to predict their grades at the end of Key Stage 4 (see Table 23.2 and Figure 23.1).

Table 23.2 Old and new GCSE grades and points

Old GCSE Grades	Points Equivalent before 2016	*New* GCSE Grades	Points Equivalent from 2016
		9	9
A*	58	8	8
A	52	7	7
B	46	6	6
C	40	5	5
D	34	4	4
E	28	3	3
F	22	2	2
G	16	1	1
u	0	u	0

Consider Pupil A. Her National Test scores placed her in the top 10% of all students. When plotted on the progression line this may generate a prediction of 60 points in her best eight GCSE grades (using the post 2016 points system). In contrast, Pupil B

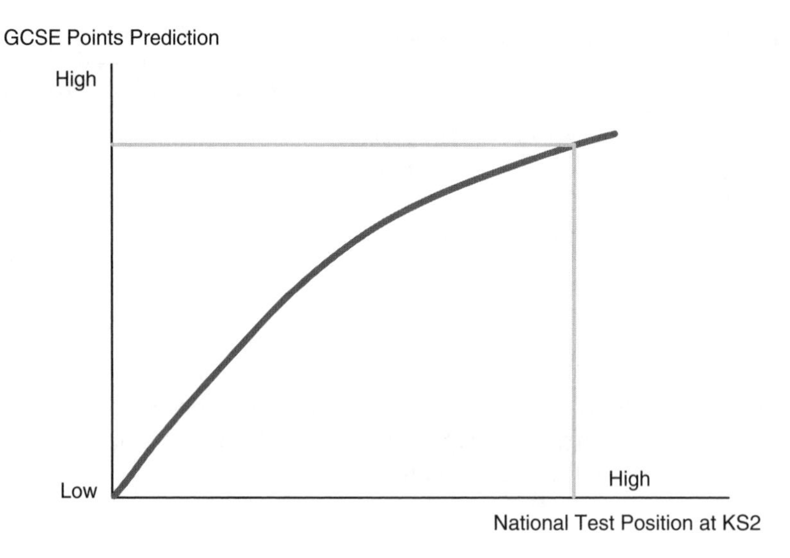

Figure 23.1 A progression graph

achieved National Test scores that placed him in the 50th percentile. This could generate a prediction of 40 points at GCSE.

At the end of Year 11, if Pupil A gained results with a 'best 8' points equivalent of 64, she will have exceeded her prediction. This would result in a *positive* score of 4. Pupil B, however, only achieved a points total of 30, a *negative* score of 10.

This is known as *value-added analysis*. By averaging the positive and negative scores of all pupils in a cohort, each school can be awarded a *value-added score* for its results at the end of a key stage. Consequently, a school with a small percentage of pupils gaining five *good* grades and a positive value-added score could be regarded as outperforming a school with a large percentage of five *good* grades and a negative value-added score.

In the past, value-added scores were further refined to take account of the social and economic context of the institution. The census data collected electronically from a school's computer management system contain details of every pupil on the roll. Adjustments are made to pupil predictions according to age, gender, ethnicity, eligibility for free school meals, home language, and even the social characteristics of a students' home address derived from census data. This complex statistical manipulation of the data was known as *contextual value-added analysis (CVA)*.

Despite these attempts to refine the ways in which schools' performances were compared, *threshold measures* remained, in the minds of the public at large, the most significant measure of a school's effectiveness. This, aligned with the complexity and cost of CVA analysis, led to its discontinuation as a performance measure in 2011.

Remember, however, that judging a school only by threshold measure alone will tell you little about the progress its pupils are making, nor about the quality of learning and teaching within its classrooms.

The 'English Baccalaureate' and '8' Measures.

You may remember that, before 2014, attainment within the National Curriculum was graded on a scale from 1 to 8. At GCSE, before 2017, the grades awarded ranged from A* to G. Under this system a student was expected to make four levels of progress across the primary phase and three levels of progress during their secondary education. Recent reform, however, has seen the abolition of National Curriculum levels and a change in the classification of future GCSE grades that does not easily equate to the previous system. This makes the measurement of progress difficult.

Similarly, in 2010, the DfE introduced the concept of an 'English Baccalaureate'. Though not a qualification in its own right, it is a suite of approved qualifications that have a greater significance in the assessment of a secondary schools performance. The 'E-Bacc' subjects are Mathematics, English Language, English Literature, the Sciences (including Computer Science), History, Geography, and Modern or Ancient Languages.

From 2016 performance data will adapt to take account of these legislative changes. Threshold measures, however, will remain. Primary schools will continue to judge on the percentage of students who achieve the expected standard in Mathematics and English (the latter being sub-divided into reading and writing). For secondary schools a key indicator will be the percentage of students who 'pass' both GCSE English Language and GCSE Mathematics.

The most significant change, for the secondary sector, involves two new measures that combine the measurement of progress with value added analysis whilst enhancing the importance of the 'E-Bacc' subjects.

These measures have complex aggregation rules involving eight examination subjects contributing ten-point scores from the grades achieved that are distributed into three 'pots' (see Table 23.3).

GCSE Mathematics and English are both 'double-weighted'. This means that the points allocated to student grades are multiplied by two. For English to be 'double-weighted', however, a student must have studied and be examined in both GCSE English Language and GCSE English Literature. The higher of these two grades will be the one selected and doubled. Maths and English grades, therefore, contribute four scores to *Pot 1*.

Pot 2 contributes three scores. To 'fill' Pot 2 the student must have studied at least three of the 'E-Bacc' subjects to GCSE standard.

Pot 3 also contributes three scores. Pot 3 can be filled by any other GCSE or Level 2 vocational qualification that appears on the DfE approved qualifications list. It can also include any other qualifications left over from Pots 1 and 2.

Table 23.3 'Attainment 8' Aggregation

Pot 1	Pot 2	Pot 3
GCSE Mathematics × 2 GCSE English Language or GCSE English Literature × 2	Best three results from: GCSE Sciences GCSE Computer Science GCSE History GCSE Geography GCSE Modern or Ancient Language	Best three results from: Any GCSE or approved Vocational Qualification Or Any 'E-Bacc' qualification unused in pots 1 or 2
4 scores	**3 scores**	**3 scores**

These ten scores will generate a combined points total for each student known as the 'Attainment 8 score'. When this is compared to the points score predicted from National Progression Lines the difference between the two is known as the pupil's 'Progress 8' score. These scores can be averaged to create 'Attainment 8' and 'Progress 8' measures for the school which when compared to the results of all schools will assess the relative performance of the institution in terms of national rankings.

Application to secondary teaching

Consider the following results gained by Kate and work out her **Attainment 8** score. If her Key Stage 2 National Test prediction was 5.5, what would be her **Progress 8** score? Do you think that the school would be happy with this?

Kate achieved the following GCSE (or equivalent) grades at the end of Year 11:

GCSE Mathematics	C
GCSE English Language	B
GCSE English Literature	A
GCSE French	B
GCSE Biology	B
GCSE Chemistry	B
GCSE Physics	D
GCSE Art	D
Vocational ICT	Pass
Vocational Business Studies	Pass

(The answer and its associated calculation can be found at the end of this chapter.)

How schools assess their own performance – the measurement and comparison of progression

Today's performance data run to many pages. Rankings and analyses are applied not only to each key stage but to all subjects. Similarly pupils' achievements are delineated by gender, ethnicity, free school meals, and special educational needs. Detailed consideration of this information certainly enables schools to identify areas of strength and weakness and formulate plans to improve the performance of future cohorts. It tells them little, however, about the pupils *currently* in a school.

Consequently, the majority of educational institutions have introduced systems to monitor the academic progress each student makes as they pass through a school. By doing so, potential underachievement can be spotted early and interventions taken to ensure that individual pupils achieve or exceed the grades expected of them.

In the past, schools could construct tables of progress based on the national expectation of two or three levels dependent on the key stage or primary or secondary phase. Usually the suffix a, b or c was added after the historic National Curriculum level (where 'a' means *level fully achieved*, 'b' means *working securely at this level but not all assessment criteria have been met*, and 'c' means *beginning to work at this level*).

Table 23.4 is an example of a historic progression table for Key Stage 2.

Grids such as this break down the expected levels of progression across a key stage. After the class teacher had assessed their students (usually once a term), they could compare their current level of attainment with the expected standard and see if each child was on target to make the appropriate levels of progress.

Can we, however, expect students of different abilities to make the same degree of progress? A child who has achieved only a Level 1 after two years of Key Stage 1 may continue to make slower than expected progress. Similarly, a pupil who has already gained Level 3 at the end of Year 2 should be encouraged to exceed the expected two levels improvement through Key Stage 2.

Fischer Family Trust

Many schools, therefore, require more individualised data and look to external agencies for support. The Fischer Family Trust (FFT) is a registered charity undertaking and supporting projects addressing the development of education in the United Kingdom. The FFT Data Analysis Project provides statistical information to assist local authorities and schools in the monitoring of performance.

Each year a school will receive FFT data about the children currently on roll. These data include predictions about each pupil's performance in future key stages and the school's performance.

Whilst still using national progression lines, the individual predictions are presented in a more 'user friendly' format. Instead of points scores the predictions are presented as potential rankings in National Tests or GCSE grades. These predictions are often divided into three 'sub-levels' using the suffix a, b or c after each grade (see Tables 23.4 and 23.5). With the majority of pupils improving by less than one grade in one academic year, the use of sub-levels is popular, because they facilitate the measurement of progress.

FFT predictions can also be manipulated by the school. A sliding scale may be used to increase the 'demand' of student predictions. An institution wishing to improve its national rankings can adjust student target grades to reflect those of the highest achieving schools, in the hope that higher expectations will lead to an improved performance.

Table 23.4 A *historic* progression table for Key Stage 2

KS1 Teacher Assessment Level	Year 3			Year 4			Year 5			Year 6		
	Autumn	Spring	Summer	Autumn	Spring	Summer	Autumn	Spring	Summer	Autumn	Spring	Summer
	Expected Attainment Level											
3a	3a	4c	4c	4b	4b	4a	4a	5c	5c	5b	5b	5a
3b	3b	3a	3a	4c	4c	4b	4b	4a	4a	5c	5c	5b
3c	3c	3b	3b	3a	3a	4c	4c	4b	4b	4a	4a	5c
2a	2a	3c	3c	3b	3b	3a	3a	4c	4c	4b	4b	4a
2b	2b	2a	2a	3c	3c	3b	3b	3a	3a	4c	4c	4b
2c	2c	2b	2b	2a	2a	3c	3c	3b	3b	3a	3a	4c
1a	1a	2c	2c	2b	2b	2a	2a	3c	3c	3b	3b	3a
1b	1b	1a	1a	2c	2c	2b	2b	2a	2a	3c	3c	3b
1c	1c	1b	1b	1a	1a	2c	2c	2b	2b	2a	2a	3c

Table 23.5 GCSE predictions with sub-levels

***New* GCSE Grades**	4	5	5	5	6	6	6	7	7	7	8	8
Sub-level Predictions	4a	5c	5b	5a	6c	6b	6a	7c	7b	7a	8c	8b

The senior managers of a school will, therefore, generate data appropriate to their institutional goals and from those predictions formulate *performance targets* at different levels throughout the organisation (see Figure 23.2).

FFT data have been used extensively at the primary and secondary levels to set targets for the local authority, the school, and individual pupils. As teachers we must remember, however, that these predictions are based on prior attainment. At the pupil level this could be problematic. A child who attended a successful primary school who was prepared by parents for the Key Stage 2 examinations may achieve excellent marks, and, therefore be predicted to achieve the highest grades at GCSE. In contrast, however, the child could have attended a school with a history of under-achievement and live in less supportive circumstances. Thus attainment may be lower, and consequently, FFT predictions reduced.

Many schools, therefore, also use mechanisms to generate pupil predictions based not on prior attainment but on a standardised measure of academic potential. Most primary schools use 'base-line' tests to assess the abilities of children entering their reception classes. In the secondary phase, the most commonly used measures are the Cognitive Ability Tests (CATs) provided by the National Foundation for Education Research (NFER). These tests are usually attempted in the first few weeks of Year 7.

The CATs require pupils to sit three papers on three consecutive days. Paper 1, the Verbal Test, attempts to assess a child's linguistic ability. Paper 2, the Quantitative Test, is a measure of numerical ability, whilst Paper 3, the Non-Verbal Test, gauges spatial reasoning and sequential decision making.

Each test is given a numerical score and all three tests are averaged to give an overall measure known as the Standard Age Score (SAS). In all cases, a score of 100 would be regarded as the result for a student of average ability. Consider Table 23.6.

Table 23.6 SAS scores

Pupil	Verbal Score	Quantitative Score	Non-Verbal Score	Standard Age Score
A	99	101	100	100
B	118	108	120	115
C	794	95	78	84

Pupil A has an SAS of 100 with a similar score in all areas; this pupil could be regarded as a student of average ability. The results for Pupil B would be commensurate with a pupil of greater academic potential. The score for the Quantitative paper, however, indicates that numerical ability is only slightly above average. In contrast, Pupil C has achieved scores that suggest an academic potential that is significantly lower. The Quantitative score is better than the other results, indicating that, for this pupil, numeracy is a strength.

In addition to this raw statistical data, the NFER will convert individual scores into predicted grades for GCSE examinations. Individual schools will use their own unique combination of FFT predictors, CAT scores and CAT predictors to generate targets for their pupils. As teachers it is important that we remember the essential distinction between the two sources of data. Predictions made from prior attainment are fundamentally different from those made from assessments of academic potential.

When presented with predictive data for the pupils in our class, only by understanding how this information has been generated can we make appropriate judgements about their abilities.

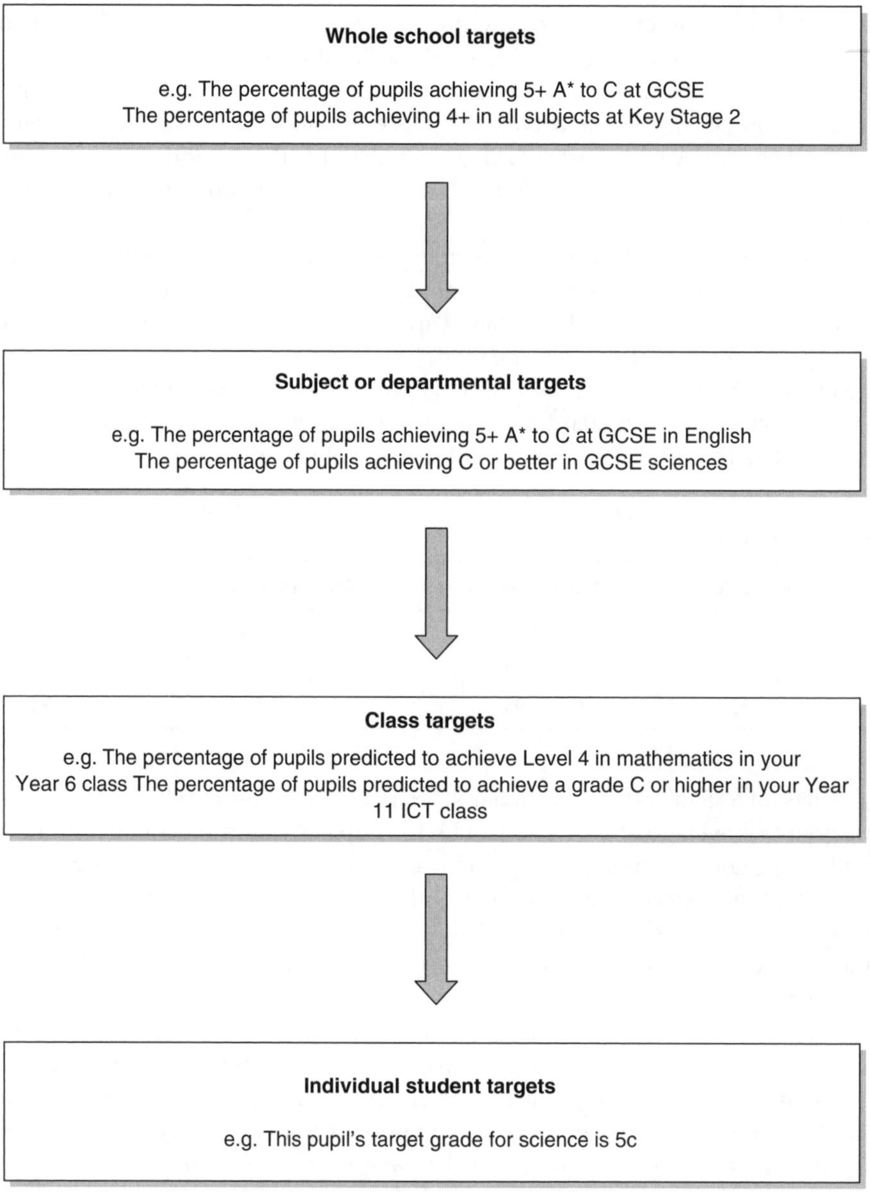

Whole school targets

e.g. The percentage of pupils achieving 5+ A* to C at GCSE
The percentage of pupils achieving 4+ in all subjects at Key Stage 2

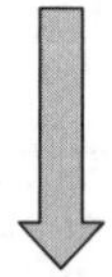

Subject or departmental targets

e.g. The percentage of pupils achieving 5+ A* to C at GCSE in English
The percentage of pupils achieving C or better in GCSE sciences

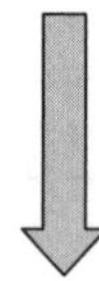

Class targets

e.g. The percentage of pupils predicted to achieve Level 4 in mathematics in your Year 6 class The percentage of pupils predicted to achieve a grade C or higher in your Year 11 ICT class

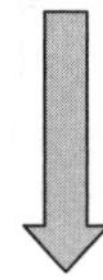

Individual student targets

e.g. This pupil's target grade for science is 5c

Figure 23.2 Formulation of performance targets

GROUP EXERCISE

Consider these predictive data.

Table 23.7 Predictive data

Pupil	FFT GCSE English prediction	FFT GCSE maths prediction	FFT GCSE science prediction	NFER CATs SAS	NFER CATs GCSE English prediction	NFER CATs GCSE maths prediction	NFER CATs GCSE science prediction
A	6a	6c	6b	102	6b	6b	6b
B	5a	5a	5b	120	7c	7b	7c
C	6b	6c	6b	92	4a	4a	5c

With colleagues decide what this information tells you about each pupil. How would you account for the differences between the FFT predictions and NFER predictions for pupils B and C? Discuss how (and why) these predictions would impact on your own subject, whether or not it is maths, English, science or other.

The contradictions in predictions made by different systems, illustrated by the example above, have made some schools uncomfortable with a 'grade specific' interpretation of the data. Similarly, teachers of art, music or PE often have little confidence in predictive grades for their subjects. This is because both FFT and NFER base their predictions on the results from tests of numeracy and literacy that take little account of a child's natural artistic, musical or physical abilities. For some, the answer lies in the use of Jesson Bands.

Originally designed by David Jesson, a mathematician from York University, this approach analyses a pupil's results at age 11 and uses these scores to predict the chances of achieving threshold measures at GCSE. He took the scores from National

Table 23.8 Jesson Bands

Jesson Band	Ability	Chance of Achieving 5 or More Good Grades at GCSE
1	High	96%
2	Above average	84%
3	Average	60%
4	Below average	30%
5	Low ability	10%

Test and delineated them into five ability bands, each with different probabilities for achieving 'good' results at GCSE (see Table 23.7).

Jesson Banding encourages teachers to view a pupil's progress across the whole curriculum rather than focusing on individual subject grades. For example, a child in Band 3 sitting ten GCSEs and currently achieving good grades or above in six subjects (60%) would be 'on target'. Similarly, a student in Band 5 sitting five GCSEs but gaining good grades in two subjects (40%) would have exceeded expectations.

INDIVIDUAL REFLECTION

Class teachers can still use Jesson Bands to help set targets. Look at the dataset for the class below.

Table 23.9 Jesson Band dataset

Student	Jesson Band	Chance of Achieving an Good Grade
1	1	96%
2	4	30%
3	3	60%
4	3	60%
5	2	84%
6	1	96%
7	2	84%
8	3	60%
9	4	30%
10	3	60%
11	3	60%
12	4	30%
13	2	84%
14	5	10%
15	3	60%
16	4	30%
17	1	96%
18	5	10%
19	3	60%
20	3	60%

How many students should achieve at least a *Good* grade? (Hint: average the percentage chances.) How many students should achieve the highest grades? How useful do you think data sets like this are?

Using data to improve pupil performance

As Farmer Giles knows, 'Weighing pigs don't fatten them.' Prior attainment data and predictions of ability provide the teacher with the information required to make judgements about the potential of each individual pupil. This, however, is just the starting point. Using the data to ensure children meet or exceed their potential is one of the major tenets for effective teaching in today's schools.

As previously described, the vast majority of schools now use predictive data to generate end of key stage targets for their pupils. These are often referred to as Minimum Target Grades (MTG). Sometimes these predictions will be used to set or stream children into different ability groups; equally often, however, your class will be of 'mixed ability'. In either case, we can use the statistical data to assess the range of ability within our teaching groups and 'pitch' the content of each lesson at a level appropriate to 'pupil ability.

Application to primary and EYFS teaching

Since 2014, teachers have had to come to terms with 'life without levels'. Now that National Curriculum content is no longer delineated by difficulty, teachers must look more closely at the demands of the topics they are teaching. At primary and early years level you are likely to have classes that show a wide range of abilities. There will also be uneven development, such as early readers (home taught) or those who grasp number concepts easily. Choose a topic or theme that you might teach to a class over a four to six week period. Define concepts by *high*, *medium* and *low* demand. Write differentiated objectives and learning outcomes for a mixed ability class with pupils that contains a mixture of 'high' and 'low' attainers. Write a short scheme of work to cover how each topic will be taught to each level of ability, to ensure that lower ability learners are not 'left behind' and the higher ability are 'stretched'.

For example, when writing schemes of work and planning individual lessons it is useful to compare the statistical data with National Curriculum programmes of study or GCSE subject specifications. By doing so it is easier to generate lesson objectives and learning outcomes that focus on the knowledge and skills required of the pupils if they are to meet or exceed their target grades. In this way, statistical data can facilitate more effective differentiation by generating different learning outcomes for different sets or individual children within a mixed ability group.

Government initiatives designed to improve the effectiveness of teaching stress the importance of lesson objectives and learning outcomes for ensuring pupil progression. The outcomes for each lesson can be viewed as the rungs on the ladder each child needs to climb as they move through a topic. At the end of each unit of work, we can measure a pupil's progress by a formal or informal assessment of the learning outcomes we have generated. In this way we can judge if individual pupils are on course to meet or exceed their targets. More importantly, however, by identifying those learning outcomes that have been forgotten or misunderstood, we can identify potential barriers to progress and apply intervention strategies to get the student 'back on track' (see Figure 23.3). The interventions that you make should be effective in moving pupils to higher bands, but don't forget that progress may then decline again post-intervention or there may, as a result of a really effective intervention, be continued improvement. If interventions are good enough, and sustained enough, further progress will occur (McNaughton et al., 2009).

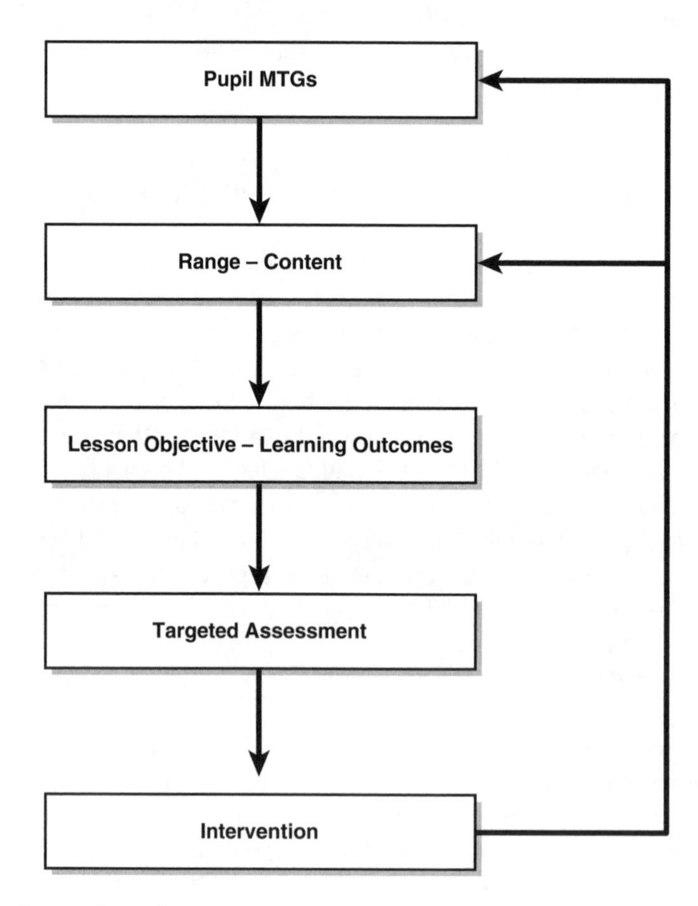

Figure 23.3 Intervention cycles

As teachers, therefore, we will be expected to not only be familiar with the levels of attainment each of our pupils is expected to achieve by the end of their current key stage, we will also be expected to accurately judge the progress they are making towards achieving those targets and identify areas for improvement. An understanding of the ways in which statistical data are generated can help us meet these expectations but it can also provide an important perspective on the whole process.

We must always remember that these statistically generated targets are just predictions. Whilst they may have the validity of large numbers at the local authority or whole school level, they can only be regarded as a rough guide when considering each individual pupil. Predictions made from a child's performance in a few hours of written testing over a limited period of time can never be more than a snapshot that could easily be affected by factors such as illness, bereavement, the misreading of a major question, or even lucky guessing! Teachers who know their pupils well soon become aware of those children who are not being stretched because their targets are too low, or conversely, are developing a sense of failure because their targets are unrealistically high. By understanding the limitations of the data, we should feel able to temper our expectations of these pupils accordingly. However useful statistical data have become, they can never replace the professional judgement of an effective classroom teacher.

Summary

- The performance of all public sector schools is assessed annually. This performance is measured through a combination of threshold, attainment and progress measures.
- Most schools set targets at all levels of the institution using predictions generated by the Fischer Family Trust, NFER CATs or Jesson Bands.
- As a teacher, you will almost certainly have performance targets for your classes and the individual pupils they contain. You will be expected to regularly assess your pupils to see if they are on course to achieve their predicted grades and identify areas for improvement for those students who are not 'on target'.

Key reading

Downey, C. and Kelly, A. (2010) 'Value-added measures for schools in England: looking inside the "black box" of complex metrics', *Educational Assessment, Evaluation and Accountability,* 22 (3): 181–98.

Fischer Family Trust (2014) *Start with intelligent benchmarking, end with intelligent targets.* Available at www.egfl.org.uk/sites/default/files/imported/categories/data/danda/_docs/fft/FFT_LA_E-Flyer_FINAL_March_14.pdf

NGA (2104) *Knowing your school: RAISEonline for governors of primary schools.* Available at www.nga.org.uk/getattachment/Can-we-help/Knowing-Your-School/Knowing-Your-School-Primary-RAISE-(Jan-14)-FINAL.pdf.aspx

References and bibliography

DfE (2014) *Progress 8 measure in 2016: a technical guide for maintained secondary schools, academies and free schools*. London: HMSO.

Douglas, J.W.B. (1964) *The home and the school*. London: Panther.

McNaughton, S., Lai, M.K., Timperley, H. and Hsiao, S. (2009) 'Sustaining continued acceleration in reading comprehension achievement following an intervention', *Educational Assessment, Evaluation and Accountability,* 21 (1): 81–100.

Webber, R. and Butler, T. (2005) *Classifying pupils by where they live: how well does this predict variations in GCSE results?*, UCL Working Paper Series, Paper 99.

Answer to Attainment 8 exercise on page 342.

To calculate her *Attainment 8* score you would select GCSE Mathematics and GCSE English Literature (as her best 'English result') for 'Pot 1'. Both of these scores are doubled. There are four potential 'E-Bacc' subjects to use in Pot 2 (French and the three sciences). The best three grades would be selected. There are five unused results that are all eligible for 'Pot 3' – including the two approved vocational qualifications. You would select these for this open group because a vocational *Pass* grade is equivalent to a C grade at GCSE. The final place is filled by English Language because the B grade achieved is higher than the results for Physics and Art (see Table 23.7).

The combined Attainment 8 total of 58 is divided by ten to give an average score of 5.8. Based on her results in the Key Stage 2 National Tests, this student was predicted to gain an average score of 5.5. By exceeding this prediction she has a Progress 8 score of +0.3 – steady progress and beyond expectations, but not spectacular.

Table 23.10 Solutions

Category	Subject Selected	GCSE Points	Attainment 8 Score
Pot 1 Maths and English selection (double score)	GCSE Mathematics	5	10
	GCSE English Literature	7	14
Pot 2 'E-Bacc' selection	GCSE French	6	6
	GCSE Biology	6	6
	GCSE Chemistry	6	6
Pot 3 Open selection of approved subjects.	GCSE English Language	6	6
	Vocational ICT	5	5
	Vocational Business Studies	5	5
Total Attainment 8 Score			58
Average Attainment 8 Score			5.8
Predicted Attainment 8 Score			5.5
Progress 8 Score			+ 0.3

Visit https://study.sagepub.com/denby3e for extra resources related to this chapter.

CHAPTER 24

YOUR FIRST TEACHING POST: APPLICATIONS, INTERVIEWS AND INDUCTION

John Trafford

Standards linked to this chapter include...

All the Standards are relevant to this chapter, but particularly the Teachers' Standards Part 2: Personal and Professional Conduct:

- Teachers uphold public trust in the profession and maintain high standards of ethics and behaviour, within and outside school, by:
  - treating pupils with dignity, building relationships rooted in mutual respect, and at all times observing proper boundaries appropriate to a teacher's professional position
  - having regard for the need to safeguard pupils' wellbeing, in accordance with statutory provisions

- showing tolerance of and respect for the rights of others
- not undermining fundamental British values, including democracy, the rule of law, individual liberty and mutual respect, and tolerance of those with different faiths and beliefs
- ensuring that personal beliefs are not expressed in ways which exploit pupils' vulnerability or might lead them to break the law.

- Teachers must have proper and professional regard for the ethos, policies and practices of the school in which they teach, and maintain high standards in their own attendance and punctuality.

Teachers must have an understanding of, and always act within, the statutory frameworks which set out their professional duties and responsibilities.

As you progress through your initial teacher training, consideration of your next steps will start to loom large. Even amongst the myriad requirements of you during training (assignments, observations, standards…) it is never too early to think about applying for your first job. You need to be aware of when and where to look for your first post and how to prepare your first application, so that when a suitable job appears, you are poised. Also be aware that a first appointment is not, yet, the end of the journey. To become a fully-fledged teacher with QTS, you must also complete an induction period. This chapter explores when to apply, how to apply, how to succeed at interview, and how to complete your first year successfully.

Timing

You are likely to complete your training in June or July and be looking to start your first post at the beginning of the September term. In some circumstances, a school will be able to recruit a new teacher to be in post as soon as training finishes if a staff vacancy already exists, and therefore offer continuous employment for the last part of the summer term through into the new school year. This is the exception rather than the rule.

Some School Direct training programmes recruit on the basis that a post will be offered within the school in which training is carried out, or in the alliance of schools in the training partnership. You should ascertain at as early a stage as possible whether this is the case, whether a formal application process will take place, and what is required of you to engage with this.

A thought

If you can persuade the school to begin your contract in June or July, this means that you are in employment throughout the summer holidays and so entitled to be paid during the six-week break. It is therefore well worth investigating the possibility of starting early.

An important date in the calendar is 31 May. Under most contractual arrangements, this is the date by which serving teachers must hand in their resignation if they do not wish to be in post the following September. Therefore, interviews for promoted posts usually happen before this deadline, so that the appointed candidate, if they are moving school, can resign their post in time. Teachers who are taking retirement, leaving the profession or relocating should also indicate this before the May deadline. Occasionally head teachers will accept late resignations, especially if an unforeseen reason has occurred, but again, this is exceptional.

It follows, therefore, that it is not until June that head teachers will know with reasonable certainty their requirements for the following school year. Over the preceding months, the staffing situation will become clearer. School budgets, which can be an important consideration, are finalised in the spring, and appointments for promoted posts are being made regularly throughout the year.

In practice, most newly qualified teacher appointments are made in the period between March and June, with the majority made towards the end of this period. However, as early as the late autumn of the previous year, a handful of posts will be advertised. Some independent schools, in particular, like to advertise early, and it has become more common in recent years for there to be a trickle of job advertisements for September appointments throughout the year.

The recommendation, therefore, is for you to be on the lookout for what is coming up from, say, December or January onwards, but not to feel disappointed if for several weeks there appears to be nothing suitable. As the year advances, this situation should change. Experience tells us that even by the end of teacher training, a number of trainees will not have secured their first appointment, but that during the last weeks of the school summer term, many fall into place. Remember also that if you have been unlucky enough not to find a post, do not be discouraged – keep on looking into the autumn term and if necessary beyond. There are unpredicted reasons why vacancies occur at all times in the year.

Where to look

Schools will make every effort to ensure they reach their desired audience and attract as good a field as possible, so it is not in their interest to make their advertisements obscure or difficult to find. Advertising, though, is costly, and it is wise to bear in mind that schools do not have unlimited budgets for this purpose; not all will be in a position to place prominent advertisements in national publications for every post they offer.

An online search will reveal a number of organisations whose business includes the advertising of teaching posts. It is worth exploring these to gain a sense of how widely they are used, how easily navigable the websites are, and how the quantity of job details they carry compares with other websites.

The most established and best known source of information about teaching posts is the *Times Educational Supplement* (TES), which in addition to its well-known weekly print publication offers a comprehensive online digest of vacancies (www.tes.co.uk/jobs). It is worthwhile becoming familiar with both of these. They offer the traditional advantages of printed and online material – the print version will allow you to browse, and gain some insight into the different style of advertisements that schools place, whereas the online version allows you to choose to view specific posts that may be of interest, selected by age group, subject and geographical region. Online advertisements will often contain links to more detailed post descriptions, school information and application forms. Printed advertisements will give you information on how to obtain further details, usually by telephone or email. Increasingly, schools are turning to online advertisements rather than print media. This is where they expect potential candidates to be searching for posts, and print advertising, especially in national publications, is considerably more expensive.

Other national newspapers will also carry some job advertisements in their education pages, and it is worthwhile familiarising yourself with the local press if you are clear about the area in which you would like to work. Local daily newspapers often have a particular day of the week on which they carry advertisements, though these are usually for temporary or part-time appointments rather than for established full-time posts. This is not a hard and fast rule, however, and it is even the case in some areas that free newspapers will contain occasional teaching post details that may be of interest.

As a newly qualified teacher, you will be looking for a post advertised as 'Main Scale'. Promoted posts above the main scale are designated as 'TLR' – staff appointed to these posts are paid for extra responsibilities for an aspect of teaching and learning, for example as the head of a subject department or a Key Stage. State maintained schools pay their staff according to a national 'Teachers' Pay and Conditions' agreement; independent schools, academies and 'free' schools are under no obligation to do so, though many choose to. It is worth checking on this before you apply, and certainly before accepting a post.

It is becoming increasingly common for agencies to handle recruitment for schools so it is worth registering with, for example, supply agencies in your area. Make sure, however, when you go for a job, that it is the school employing you and not the agency, otherwise your salary will be lower.

Where local authorities have retained a strong role in the administration of schools, their websites will have a section devoted to employment opportunities. It may be possible for you to submit a generic application which will be forwarded by the local authority to schools advertising posts suitable to your expertise and training. This can be a valuable timesaver, but experience suggests it should not be relied upon – if you see a suitable post, apply for it rather than rely on their receiving your generic application. This gives you the opportunity to personalise the application to the post.

The application process

Note how to apply, and importantly, the deadline by which your application should be received. A good level of organisation is required – it is better for a number of reasons if you can submit your application a few days ahead of the published deadline. The scenario to avoid is the last minute dash to the school on the morning applications close to deliver it by hand!

You may be asked to submit your application as a curriculum vitae with a covering letter, or on an application form provided. The latter may contain space for a 'personal statement', which will contain very similar information to a covering letter. Ensure your prospective employer has all the information needed to convince them that you are the person for the job.

Curriculum vitae

Long before you are ready to make your first job application, you should think about preparing your curriculum vitae, or 'cv', and making sure it is up to date. There is no hard and fast rule about how a cv should be presented. Much advice is available through online searches, and careers services in higher education are well equipped to offer help and guidance. Senior managers in your placement schools will be experienced in assessing applications, and can also offer valuable advice.

Your cv should contain relevant personal information, including full contact details, a list of your academic achievements with grades and dates, and your full employment record, with all periods of time accounted for. It is also an opportunity for you to mention outside interests and achievements, for example in sport or music, especially if these evidence skills which will be of relevance to your role as a teacher.

Clarity is key. If, for example, you have carried out teaching placements in three schools, list these, and make sure it is clear that these were placements undertaken as part of your initial teacher training course, rather than periods of paid employment. It stands to reason that the younger you are, the shorter your cv will be, and this should not cause you any concern. If you are an older entrant with a previous career behind you, mention how the skills and experience you acquired have helped you become a better teacher.

It has become accepted practice in some areas of employment to preface a cv with an upbeat statement such as 'I am a highly motivated, conscientious individual committed to giving my best to your organisation …'. This is perhaps best avoided as such statements end up sounding very similar to each other, and your enthusiasm and commitment should come through in other ways.

Application forms

Application forms will ask you for the same information as you would include in your cv, and are usually reasonably straightforward, if time-consuming, to fill in. Not all application forms can be completed and submitted online, so ensure that handwritten forms are neat and well presented. It may be a good idea to photocopy the form and fill in the copy for yourself, to ensure that you can fit everything in the space provided, and that all the information is included in the right sections. However you are submitting a form, careful proof-reading is essential. No employer is impressed by poor spelling, punctuation, incorrect dates or inconsistencies in a CV.

A thought

Application forms, especially if they are designed by, for example, a Local Authority, are used for the full range of teaching posts at all levels. This means that applicants for a first post will not be able to complete many sections, for example 'Previous teaching posts held', or 'In-service courses attended'. Your completed application form may contain what looks like a worrying amount of white space! This should not concern you. Your prospective employer will realise that you are a new entrant to teaching, and therefore expects to see much less detail than would be the case for, say, the appointment of an assistant head teacher.

Referees

An application form will usually contain a request for you to name two referees. If your application is not made on a form, include referees at the end of your cv. Include full contact details: name, job title, postal address, phone and fax numbers, and email address. The best referees are professionals who have good, recent insight into your work as a trainee teacher. Normally (on higher education-based routes), these are a university tutor who has seen you teach and a school-based mentor. On employment-based routes, it will probably be two school-based tutors, though this will vary.

Consider who knows you and your teaching best – these are the most suitable people to nominate. University-based tutors expect to do this as part of their role; it is courteous to check with school-based mentors if they are willing to do it, though most agree. A further courtesy, sometimes overlooked, is to let your referees know when you have obtained a post, especially if you are no longer in day-to-day contact with them, for example if you have completed your placement at their school.

Covering letters/personal statements

Supplement the factual information on your cv or form with a letter/statement expanding on your experience, strengths and beliefs about the profession. Try to match your experience to the details of the post. Talk about your experience to date, and how relevant this has been. Many applicants talk only about their classroom experience, but don't forget the other experiences you have had as a trainee teacher – you may have investigated a particular area of practice, such as special educational needs, assessment for learning or phonics, for a course assignment. You may have secured a number of 'M' level credits, and can describe what you researched.

It is tempting to try to encapsulate everything you have learnt into a covering letter, but this is neither feasible nor desirable. As a guideline, between one and two pages of A4 typescript should be ample. Again, the rule of thumb to apply is – have I, in my cv/application form plus my letter/personal statement, said everything about myself and my experience that the appointing panel would like to know? Avoiding repetition is important. Bear in mind that the panel members have to read and digest a number, possibly a large number, of applications. Do not send them to sleep!

Leave the panel with some questions to ask you – an over-detailed statement, listing every class and teaching technique you have used, leaves you with nothing to expand on at interview. It is good to get a buddy to read your efforts before you submit – he or she may spot mistakes that you miss, or point out omissions.

Finally, if posting your application, leave enough time for it to be delivered, and send it in a big enough envelope that you do not need to fold anything. You want it to emerge in pristine condition – first impressions do count.

Application to primary and secondary teaching

Think about what the panel wants to see of you in a lesson taught as part of the interview process and you can do some preparation in advance. Remember that outstanding lessons are creative, innovative, and varied in pace. They contain a variety of approaches and clear (and well managed) transitions between activities. Keep a list of activities, approaches and transitions that have been particularly successful during training and be prepared to adapt these to the lesson you have to teach.

Interviews

The next move will be the school shortlisting the candidates they would like to interview. If you are not shortlisted, it may well be that you will hear nothing, and you must eventually assume that you have been unsuccessful. Those candidates who are shortlisted will be invited for interview. The conventional way of organising interviews for teaching posts varies from practice common in other professions, where candidates never meet each other. In schools, it is the norm for all the candidates to be invited together, perhaps be shown round in a group, and in some cases take part in selection activities with each other. This has its advantages and disadvantages – you can assess the opposition, but can be put off by how accomplished the other candidates appear!

Often candidates are invited for a full day, and will spend the morning on a variety of activities. This usually means having a look around the school, and the opportunity to ask relevant questions. Sometimes you will be told that this part of the day is 'informal', but the fact is that you will be under scrutiny throughout. You may be interviewed by different groups of staff, and sometimes by pupils, perhaps School Council members. Take this seriously – they will!

Usually there is the requirement to teach a lesson. Details of this should have been made clear to you in advance, for example the topic, year group, the size of the class and available resources, such as projectors. If you are unsure of anything when you receive the brief, ring the school and ask for clarification. One or more of the appointing panel or another colleague will observe your lesson and report back. Some candidates find this an intimidating part of the process, but the important thing is to plan well and be natural. Your ability to communicate well, prepare appropriately and engage a group of pupils unfamiliar to you is the main priority.

Formal interviews will often take place in the afternoon, one after the other. A certain amount of nervous waiting around is endemic to teaching interviews. The size of the panel will vary – it is reasonable to expect three, four or five people. Their priority is to appoint the best person for the job, and they will ask questions to find out more about you, your experience, your potential, and what contribution you could make to the school. As preparation for this part of the process, your mentors and tutors will give you advice about the kinds of question to prepare for. Some could be specifically subject related – for a modern languages post, for example, you may well be asked to answer some questions in your foreign language(s), others may relate to your interest in extracurricular activities or cross-curricular issues. You may be asked to describe your best or worst lesson ever, and to say how you analysed the reasons for this.

Whatever you are asked, try to gather your thoughts and give a detailed, but not overlong, answer. If you are unsure as to whether you have said enough, ask if they would like you to add anything. If you do not understand a question, or through nervousness forget it halfway through your answer, ask for it to be rephrased or repeated. Some humour is usually welcomed, as long as it is not flippant. Above all, be as natural and honest as possible. Saying what you think they want to hear is not usually a good policy.

At some stage during the interview, you will be asked to confirm whether or not you would accept the job if it is offered. This could be phrased in a number of ways, for example, 'Are you still a serious candidate for the post?' An honest answer is expected at this stage – the panel do not want their time wasted in deliberating, offering the post, and then having it turned down.

INDIVIDUAL REFLECTION

If you are offered a job a complication at this stage could be if you have another interview lined up a few days later, for a post you would prefer. Here, honesty is the best policy. Give the panel this information, and that you would like to attend that interview if possible. Sometimes they will allow you to do that and suspend a decision. More often, though, they will ask for a decisive yes or no, so that an appointment can be made that day.

Acceptance of a post, even verbally, means just that, and is seen as contractually binding. There is a strong ethic in the profession that it is not acceptable to take a post, and then continue to pursue others. This would be viewed very badly, and could rebound on you later.

How do you think this could affect your career?

After the interview

You will often know on the same day whether or not you have been successful. If you are not the first choice you will feel disappointed, but pick yourself up and go on to the next. Eventually your face will fit, and every interview experience is something to reflect on and store away for the future. Heads are often willing to give feedback to unsuccessful candidates, and this can be useful to help you perform better next time.

If you are successful, it is strange that you may often feel rather deflated rather than elated. The process will have been stressful, and everyone has natural doubts about whether they have accepted the right job for them. The good news is that most NQTs, once they settle into their new role, make a success of it. The hard work, of course, is never over, as every teacher will tell you. But by this stage, you will have taken a significant step into this demanding yet rewarding profession.

Induction

Once you have successfully completed your initial teacher training, you will receive an academic award, provided you trained in HE, and your provider will recommend you for qualified teacher status (QTS). This is a formality once you have passed your training course, and in due course you will receive official confirmation. The award of QTS is made at this point, and before you begin your induction period. However, the induction year is an important sequel to your training, and must be negotiated successfully before you can remain in teaching.

The induction is not just a further hurdle to jump, but a time when there is recognition that you have successfully taken the first steps in teaching, but can still benefit from additional support, training, monitoring and encouragement. To ensure that this happens, the Department for Education issues statutory guidance to assist both NQTs and schools to navigate the requirements for the year. Be familiar with this guidance in advance of your NQT year and at regular intervals during it.

Technically, it is not necessary to complete induction if you are appointed to an academy, 'free' school or independent school. In practice, the opportunity to complete the induction year will be usually be offered to you. It makes good sense to complete the induction year to prevent any need to start it much later in your career, should you transfer to a maintained school where it is a legal requirement. Information about induction can be found on the web (see below).

The official guidance is revised at intervals, so do make sure you are consulting the current version. Your school will appoint an induction tutor who will normally be a senior member of staff to oversee your induction arrangements – check with him or her at an early stage that you are both reading the same document.

Contrary to popular myth, there is no time limit on starting induction. You are under no obligation, therefore, to start your induction period immediately after completing training. It may be that for a variety of reasons, for example family responsibilities or a wish to take time out for travelling, you do not want to embark on your NQT year at once. Short-term supply teaching may be an option you want to consider instead. This is possible, but keep an eye on the regulation which at present only allows you to teach on a supply basis for up to five years before you are obliged to start induction, which must involve contracts of one term or more. Also, be aware of the limited job satisfaction that supply teaching brings, especially at this stage in your career. It does not normally allow you to build the relationships with pupils on the longer-term basis that most teachers, and pupils, value. Extending your experience by travelling has great merits, provided you take account of the practical issues of finding a post when you return, and also the time that may elapse between the successful end to your training and the day you embark on induction. The longer this time is, the steeper the learning curve may be. None of these are insuperable difficulties, but are well worth thinking through in advance.

As an NQT you will be required to teach less than established members of staff – you should teach no more than 90% of the timetable of other teachers who are on the main pay scale. This is in addition to the normal allocation of non-teaching time for the purposes of planning, preparation and assessment (PPA). This reduction is of course welcome, and means that that the jump in teaching hours that you will experience between your training and full-time work is easier to manage. However, it is intended to be used constructively for professional development. It may result in, for example, a block of time being available during which you could observe colleagues, or familiarise yourself with particular areas of expertise within the school, such as special needs provision. If timetabling permits, you may be able to visit other schools if there is particular practice it would be beneficial to see. This can all be negotiated with your induction tutor. As well as an induction tutor you should also have a named contact within the 'appropriate body' overseeing induction. This may be a Local Authority or teaching school to whom you have recourse if problems arise. Find out at an early stage who this named contact is, even though you may never need to liaise with them, provided arrangements are put in place efficiently.

Your professional development needs, especially at the beginning of your NQT year, will be identified more easily if you finish your training with a clear idea of those areas of practice which you would like to develop more substantially. This should be assisted by your training provider – in partnership with your tutors and mentors. Based on the experiences you have had during training, you should be able to set yourself some targets to meet during your NQT year. These could be based around areas of particular strength, or aspects of practice where you feel you would benefit from further training and development. Some providers continue to use the Career Entry and Development Profile format developed as a national template, but which is no longer obligatory.

The continuity of experience between training and induction has become a focus of Ofsted's current inspection framework, and if your training provider is inspected, you may be visited at your new school.

Your responsibilities as an NQT

Your responsibilities are expressed in the government's guidance, giving a good indication of the spirit in which you should approach the NQT year.

> NQTs should:
>
> - provide evidence that they have QTS and are eligible to start induction;
> - meet with their induction tutor to discuss and agree priorities for their induction programme and keep these under review;
> - agree with their induction tutor how best to use their reduced timetable allowance;
> - provide evidence of their progress against the relevant standards;
> - participate fully in the agreed monitoring and development programme;
> - raise any concerns with their induction tutor as soon as practicable;
> - consult their appropriate body named contact at an early stage if there are or may be difficulties in resolving issues with their tutor/within the institution;

- keep track of and participate effectively in the scheduled classroom observations, progress reviews and formal assessment meetings;
- agree with their induction tutor the start and end dates of the induction period/part periods and the dates of any absences from work during any period/part period; and
- retain copies of all assessment forms. (Weblink a)

INDIVIDUAL REFLECTION

How does this checklist of responsibilities compare with those you feel you have been fulfilling during your initial teacher training? Are there any changes of emphasis? How will you organise yourself to ensure that you are meeting the requirements on you?

If there is an overall message contained in the checklist of an NQT's responsibilities, it is perhaps the need to remain proactive throughout the process. Diligent induction tutors will ensure that the induction year unfolds smoothly, with all requirements met in timely fashion, paperwork completed, and teaching observations carried out at appropriate times and recorded. Experience shows, however, that the job of an induction tutor is made considerably more straightforward if the NQT also takes responsibility for ensuring that requirements are met. You will have developed good habits of evidencing your progress through meeting the Teachers' Standards during your training, and it is important to ensure that this continues throughout your induction year.

Head teachers' responsibilities

It is incumbent on your school to ensure that they make good provision for you as a newly qualified colleague, and the government's guidance specifies clearly what head teachers must do to play their part in the process:

> The head teacher/principal is, along with the appropriate body, jointly responsible for the monitoring, support and assessment of the NQT during induction, and should:
>
> - check that the NQT has been awarded QTS;
> - clarify whether the teacher needs to serve an induction period or is exempt;
> - agree, in advance of the NQT starting the induction programme, which body will act as the appropriate body;
> - notify the appropriate body when an NQT is taking up a post in which they will be undertaking induction;

- meet the requirements of a suitable post for induction;
- ensure the induction tutor is appropriately trained and has sufficient time to carry out their role effectively;
- ensure an appropriate and personalised induction programme is in place;
- ensure the NQT's progress is reviewed regularly, including through observations and feedback of their teaching;
- ensure that termly assessments are carried out and reports completed and sent to the appropriate body;
- maintain and retain accurate records of employment that will count towards the induction period;
- make the governing body aware of the arrangements that have been put in place to support NQTs serving induction;
- make a recommendation to the appropriate body on whether the NQT's performance against the relevant standards is satisfactory or requires an extension;
- participate appropriately in the appropriate body's quality assurance procedures; and
- retain all relevant documentation/evidence/forms on file for six years.

There may also be circumstances where the head teacher/principal should:

- obtain interim assessments from the NQT's previous post;
- act early, alerting the appropriate body when necessary, in cases where an NQT may be at risk of not completing induction satisfactorily;
- ensure third-party observation of an NQT who may be at risk of not performing satisfactorily against the relevant standards;
- notify the appropriate body as soon as absences total 30 days or more;
- periodically inform the governing body about the institution's induction arrangements;
- advise and agree with the appropriate body in exceptional cases where it may be appropriate to reduce the length of the induction period or deem that it has been satisfactorily completed;
- provide interim assessment reports for staff moving in between formal assessment periods; and
- notify the appropriate body when an NQT serving induction leaves the institution. (Weblink a)

This appears an intimidating list, but includes provision for circumstances which occur infrequently. It should provide some reassurance for you as a prospective NQT as it illustrates the considerable responsibilities on schools to ensure that proper and continuing provision is made for you. If at any stage you feel that this is not happening, you must explore this with appropriate senior colleagues. Taking responsibility for your own professional progress is essential.

Remember, you can fail the induction year, with no right to repeat it, unless it can be demonstrated that procedures have not been followed correctly. This rarely happens.

Wellbeing

Keep an emphasis on your wellbeing, as if you are overtired you will not perform as well as you can. Good organisation is paramount, and this needs to include planning ahead – predicting when particularly busy weeks are going to occur, for example, thanks to assessment deadlines, public examination requirements, internal data collection exercises, or parent consultations. If you teach a timetable which carries a heavy and time-consuming marking load, try to ensure that this is reasonably spaced out. At the same time, give yourself the opportunity to take part in the life of the school in ways that your training experiences might not have permitted, through, for example, extra-curricular activities, school visits, community involvement inter alia. Again, planning and using time well are key to success.

Unless you have followed a salaried training route, in which you have had responsibility for pupil progress from a very early stage in your training, you may have had a sense that the pupils you have taught so far have been in a sense on loan to you, and have really 'belonged' to their regular teacher. This has its advantages – you have been able to take your first steps in teaching without total accountability for the pupils' academic progress. However, you are ready now to take the next step and take on the, albeit daunting, responsibility for pupils who will be 'yours'. Success in your training means that teachers and tutors who have assessed you believe that you are well placed to take this step in your induction year. The pupils will depend on you for good teaching, good pastoral care, and an accurate assessment of their needs and progress. Good luck in taking this next step in your professional career in teaching.

Summary

- 31 May is the usual date by which teachers must hand in resignations – this is when most job opportunities arise.
- Look in a variety of media for job opportunities.
- The application process usually involves a cv and some kind of personal statement – use this to emphasise your strengths.
- Interviews are often full-day affairs and involve the teaching of a lesson.
- Your first year of teaching includes a statutory induction period.

- You must be provided with an individualised programme of support which is reviewed regularly, at least every half term.
- You must be provided with an induction tutor who will observe, monitor, assess and mentor you, providing you with opportunities to learn from more experienced teachers and giving you and the head teacher reviews of your progress.
- You should keep an evidence file showing your progress and results of assessment reviews.
- You should know what to do in case of grievance or if things go wrong.

Key reading

Bubb, S. (2003) *The insider's guide for new teachers*. London: Routledge.
Bubb, S. (2007) *Successful induction for new teachers*. London: Sage.

References

Bubb, S. (2009) 'Ten for the top', *Professional Teacher* 3, Autumn, p. 17.

Useful website

Induction for newly qualified teachers (England): Statutory guidance for appropriate bodies, headteachers, school staff and governing bodies: www.gov.uk/government/uploads/system/uploads/attachment_data/file/375304/Statutory_induction_for_newly_qualified_teachers_guidance_revised_October_2014.pdf

Visit https://study.sagepub.com/denby3e for extra resources related to this chapter.

APPENDIX I: LIST OF COMMON EDUCATIONAL ACRONYMS

AfL	Assessment for Learning (formative assessment)
AoL	Assessment of Learning (summative assessment)
APP	Assessing Pupils' Progress
AQA	Assessment and Qualifications Alliance (Examination Board)
ASDAN	Award Scheme Development and Accreditation Network
ASK	Attitudes, Skills and Knowledge
AST	Advanced Skills Teacher
BSF	Building Schools for the Future
BTEC	Business and Technology Education Council
CAT	Cognitive Ability Test
CCEA	Council for Curriculum, Examinations and Assessment
CEOP	Child Exploitation and Online Protection Centre
CfLaT	Centre for Learning and Teaching
CIDA	Certificate in Digital Applications
CLAIT	Computer Literacy and Information Technology

CLASI	Capable, Listened to, Accepted, Safe and Included
CPD	Continuing Professional Development
CTC	City Technology College
CUREE	Centre for the Use of Research and Evidence in Education
CVA	Contextual Value Added
DBS	Disclosure and Barring Service
DCSF	Department for Children, Schools and Families
DfE	Department for Education
DIDA	Diploma in Digital Applications
EAL	English as an Additional Language
EBP	Education Business Partnership
Edexcel/ Pearson	(examination board, not an acronym)
ESTYN	Education and Training Inspectorate for Wales (not an acronym)
ETI	Education and Training Inspectorate (Northern Ireland)
GTC	General Teaching Council
GTP	Graduate Teacher Programme
HEI	Higher Education Institution
HMI	Her Majesty's Inspector
IAG	Information Advice and Guidance
ICT	Information and Communication Technology
IEP	Individual Education Plan
ILP	Individual Learning Plan
INSET	In-Service Training
KS	Key Stage
KTP	Knowledge Transfer Partnership
LADO	Local Authority Designated Officer
LiL	Leading in Learning
LSA	Learning Support Assistant
LSC	Learning and Skills Council
MFL	Modern Foreign Languages
MIS	Management Information System
MLD	Moderate Learning Difficulties
NCSL	National College for School Leadership
NFER	National Foundation for Educational Research
NQT	Newly Qualified Teacher
NUT	National Union of Teachers
OCR	Oxford Cambridge and RSA (Examination Board)
P4C	Philosophy for Children
PASS	Pupil Attitude to Self and School
PGCE	Post Graduate Certificate in Education
PGDE	Post Graduate Diploma in Education

PLTS	Personal, Learning and Thinking Skills
PPA	Planning, Preparation and Assessment (time)
PSHE	Personal, Social and Health Education
QCA	Qualifications and Curriculum Authority
QTS	Qualified Teacher Status
QTLS	Qualified Teacher, Learning and Skills
RAG	Red, Amber, Green (progress indicators)
RE	Religious education
RSA	Royal Society for the Arts (examination board)
RTP	Registered Teacher Programme
SAT	Standard Assessment Task
SCiTT	School-based Initial Teacher Training
SEAL	Social and Emotional Aspects of Learning
SEELS	School Emotional Environment for Learning Survey
SEF	Self-Evaluation Form
SEN	Special Educational Needs
SENCo	Special Educational Needs Coordinator
SEND	Special Educational Needs and Disabilities
SLT	Senior Leadership Team
SMART	Specific, Measurable, Achievable, Realistic and Time-related
SMSC	Spiritual, Moral, Social and Cultural education
SMT	Senior Management Team
SSAT	Specialist Schools and Academies Trust
STPCD	The School Teachers' Pay and Conditions Document (2014)
T&L	Teaching and Learning
TES	*Times Educational Supplement*
TLR	Teaching and Learning Responsibility
TLRP	Teaching and Learning Research Programme
TSPC	Thinking Skills and Personal Capabilities
VAK	Visual Aural and Kinaesthetic learning
VLE	Virtual Learning Environment
WAGOLL	What A Good One Looks Like
YST	Youth Sport Trust
ZPD	Zone of Proximal Development

APPENDIX II: THE TEACHERS' STANDARDS

The Teachers' Standards apply to all of those who began their training for QTS on or after 1 September 2012.

The **Part One Standards** refer to teaching and responsibilities. Although not numbered by the government, the numbering system used here helps to show exactly where each Standard or part Standard is discussed in the text. Chapters appropriate to each point are given in brackets.

The table which follows lists each chapter with the appropriate Standards next to it. This does not mean that this is the only place where that Standard will be found, but that it is a key focal point.

Standards for qualified teachers

Preamble

Teachers make the education of their pupils their first concern, and are accountable for achieving the highest possible standards in work and conduct. Teachers act with honesty and integrity; have strong subject knowledge; keep their knowledge and skills as teachers up-to-date and are self-critical; forge positive professional relationships; and work with parents in the best interests of their pupils.

Part one: teaching

A teacher must:

1. Set high expectations which inspire, motivate and challenge pupils

1. establish a safe and stimulating environment for pupils, rooted in mutual respect (Chapters 2, 3, 4, 20)
2. set goals that stretch and challenge pupils of all backgrounds, abilities and dispositions (Chapters 9, 10, 14, 15, 16, 20)
3. demonstrate consistently the positive attitudes, values and behaviour which are expected of pupils (Chapters 2, 3, 4, 5, 7, 9, 10).

2. Promote good progress and outcomes by pupils

1. be accountable for pupils' attainment, progress and outcomes (Chapters 11, 12, 13, 14, 17)
2. be aware of pupils' capabilities and their prior knowledge, and plan teaching to build on these (Chapters 9, 10, 11, 17, 18, 23)
3. guide pupils to reflect on the progress they have made and their emerging needs (Chapters 7, 9, 10, 11, 12, 13, 14)
4. demonstrate knowledge and understanding of how pupils learn and how this impacts on teaching (Chapters 9, 10, 11, 12, 13, 14, 15)
5. encourage pupils to take a responsible and conscientious attitude to their own work and study (Chapters 9, 10, 11, 17, 18, 21).

3. Demonstrate good subject and curriculum knowledge

1. have a secure knowledge of the relevant subject(s) and curriculum areas, foster and maintain pupils' interest in the subject, and address misunderstandings (Chapters 6, 9, 10, 11, 12, 13, 14, 15, 17, 18)
2. demonstrate a critical understanding of developments in the subject and curriculum areas, and promote the value of scholarship (Chapters 3, 5, 6, 8, 24)
3. demonstrate an understanding of and take responsibility for promoting high standards of literacy, articulacy and the correct use of standard English, whatever the teacher's specialist subject (Chapters 6, 7, 11, 12, 13, 14, 19, 21, 22)

4. if teaching early reading, demonstrate a clear understanding of systematic synthetic phonics (Chapters 6, 11)
5. if teaching early mathematics, demonstrate a clear understanding of appropriate teaching strategies (Chapters 6, 11).

4. Plan and teach well-structured lessons

1. impart knowledge and develop understanding through effective use of lesson time (Chapters 9, 10, 11, 12, 13, 14, 15, 18, 19)
2. promote a love of learning and children's intellectual curiosity (Chapters 9, 10, 11, 12, 13, 14, 15, 18, 19)
3. set homework and plan other out-of-class activities to consolidate and extend the knowledge and understanding pupils have acquired (Chapters 3, 9, 11,21, 22)
4. reflect systematically on the effectiveness of lessons and approaches to teaching (Chapters 5, 6, 7, 8, 9, 10, 17, 23)
5. contribute to the design and provision of an engaging curriculum within the relevant subject area(s) (Chapters 3, 5, 6, 7, 8, 9, 15, 17, 18, 19, 21,22).

5. Adapt teaching to respond to the strengths and needs of all pupils

1. know when and how to differentiate appropriately, using approaches which enable pupils to be taught effectively (Chapters 14, 15, 16, 18, 19)
2. have a secure understanding of how a range of factors can inhibit pupils' ability to learn, and how best to overcome these (Chapters 4, 5, 9, 10, 11, 12, 13, 14, 15)
3. demonstrate an awareness of the physical, social and intellectual development of children, and know how to adapt teaching to support pupils' education at different stages of development (Chapters 4, 5, 9, 10, 11, 12, 13, 14, 15, 24)
4. have a clear understanding of the needs of all pupils, including those with special educational needs; those of high ability; those with English as an additional language; those with disabilities; and be able to use and evaluate distinctive teaching approaches to engage and support them (Chapters 4, 9, 10, 11, 12, 13, 14, 15, 16, 20, 21, 22).

6. Make accurate and productive use of assessment

1. know and understand how to assess the relevant subject and curriculum areas, including statutory assessment requirements (Chapters 17, 21, 23)
2. make use of formative and summative assessment to secure pupils' progress (Chapters 17, 23)

3. use relevant data to monitor progress, set targets, and plan subsequent lessons (Chapters 17, 23)
4. give pupils regular feedback, both orally and through accurate marking, and encourage pupils to respond to the feedback (Chapters 5, 6, 7, 17, 23).

7. Manage behaviour effectively to ensure a good and safe learning environment

1. have clear rules and routines for behaviour in classrooms, and take responsibility for promoting good and courteous behaviour both in classrooms and around the school, in accordance with the school's behaviour policy (Chapters 2, 3, 4, 5, 6, 7, 9, 10)
2. have high expectations of behaviour, and establish a framework for discipline with a range of strategies, using praise, sanctions and rewards consistently and fairly (Chapters 2, 3, 4, 5, 6, 7, 9, 10)
3. manage classes effectively, using approaches which are appropriate to pupils' needs in order to involve and motivate them (Chapters 2, 3, 4, 5, 6, 7, 9, 10, 11, 12, 13, 14)
4. maintain good relationships with pupils, exercise appropriate authority, and act decisively when necessary (Chapters 2, 3, 4, 5, 6, 7, 9, 10).

8. Fulfil wider professional responsibilities

1. make a positive contribution to the wider life and ethos of the school (Chapters 2, 5, 6, 7, 8, 20, 24)
2. develop effective professional relationships with colleagues, knowing how and when to draw on advice and specialist support (Chapters 5, 6, 7, 8, 16, 20, 24)
3. deploy support staff effectively (Chapters 5, 6, 7, 16, 20, 24)
4. take responsibility for improving teaching through appropriate professional development, responding to advice and feedback from colleagues (Chapters 3, 5, 6, 7, 8)
5. communicate effectively with parents with regard to pupils' achievements and well- being (Chapters 3, 5, 7).

Part two: personal and professional conduct

A teacher is expected to demonstrate consistently high standards of personal and professional conduct. The following statements define the behaviour and attitudes which set the required standards for conduct throughout a teacher's career.

1. Teachers uphold public trust in the profession and maintain high standards of ethics and behaviour, within and outside school, by:

   - treating pupils with dignity, building relationships rooted in mutual respect, and at all times observing proper boundaries appropriate to a teacher's professional position
   - having regard for the need to safeguard pupils' wellbeing, in accordance with statutory provisions
   - showing tolerance of and respect for the rights of others
   - not undermining fundamental British values, including democracy, the rule of law, individual liberty and mutual respect, and tolerance of those with different faiths and beliefs
   - ensuring that personal beliefs are not expressed in ways which exploit pupils' vulnerability or might lead them to break the law.

2. Teachers must have proper and professional regard for the ethos, policies and practices of the school in which they teach, and maintain high standards in their own attendance and punctuality.
3. Teachers must have an understanding of, and always act within, the statutory frame-works which set out their professional duties and responsibilities.

   (Source: Department for Education, *Teachers' Standards*, pp. 5–8)

The following table sets each chapter in the context of the Standards linked to it.

Part 1. Professional attributes	**Link to Standards ...**
2. Relationships with children and young people	1.1, 1.2, 1.3; Part 2 Standards
3. Professionalism, the professional duties of teachers	7.1, 7.2, 7.3, 7.4, 8.5; Part 2 Standards
4. Child protection issues	1.1, 5.2, 5.3, 7.1, 7.2, 7.3, 7.4 Part 2 Standards
5. Communication and collaboration	5.1, 5.2, 5.3, 5.4; 6.4, 8.1, 8.2, 8.3, 8.4; Part 2 Standards
6. School-based training	4.4, 4.5; 5.3; 8.2, 8.4; Part 2 Standards
7. Understanding the roles of specialist colleagues	7.1, 7.2, 7.3, 7.4, 8.1, 8.2, 8.3, 8.4, 8.5; Part 2 Standards
8. Developing skills for career progress	3.2, 4.2, 4.4, 8.4; Part 2 Standards

Part 2. Strategies for teaching and learning and for developing pupils	
9. Managing your classroom environment	1.1, 1.2, 1.3; 7.1, 7.2, 7.3, 7.4
10. Behaviour strategies in challenging classrooms	1.1, 1.2, 1.3; 7.1, 7.2, 7.3, 7.4
11. Beginning to understand how young people learn	1.2, 1.3; 2.4, 2.5; 3.1, 3.4, 3.5; 4.1, 4.3; 5.3
12. Teaching and learning 1: developing a range	2.3, 2.5, 3.1, 3.3, 4.1, 4.3; 5.1, 5.2
13. Teaching and learning 2: planning and progression	2.1, 2.2, 2.3, 2.4, 2.5,;4.1, 4.2, 4.3
14. Differentiation and personalisation	1.2, 5.1, 5.2, 5.3, 5.4; 6.2; 7.3
15. Inclusion	5.1, 5.2, 5.3, 5.4;
16. Pupils with English as an additional language	1.2, 2.3, 5.1, 5.2, 5.4, 8.3
Part 3. Building knowledge and skills	
17. Assessment and delivering feedback	1.2, 2.2, 2.5, 3.1, 4.1, 5.4, 6.1, 6.2, 6.4
18. Creativity	2.3, 2.5; 4.1, 4.2, 4.4, 4.5
19. Using digital technologies	2.1, 2.2; 4.1, 4.2, 4.4, 4.5
20. The rights of the child	1.1; 2.5; Part 2 Standards
21. Cross-curricular planning issues	1.2, 2.4, 2.5, 4.1, 8.3
22. Cross-curricular teaching issues	1.2, 2.4, 2.5, 4.1, 8.3
23. Accessing statistical information	1.2; 2.1, 2.2; 6.1, 6.2, 6.3, 6.4
24. Applications, interviews and induction	All standards, especially Part 2 standards

REFERENCES AND BIBLIOGRAPHY

Aaronson, D., Barrow, L. and Sander, W. (2007) 'Teachers' and student achievement in the Chicago public high schools', *Journal of Labor Economics*, 25 (1): 95–135.

Addi-Raccah, A. and Ainhoren, R. (2009) 'School governance and teachers' attitudes to parents' involvement in schools', *Teaching and Teacher Education,* 25 (6): 805–13.

Ainscow, M. (2000) 'Profile', in P. Clough and J. Corbett (eds), *Theories of inclusive education: a students' guide*. London: Paul Chapman.

Ainscow, M., Booth, T. and Dyson, A. (2006) 'Inclusion and the standards agenda: negotiating policy pressures in England', 10 (4/5): 295–308.

Ajegbo, K. (2007) *Diversity and citizenship: curriculum review*. Nottingham: DfES.

Alexander, R. (ed.) (2009) *Children, their world, their education: final report and recommendations of the Cambridge Primary Review*. London: Routledge.

Allan, J. (2000) 'Reflection: inconclusive education? Towards settled uncertainty', in P. Clough and J. Corbett (eds), *Theories of inclusive education: a students' guide*. London: Paul Chapman.

Allan, J. (2006) 'The repetition of exclusion', *International Journal of Inclusive Education*, 10 (2/3): 121–33.

Allan, J. (2008) *Rethinking inclusion: the philosophers of difference in practice*. Dordrecht: Springer.

Anderson, L. and Krathwohl, D. (eds) (2001) *A taxonomy for learning, teaching, and assessing: a revision of Bloom's taxonomy of educational objectives*. New York: Longman.

Argyris, C. and Schön, D.A. (1975) *Theory in practice: increasing professional effectiveness*. San Francisco, CA: Jossey-Bass.

Armstrong, D. (2005) 'Reinventing "inclusion": New Labour and the cultural politics of special education', *Oxford Review of Education*, 31 (1): 135–51.

Armstrong, D., Armstrong, A.C. and Spandagou, I. (2011) 'Inclusion: by choice or chance?', *International Journal of Inclusive Education*, 15 (1): 29–39.

Avramidis, E., Bayliss, P. and Burden, R. (2002) 'Inclusion in action: an in-depth case study of an effective inclusive secondary school in the south-west of England', *International Journal of Inclusive Education*, 6 (2): 143–63.

Azzopardi, A. (2010) *Making sense of inclusive education: where everyone belongs*. Saarbrucken: VDM.

Ball, S.J. (2003) 'The teacher's soul and the terrors of performativity', *Journal of Education Policy*, 18 (2): 215–28.

Bandura, A. (1986) *Social foundations of thought and action: a social cognitive theory*. Englewood Cliffs, NJ: Prentice-Hall.

Barber, M. (1996) *The learning game*. London: Gollancz.

Barnard, C. (1948) *Organisation and management*. Cambridge, MA: Harvard University Press.

Barnes, J. (2011) *Cross-curricular learning 3–14* (2nd edn). London: Sage.

Baumert, J., Kunter, M., Brunner, M., Tsai, Y., Krauss, S. and Klusmann, U. (2008) 'Students' and mathematics teachers' perceptions of teacher enthusiasm and instruction', *Learning and Instruction,* 18 (5): 468–82.

Beckett, L. and Wrigley, T. (2014) *Improving Schools,* 17 (3): 217–30.

Belbin, R.M. (1981) *Management teams: why they succeed or fail*. London: Heinemann.

Bell, B. and Gilbert, J. (1996) *Teacher development: a model from science education*. London: Falmer.

Benjamin, S. (2002a) 'Valuing diversity: a cliché for the 21st century?', *International Journal of Inclusive Education*, 6 (4): 309–23.

Benjamin, S. (2002b) *The micropolitics of inclusive education*. Buckingham: Open University Press.

Bennett, T. (2010) *The behaviour guru: behaviour management solutions for teachers*. London: Continuum.

Bernstein, B. (1981) 'Codes, modalities, and the process of cultural reproduction: a model', *Language in Society,* 10: 327–63.

Bernstein, B. (2000) *Pedagogy, symbolic control, and identity: theory, research, critique* (4th edn). Maryland: Rowman & Littlefield.

Bigger, S. and Brown, E. (2013) *Spiritual, moral, social, & cultural education*. London: David Fulton.

Biggs, J. and Collis, K. (1982) *Evaluating the quality of learning: the SOLO taxonomy*. New York: Academic Press.

Biglan, A. (1973) 'The characteristics of subject matters in different academic areas', *Journal of Applied Psychology,* 57: 195–203.

Bines, H. (2000) 'Inclusive standards: current developments in policy for special educational needs in England and Wales', *Oxford Review of Education*, 26 (1): 21–33.

Birkett, V. (2003) *How to support and teach children with special educational needs*. Hyde: LDA.

Black-Hawkins, K., Florian, L. and Rouse, M. (2007) *Achievement and inclusion in schools*. London: Routledge.

Black, P. and Wiliam, D. (1998a) 'Assessment and classroom learning', *Assessment in Education,* March: 7–74.

Black, P. and Wiliam, D. (1998b) *Inside the black box: raising standards through classroom assessment*. London: King's College.

Black, P., Harrison, C., Lee, C., Marshall, B. and Wiliam, D. (2004) 'Working inside the black box: assessment for learning in the classroom', *Phi Delta Kappan*, 86 (1): 8–21.

Blanden, J. and Machin, S. (2007) *Recent changes in intergenerational mobility in Britain*. London: Sutton Trust.

Blandford, S. (2001) 'Professional development in schools', in A. Banks and A.S. Mayers (eds), *Early professional development for teachers*. London: David Fulton.

Bloom, B. (ed.) (1956) *Taxonomy of educational objectives, the classification of educational goals – Handbook I: Cognitive domain*. New York: McKay.

Bloom, B. (1984) *Taxonomy of educational objectives*. Boston, MA: Pearson.

Boekaerts, M., Oortwijn, M. and Vedder, P. (2008) 'The impact of the teacher's role and pupils' ethnicity and prior knowledge on pupils' performance and motivation to cooperate', *Instructional Science*, 36 (3): 251–68.

Boler, M. (1999) *Feeling Power: Emotions and Education*. New York: Psychology Press.

Boliver, V. (2011) 'Expansion, differentiation, and the persistence of social class inequalities in British higher education', *Higher Education*, 61 (3): 229–42.

Bosch, K. (2006) *Planning classroom management: a five-step process to creating a positive learning environment*. Thousand Oaks: Corwin.

Boston, K. (2006) 'Tipping points in education and skills', speech to QCA Annual Review 2006. Available online at: http://webarchive.nationalarchives.gov.uk/20081117153621/qca.org.uk/qca_11250. aspx

Boud, D. (1995) *Enhancing learning through self-assessment*. London: Kogan Page.

Bourdieu, P. (1989) 'Social space and symbolic power', *Sociological Theory*, 7 (1): 14–25.

Bransford, J., Darling-Hammond, L. and LePage, P. (2005) *Preparing teachers for a changing world: what teachers should learn and be able to do*. San Francisco, CA: Jossey-Bass.

Brooks, V. and Sikes, P. (1997) *The good mentor guide: initial teacher education in secondary schools*. Buckingham: Open University Press.

Brown, M., Boyle, B. and Boyle, T. (1999) 'Commonalities between perception and practice in models of school decision-making in secondary schools', *School Leadership & Management*, 19 (3): 319–30.

Bruner, J. (1960) *The process of education*. Cambridge, MA: Harvard University Press.

Bruner (1974) *Beyond the information given: studies in the psychology of knowing*. London. Allen & Unwin.

Bruner, J. (1996) *The culture of education*. Cambridge, MA: Harvard University Press.

Bubb, S. (2003) *The insider's guide for new teachers*. London: Routledge.

Bubb, S. (2007) *Successful induction for new teachers*. London: Sage.

Bubb, S. (2009) 'Ten for the top', *Professional Teacher*, 3: 17.

Buitink, J. (2008) 'What and how do student teachers learn during school-based teacher education?', *Teaching and Teacher Education*, 25 (1): 118–27.

Burton, D. and Bartlett, S. (2005) *Practitioner research for teachers*. London: Sage.

Butroyd, R. (2007) 'Denial and distortion of instrumental and intrinsic value in the teaching of science and English: its impact upon fifteen Year 10 teachers', *Forum* 49 (3): 313–29.

Buzan, T. (1995) *Use your head*. London: BBC Books.

Buzzelli, C. A., Donnelly, L. A. and Akerson, V. L. (2008) 'Early childhood teachers' views of nature of science: the influence of intellectual levels, cultural values, and explicit reflective teaching', *Journal of Research in Science Teaching*, 45 (6): 748–70.

Byron, T. (2008) *Safer children in a digital world: a summary for children and young people*. Nottingham: DCSF.

Cairns, J. (2000) 'Schools, community and the developing values of young adults: towards an ecology of education in values', in J. Cairns, R. Gardiner and D. Lawton (eds), *Values and the curriculum*. London: Woburn. pp. 52–73.

Caldwell, B. and Spinks, J. (1998) *Beyond the self-managing school*. London: Falmer.

Capel, S., Leask, M. and Turner, T. (eds) (2009) *Learning to teach in the secondary school* (5th edn). London: RoutledgeFalmer.

Carr, D. (2003) *Making sense of education*. London: Routledge.

Chaplain, R. (2014) 'Managing classroom behaviour', in T. Cremin and J Arthur (eds), *Learning to teach in the primary school*. London: Routledge

Cheminais, R. (2008) *Engaging pupil voice to ensure that every child matters: a practical guide*. London: David Fulton.

Child, A. and Merrill, S. (2005) *Developing as a secondary school mentor: a case study approach for trainee mentors and their tutors*. Exeter: Learning Matters.

Chiu, S. (2010) 'Students' knowledge sources and knowledge sharing in the design studio – an exploratory study'. *International Journal of Technology and Design Education*, 20 (1): 27–42.

Clarke, S. (2014) *Outstanding formative assessment: culture and practice*. London: Hodder Education.

Claxton, G. (1997) *Hare brain, tortoise mind: why intelligence increases when you think less*. London: Fourth Estate.

Clough, P. (2000) 'Routes to inclusion', in P. Clough and J. Corbett (eds), *Theories of inclusive education: a students' guide*. London: Paul Chapman.

Coe, R. et al. (2014a) 'What makes great teaching?' The Sutton Trust at www.suttontrust.com/wp-content/uploads/2014/10/What-Makes-Great-Teaching-REPORT.pdf

Coe, R., Aloisi, C., Higgins, S. and Elliot Major, L. (2014b) *What makes great teaching?* Durham: The University of Durham.

Cohen, L., Manion, L. and Morrison, K. (2004) *A Guide to teaching practice*. London: Routledge.

Cole, B. (2005) 'Good faith and effort? Perspectives on educational inclusion', *Disability and Society*, 20 (3): 331–44.

Collier, V.P. and Thomas, W.P. (1989) 'How quickly can immigrants become proficient in school English?', *Educational Issues of Language Minority Students*, 5.

Conole, G., Oliver, M., Falconer, I., Littlejohn, C. and Harvey, J. (2007) *Designing for learning: contemporary perspectives in e-learning research: themes, methods and impact on practice*. London: RoutledgeFalmer.

Cooke, C. (2011) 'Personal, learning and thinking skills and functional skills', in J. Price and M. Savage (eds), *Teaching secondary music*. London: Sage.

Cooke, N. J., Rosen, M. A. and Salas, E. (2008) 'On teams, teamwork, and team performance: discoveries and developments', *Human Factors: The Journal of the Human Factors and Ergonomics Society*, 50 (3): 540–7.

Corbett, J. (1992) 'Careful teaching: researching a special career', *British Educational Research Journal*, 18 (3): 235–43.

Corbett, J. (2000) 'Profile', in P. Clough and J. Corbett (eds), *Theories of inclusive education*. London: Sage. pp. 69–73.

Corbett, J. (2001) 'Teaching approaches which support inclusive education: a connective pedagogy', *British Journal of special Education*, 28 (2): 55–9.

Corbett, J. and Slee, R. (2000) 'An international conversation on inclusive education', in F. Armstrong, D. Armstrong and L. Barton (eds) *Inclusive education: policy, contexts and comparative perspectives*. London: Fulton.

Craft, A. (2001) 'Little c creativity', in A. Craft, B. Jeffrey and M. Leibling (eds), *Creativity in education*. London: Continuum.

Craft, A. (2003) 'The limits to creativity in education: dilemmas for the educator', *British Journal of Education Studies*, 51 (2): 113–27.

Craft, A. and Jeffrey, B. (2008) 'Creativity and performativity in teaching and learning: tensions, dilemmas, constraints, accommodations and synthesis', *British Education Journal*, 334 (5): 577–84.

Cremin, H., Mason, C. and Busher, H. (2011) 'Problematising pupil voice using visual methods: findings from a study of engaged and disaffected pupils in an urban secondary school', *British Educational Research Journal*, 37 (4): 585–603.

Cremin, T. (2006) ' Creativity, uncertainty and discomfort', *Cambridge Journal of Education*, 36 (3): 415–33.

Crick, B. (1998) *Education for citizenship and the teaching of democracy in schools: final report of the Advisory Group on Citizenship*. London: QCA.

Csikszentmihalyi, M. (1996) *Creativity: flow and the psychology of discovery and intervention*. New York: Harper.

Cullingford, C. (1990) *The nature of learning*. London: Cassell.

Cullingford, C. (1991) *The inner world of the school*. London: Cassell.

Cullingford, C. (2006) 'Children's own vision of schooling', *Education 3–13*, 34 (3): 211–21.

Cummins, J. (2000) *Language, power, and pedagogy: bilingual children in the crossfire*. Bristol: Multilingual Matters.

Day, C. (2002) 'Revisiting the purposes of Continuing Professional Development', in G. Trorey and C. Cullingford (eds), *Professional development and institutional needs*. Aldershot: Ashgate.

Day, C. (2004) *A passion for teaching*. London: RoutledgeFalmer.

Day, C., Kington, A., Stobart, G. and Sammons, P. (2006) 'The personal and professional lives of teachers: stable and unstable identities', *British Educational Research Journal*, 32 (4): 601–16.

Denby, N. (2007) 'Ensuring more accurate responses from child respondents in school-based research', Hawaii International Conference on Education, Pepperdine University, CA.

Denby, N. (2014) *Working together*. L'Avenir (Training) publications, West Yorkshire, UK.

Denby, N., Butroyd, R., Swift, H., Price, J. and Glazzard, J. (2008) *Master's level study in education*. Minehead: OUP.

Department for Children, Education, Lifelong Learning and Skills (DCELLS) (2008) *Framework for children's learning (aged 3-7 years) in Wales*. Cardiff: Welsh Assembly Government.

Department for Children, Schools and Families (DCSF) (2010) *Working together to safeguard children: a guide to inter-agency working to safeguard and promote the welfare of children*. Nottingham: DCSF.

Department for Education (DfE) (2010) *The importance of teaching schools* (White Paper). London: DfE.

Department for Education (DfE) (2011a) *Review of vocational education – The Wolf Report* (DfE-00031-2011). London: DfE.

Department for Education (DfE) (2011b) *Support and aspiration: a new approach to special educational needs and disability: a consultation*. London: DfE.

Department for Education (DfE) (2012) *Standards for qualified teachers*. Available online at www.gov.uk/government/publications/teachers-standards

Department for Education (DfE) (2013) *The national curriculum in England: Key Stages 1 and 2 Framework Document*. London: DfE.

Department for Education (DfE) (2014a) *Keeping children safe in education: statutory guidance for schools and colleges*. London: DfE.

Department for Education (DfE) (2014b) *Special educational needs and disability code of practice: 0 to 25 years: Statutory guidance for organisations who work with and support children and young people with special educational needs and disabilities*. London: DfE.

Department for Education (DfE) (2014c) *Progress 8 measure in 2016: a technical guide for maintained secondary schools, academies and free schools*. London: HMSO.

Department for Education and Skills (DfES) (2001) *Special educational needs code of practice*. London: DfES.

Department for Education and Skills (DfES) (2003) *Towards a unified e-learning strategy*. London: DfES.

Department for Education and Skills (DfES) (2004a) *Every child matters: change for children*. London: DfES.

Department for Education and Skills (DfES) (2004b) *Pedagogy and practice: unit 12: assessment for learning*. London: DfES.

Department for Education and Skills (DfES) (2004c) *Pedagogy and practice: teaching and learning in secondary schools*. London: HMSO.

Department for Education and Skills (DfES) (2004d) *Excellence and enjoyment: learning and teaching in the primary years*. London: HMSO.

Department for Education and Skills (DfES) (2005) *Learning behaviour: the report of the practitioners' group on school behaviour and discipline*. London: HMSO.

Department for Education and Skills (DfES) (2006) 'Coaching in secondary schools' (DVD-ROM), *Secondary National Strategy for School Improvement*. Norwich: DfES.

Department for Education and Skills (DfES) (2007) *Safeguarding children and safer recruitment in education*. London: DfES.

Deuchar, R. (2009) 'Seen and heard, and then not heard: Scottish pupils' experience of democratic educational practice during the transition from primary to secondary school', *Oxford Review of Education*, 35 (1): 23–40.

Dewey, J. (1938) *Experience and education*. New York: Macmillan.

Dewey, J. (1966) *Democracy in education*. New York: The Free Press.

Dillenburger, K. and McKee, B. (2009) 'Child abuse and neglect: training needs of student teachers', *International Journal of Educational Research*, 48 (5): 320–30.

Dillon, J. and Maguire, M. (2011) *Becoming A teacher: issues in secondary education*. Maidenhead: Open University Press.

Dix, P. (2010) *The essential guide to taking care of behaviour* (2nd edn). Harlow: Pearson Education.

Douglas, J.W.B. (1964) *The home and the school*. London: Panther.

Downey, C. and Kelly, A. (2010) 'Value-added measures for schools in England: looking inside the "black box" of complex metrics', *Educational Assessment, Evaluation and Accountability*, 22 (3): 181–98.

Dunne, L. (2009), 'Discourses of inclusion: a critique', *Power and Education*, 1 (1): 42–56.

Dweck, C.S. (2007) *Mindset: the new psychology of success*. New York: Ballantine.

Dyson, A. (2001) 'Special needs education as the way to equity: an alternative approach?', *Support for Learning*, 16 (3): 99–104.

Elwood, J. (2013) 'Educational assessment policy and practice: a matter of ethics', *Assessment in Education: Principles, Policy & Practice*, 20 (2): 205–20.

Erten, O. and Savage, R.S. (2012) 'Moving forward in inclusive education research', *International Journal of Inclusive Education*, 16 (2): 221–33.

Ertmer, P.A. and Newby, T.J. (1993) 'Behaviorism, cognitivism, constructivism: comparing critical features from an instructional design perspective', *Performance Improvement Quarterly*, 6 (4): 50–72.

Farrell, P. (2001) 'Special education in the last twenty years: have things really got better?', *British Journal of Special Education*, 28 (1): 3-9.

Farrell, T.S.C. (2004) *Reflective practice in action: 80 reflection breaks for busy teachers*. London: Sage.

Fielding, M., and Bragg, S. (2003) *Students as researchers: making a difference*. Cambridge: Pearson.

Flutter, J. and Rudduck, J. (2004) *Consulting pupils: what's in it for schools?* London: RoutledgeFalmer.

Franklin, B. (2002) *The new handbook of children's rights*. London: Routledge.

Franson, C. (2009) *Bilingualism and second language acquisition*. Available at www.naldic. org. uk/ITTSEAL2/teaching/bilingualism.cfm

Fuller, F. (1969) 'Concerns of teachers: a developmental conceptualization', *American Educational Research Journal*, 6: 207–26.

Gabel, S.L. (2010) 'Foreward: disability and equity in education and special education', in A. Azzopardi (ed), *Making sense of inclusive education: where everyone belongs*. Saarbrucken: VDM. pp. 9–10.

Galton, M., Steward, S., Hargreaves, L., Page, C. and Pell, A. (2009) *Motivating your secondary class*. London: Sage.

Gardner, H. (1993) *Frames of mind: the theory of multiple intelligences* (2nd edn). New York: Basic.

General Teaching Council for England (2004) *The learning conversation*. London: GTCE.

Gertrudix, M. and Gertrudix, F. (2010) 'La utilidad de los formatos de interacción músico-visual en la enseñanza' [The utility of musico-visual formats in teaching], *Comunicar*, 17 (34): 99–107.

Ghaye, T. and Ghaye, K. (1998) *Teaching and learning through critical reflective practice*. London: David Fulton.

Giroux, H.A. (2003) 'Public pedagogy and the politics of resistance: notes on a critical theory of educational struggle', *Educational Philosophy and Theory*, 35 (1): 5–16.

Glazzard, J. (2010) 'The impact of dyslexia on pupils' self-esteem', *Support for Learning*, 25 (2): 63–9.

Glazzard, J., Chadwick, D., Webster, A. and Percival, J. (2010) *Assessment for learning in the early years foundation stage*. London: Sage.

Glazzard, J., Hughes, A., Netherwood, A., Neve, L. and Stokoe, J. (2015) *Teaching and supporting children with special educational needs and disabilities in primary schools*. London: Sage.

Goepel, J. (2009) 'Constructing the individual education plan: confusion or collaboration?', *Support for Learning*, 24 (3): 126–32.

Goepel, J. (2012) 'Upholding public trust: an examination of teacher professionalism and the use of teachers' standards in England', *Teacher Development: An International Journal of Teachers' Professional Development*, 16 (4): 489–505.

Goodley, D. (2007) 'Towards socially just pedagogies: Deleuzoguattarian critical disability studies', *International Journal of Inclusive Education*, 11 (3): 317–34.

Goodley, D. and Runswick-Cole, K. (2011) 'Len Barton, inclusion and critical disability studies: theorizing disabled childhoods', *International Studies in Sociology of Education*, 20 (4): 273–90.

Graham, L.J. and Slee, R. (2008) 'An illusory interiority: interrogating the discourse/s of inclusion', *Educational Philosophy and Theory*, 40 (2): 247–60.

Grasha, A. (1996) *Teaching with style*. Pittsburgh, MA: Alliance.

Gray, J., Hopkins, D., Reynolds, D., Wilcox, B., Farrell, S. and Jesson, D. (1999) *Improving schools: performance and potential*. Buckingham: Open University Press.

Grossman, P. and Thompson, C. (2008) 'Learning from curriculum materials: scaffolds for new teachers?', *Teaching and Teacher Education*, 24 (8): 2014–26.

Groundwater-Smith, S. and Sachs, J. (2002) 'The activist professional and the reinstatement of trust', *Cambridge Journal of Education*, 32 (3): 341–58.

Hall, E. and Moseley, D. (2006) 'Is there a role for learning styles in personalised education and training?', *International Journal of Lifelong Education*, 24 (3): 243–55.

Hall, V. (2001) 'Management teams in education: an unequal music', *School Leadership and Management*, 21 (3): 327–41.

Hannam, A. (1998) cited in Ruddock, J. and Flutter, J. (2000) 'Pupil participation and pupil perspective: "carving a new order of experience"', *Cambridge Journal of Education* 30 (1): 75–89.

Hansen, J.H. (2012) 'Limits to inclusion', *International Journal of Inclusive Education*, 16 (1): 89–98.

Hargreaves, D. (1994) 'The new professionalism: the synthesis of professional and institutional development', *Teaching and Teacher Educator,* 10 (4): 423–38.

Hattie, J. (2008) *Visible learning: a synthesis of over 800 meta-analyses relating to achievement.* London: Routledge.

Hattie, J. (2012) *Visible learning for teachers.* New York and London: Routledge.

Hattie, J. and Timperley, H. (2007) ' The power of feedback', *Review of Educational Research,* 77 (1): 81–112.

Hegarty, S. (2001) 'Inclusive education: a case to answer', *Journal of Moral Education,* 30 (3): 243–49.

Helsby, G. (1996) 'Defining and developing professionalism in English secondary schools', *Journal of Education for Teaching,* 22 (2): 135–48.

Hilferty, F. (2008) 'Theorising teacher professionalism as an enacted discourse of power', *British Journal of Sociology of Education,* 29 (2): 161–73.

Hirsch, E.D. (1999) *The schools we need and why we don't have them.* New York: Anchor Books (Random House).

Hirst, P.H. (1974) *Knowledge and the curriculum.* London: Routledge and Kegan Paul.

HMI (2005) *Citizenship in secondary schools: evidence from Ofsted inspections (2003/04),* HMI 2335.

HMSO (2007) *The Children's Plan: building brighter futures,* Cm 7280.

Hodkinson, A. (2012) '"All present and correct?": Exclusionary inclusion within the English education system', *Disability and Society,* 27 (5): 675–88.

Hodkinson, A. and Vickerman, P. (2009) Key issues in special educational needs and inclusion. London: Sage.

Holt, J. (1982) *How children fail.* New York: Delacorte/Seymour Lawrence.

Honey, P. and Mumford, A. (1982) *Manual of learning styles.* London: Peter Honey Publications.

Hook, P. and Mills, J. (2011) *SOLO taxonomy: a guide for schools. Book 1. A common language of learning.* New Zealand: Essential Resources Educational Publishers Limited.

Hout, M. (2006) 'Maximally maintained inequality and essentially maintained inequality: cross-national comparisons', *Sociological Theory and Methods,* 21 (2): 237–52.

Hout, M. (2007) 'Maximally maintained inequality revisited: Irish educational mobility in comparative perspective', in B. Hilliard and M.N.G. Phadraig (eds), *Changing Ireland in international comparison.* Dublin: The Liffey Press.

Hoyle, E. (2001) 'Teaching: prestige, status and esteem', *Educational Management & Administration,* 29 (2): 139–52.

Hoyle, E. and John, P. (1995) *Professional knowledge and professional practice.* London: Cassell.

Hughes, S. (2010) 'Mentoring and coaching: the helping relationship', in Wright T (ed.), *How to be a brilliant mentor: developing outstanding teachers.* London: Routledge. Chapter 7.

Humphreys, M. and Hyland, T. (2002) 'Theory, practice and performance in teaching: professionalism, intuition, and jazz', *Educational Studies,* 28 (1): 5–15.

Hutchin, V. (2006) 'Meeting individual needs', in T. Bruce (ed.), *Early childhood: a guide for students.* London: Sage. Chapter 4.

Jeffrey, B. and Craft, A. (2004) 'Teaching creatively and teaching for creativity: distinctions and relationships', *Educational Studies,* 30 (1): 77–87.

Jennings, P.A. (2014) 'Early childhood teachers' well-being, mindfulness, and self-compassion in relation to classroom quality and attitudes towards challenging students', *Mindfulness,* 1–12.

Jones, B. & Flannigan, S. (2006) 'Connecting the digital dots: literacy of the 21st century', *Educause Quarterly,* 1–35.

Jones, P. and Welch, S. (2010) *Rethinking children's rights: attitudes in contemporary society.* London: Continuum.

Joyce, B., Calhoun, E. and Hopkins, D. (1997) *Models of learning – tools for teaching*. Buckingham: Open University Press.

Kearns, L. R. and Frey, B. A. (2010) 'Web 2.0 technologies and back channel communication in an online learning community', *TechTrends*, 54 (4): 41–51.

Keating, A., Kerr, D., Lopes, J., Featherstone, G. and Benton, T. (2009) *Embedding citizenship education in secondary schools in England (2002-08): Citizenship Education Longitudinal Study Seventh Annual Report*. National Foundation for Educational Research, DCSF RR172.

Kelly, R. (2012) *Educating creativity: a global conversation*. Edmonton, Canada: Brush Education Inc.

Kennewell, S. (2013) *Meeting the standards in using ICT for secondary teaching: a guide to the ITTNC*. London: Routledge.

Kerr, D., Lopes, J., Nelson, J., White, K., Cleaver, E. and Benton, T. (2007) *Vision versus pragmatism: citizenship in the secondary school curriculum in England: citizenship education longitudinal study: Fifth Annual Report*. National Foundation for Educational Research, DfE RR845.

Kirschner, P., Sweller, J. and Clark, R. (2006) 'Why minimal guidance during instruction does not work: an analysis of the failure of constructivist, discovery, problem-based, experiential and inquiry-based teaching', *Educational Psychologist*, 41 (2): 75–86.

Knight, O. and Benson, D. (2013) *Creating outstanding classrooms: a whole-school approach*. London: Routledge.

Koedel, C. and Betts, J.R. (2007) 'Re-examining the role of teacher quality in the educational production function' (Working Paper 07-08). Columbia: University of Missouri.

Kolb, D.A. (1984) *Experiential learning: experience as the source of learning and development*. Englewood Cliffs, NJ: Prentice-Hall.

Kortman, S.A. and Honaker, C.J. (2002) *The best mentoring experience*. Dubuque, IA: Kendall Hunt.

Krathwohl, D. (2002) 'A revision of Bloom's taxonomy: an overview', *Theory into Practice*, 41 (4): 212–18.

Lankshear, C. (2010) 'The challenge of digital epistemologies', *Education, Communication & Information*, 167–86.

Laurie, J. (2011) 'Curriculum planning and preparation for cross-curricular teaching', in T. Kerry (ed.), *Cross-curricular teaching in the primary school*. Abingdon: Routledge.

Laurillard, D. (1993) *Rethinking university teaching: a framework for the effective use of educational technology*. London: Routledge.

Lave, J. and Wenger, E. (1991) *Situated learning: legitimate peripheral participation*. Cambridge: Cambridge University Press.

Layder, D. (2006) *Understanding social theory* (2nd edn). London: Sage.

Leask, M. (2009) 'The student teacher's role and responsibilities', in S. Capel, M. Leask and T. Turner (eds), *Learning to teach in the secondary school* (5th edn). London: RoutledgeFalmer. pp.18–28.

Leask, M. and Pachler, N. (2014) *Learning to teach using ICT in the secondary school* (3rd edn). Abingdon: Routledge.

Leaton Gray, S. and Whitty, G. (2010) 'Social trajectories or disrupted identities? changing and competing models of teacher professionalism under New Labour', *Cambridge Journal of Education*, 40 (1): 5–23 (DOI: 10.1080/03057640903567005).

Lee, B. (2002) *Teaching assistants in schools: the current state of play*. Windsor: NFER.

Leonard, L. and Leonard, P. (2003) 'The continuing trouble with collaboration: teachers talk', *Current Issues in Education* [online], 6 (15): Available at http://cie.ed.asu.edu/volume6/ number15/

Lewis, P. (2007) *How we think but not in school*. Rotterdam: Sense Publishers.

Lightman, A. and Sadler, P. (1993) 'Teacher predictions versus actual student gains', *The Physics Teacher*, 31: 162–67.

Lindon, J. (2008) *Safeguarding children and young people*. London: Hodder.

Lindsay, G. (2003) 'Inclusive education: a critical perspective', *British Journal of Special Education*, 30 (1): 3–12.

Lloyd, C. (2008) 'Removing barriers to achievement: a strategy for inclusion or exclusion?', *International Journal of Inclusive Education*, 12 (2): 221–36.

Lucas, S.R. (2001) 'Effectively maintained inequality: education transitions, track mobility, and social background effects', *American Journal of Sociology*, 106: 1642–90.

Lucas, S.R. (2009) 'Stratification theory, socioeconomic background, and educational attainment: a formal analysis', *Rationality and Society*, 21 (4): 459–511.

Lyotard, J.F. (1984) *The postmodern condition: a report on knowledge*, Vol. 10, Manchester: Manchester University Press.

MacBeath, J., Demetriou, H., Rudduck, J. and Myers, K. (2003) *Consulting pupils: a toolkit for teachers*. Cambridge, Pearson.

MacGilchrist, B., Myers, K. and Reed, J. (2005) *The intelligent school* (2nd edn). London: Sage.

MacLennan, N. (1999) *Coaching and mentoring*. Aldershot: Gower.

Macpherson, P. (2011) 'Safeguarding children', in A. Hansen (ed.), *Primary professional studies*. Exeter: Learning Matters. pp. 134–49.

Mansell, W. and James, M. (2009) *Assessment in schools. Fit for purpose?* The Assessment Reform Group. Available at www.tlrp.org/pub/documents/assessment.pdf

Maslow, A.H. (1943) 'A theory of human motivation', *Psychological Review*, 50: 370–96.

Maynard, T. and Furlong, J. (1994) 'Learning to teach and models of mentoring', in D. McIntyre, H. Hagger and M. Wilkin (eds), *Mentoring: perspectives on school-based teacher education*. London: Kogan Page.

Maynard, T. and Furlong, J. (1995) *Mentoring student teachers: the growth of professional knowledge*. London: Routledge.

McEntee, G.H., Appleby, J., Dowd, J., Grant, J., Hole, S. and Silva, P. (2003) *At the heart of teaching: a guide to reflective practice*. New York and London: Teachers College Press.

McNaughton, S., Lai, M.K., Timperley, H. and Hsiao, S. (2009) 'Sustaining continued acceleration in reading comprehension achievement following an intervention', *Educational Assessment, Evaluation and Accountability*, 21 (1): 81–100.

McNeill, L. and Hook, P. (2012) *SOLO taxonomy and making meaning. Books 1, 2, 3. Text purposes, audiences and ideas*. New Zealand: Essential Resources Educational Publishers Limited.

Mehrabian, A. (1971) *Silent messages*. Belmont, CA: Wadsworth.

Mehrabian, A. (1981) *Silent messages: implicit communication of emotions and attitudes*, 2nd edn. Belmont, CA: Wadsworth.

Miliband, D. (2004) 'Personalised learning: building a new relationship with schools', speech delivered at the North of England Education Conference, 8 January.

Miller, C. and Doering, A. (eds) (2014) *The new landscape of mobile learning: redesigning education in an app-based world*. London: Routledge.

Mitchell, N. and Pearson, J. (eds) (2012) *Inquiring in the classroom*. London: Continuum.

Mitra, D.L. and Gross, S.J. (2009) 'Increasing student voice in high school reform: building partnerships, improving outcomes', *Educational Management Administration and Leadership*, 37 (4): 522–43.

Mittler, P. (2000) *Working towards inclusive education: social contexts*. London: David Fulton.

Monteith, M. (ed.) (2004) *ICT for curriculum enhancement*. Bristol: Intellect Books.

Moylett, H. (2006) 'Supporting children's development and learning', in T. Bruce (ed.), *Early childhood*. London: Sage, pp. 106–26.

Muijs, D. and Reynolds, D. (2010) 'Collaborative small group work', in *Effective teaching evidence and practice* (3rd edn). London: Sage.

Murphy, J.F., Hallinger, P. and Heck, R.H. (2013) 'Leading via teacher evaluation: the case of missing clothes?', *Educational Researcher*, 42 (6): 349–54.

Murray, M. (2001) *Beyond the myths and magic of mentoring: how to facilitate an effective mentoring process*. San Francisco, CA: Jossey-Bass.

National Advisory Committee on Creativity and Cultural Education (1999) *All our futures: creativity, culture and education*. London: Department for Education and Employment & Department for Culture, Media and Sport.

Newton, P. (2007) 'Clarifying the purposes of educational assessment', *Assessment in Education: Principles, Policy and Practice*, 14 (2): 149–70.

NGA (2104) *Knowing Your School: RAISEonline for Governors of Primary School*. Available at www.nga.org.uk/getattachment/Can-we-help/Knowing-Your-School/Knowing-Your-School-Primary-RAISE-(Jan-14)-FINAL.pdf.aspx

Nias, J. (1989) *Primary teachers talking*. London: Routledge & Kegan Paul.

Nias, J. (1996) 'Thinking about feeling: the emotions in teaching', *Cambridge Journal of Education*, 26 (3): 293–306.

Nilholm, C. (2006) 'Special education, inclusion and democracy', *European Journal of Special Needs Education*, 21 (4): 431–45.

Nind, M. (2005) 'Inclusive education: discourse and action', *British Educational Research Journal*, 31 (2): 269–75.

Nind, M., Rix, J., Sheehy, K. and Simmons, K. (2003) *Inclusive education: diverse perspectives*. London: David Fulton.

Nutbrown, C. and Clough, P. (2006) *Inclusion in the early years*. London: Sage.

O'Hanlon, C. (2003) *Educational inclusion as action research*. Maidenhead: McGraw-Hill Education.

Ofsted (2011) *The impact of the 'Assessing pupils' progress' initiative*. Available at www.ofsted.gov.uk/publications/100226

Olsen, L. (2000) 'Learning English and learning America: immigrants in the centre of a storm', *Theory into Practice*, 39 (4): 196–202.

Park, S. and Oliver, J.S. (2008) 'Revisiting the conceptualisation of pedagogical content knowledge (PCK): PCK as a conceptual tool to understand teachers as professionals', *Research in Science Education*, 38: 261–84.

Parsloe, E. (1999) *The manager as coach and mentor*. London: Institute of Personnel & Development.

Pellino, K. (2010) *Effective strategies for teaching English language learners*. Available at www.teach-nology.com/tutorials/teaching/esl

Perkins, D. (1993) 'Teaching for understanding', *Journal of the American Federation of Teachers*, 17 (3): 28–35.

Phillips, C., Tse, D. and Johnson, F. (2011) *Community cohesion and PREVENT: how have schools responded?* Research Report DFE-RR085 2011.

Piaget, J. (2000) *The language and thought of the child* (3rd edn). London and New York: Routledge Classics.

Pianta, R.C. and Hamre, B.K. (2009) 'Classroom processes and positive youth development: conceptualizing, measuring, and improving the capacity of interactions between teachers and students', *New Directions in Youth Development*, 121: 33–46.

Pollard, A. (2014) *Reflective teaching in schools*. London: Bloomsbury.

Pollard, A. and Triggs, P., with Broadfoot, P., McNess, E., and Osborn, M. (2000) *What pupils say: changing policy and practice in primary education*. London and New York: Continuum.

Powell, S. and Tod, J. (2004) 'A systematic review of how theories explain learning behaviour in school context', in *Research Evidence in Education Library*. London: EPPI-Centre, Social Science Research Unit, Institute of Education.

Purkey, W.W., Schmidt, J.J. and Novak, J.M (2010) *From conflict to conciliation: how to defuse difficult situations*. Thousand Oaks, CA: Corwin.

Qualifications and Curriculum Authority (QCA) (2007) *The new secondary curriculum: what has changed and why?* London: QCA.

Qualifications and Curriculum Authority (QCA) (2009a) 'Guidance on cross-curriculum dimensions'. News release, 12 March. Available at www.qcda.gov.uk/news/1024.aspx

Qualifications and Curriculum Authority (2009b) *Get to grips with assessing pupils' progress*. London: Department for Children, Schools and Families.

Race Relations (Amendment) Act (2000) London: HMSO.

Reimer, E. (1971) '"Peanuts", quoted in "School is dead: an essay on alternatives to education"', *Interchange*, 2(1).

Robertson, J. (1996) *Effective classroom control: understanding teacher–pupil relationships*. London: Hodder & Stoughton.

Robinson, C. and Kellett, M. (2004) in S. Fraser (ed.), *Doing research with children and young people*. London: Sage.

Robinson, K. (2001) *Out of our minds*. London: Capstone.

Robson, C. and Fielding, M. (2010) 'Children and their primary schools: pupils' voices', in R. Alexander (ed.), *The Cambridge primary review research surveys*. London: Routledge. pp.17–48.

Rogers, B. (2006) *Classroom behaviour: a practical guide to effective teaching, behaviour management and colleague support* (2nd edn). London: Sage.

Rogers, B. (2011) *Classroom behaviour: a practical guide to effective teaching, behaviour management and colleague support* (3rd edn). London: Sage.

Rose, J. (2009) *Independent review of the primary curriculum: final report*. London: DCSF.

Roulstone, A. and Prideaux, S. (2008) 'More policies, greater inclusion? Exploring the contradictions of New Labour inclusive education policy', *International Studies in Sociology of Education*, 18 (1): 15–29.

RSA (2008) *Opening Minds impact update: Autumn 2008*. Available at http://.thersa.org/-data/assets/pdf-file/0003/139764/Microsoft-word...Opening-Minds-impact-update-Autumn-2008-v.2.pdf

Rudduck, J. and Flutter, J. (2000) 'Pupil participation and pupil perspective: carving a new order of experience', *Cambridge Journal of Education*, 30 (1): 75–89.

Rudduck, J. and Flutter, J. (2004) *How to improve your school*. London: Continuum.

Rudduck, J. and McIntyre, D. (2007) *Improving learning through consulting pupils*. Abingdon: Routledge.

Sachs, J. (2003) *The activist teaching profession*. Oxford: Oxford University Press.

Sachs, J. and Smith, R. (1988) 'Constructing teacher culture', *British Journal of Education*, 9 (4): 423–36.

Safford, K. (2005) *Teaching language and curriculum*. Available at www.naldic.org.uk/ITTSEAL2/teaching/Teachingapproaches.cfm

Salo, P. (2008) 'Decision making as a struggle and a play', *Educational Management Administration and Leadership*, 36 (4): 495–510.

Savage, J. (2011) *Cross curricular teaching and learning in the secondary school*. Abingdon: Routledge.

Saylor, C. (2010) 'Learning theories applied to curriculum development', in S. Keating (ed.), *Curriculum development and evaluation in nursing* (2nd edn). New York: Springer.

Schmuck, T. H., Haber, P., Mayr, M. and Lampoltshammer, T. (2014) 'Management of collaboration in education', *INTED2014 Proceedings*, 1588–95.

Schön, D.A. (1983) *The reflective practitioner*. London: Temple Smith.

Schunk, D.H. and Pajares, F. (2002) 'The development of academic self-efficacy', in A. Wigfield and J.S. Eccles (eds), *Development of achievement motivation*. San Diego, CA: Academic Press. pp. 15–31.

Scrivener, J. (2012) *Classroom management techniques*. Cambridge: Cambridge University Press

Secretary of State for Education and Employment (1997) *Excellence in Schools*, CM368. London: HMSO.

Seipold, J., Pachler, N., Bachmair, B. and Honegger, B.D. (2014) 'Mobile learning: strategies for planning and implementing learning with mobile devices in secondary school contexts', in M. Leask and N. Pachler (eds), *Learning to teach using ICT in the secondary school*. Abingdon: Routledge. pp. 185–204.

Sellars, M. (2014) *Reflective practice for teachers*. London: Sage.

Shier, H. (2001) 'Pathways to participation: openings, opportunities and obligations', *Children and Society*, 15 (2): 107–17.

Shoffner, M. (2008) 'The place of the personal: exploring the affective domain through reflection in teacher preparation', *Teaching and Teacher Education*, 25 (6): 783–89.

Shulman, L.S. (1987) 'Knowledge and teaching: foundation of the New Reform', *Harvard Educational Review*, 59 (1): 1–22.

Shute, V.J. (2007) *Focus on formative feedback research report*. Princeton, NJ: Educational Testing Service. Available at www.ets.org/Media/Research/pdf/RR-07-11.pdf

Shute, V.J. (2008) 'Focus on formative feedback', *Review of Educational Research*, 78 (1): 153–89.

Siemens, G. (2005) 'Connectivism: A learning theory for the digital age', *International Journal of Instructional Technology and Distance Learning*, 2 (1) January.

Sikes, P. (1997) *Parents who teach: stories from home and from school*. London: Cassell.

Sikes, P., Lawson, H. and Parker, M. (2007) 'Voices on: teachers and teaching assistants talk about inclusion', *International Journal of Inclusive Education*, 11(3): 355–70.

Skidmore, D. (2004) *Inclusion: the dynamic of school development*. Maidenhead: Open University Press.

Slee, R. (2001a) 'Social justice and the changing directions in educational research: the case of inclusive education', *International Journal of Inclusive Education*, 5 (2/3): 167–77.

Slee, R. (2011) *The irregular school: exclusion, schooling and inclusive education*. London: Routledge.

Slee, R. and Allan, J. (2001) 'Excluding the included: a reconsideration of inclusive education', *International Studies in Sociology of Education*, 11 (2): 173–91.

Slee, R. (2001) 'Inclusion in practice: does practice make perfect?', *Educational Review*, 53 (2): 113–23.

Smith, C., Dakers, J., Dow, W., Head, G., Sutherland, M. and Irwin, R. (2005) 'A systematic review of what pupils, aged 11–16, believe impacts on their motivation to learn in the classroom', in *Research Evidence in Education Library*. London: EPPI-Centre, Social Science Research Unit, Institute of Education, University of London.

Smith C. and Laslett R. (1993) *Effective classroom management: a teacher's guide*. London: Routledge.

Sousa, D.A. (2012) *How the brain learns* (4th edn). London: Sage.

South, H. (1999) *Working paper 5. The distinctiveness of EAL: a cross-curriculum discipline.* Watford: NALDIC.

Stenhouse, L. (1975) *An introduction to curriculum research and development.* London: Heinemann.

Stobart, G. (2008) *Testing times: the uses and abuses of assessment.* London: Routledge.

Stopp, P (2008) 'From feedback to dialogic review: an approach to appropriate matching of mentoring and coaching feedback'. Paper presented at BERA, Heriot Watt University, Edinburgh, 3–6 September.

Summey, D. C. (2013). *Developing digital literacies – a framework for professional learning.* London: Sage.

Sylva, K., Melhuish, E., Sammons, P., Siraj-Blatchford, I., Taggart, B. and Elliot, K. (2003) *Research brief: The Effective Provision of Pre-School Education (EPPE) Project: findings from the pre-school period.* Available at www.ioe.ac.uk/projects/eppe

The 2020 Group (2006) *A vision for teaching and learning in 2020.* London: HMSO.

The Royal Society (2012) *Shut down or restart? The way forward for computing in UK schools.* London: The Royal Society.

Thody, A., Gray, B. and Bowden, D. (2000) *The teacher's survival guide.* London: Continuum.

Tucker, S. (2014) *Pastoral care in education: an international journal of personal, social and emotional development.* Birmingham: Routledge Taylor Francis Group.

Tuckman, B. W. (1965) 'Development sequence in small groups', *Psychological Bulletin,* 63 (6): 384–99.

UNESCO (1994) 'The Salamanca Statement and Framework for Action on Special Needs Education', World Conference on Special Needs Education Access and Quality. Available at www.unesco.org/education/pdf/SALAMA_E.PDF (accessed 01.08.13).

United Nations (1989) *United Nations Convention on the Rights of the Child.* Geneva: UN.

Van de Watering, G., Gijbels, D., Dochy, F. and Van der Rijt, J. (2008) 'Students' assessment preferences, perceptions of assessment and their relationships to study results', *Higher Education,* 56 (6): 645–58.

Vekiri, I. (2010) 'Boys' and girls' ICT beliefs: do teachers matter?', *Computers & Education,* 55 (1): 16–23.

Vygotsky, L. S. (1978) *Mind and society: the development of higher mental processes.* Cambridge, MA: Harvard University Press.

Vygotsky, L. S. (1986) *Thought and language.* Revised and edited by Alex Kozulin. Cambridge, MA: The Massachusetts Institute of Technology Press.

Wallace, M. and Poulson, L. (eds) (2003) *Learning to read critically in teaching and learning.* London: Sage.

Waters, M. (2007) 'New curriculum, exciting learning', Comment, *Guardian,* 5 February.

Webber, R. and Butler, T. (2005) *Classifying pupils by where they live: how well does this predict variations in GCSE results?* UCL Working Paper Series, Paper 99.

Wedell, K. (2008) 'Confusion about inclusion: patching up or system change?', *British Journal of Special Education,* 35 (3): 127–35.

Welding, J. (1998) 'The identification of able children in a secondary school: a study of the issues involved and their practical implications', *Educating Able Children,* 2.

Weller, S. (2006) 'Tuning-in to teenagers! Using radio phone-in discussions in research with young people', *Social Research Methodo*logy, 9 (4): 303–15.

Wilson, J. (2000) 'Doing justice to inclusion', *European Journal of Special Needs Education,* 15 (3): 297–304.

Winch, C. (2004) 'What do teachers need to know about teaching? A critical examination of the occupational knowledge of teachers', *British Journal of Educational Studies,* 52 (2): 180–96.

Wood, E. (2003) 'The power of pupil perspectives in evidence-based practice: the case of gender and underachievement', *Research Papers in Education,* 18 (4): 365–83.

Woods, P. (1979) *The divided school.* London: Routledge & Kegan Paul.

Woods, P. (ed.) (1980) 'Pupil strategies', in *Explorations in the sociology of the school.* London: Croom Helm.

Woods, P. (1990) *The happiest days? How pupils cope with school.* London: Falmer.

Woolfolk, A. (2010) *Educational psychology* (11th edn). Upper Saddle River, NJ: Pearson Education.

Worm B. S. and Buch S. V. (2014) 'Does competition work as a motivating factor in e-learning? A randomized controlled trial', *PLoS ONE* 9 (1): e85434 (doi: 10.1371/journal.pone)

Wragg, E. (1994) *An introduction to classroom observation.* London: Routledge.

Wright, T. (ed.) (2010) *How to be a brilliant mentor: developing outstanding teachers.* London: Routledge.

Wubbels, T. and Levy, J. (1993) *Interpersonal relationships in education.* London: Falmer.

Young, M. (1971) *Knowledge and control.* London: Collier Macmillan.

Zey, M. G. (1988) 'A mentor for all reasons', *Personnel Journal,* 67 (1): 46–51.

INDEX